TEXTILE PROTEST

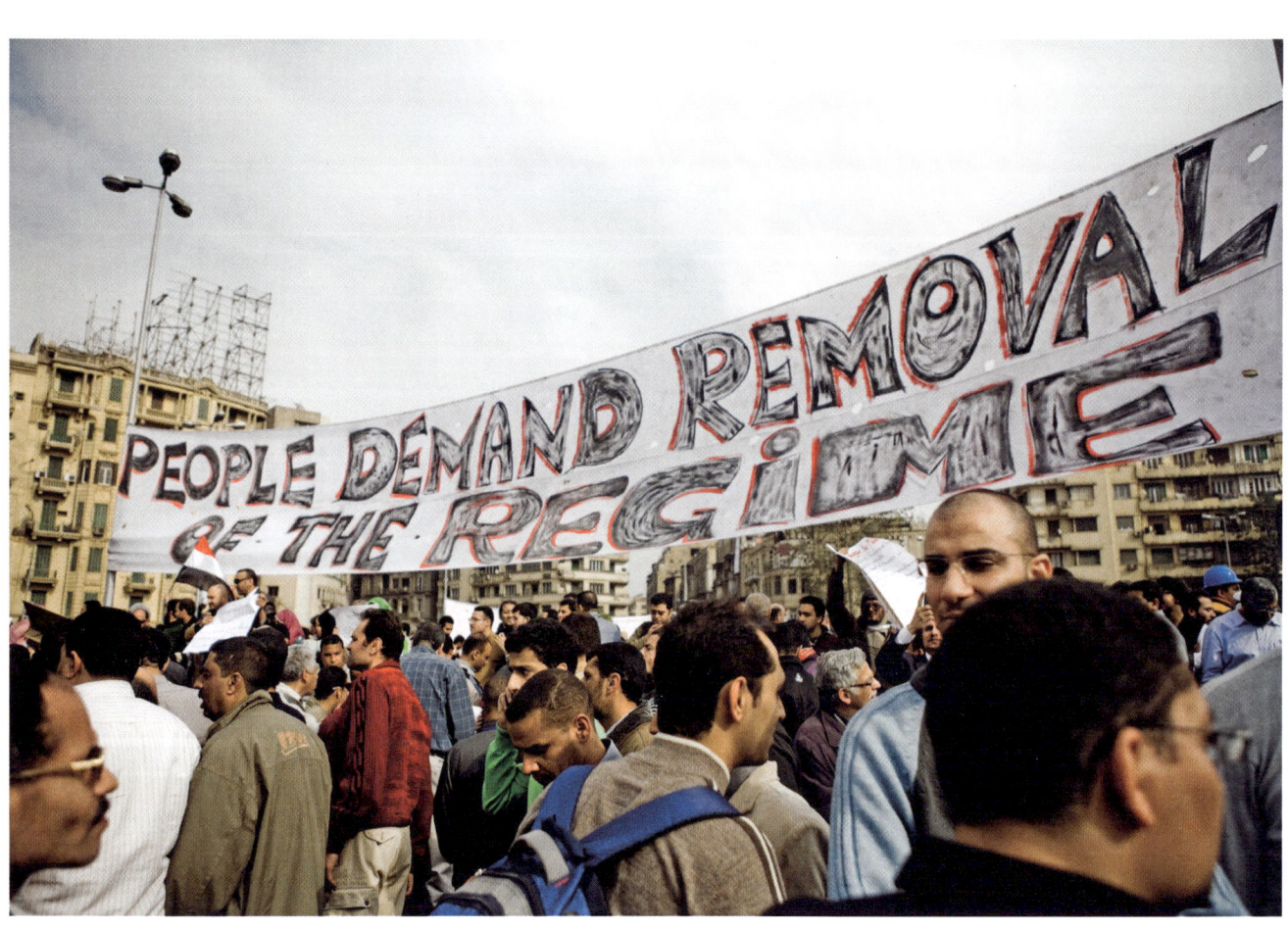

TEXTILE PROTEST

ARTISTS, ACTIVISM AND THE HISTORICAL POWER OF CLOTH IN PROTEST

JULIA TRISTON

BATSFORD

CONTENTS

INTRODUCTION

Textile Protest celebrates and showcases the international visual language of stitch and cloth through the richness and diversity of textiles that have been used to express resistance in its many forms.

In declarations of protest, textiles can be confrontational and explicit, satirical and subversive, ironic and humorous. Creatively, protest textiles can be used to heal and bridge the gaps following conflicts, or comment in a thought-provoking way to challenge the contentious issues of language, 'isms' or imbalances of power. Whether for social justice or peace, to demonstrate opposition to oppression, to celebrate liberty, to honour hope and equality, or to express solidarity with others fighting for their rights or for radical change, people have made and united behind protest textiles for hundreds of years.

Drawing on a comprehensive collection of international textile artworks across different movements and campaigns, continents and centuries, *Textile Protest* is an appreciation of how textiles are used in powerful and radical ways to communicate messages of solidarity and defiance, to challenge injustices and inequalities, to give a voice to the marginalized and to effect change.

Textile Protest documents and reflects upon how everyday materials can be repurposed and transformed to make quilts, flags, banners and garments that carry a message of protest. Whilst some artists, activists and craftivists show their commitment to highlighting inequalities through artworks that embrace issues of gender, LGBTQIA+ rights or the climate crisis, others express their individual frustrations about expectations faced daily in society with profanities and humour whilst commenting on their dissatisfaction with the status quo, misogynistic language or issues surrounding consent.

Laid out in accessible chapters, *Textile Protest* catalogues a range of artworks which convey messages of love and longing or hope and justice, alongside reactions to war or oppression, violence and exclusion. Some protest textiles ask questions and demand answers, whilst others call for action or amnesty; all unite people and voices across campaigns, communities and countries.

From early trade union banners and women's suffrage sashes to contemporary wearable textiles which highlight recent campaigns, *Textile Protest* investigates the concept of protest through the medium of textiles, examining its importance and significance,

Bleeding (From the mini banner series 2023–4)

Julia Triston

60×46cm (23.6×18.1in). Appliquéd text with machine stitch on vintage French linen tea-towel.

The mini banner series explores a range of feminist themes, political slogans and personal viewpoints which are translated into bold statements to draw attention to these issues and inequalities, several of which are featured in this book. (See also pages 114, 205, 220, 227.)

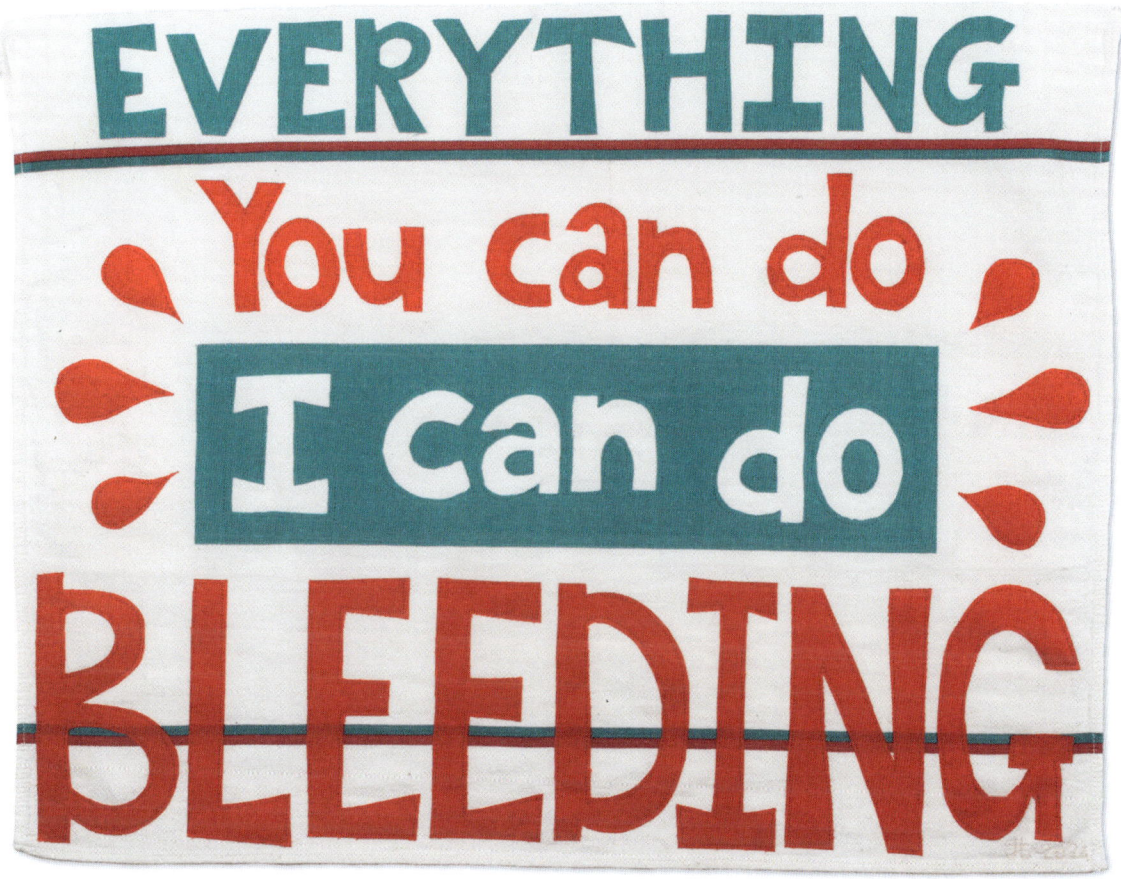

and contextualizing how textiles are used to raise awareness of everything from local issues that are protested by a few, to global issues that affect us all.

Textile Protest also includes a contemporary review of current works which demonstrate a subversion of what has traditionally been deemed the domain of women: stitch in its many forms. Moving beyond traditional realms, embroidery, appliqué and quilt-making processes have become creative forms of embracing individual and collective expression connecting people with like minds, to educate, inspire and initiate debate.

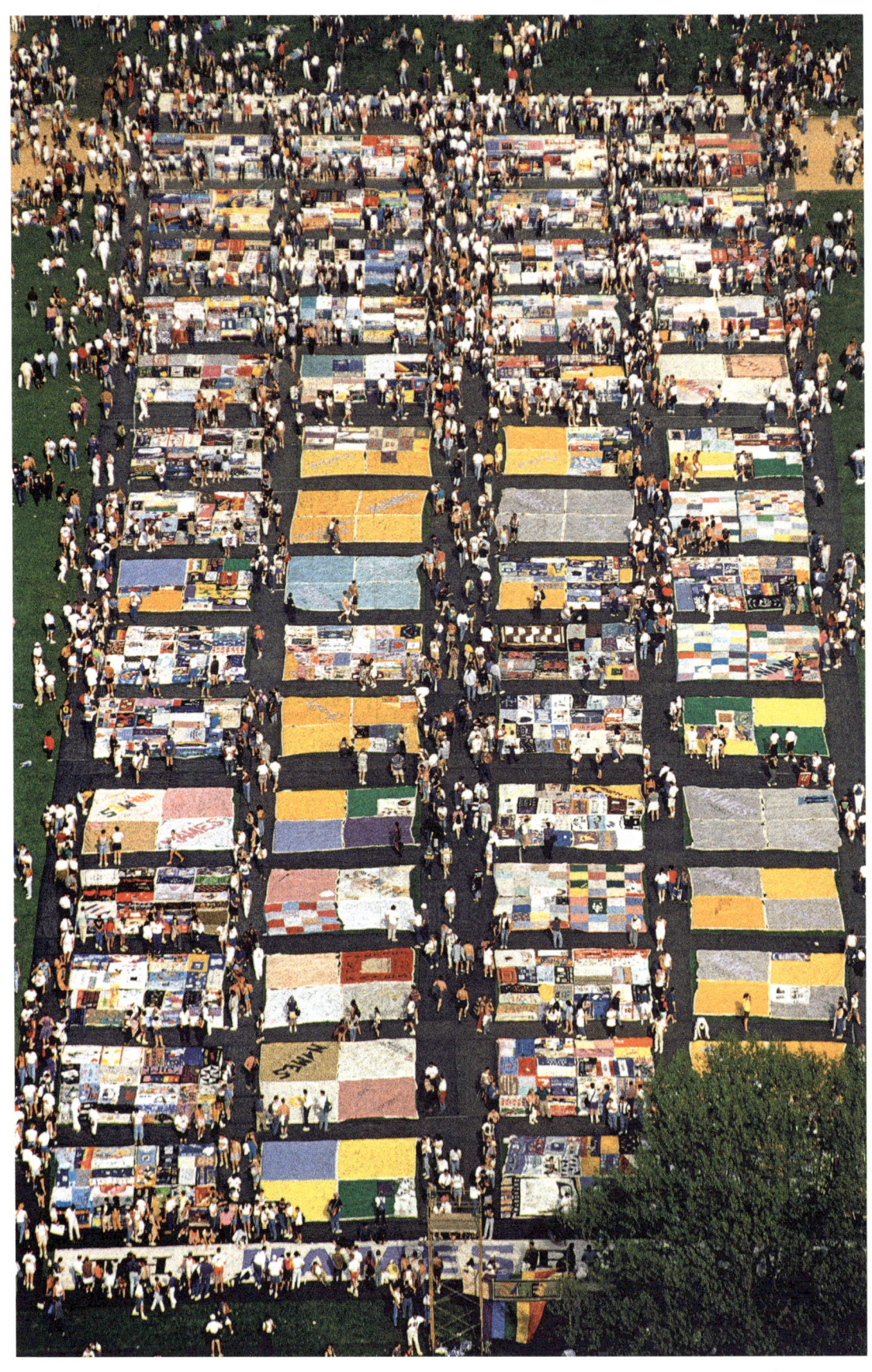

IN MEMORIAM

IN MEMORIAM

'Lit up at night Grenfell Tower was like a twinkling mosaic in the sky. We sew for justice for those whose lights and lives have been extinguished forever.' TUESDAY GREENIDGE

OPPOSITE

Aerial shot of the AIDS Memorial Quilt.

As soon as we are born we are wrapped in textiles; perhaps a special cloth, a hospital sheet, or a lovingly knitted blanket. As we exit this world we are laid out in different textiles too – our best clothes, a commemorative fabric or a significant or simple shroud.

Between our birth and death we experience textiles on a daily basis without giving many a second thought. From the towels that dry our skin and the bedclothes that cover our tired bodies, to the clothes we choose to convey our identity and celebrate our cultural heritage, we are surrounded by fabrics in a plethora of colours, textures and patterns, for a myriad of purposes. In ceremonies and rites of passage, in both creative and utilitarian ways, textiles are integral to our lives.

It is fitting, therefore, that textiles are not just used as a medium to celebrate life, but are also used to highlight and protest against death, particularly when a death is untimely, unnatural or unexplained. The voids left by loved ones, and the tragedies and disasters surrounding them – such as a public health catastrophe, a pandemic, or a major flaw in legislation – have been illuminated and questioned through the medium of textiles for generations. Personal details of victims printed, embroidered, appliquéd or quilted onto cloth are some of the most haunting; they serve as a permanent reminder of lives cut short by murder or genocide, suicide or accident, disease or conflict.

Many protest textiles about death focus not only on the deceased, but also aim to draw attention to the toxicity or flaws in a system, and the negligence, exploitation, greed and abuse of power that allowed these tragedies to happen. They vigorously protest against injury and resolutely demand a communal quest for justice and a desire to bring those responsible to account.

As well as expressing rage, disbelief, grief and loss, these protest textiles, often made collaboratively, serve as a permanent and collective remembrance, a lasting testament to those missing, dead or bereaved. They are also a symbol of hope and love; they honour the memory of the victims – both visually and viscerally – keeping their names and memories alive whilst keeping the causes of their deaths or disappearances in the media spotlight.

Some protest textiles have changed outlooks and attitudes globally, galvanizing politicians and lawyers into action.

The NAMES Project AIDS Memorial Quilt

This fabric memorial, often abbreviated to the AIDS Memorial Quilt, is a record-breaking protest textile representing lost lives. Cleve Jones, a prominent human rights activist and LGBTQIA+ campaigner in San Francisco, conceived the idea of a patchwork quilt in 1985, to commemorate the thousand-plus San Franciscans lost to AIDS and to provide creative therapy for those living with their grief. His idea, based on cardboard placards depicting names of deceased loved ones, taped to the San Francisco Federal Building at the end of the 1985 Candlelight Parade, took a couple of years to come to fruition. It then took off exponentially to become the world's largest community arts project to date, and the biggest textile expression of remembrance ever made.

The AIDS Memorial Quilt began in 1987, with a single panel to celebrate the life of Marvin Feldman, a friend of Jones. The original panel size was a template for those that followed – 0.9×1.8m (3×6ft) – approximately the size of a human grave. Each panel displays a name and imagery associated with that person, and is sewn together with another seven to constitute a 'block'. At every display the blocks are ceremoniously unwrapped, and the names of the loved ones read out. It is a beautiful monument lovingly sewn in cloth and thread which serves as a permanent record of lives lost to a devastating global pandemic, depicting the humans behind the statistics, who might otherwise be forgotten by history.

The inaugural display of the quilt took place on 11 October 1987 at the National Mall, Washington DC. At that time the quilt consisted of 1,920 panels and was larger than a football field.

Since its inception, the quilt has been added to by people from all over the world and can no longer be displayed all at once. Now permanently in San Francisco in the safe keeping of the National AIDS Memorial, it currently weighs 54,000kg (54tn) and consists of over 50,000 panels dedicated to more than 110,000 people; it is a living and growing memorial to a generation lost to AIDS.

The legacy of the quilt lives on. Today it serves as an online interactive educational resource and prevention tool demanding that health and social justice be taught to future generations.

OPPOSITE AND OVERLEAF

Details of the AIDS Memorial Quilt.

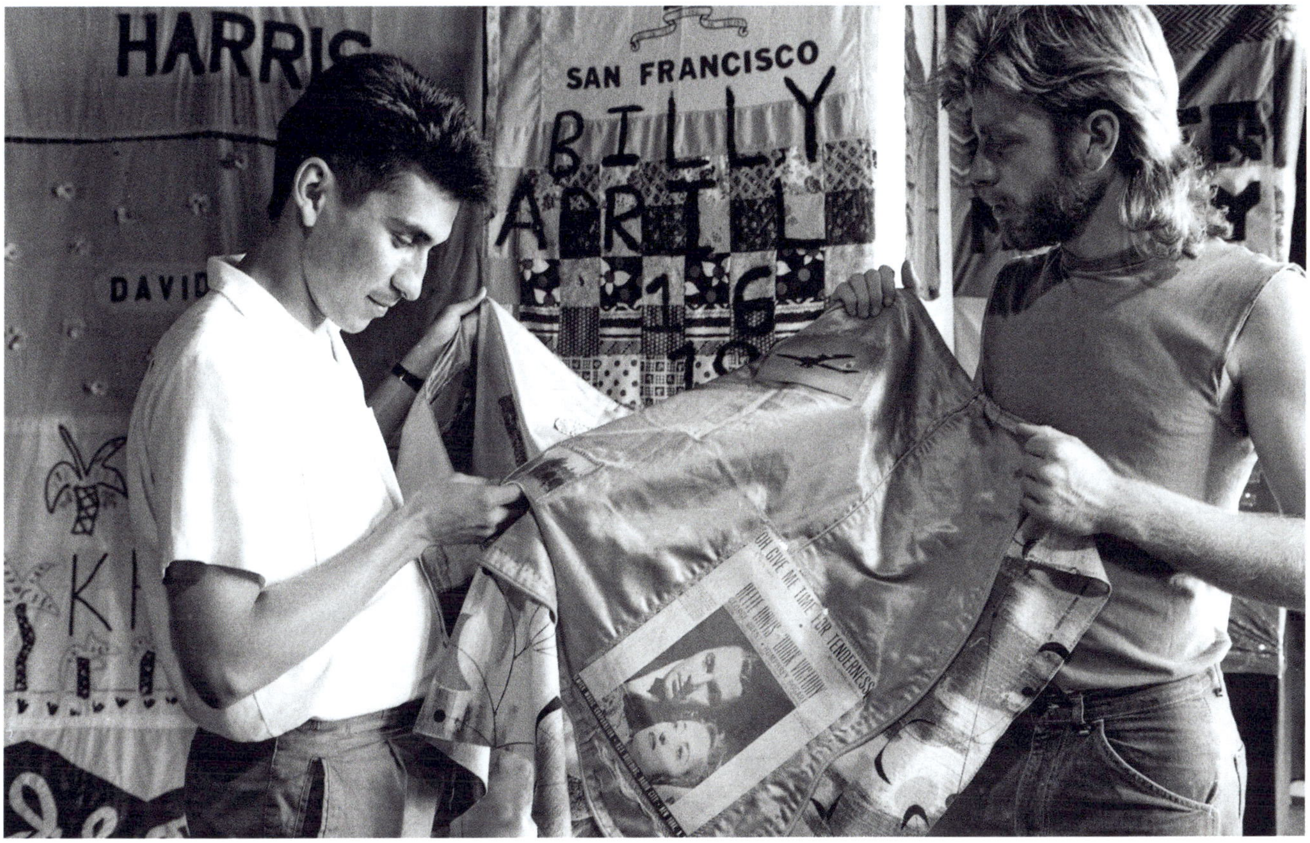

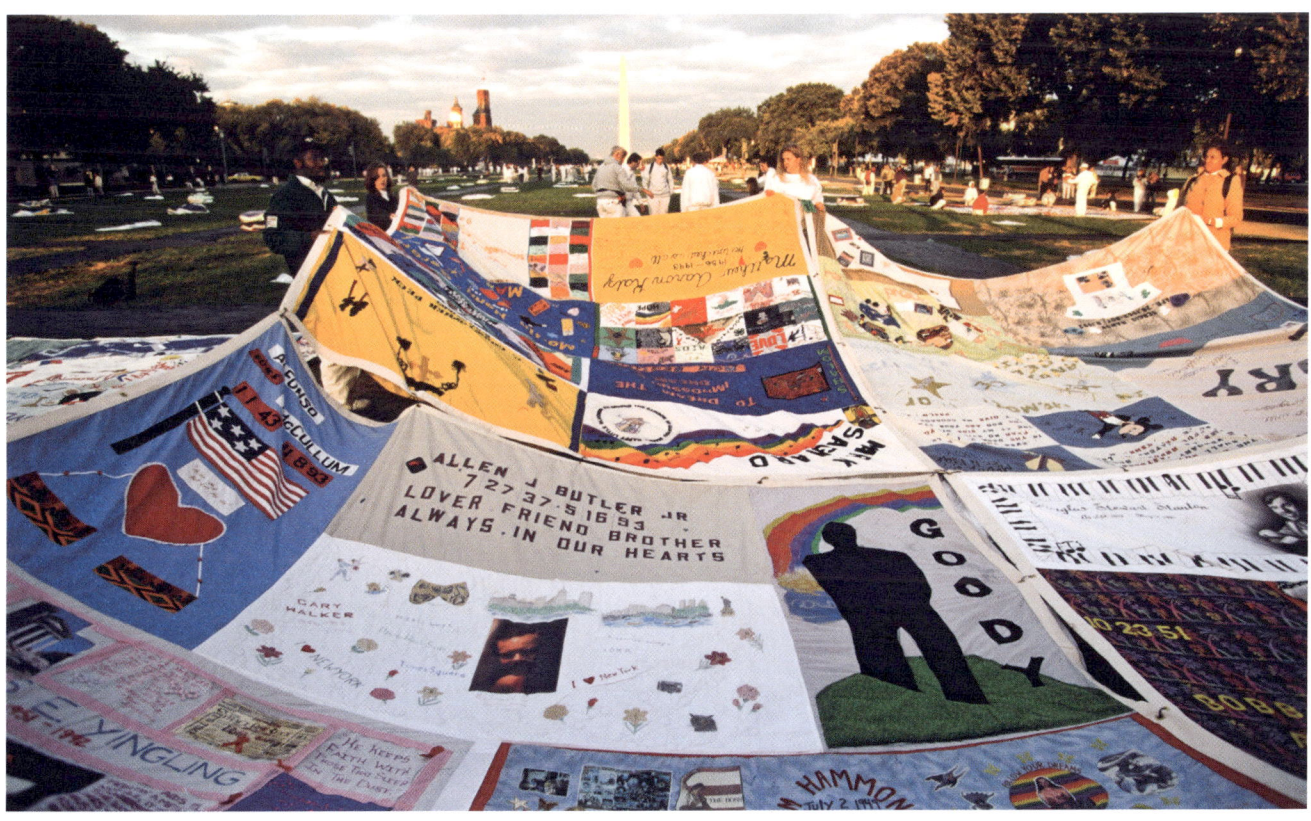

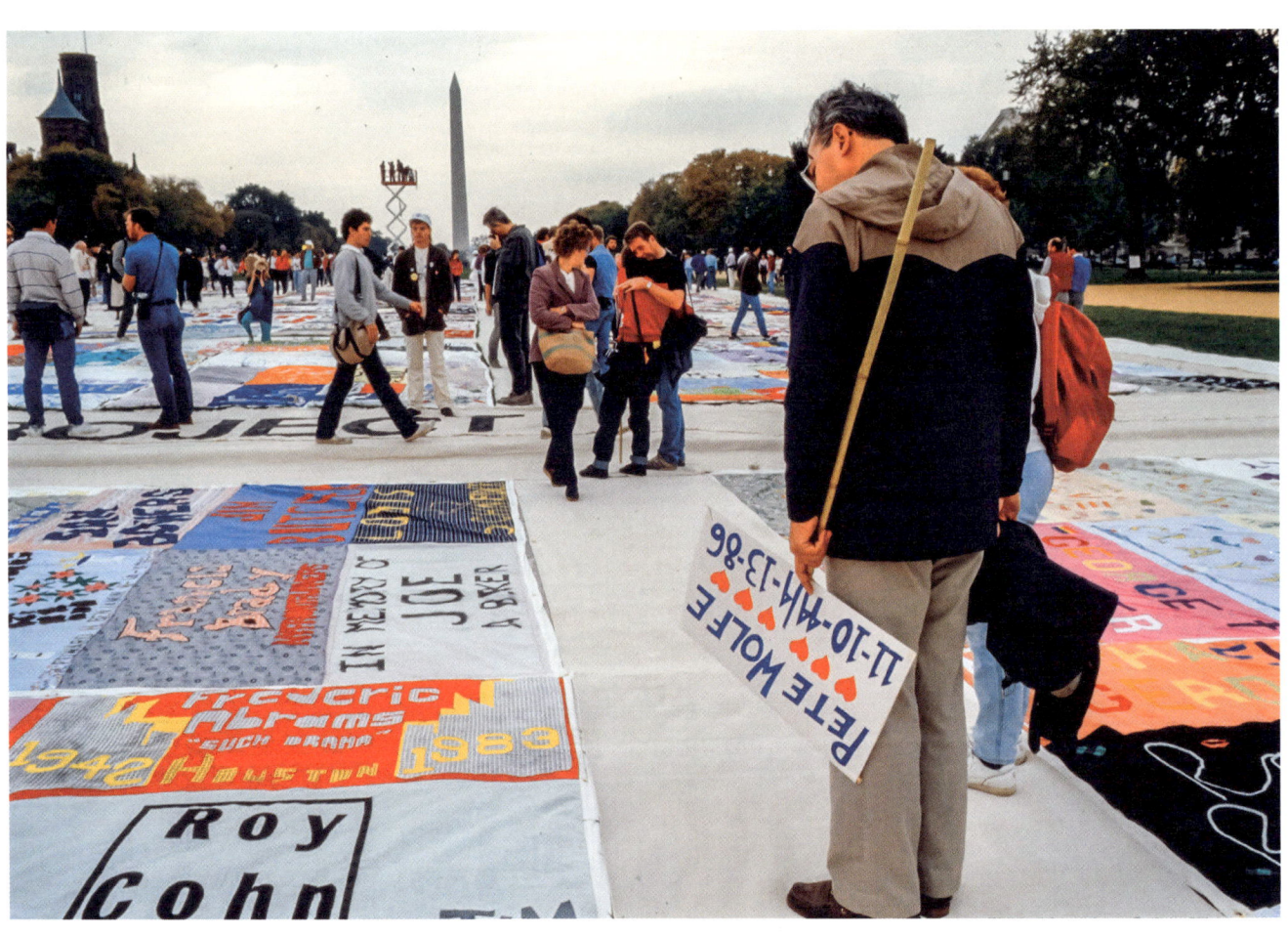

IN MEMORIAM

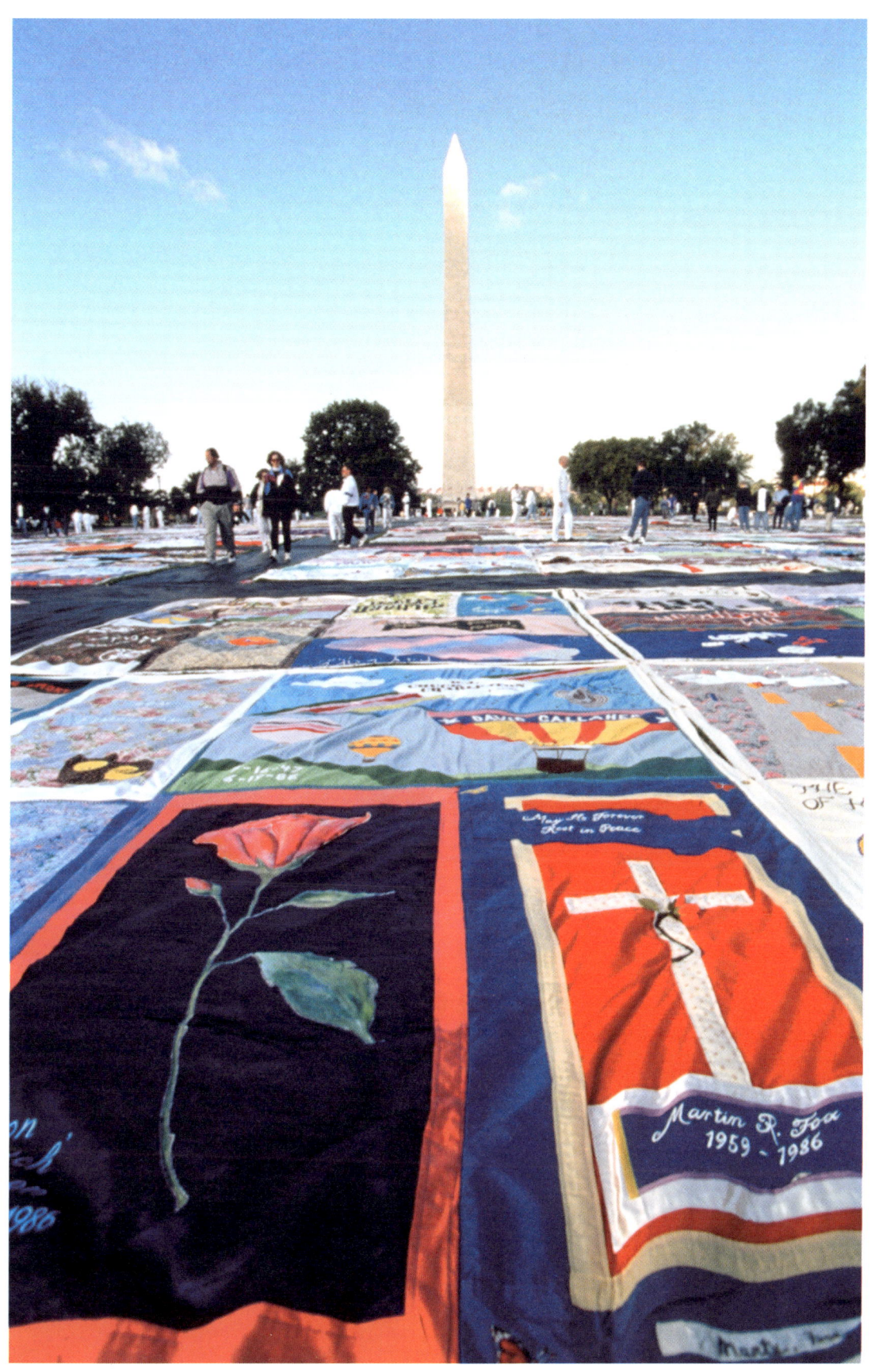

The Hillsborough Patchwork Quilt

On 15 April 1989, at Hillsborough Stadium, Sheffield, UK, just before the kick-off of the FA Cup semi-final between Liverpool and Nottingham Forest, an exit gate was opened by police to ease overcrowding outside the standing-only pens allocated to Liverpool supporters. This led to a massive influx of people into the pens, causing the death of 94 people in a human crush. A further 766 fans suffered injuries, and three more Liverpool supporters have since died from their injuries.

At the time, 'drunken fans' and 'hooligans' were blamed for causing the crush, but after tireless efforts to bring those responsible to account, and after the fans and families of those who died vehemently disputed the first inquest verdicts of accidental death, in April 2016 it was ruled that the fans who died were 'unlawfully killed'.

The Hillsborough Patchwork Quilt was created in 2014 by Merseyside artist Linda Whitfield to honour the memory of the victims and mark the 25th anniversary of the tragedy. It serves as a remembrance for the deceased Liverpool supporters and – at the time of making – highlighted the ongoing battle of the families' quest for justice. Made from donated football shirts with the iconic Liver Bird crest, the quilt originally consisted of stitched patches with the names of 96 victims. The 97th name was added in 2021, after Andrew Devine died from the life-changing injuries he suffered in the disaster. In 2022 Liverpool Football Club updated their memorial symbol to include the number 97 between two eternal flames, to commemorate the 97 who died and to represent the Hillsborough Justice Campaign, which was established in the aftermath of the tragedy. This number is included on all football shirts, in print and in all tributes by the club hereafter.

The Hillsborough Patchwork Quilt now resides in the Museum of Liverpool, after being presented as a gift by the Hillsborough Family Support Group. It is a beautiful tribute to the fans who died, those who survived and to a city that will never forget.

BELOW

The Hillsborough Patchwork Quilt.

OPPOSITE, BELOW

The number 97 features on the Liverpool Football Club shirts to commemorate the victims of the Hillsborough disaster.

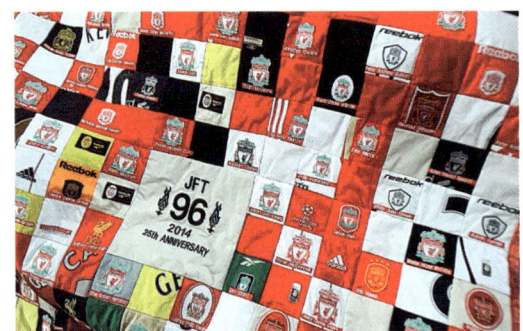

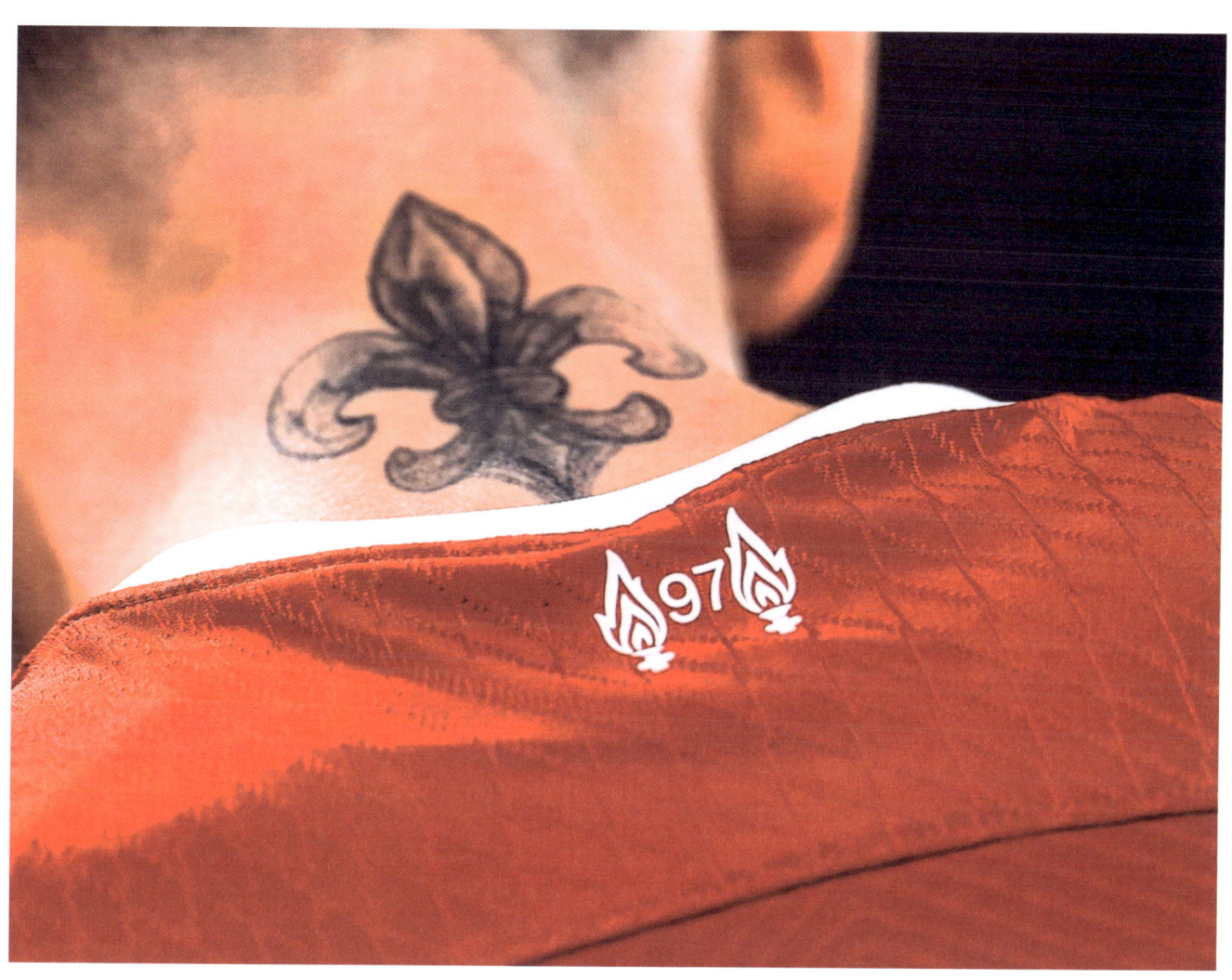

The Grenfell Memorial Quilt

OPPOSITE, ABOVE

Grenfell Tower,
London, UK.

On 14 June 2017 a catastrophic fire engulfed Grenfell Tower, a 24-storey residential building in North Kensington, London, UK, claiming the lives of 72 people. Many more victims were injured and left homeless after this devastating tragedy, which was initially started by a malfunctioning fridge in a fourth-floor apartment. The fire advanced quickly due to the cladding system on the exterior of the building that was made from flammable materials, causing an inferno that took 60 hours to extinguish fully. The cladding, which had a polyethylene core and did not meet fire safety standards, contributed significantly to the rapid spread of the blaze. In addition, the tower block had only one staircase, no sprinkler system, and a key-fob entry system which only residents could operate. These were all factors which contributed to the tragedy, along with a late call for evacuation of the building by the fire service who originally advised residents to 'stay put' when they wrongly believed they could contain the fire.

Grenfell Tower housed hundreds of people of many different nationalities and ages, and was a central landmark in the community, both physically and visually. In the aftermath of the disaster, floral tributes and handwritten messages poured in, covering the fencing surrounding the burned-out building, and regular candle-lit vigils were held by locals. As these natural and organic tributes began to fade and decay, the need was felt for a permanent memorial. The idea of a quilt was initiated by Tuesday Greenidge and her daughter Charlie Manning, a survivor of the fire, and swiftly developed into an important community-led fabric activism project to create a heartfelt tribute to all the victims of the tragedy, honouring the memories of those who lost their lives.

Stitched in a weekly sewing bee, through the collective efforts of numerous volunteers (including survivors, bereaved family members and local residents), the making process of the Grenfell Memorial Quilt has provided a source of comfort and healing, strengthening the spirit of the local community in the face of a terrible tragedy. Many of the makers have never been on a protest; this quilt is their voice, and the project offers a tangible reminder of the love and support that surrounds them.

Aptly, this quilt is made from fabric donated by the community. The fabric comes in all shapes, textures and colours, and is made

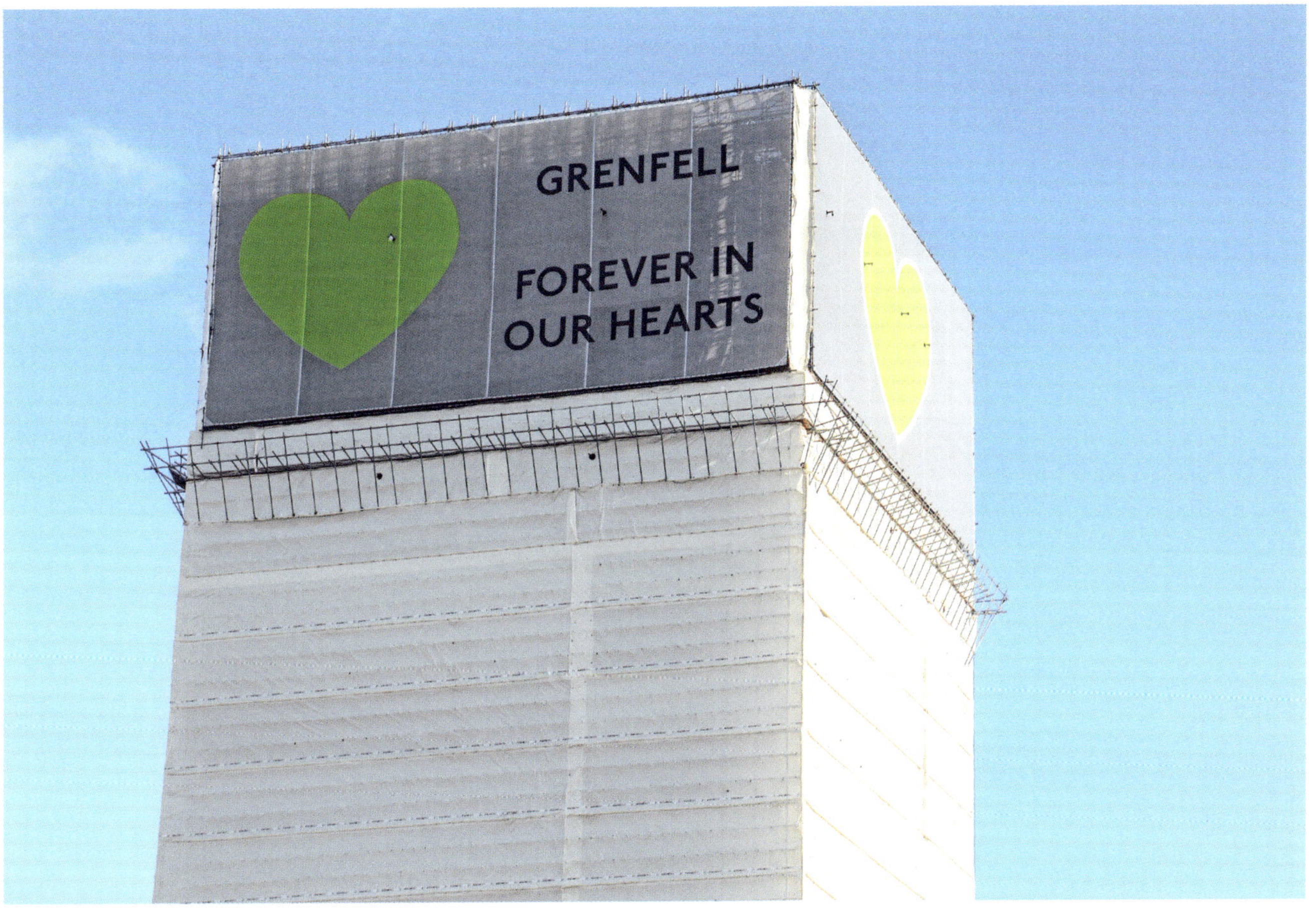
GRENFELL
FOREVER IN
OUR HEARTS

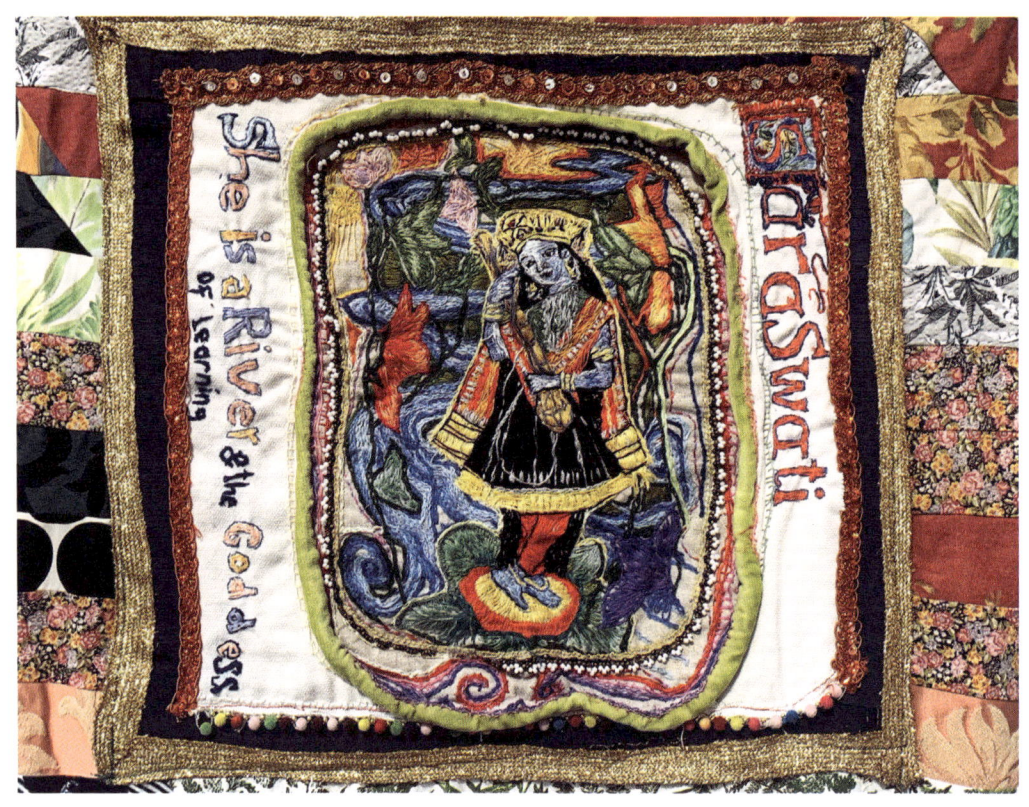

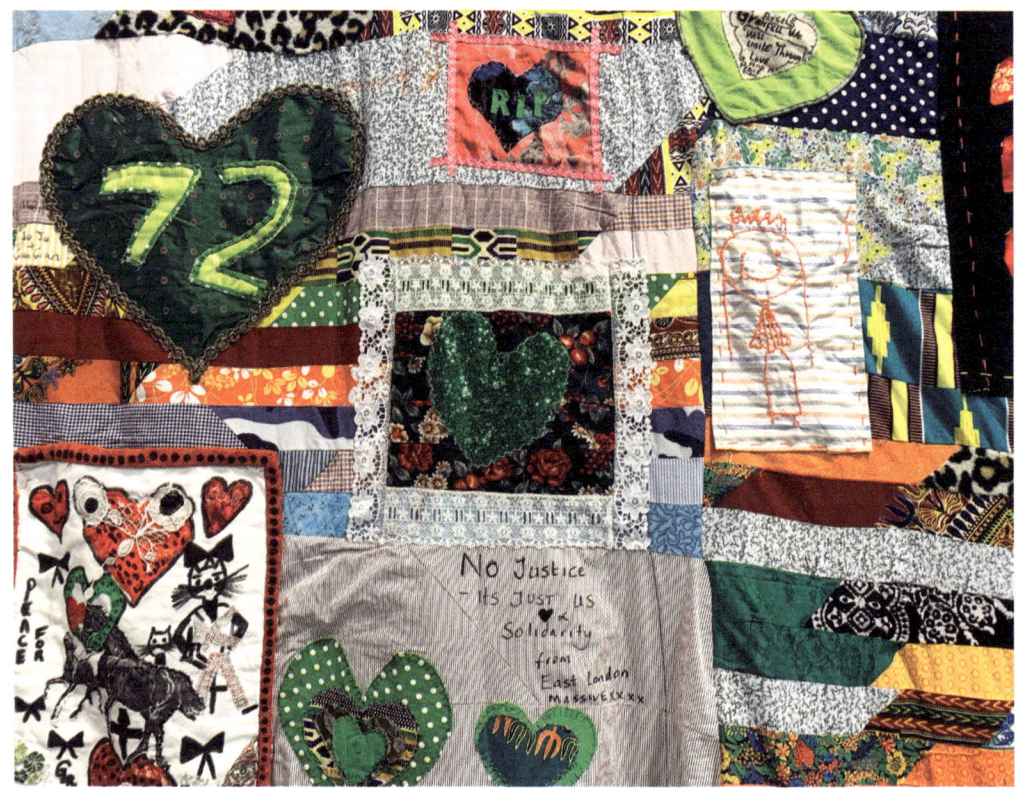

into jelly rolls before being stitched into squares and borders as the quilt grows. Green is the predominant colour chosen by Grenfell United, the group of survivors and bereaved families that formed days after the fire. Each square of the quilt represents an individual victim of the Grenfell Tower fire, with their name, floor number and a personalized message or design embroidered or painted onto the fabric. A star motif is used throughout the quilt to represent the 'star dust' we are all made from and to echo star designs in traditional patchwork used to represent protection, identity, pride and a journey to freedom. All 72 victims, of 19 different nationalities, are represented in the quilt, symbolizing unity, resilience, solidarity and remembrance.

The quilt has gained international recognition, and activists and supporters from all over the world have contributed to this ongoing textile project, which aims to raise awareness through craftivism, and to 'sew for justice' for the victims. By 2027, the tenth anniversary of the fire, it is planned that the quilt will have reached the height and width of Grenfell Tower (67×22m – 220×72ft) and have its inaugural showing as one complete piece.

Following the tragedy in 2017, a full public inquiry was launched, which uncovered systematic failures in fire safety regulations, building materials, emergency response procedures and in the management of social housing.

The Impact of Covid-19

In late January 2020 the World Health Organization (WHO) declared the outbreak of the severe acute respiratory syndrome coronavirus 2 (SARS-CoV-2) a 'public health emergency of international concern'. In February 2020 they officially named the disease Covid-19, and on 11 March 2020 it was classified as a pandemic after the deadly virus spread exponentially throughout the world.

Severe worldwide travel restrictions, school shutdowns, closures of workplaces and the entertainment and hospitality industries were enforced, and strict quarantines and international lockdowns ensued. Consequently, this greatly impacted everyone's lives, causing economic hardship, food shortages and a disruption of social systems, which ultimately led to a global recession.

Mask wearing and hand sanitization became compulsory in public places, and community testing stations and vaccination centres were commonplace. Throughout the world, makeshift morgues were set up as the ever-rising death toll exceeded the usual demand for mortuary places. In many countries funeral services were curtailed, and millions of people were not able to be present when their loved ones were buried or cremated.

On 5 May 2023, the WHO announced that the pandemic was no longer a 'public health emergency of international concern', but made it clear that the pandemic wasn't over. By April 2024, Covid-19 had claimed more than 7 million lives, making it the fifth deadliest pandemic or epidemic in history.

During this turbulent time, Alison Aye, a British collage artist, put her creative energy into recording the pandemic and its new vocabulary (such as 'furloughed' and 'PPE') in her Exile Textile series. Her astute observations of current affairs and key international moments in the ever-changing pandemic landscape were composed and stitched from found household textiles, such as her mother's dusters.

In 2020 another textile commemorating Covid-19 was conceived by 13-year-old Madeleine Fugate from California. Saddened by the impact of this deadly virus, she wanted to honour the lives of those affected to emphasize that the victims were people, not just statistics. Her Covid Memorial Quilt is a stitched 'act of love' that could take many years to complete. Volunteers will continue to compile the 20×20cm (8×8in) squares, each one a tribute to a victim, until the last square is submitted.

OPPOSITE

Exile Textile (2020)

Alison Aye

101×87cm (40×34in). Hand stitched textile.

OVERLEAF, LEFT

Exile Textile 2: The New Normal (2020)

100×87cm (39×34in). Hand stitched textile.

OVERLEAF, RIGHT

Exile Textile 3: The Prequel (2003–22)

100×91cm (39×36in). Hand stitched textile.

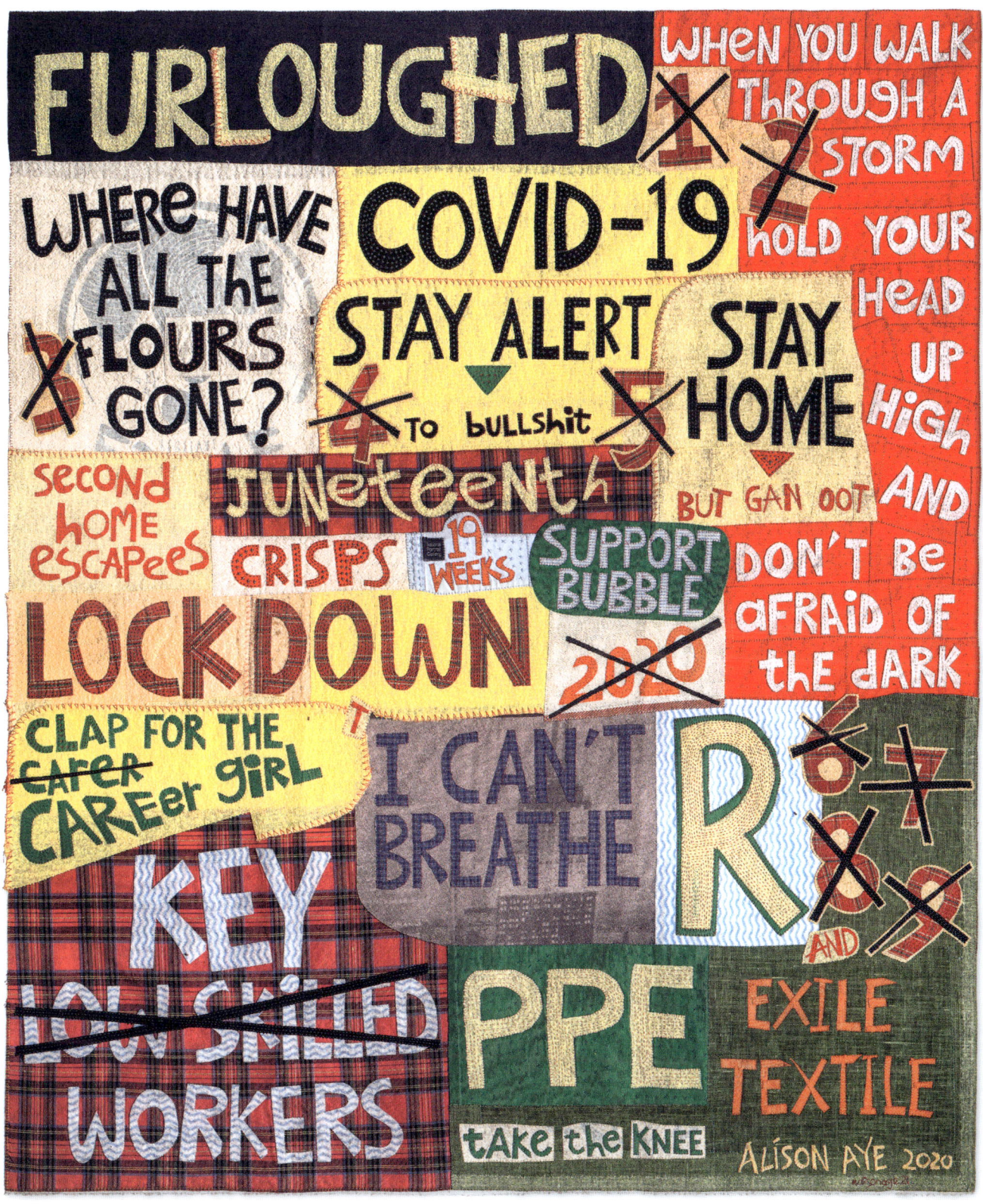

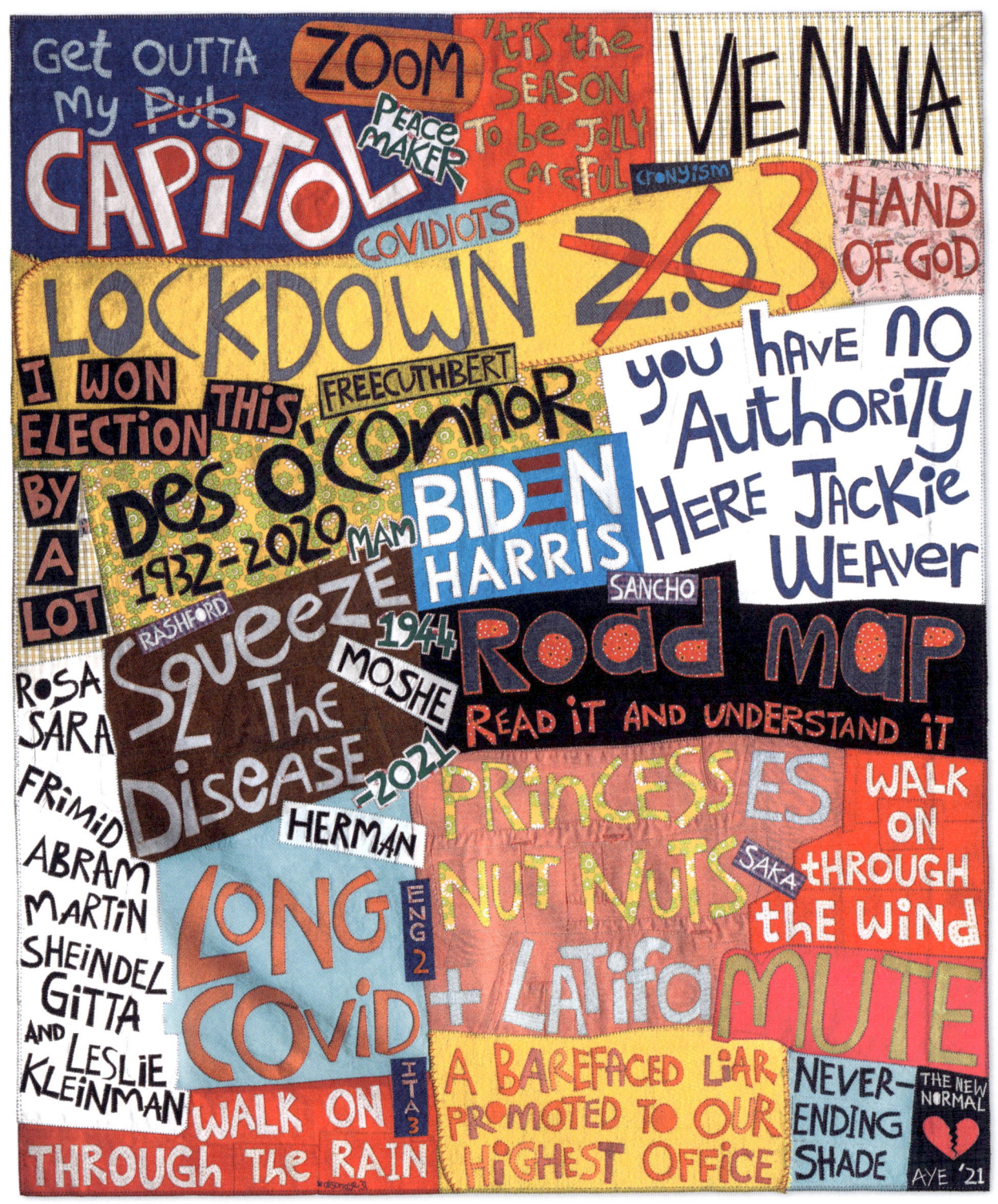

IN MEMORIAM

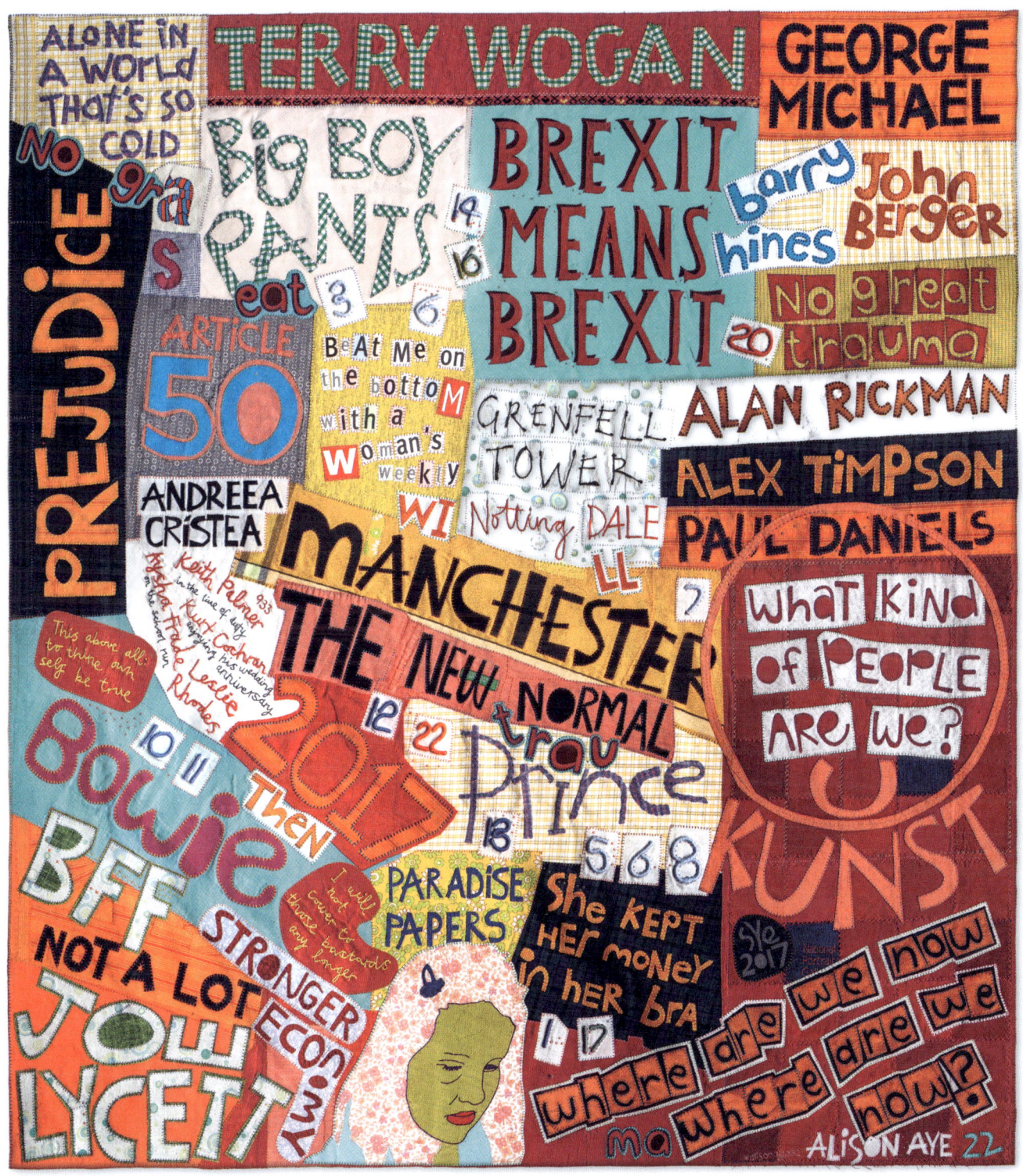

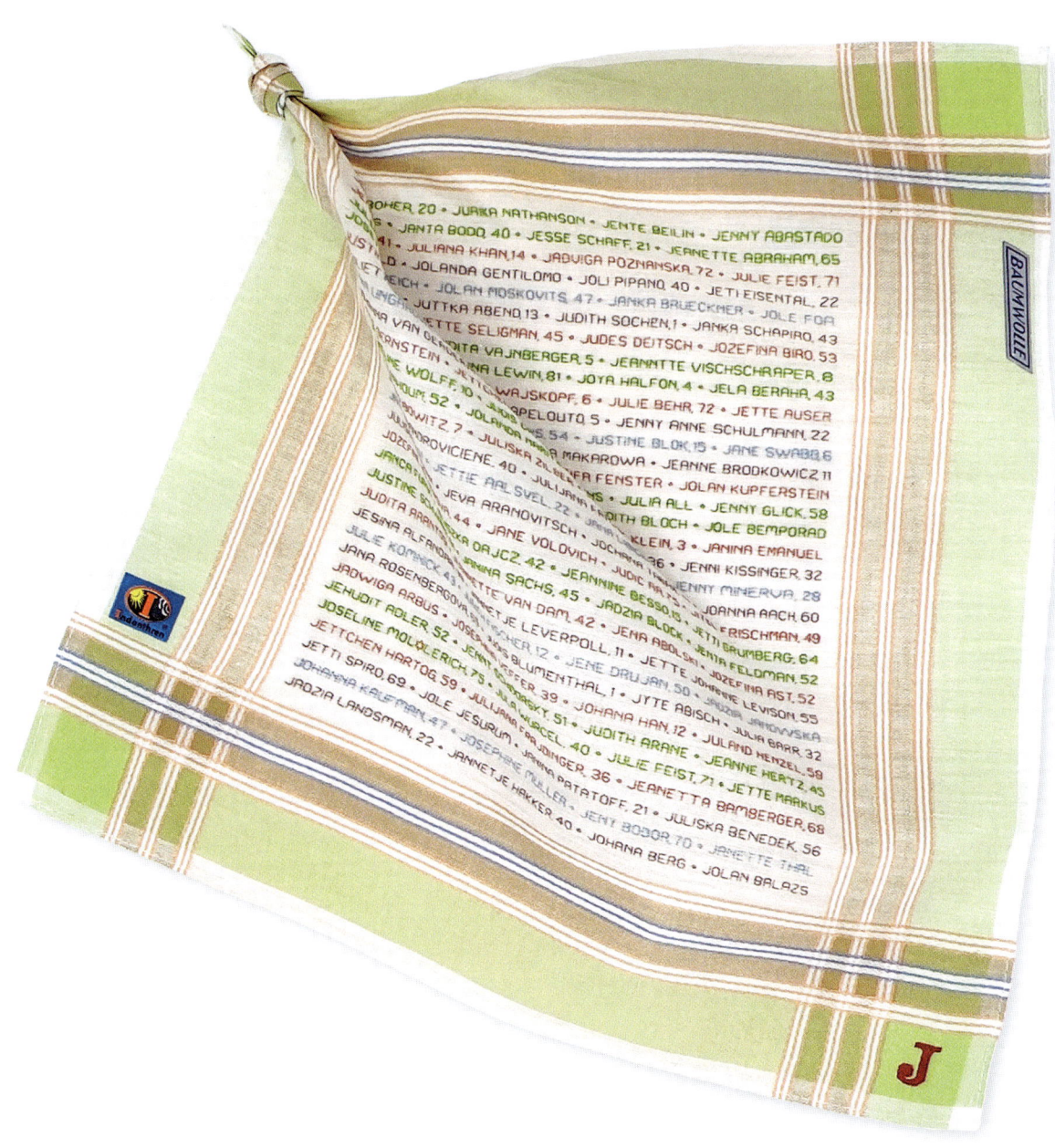

The Holocaust

OPPOSITE

Remember (2023)

Caren Garfen

28×28×4cm
(11×11×1.57in).
Vintage German
handkerchief, silk
threads. Hand stitch.

Although the word 'Holocaust' has been used in different contexts throughout history, it was adopted after World War II to specifically refer to the Nazi genocide of Jewish people in Europe during the period 1941–45. In this period the Nazis murdered six million Jews, as well as millions of other 'undesirables', such as Roma, Slavs, gay people and people with disabilities.

Adolf Hitler seized power in Germany in 1933, and antisemitic laws were passed that forced many Jewish people to emigrate, become displaced or forced to live in segregated ghettos; their lives were under constant threat.

Despite condemnation from many international leaders, the Nazis' antisemitic laws became more extreme and radical, and after Germany invaded Poland in September 1939, all German Jews were at risk of being persecuted and systematically slaughtered. The Nazi regime designed and built five 'killing centres' or extermination camps in German-occupied Poland: Chelmno, Belzec, Sobibór, Treblinka and Auschwitz-Birkenau. More than three million Jewish people were murdered with poison gas and then buried in mass graves.

Other Jews were incarcerated in concentration camps, such as Bergen-Belsen or Majdanek (which latterly became an extermination camp), where they were used as slave labour or for medical experiments, and subjected to abuse and torture. Approximately one million people died in concentration camps during the course of the Holocaust.

By the end of World War II in 1945, when the Allied forces defeated Nazi Germany, approximately two thirds of the Jewish population in Europe had been killed and ethnically cleansed by the Nazis and their collaborators. The scale of this calculated level of mass slaughter and genocide had never been seen before.

Many poignant memorials across the world have been established in memory of the millions of Jews and other minorities who were brutally murdered by the Nazis.

Caren Garfen is an internationally renowned, award-winning artist specializing in textiles. Although her work has always been issue-based, since 2019 she has focused on Holocaust-related themes. Garfen researches and investigates her lines of enquiry thoroughly. She uncovers Jewish lives of loss and turmoil, grief and resilience, courage and horror, unearthing and documenting intimate perspectives and details along the way whilst 'trying to make sense of our complex and problematic world'. Garfen translates her findings into textile and mixed-media narratives with minute and meticulous hand-stitch to create poignant, powerful and challenging artworks. Her embroidered installations are presented and sensitively contextualized within, upon or among everyday objects or personal possessions. This evokes a haunting and indelible impression of real lives and innocent victims. She has created many moving bodies of work to date and her research continues as she unveils the lives of innocent people who were 'murdered by the Nazis because they were Jewish'. Many of her works, such as her ongoing 'Selection' series, are an 'avowal of remembrance', and a 'reminder that antisemitism did not cease when World War II ended'.

In 'Shattered Dreams' (2021), Garfen stitches the story of Ernst Krebs, who was murdered in Auschwitz-Birkenau; at the end of World War II, thousands of spectacles belonging to Holocaust victims were discovered piled up in warehouses at the death camp.

In 'Remember' (2023), Garfen has stitched 130 names of Jewish women and girls, ranging in age from 5 months to 81 years, whose names all begin with 'J'. The letter is significant because all German passports held by Jews were invalid unless stamped with a red 'J' after the 1938 decree issued by the Reich Ministry of the Interior.

In 'Labelled' (2020), Garfen memorializes 73-year-old Helene Brill, who was deported from the Theresienstadt ghetto to the Treblinka extermination camp where she was murdered.

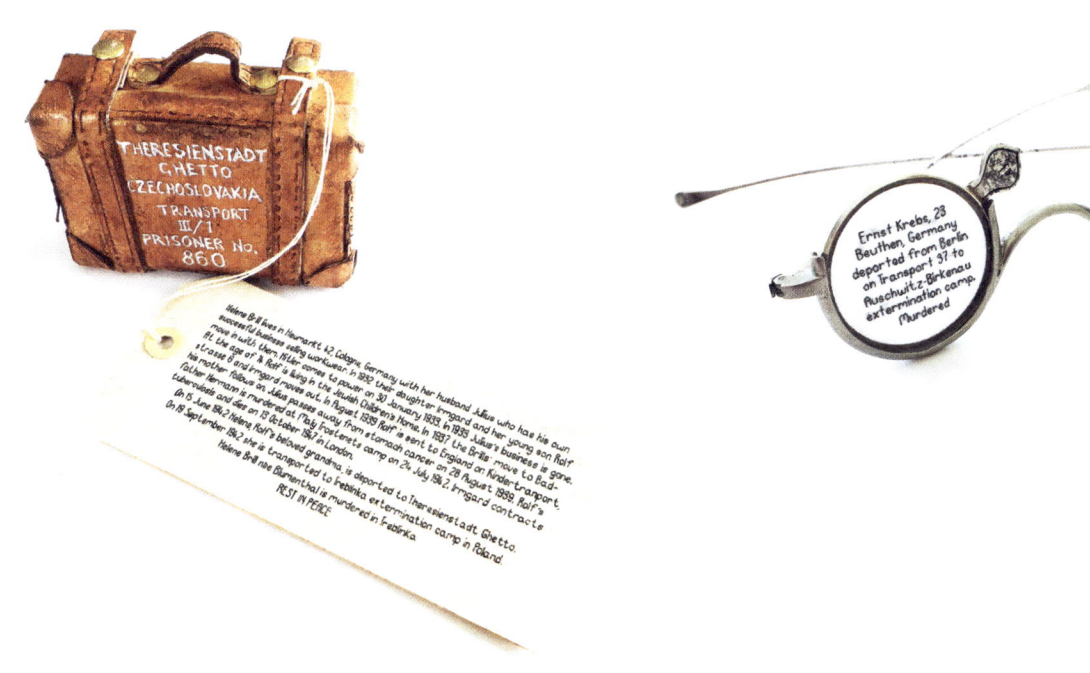

Shrouds

As many of us are increasingly recognizing how our lives make an impact on a world of limited resources, sustainability is creeping higher up the political agenda – but not as fast as many would like. Whilst some are considering making a personalized death shroud for themselves or a loved one – perhaps creatively repurposed from favourite clothes, a quilt or other sentimental materials – one prominent artist is making shrouds as a powerful protest from recycled bedding.

Vince Laws is a UK poet, artist, performer and campaigner. His ongoing textile installation 'DWP Deaths Make Me Sick' began in 2017 and often makes an appearance at rallies, in galleries and outside Parliament. His aim through this impactful project is to highlight the difficult and hostile environment faced by disabled people when dealing with the Department for Work and Pensions (DWP) – the UK government's public service department responsible for welfare, benefits, pensions and child maintenance policies (see also page 113).

'DWP Deaths Make Me Sick' consists of a series of poignant and graphic shrouds, each one naming a disabled person who has lost their life, and describing the circumstances of their death. Upon each haunting shroud, Laws succinctly describes the tragic series of events that directly led to each person's death, such as a ruling from the DWP for an immediate cut in benefits, or an utterly inappropriate 'fit for work' decision. Some shrouds highlight specific campaigns and petitions, or repeat important slogans linked to this potent protest project, such as 'Justice Not Charity', 'Rights Not Charity', 'Respect Not Charity' and 'Dead People Don't Claim'.

Laws' 'DWP Deaths Make Me Sick' shrouds began in a performance by Unlimited and came to the attention of a wider audience in the Piss on Pity exhibition – a seminal exhibition of disabled artists' work reflecting the antipathy of the disabled people's movement towards charity – when it took place in Wakefield, UK, in 2019.

OPPOSITE

DWP Jacqueline Harris (2017–23)

Vince Laws

180×122cm (72×48in) approx. Recycled bedding spraypainted.

'DWP Deaths Make Me Sick', a series of 28 shrouds protesting the deaths of disabled people who died whilst dealing with the DWP. The shrouds were created as part of a live performance, called A Very Queer Nazi Faust, supported by Unlimited and Spirit of 2012. (See also page 113.)

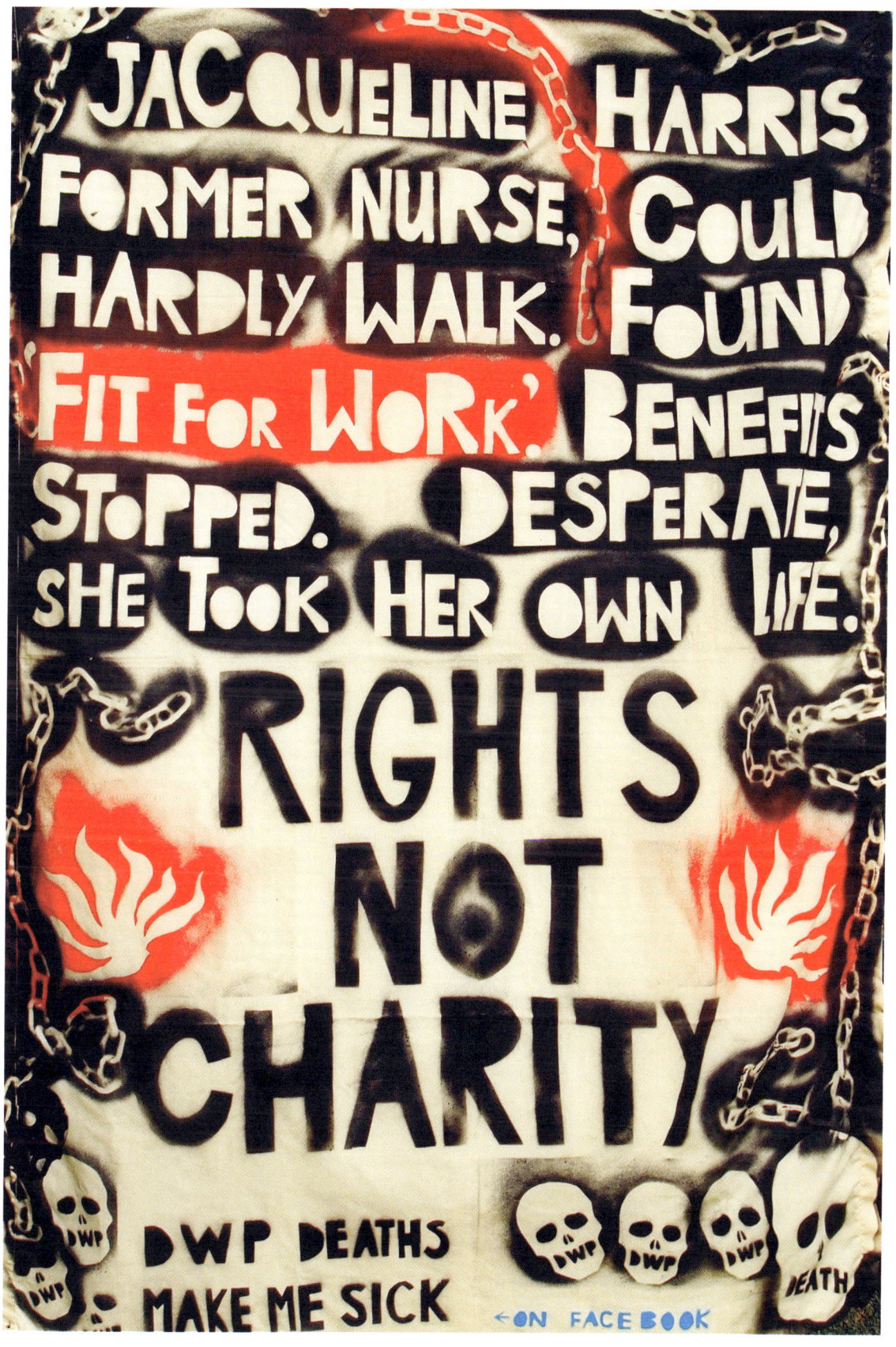

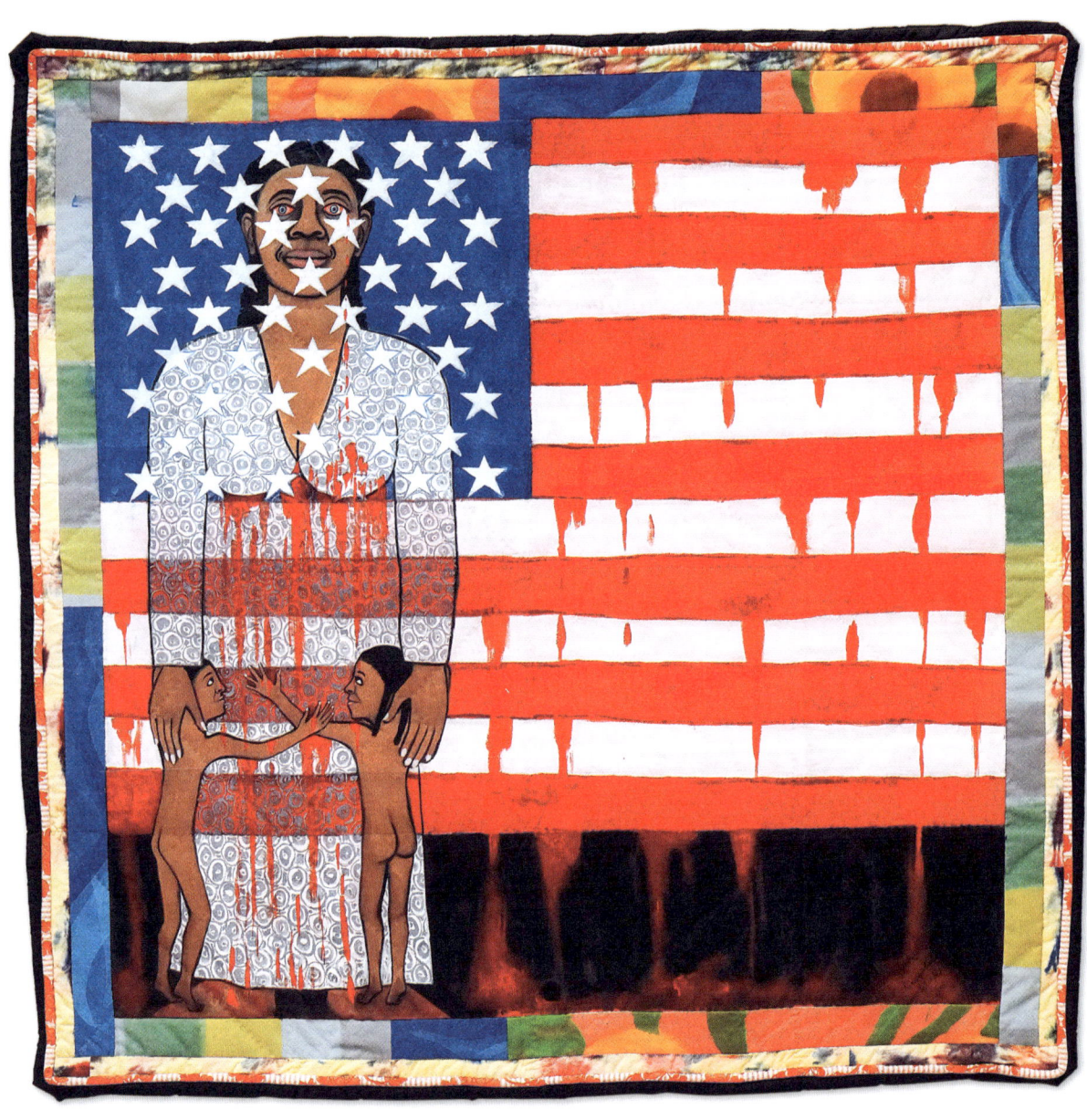

'AND STILL I RISE ...'

'I make thought-provoking artwork that comments on social and environmental injustice; strongly advocating for the protection of women and girls of colour.' NNEKA JONES

Throughout recorded history most societies have traditionally been patriarchal. Men have held the power, controlled politics and defined *'his'tory*. Those assigned female at birth, brought up as girls, or who have embraced their womanhood, have often been denied the opportunities afforded to men and boys.

Women have fought hard for suffrage and political representation, equal pay and employment opportunities, access to education and professional development, comprehensive health care, cultural representation, marital and property rights, legal protection from domestic violence, sexual assault and harassment, and the right to make choices about their own bodies and lifestyles.

But the struggle for equality has been unequal itself as, particularly during early women's suffrage campaigns, Black women frequently faced exclusion from the movement.

Protest textiles have played a significant role in these campaigns, which have been driven by outspoken activists and ordinary women that society expected to stay silent. These trailblazers have marched behind banners, worn colours and coded messages to state their cause, created artworks and installations, and proudly waved flags of resistance to challenge everything from stigmas to the status quo. They have printed, appliquéd, knitted, crocheted, embroidered and stitched their messages of defiance, rage and resistance in protest textiles, some of which have become historic artefacts and serve as a reminder that activism can bring about change.

Although much progress has been made, the fight for equality continues; progress is not linear, inequalities and challenges persist, laws are reversed, and regimes become more extreme and intolerant.

Faith Ringgold (1930–2024) was a feminist, artist, activist, and author who told stories through her mixed media and fabric artworks. Her powerful protest 'story quilts' interpreted political and personal observations of historical and current African American experiences of identity, Black life and culture, oppression and violence. Ringgold's story quilt depicts imagery of blood, tears, anger and frustration and confronts stereotypes of gender and race. The dominant, bloody American flag reflects the tension between the promise of liberty and the reality of systemic inequality.

Women's Suffrage

The Women's Social and Political Union (WSPU) was founded in 1903 in Manchester, UK, by Emmeline Pankhurst and her daughters Christabel and Sylvia. This women-only, activist organization led the movement for women's suffrage, and their members became known as the Suffragettes.

Upon their banners and regalia they presented their slogan 'Votes for Women' in their significant campaign colours chosen by Emmeline Pethick-Lawrence: Green (symbolizing hope), White (symbolizing purity) and Violet (symbolizing dignity). The first letter of the colours, G, W and V were also used as the acronym for 'Give Women Votes'. The Suffragettes demanded results, which they requested using the slogan 'Deeds Not Words'.

Suffragists pursued non-violent tactics in their fight for suffrage, using direct action and civil disobedience to bring attention to their cause. Their confrontational and militant actions included smashing shop windows, posting letter bombs, cutting railway signal lines and coordinating a bombing and arson operation. They targeted key political figures and infrastructure, but their wider campaign also threatened the safety of the general public. Emmeline Pankhurst stated that their aim was 'to make England and every department of English life insecure and unsafe'. Often labelled as 'terrorists', they killed four people in their attacks and injured more. One notable Suffragette, Emily Wilding Davison, lost her own life in the cause, when she stepped in front of King George V's horse during the Epsom Derby. She became a martyr for the suffrage movement.

Many Suffragettes were arrested and imprisoned, including Emmeline Pankhurst. Whilst imprisoned, the Suffragettes went on hunger strikes and were subject to brutal force-feeding procedures. But they never gave up. They paused their fight during World War I and eventually gained a partial victory in 1918 in the UK, when the Representation of the People Act was passed. This granted votes to women over the age of 30 who fulfilled certain property requirements. Victory, and full suffrage, was finally achieved in 1928 with the Representation of the People (Equal Franchise) Act, which gave women equal voting rights to men.

The Suffragettes' legacy still has an impact today as a model for significant activism that brought about radical change for gender equality through reformed electoral systems.

OPPOSITE, ABOVE

The Hammersmith 'Deeds Not Words' banner.

OPPOSITE, BELOW

Emmeline Pankhurst addresses a crowd.

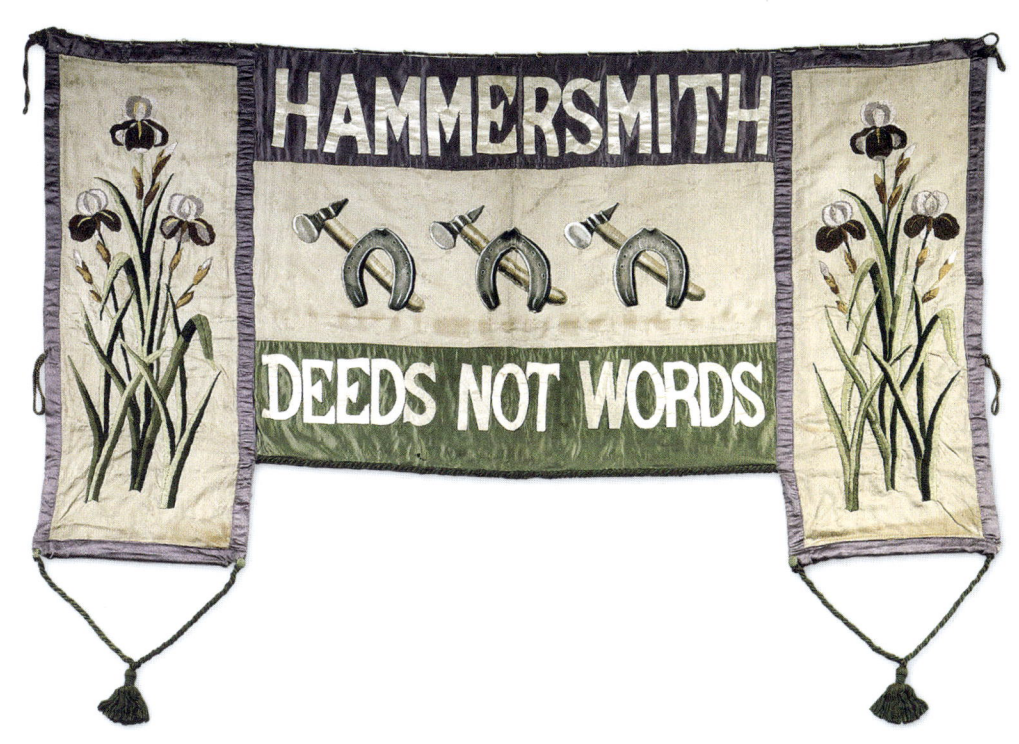

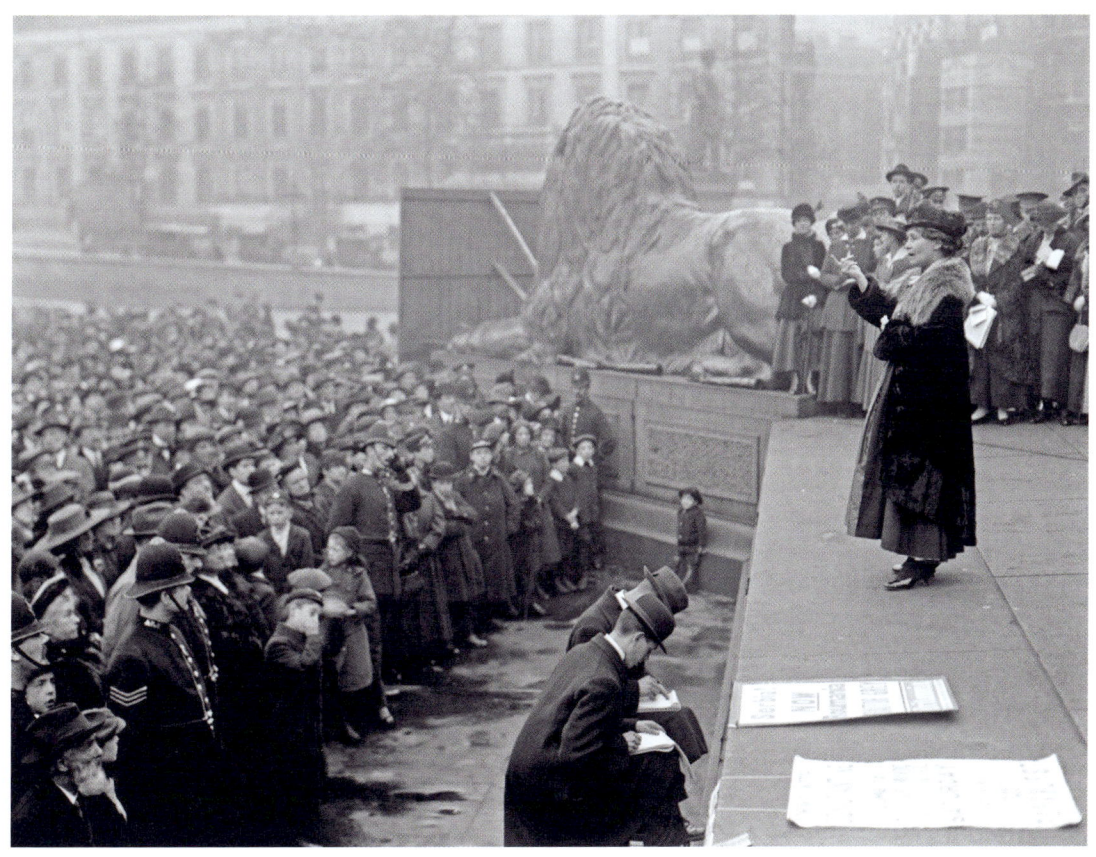

The Women's Liberation Movement

Also known as the Feminist Movement or Women's Lib, in the 1960s and 70s the Women's Liberation Movement (WLM) sought to achieve equal rights for women across social and political male-dominated spaces by closing the 'gender gap'. The Suffragettes and civil rights activists inspired and paved the way for this movement, and women mobilized to challenge patriarchal systems and address gender equality in all reaches of life.

In 1968 feminist activists disrupted the Miss America pageant in Atlantic City, condemning the event for its misogynistic and degrading attitudes towards women, reducing them only to 'objects of beauty'. Activists were encouraged to bring along beauty products and paraphernalia such as girdles, wigs, curlers, false eyelashes and bras, and symbolically discard then burn them in a 'freedom trash can' to emulate the illegal burning of the draft card by pacifists. Officials actually stopped the burning because of the flammability of the boardwalk where the hundreds of women were protesting but, to this day, the reduction of the WLM to 'bra burning' is a popular misconception of the movement.

One of the central campaigns of the WLM was access to safe contraception and the right to abortion. Birth-control pills became available on the National Health Service (NHS) in the UK in 1961, and Roe vs Wade in 1973 was a landmark case in the US Supreme Court which legalized abortion and was a significant victory for the movement.

Another campaign by the WLM was for equality in the workplace, with a demand for equal pay for equal work, and an end to sexual harassment, discriminatory hiring practices and archaic employment laws in the labour market. An Equal Pay Act was introduced in the US in 1963 and similar legislation was enacted in the UK in 1970. Despite these and similar laws, there are still huge disparities in wages, and women still fight to receive the same pay as men for equivalent work.

Women fought for cultural changes too, such as the right to have the freedom to choose a career outside the home, a domestic life as a home-maker, or both. Women's studies courses were established in universities, feminist literature came to prominence (notably from The Women's Press) and women's issues appeared on more agendas as gender stereotypes were scrutinized.

OPPOSITE

1971 New York march for women's liberation.

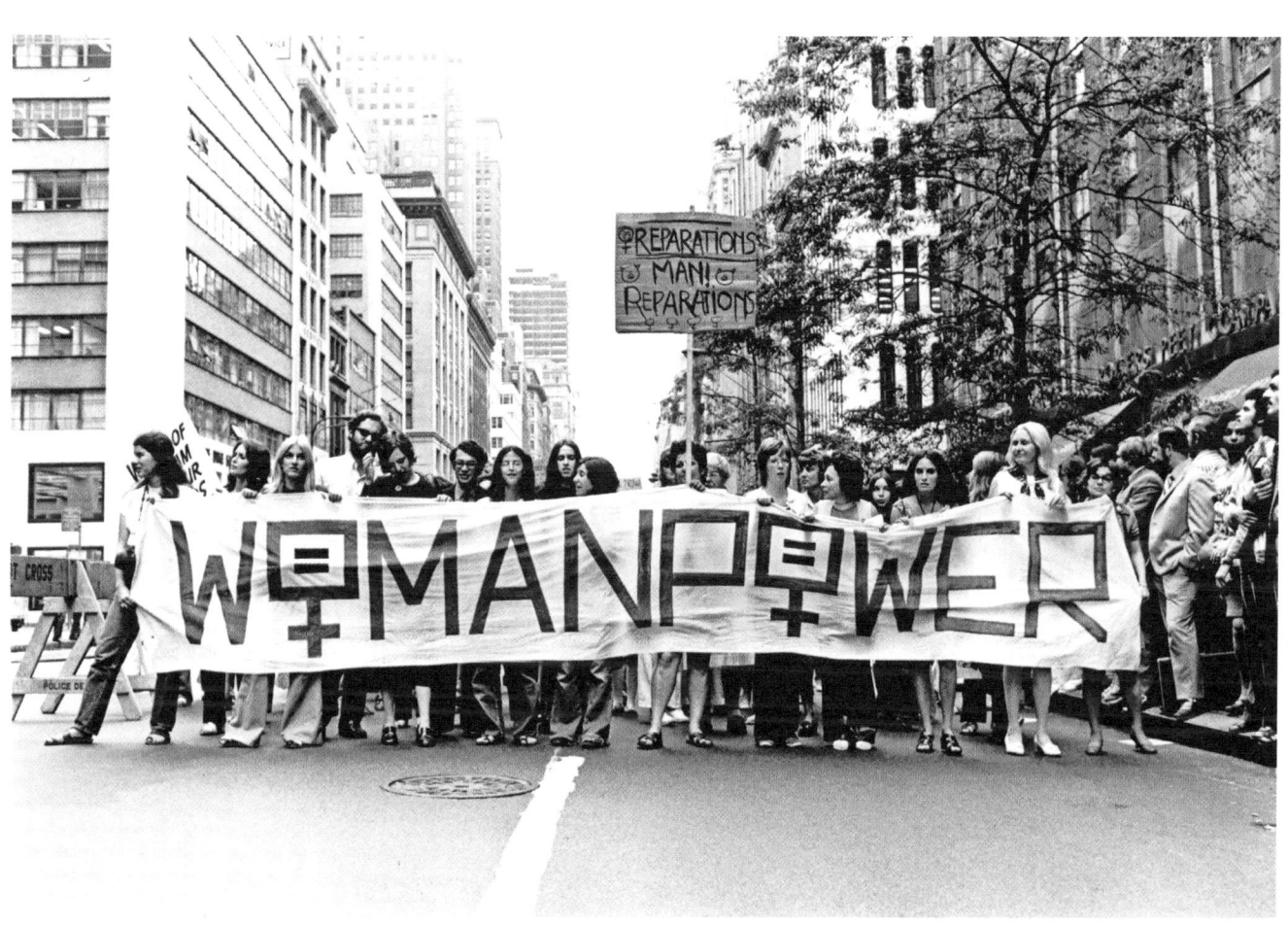

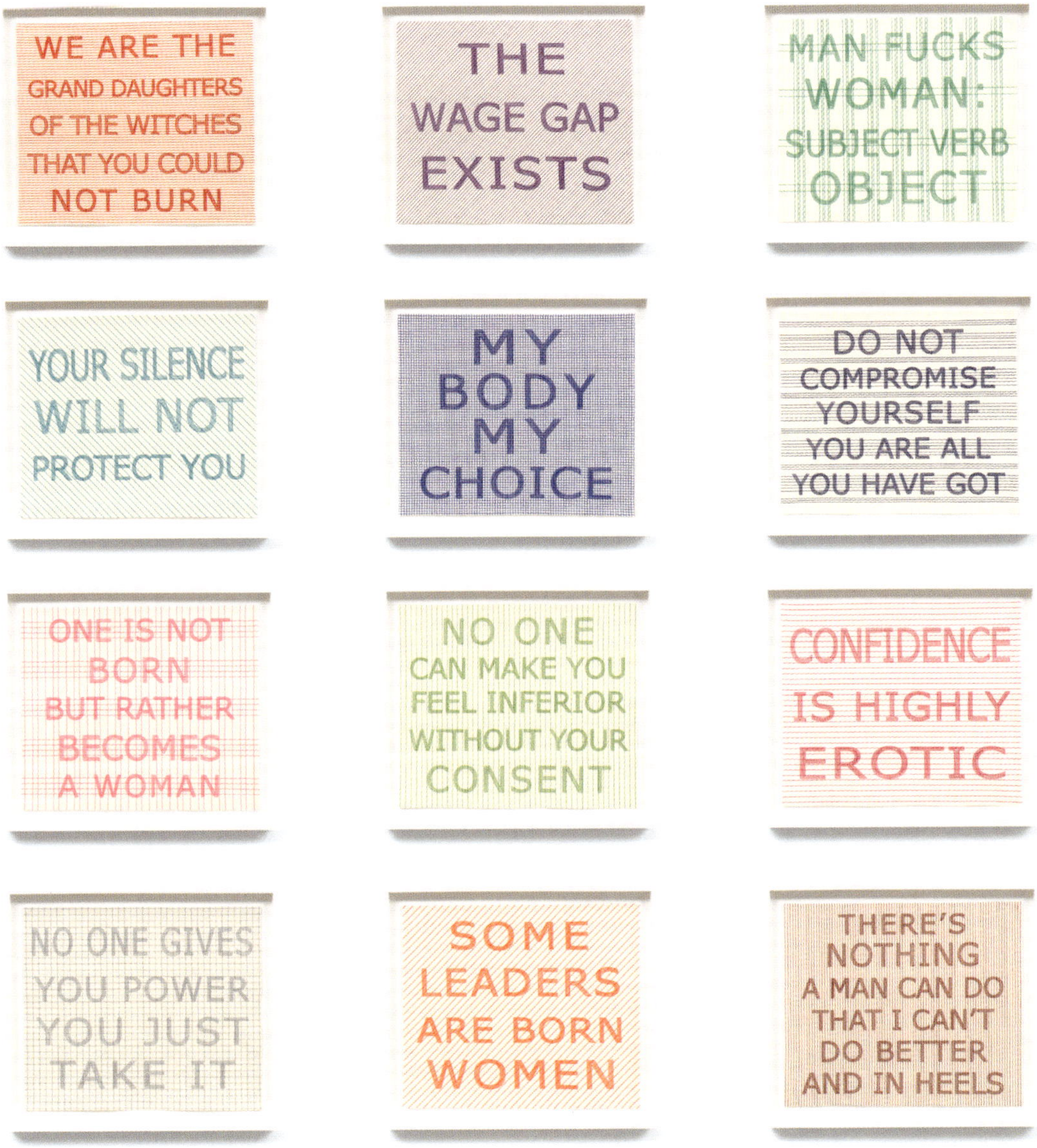

WE ARE THE
GRAND DAUGHTERS
OF THE WITCHES
THAT YOU COULD
NOT BURN

THE
WAGE GAP
EXISTS

MAN FUCKS
WOMAN:
SUBJECT VERB
OBJECT

YOUR SILENCE
WILL NOT
PROTECT YOU

MY
BODY
MY
CHOICE

DO NOT
COMPROMISE
YOURSELF
YOU ARE ALL
YOU HAVE GOT

ONE IS NOT
BORN
BUT RATHER
BECOMES
A WOMAN

NO ONE
CAN MAKE YOU
FEEL INFERIOR
WITHOUT YOUR
CONSENT

CONFIDENCE
IS HIGHLY
EROTIC

NO ONE GIVES
YOU POWER
YOU JUST
TAKE IT

SOME
LEADERS
ARE BORN
WOMEN

THERE'S
NOTHING
A MAN CAN DO
THAT I CAN'T
DO BETTER
AND IN HEELS

'AND STILL I RISE …'

Feminism

Feminism has generally been described as coming in four 'waves'. The first wave (1848–1920) was established in the UK and US and focused on obtaining women's suffrage. The second wave was in the 1960s and 70s – the period known as the Women's Liberation Movement. The third wave, starting in the 1990s, focused on intersectionality, inclusivity and the difference between sex and gender. The fourth wave of feminism, which began in the 2010s, has built on the third wave, but has also used the internet and social media to bring campaigns, such as #MeToo, to global attention.

Early waves of feminism have been criticized for not including all women in their struggle for equality – for instance no Black women were invited to attend the Seneca Falls convention in New York, 1848, where women's rights reformers advocated for the right of white women to vote – but central to all has been the deconstruction and dismantling of patriarchal systems.

Many artists and activists have made artworks that bring feminist issues to the public arena, including contemporary Egyptian artist Ghada Amer whose work is pictured here. Her delicately stitched embroideries embrace empowerment as she 'explores the dichotomies of an uneasy world' and 'repudiates first-wave feminist theory that the body must be denied to prevent victimization'.

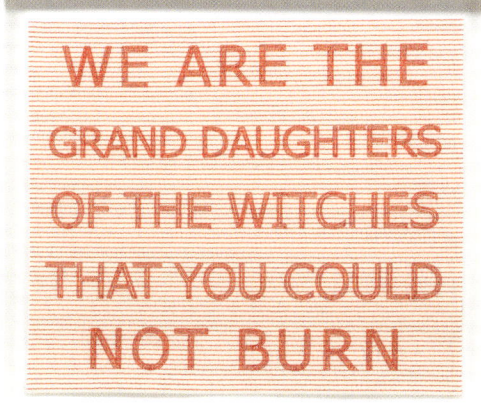

Black Feminism

Black feminism addresses the unique experiences of Black women by emphasizing the overlap of race, gender and class: a concept central to intersectionality. Black feminists in the 1960s and 70s criticized aspects of the mainstream Women's Liberation Movement for overlooking these intersections and marginalizing Black women and their concerns. Many Black feminists had been active in the American Civil Rights Movement, but had become disillusioned because of the sexism they faced within it. Black feminist groups such as the Combahee River Collective formed, as they described it, out of the need to 'develop a politics that was anti-racist, unlike those of white women, and anti-sexist, unlike those of Black and white men'.

In 1979 the collective protested the murders of 12 Black women in Roxbury in Boston, and the lack of media attention given to them. Their banner '3RD WORLD WOMEN WE CANNOT LIVE WITHOUT OUR LIVES' calls to attention a basic right that many white middle-class feminists took for granted: the right to life. The cuts into the banner draw attention to the violence that these Black women faced.

Like Maya Angelou's collection of poetry *And Still I Rise*, from which this chapter takes its name, the Combahee River Collective's feminism drew on a strong tradition of resistance of enslaved women and their descendants in the USA.

The group disbanded in 1980, but their inclusive vision for liberation, from their perspective as Black feminist lesbians, carried on and influenced later waves of feminism.

OPPOSITE

The Combahee River Collective.

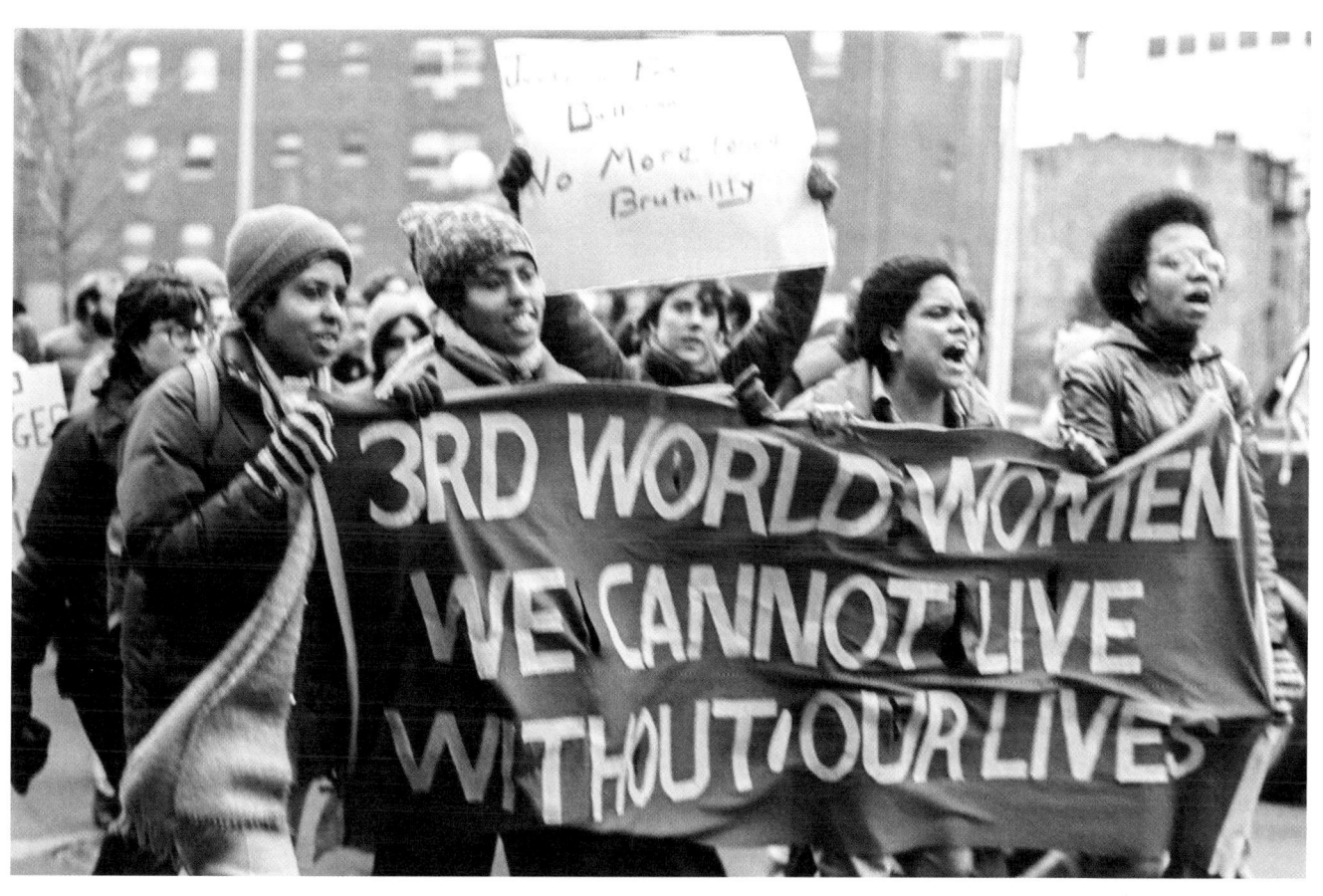

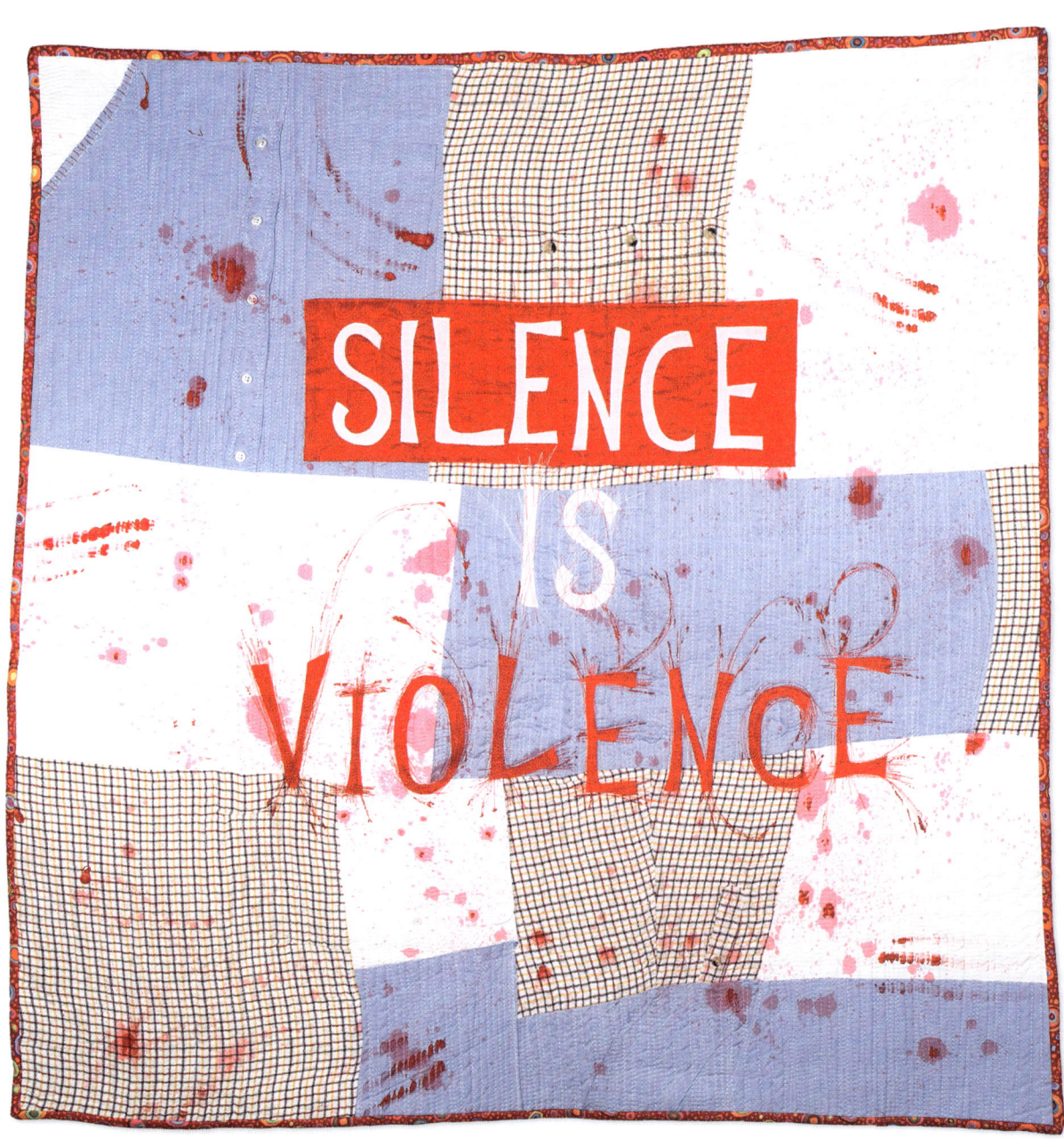

Protesting Gender-based Violence

OPPOSITE

Silence (2024)

Brenda Jane Sanders

118×114cm (46.45×44.88in). Pieced and quilted thrifted men's shirts, machine appliqué, machine embroidery and acrylic paint.

Made in response to memories of childhood (see also page 161).

Throughout their lives, women and girls are more likely to be victims of emotional, physical or sexual abuse and violence because of their gender. They can be victims of sexual assault, domestic violence, marital rape or trafficking – all of which can have devastating long-term consequences resulting in deep psychological trauma or even death.

The entrenched culture of victim blaming often leads to 'survivor silence'. Survivors are silenced for many reasons, including fear of retaliation or not being believed, the shame and stigma of being judged or blamed, and the distrust of the justice system.

Ending gender-based violence requires a monumental shift in societal attitudes: from views about safety and consent, to legal reforms and advocating for robust support systems for survivors.

In 2024 Gisèle Pelicot garnered international support and respect, and was hailed as a feminist hero during the trial of her ex-husband and 50 other men for rape and sexual assault. Pelicot's ex-husband admitted to regularly drugging and then raping Pelicot, as well as to recruiting strangers to rape her whilst she was unconscious – which he filmed over the course of a decade.

Pelicot opted for a public trial and waived her rights to anonymity to hold her abusers to account and to turn the conversation of blame and shame around, whilst demanding justice. She said 'it's not for us to have shame, it's for them; shame must change sides'.

Her courage and resilience to break the silence about sexual violence, and spark a global conversation about consent, has been applauded by women around the globe who have praised her for shedding light on gender-based violence with such dignity.

Textiles have been used in many ways to protest against gender-based violence; they are often created to draw attention to key issues that affect women every day across the world. They claim space, command attention and call for change. They are a protest against the pressure to stay silent.

In her embroidered Target series, US-based Trinidadian activist artist Nneka Jones powerfully confronts issues of gender-based violence, in particular the objectification and exploitation of women and girls of colour. These artworks potently address themes of vulnerability, exploitation, human trafficking, violence and injustice.

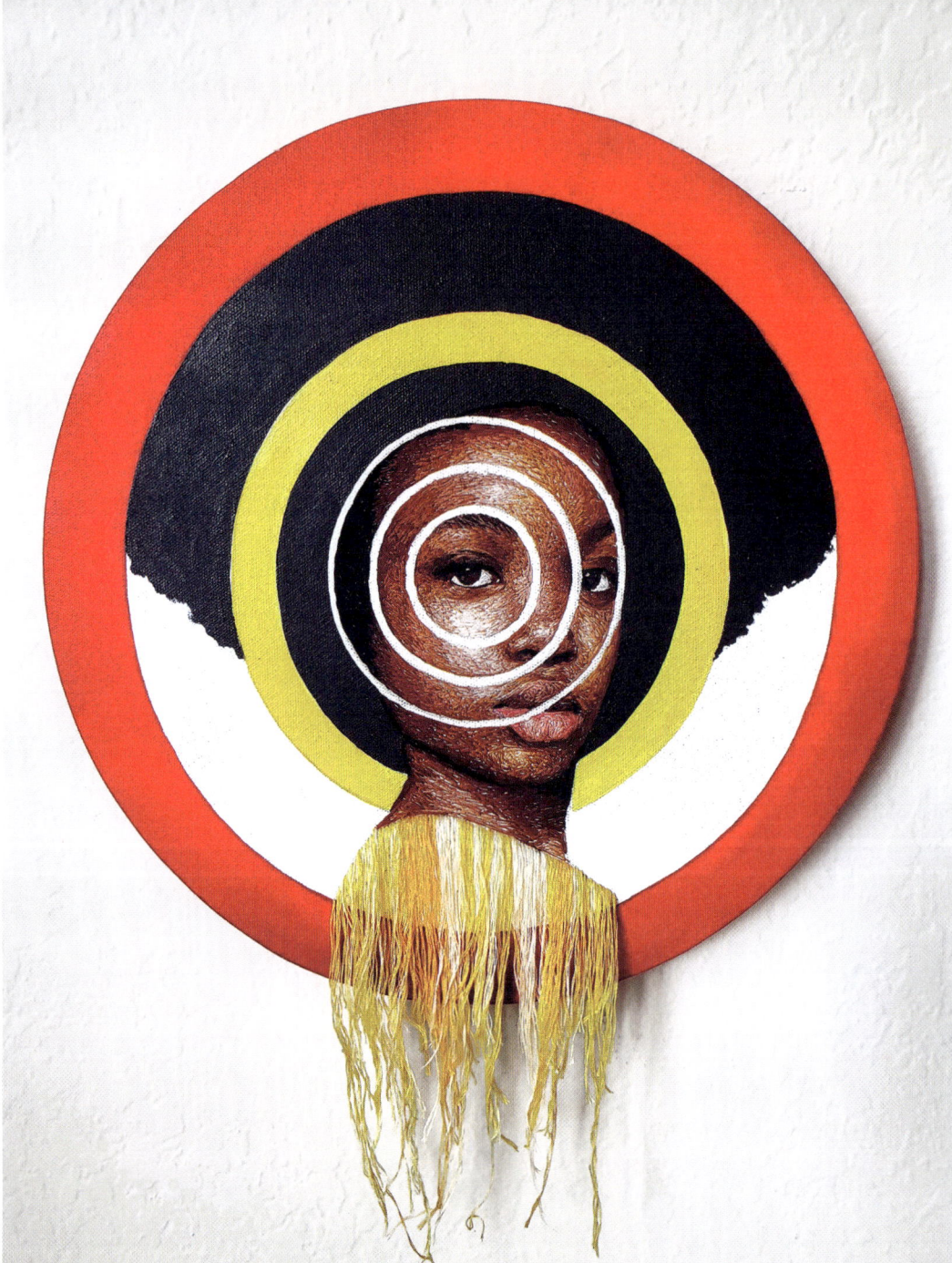

LEFT

Yellow Light (2019)

Nneka Jones

Hand-embroidery on canvas.

OPPOSITE

Shooting Range Target (2019)

Nneka Jones

Hand-embroidery on canvas.

US-based Trinidadian activist artist Nneka Jones powerfully confronts issues of gender-based violence, in particular the objectification and exploitation of women and girls of colour, in her embroidered Target series. These artworks potently address themes of vulnerability, exploitation, human trafficking, violence and injustice.

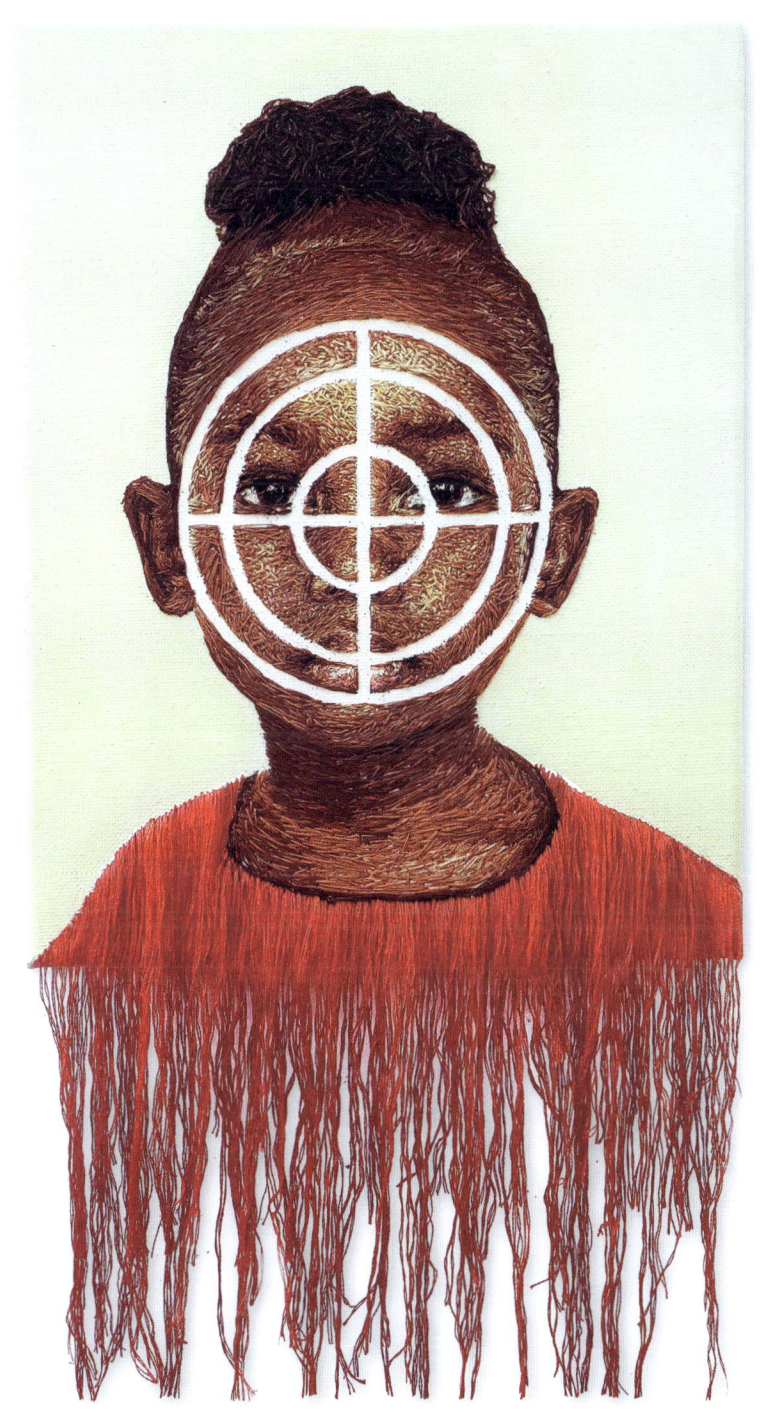

Reclaim the Night

International protests to 'Reclaim the Night' provided a platform for women to assert their right to walk safely and without fear at night and to demonstrate against continued sexual violence and harassment from men. Inspired by earlier 'Take Back the Night' demonstrations in West Germany, the first 'Reclaim the Night' march, in 1977, was organized by the Leeds Revolutionary Feminist Group in the UK.

In the midst of the Yorkshire Ripper murders the police advised women to stay indoors at night. Women, including sex workers, felt under curfew, restricted and blamed. In response, women took to the streets to reclaim their rights to walk safely in public places, carrying placards stating that men, not women, should be under curfew. Several torchlit marches were held simultaneously in Leeds, Newcastle, London, Brighton, Manchester, York and Bristol.

Half a century on, women are often still blamed for the actions of men, so the 'Reclaim the Night' marches continue to challenge victim blaming and rape culture, and demand the right to live without the fear of attack.

The kidnapping, rape and murder of Sarah Everard in London in 2021, by an off-duty Metropolitan Police officer who used his police powers to falsely arrest her under the pretence of breaching Covid-19 regulations, triggered widespread outrage and protests, and, once again, brought into the spotlight the misogynistic and violent attitudes towards women and their safety.

OPPOSITE

Protestors at a 'Reclaim the Night' march.

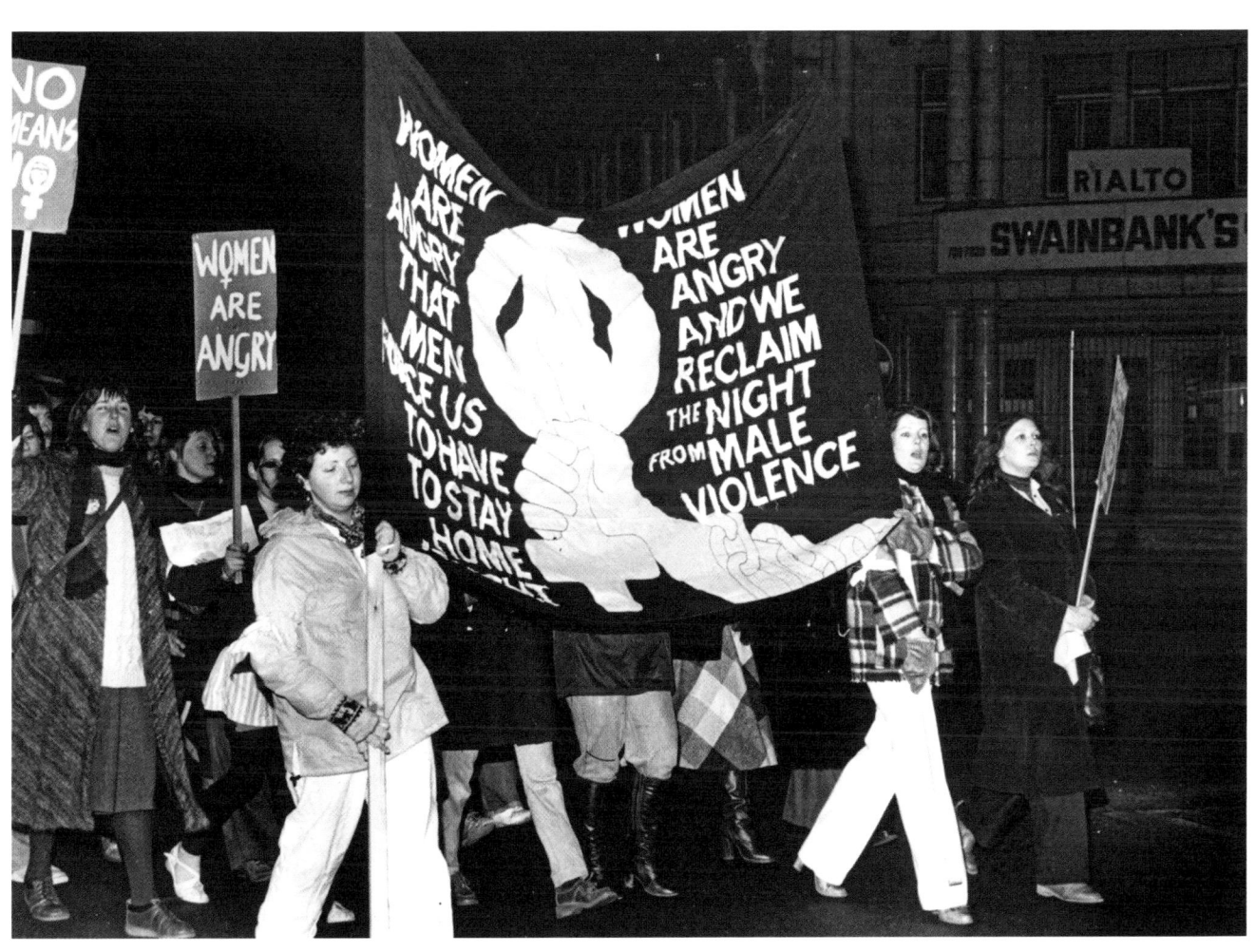

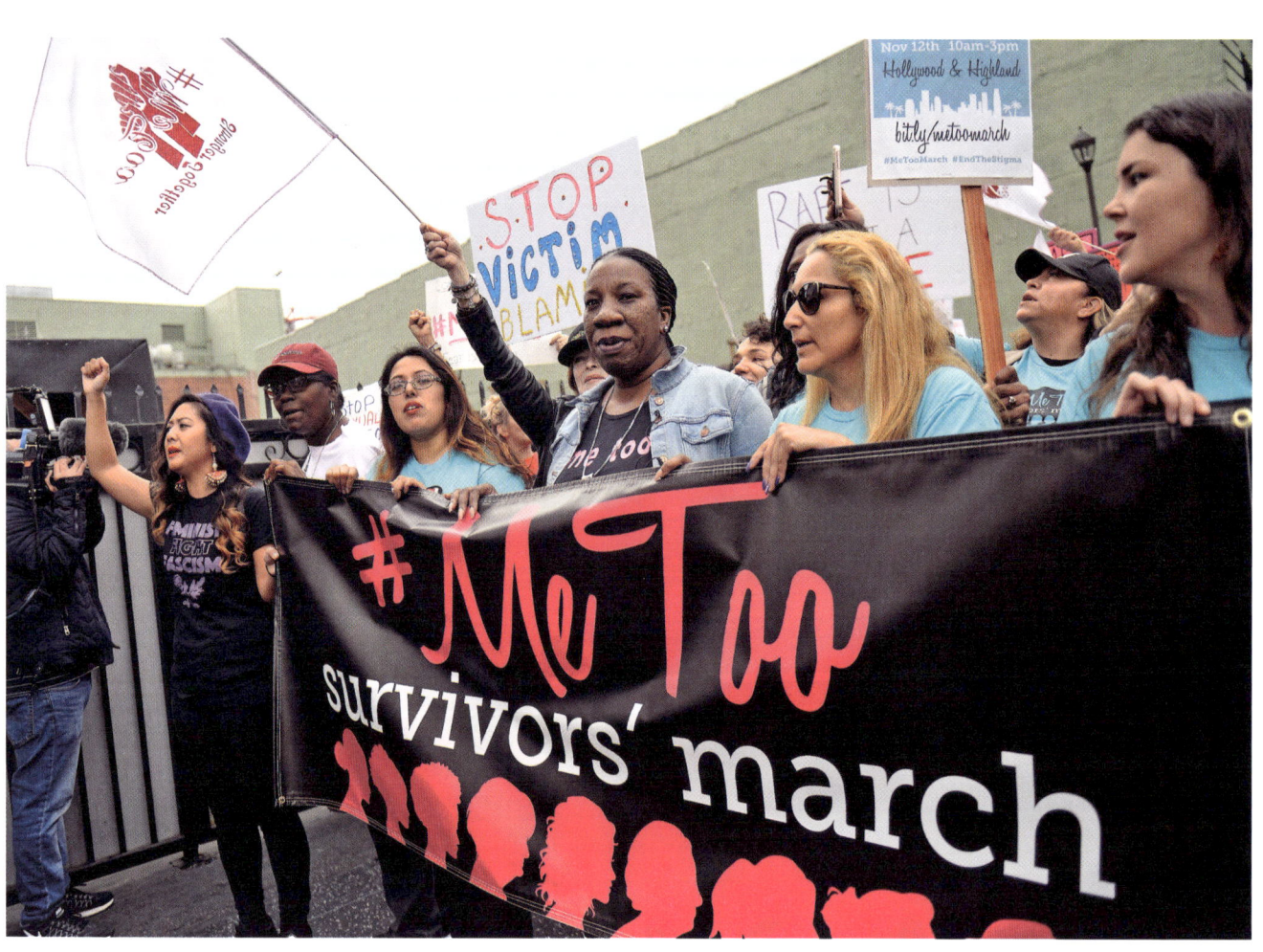

'AND STILL I RISE …'

OPPOSITE

Tarana Burke and
other protestors
with #MeToo
banner.

OVERLEAF, LEFT

Bewitched (2020)

Holly Searle

Vintage linen tea-towel
with appliquéd felt
letters stitched by hand.

OVERLEAF, RIGHT

Re Brand (2023)

Holly Searle

Vintage linen tea-towel
with appliquéd felt
letters stitched by hand.

#MeToo

The #MeToo movement is a survivor-led awareness campaign and social movement founded by the American activist Tarana Burke. Through her community work with various youth organizations, Burke worked with young African American women who were survivors of sexual violence. She first used the phrase 'me too' on MySpace in 2006. As a survivor herself, she saw this as a way of promoting 'empowerment through empathy', and also as a way of raising awareness of the extent of sexual abuse and violence in society, particularly among women of colour.

In 2017, sparked by the sexual abuse allegations against Harvey Weinstein, Alyssa Milano, an American activist, actress and producer, suggested using 'Me Too' as a hashtag in order to stand in solidarity with other women and girls who had been victims of sexual violence and to unveil 'the magnitude of the problem'. The hashtag instantly went viral as survivors, including high-profile celebrities, posted #MeToo as their status. Milano credited Burke for the origin of the phrase, and Burke supported the use of the #MeToo hashtag.

#MeToo started an international conversation, revealing the prevalence of sexual harassment, abuse and rape culture in societies throughout the world, and a global movement was born. The World Health Organization (WHO) currently estimates that one in three women worldwide are subjected to some form of physical or sexual violence during their lifetime.

British artist and activist, Holly Searle (see overleaf and page 206) embellishes vintage tea towels with phrases in felt lettering which she sews onto them to subvert their original context. She highlights issues that are 'prevalent in society', such as sexual violence against women and girls, and misogynistic comments from high-profile celebrities.

Whilst some of the artworks in her Vintage Tea Towel series are sprinkled with punchy feminist statements that can raise a nod of recognition and a smile for being well said, others portray more sobering and sinister messages.

Through this fascinating ongoing series, Searle is keeping important issues in the spotlight.

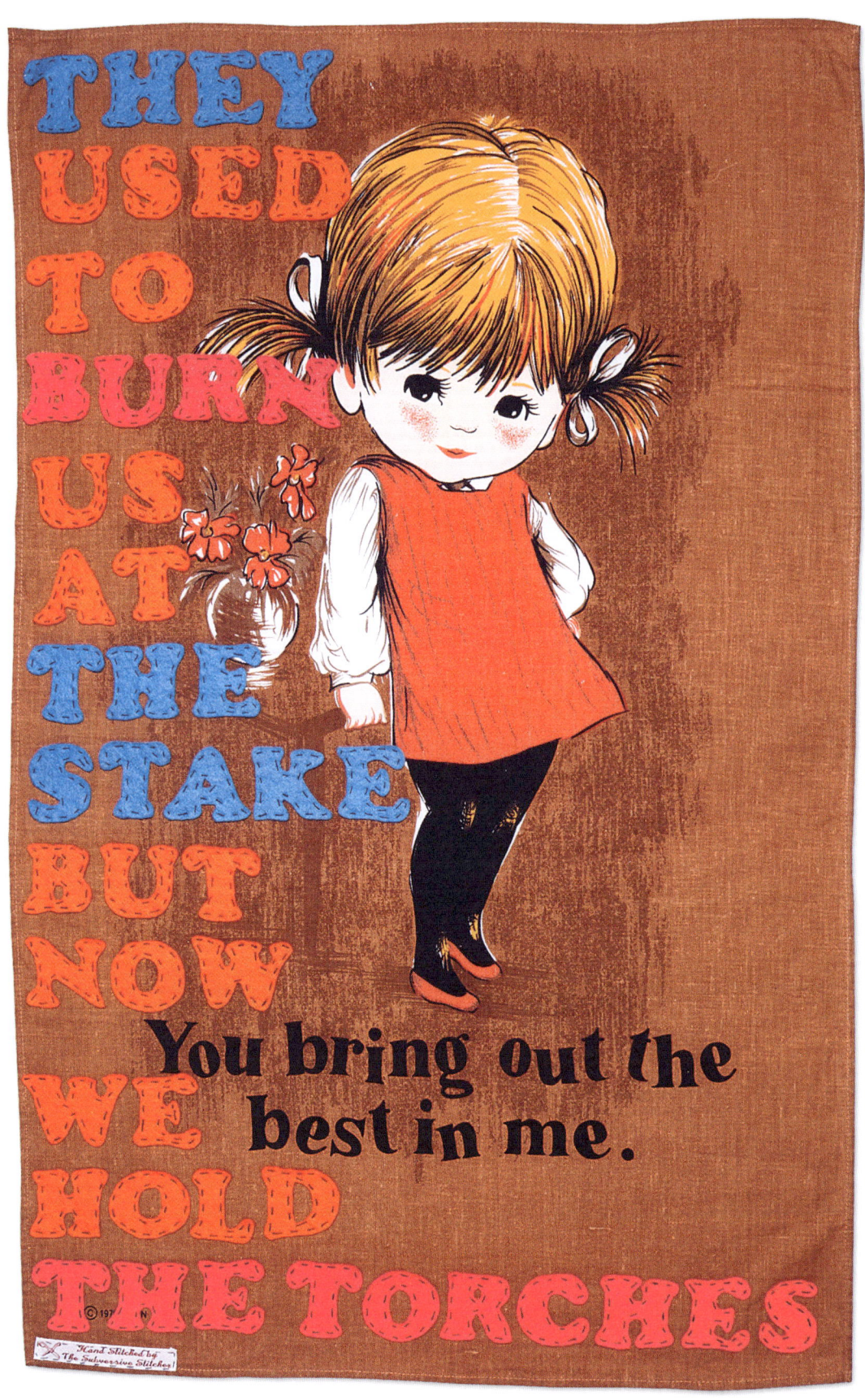

'AND STILL I RISE …'

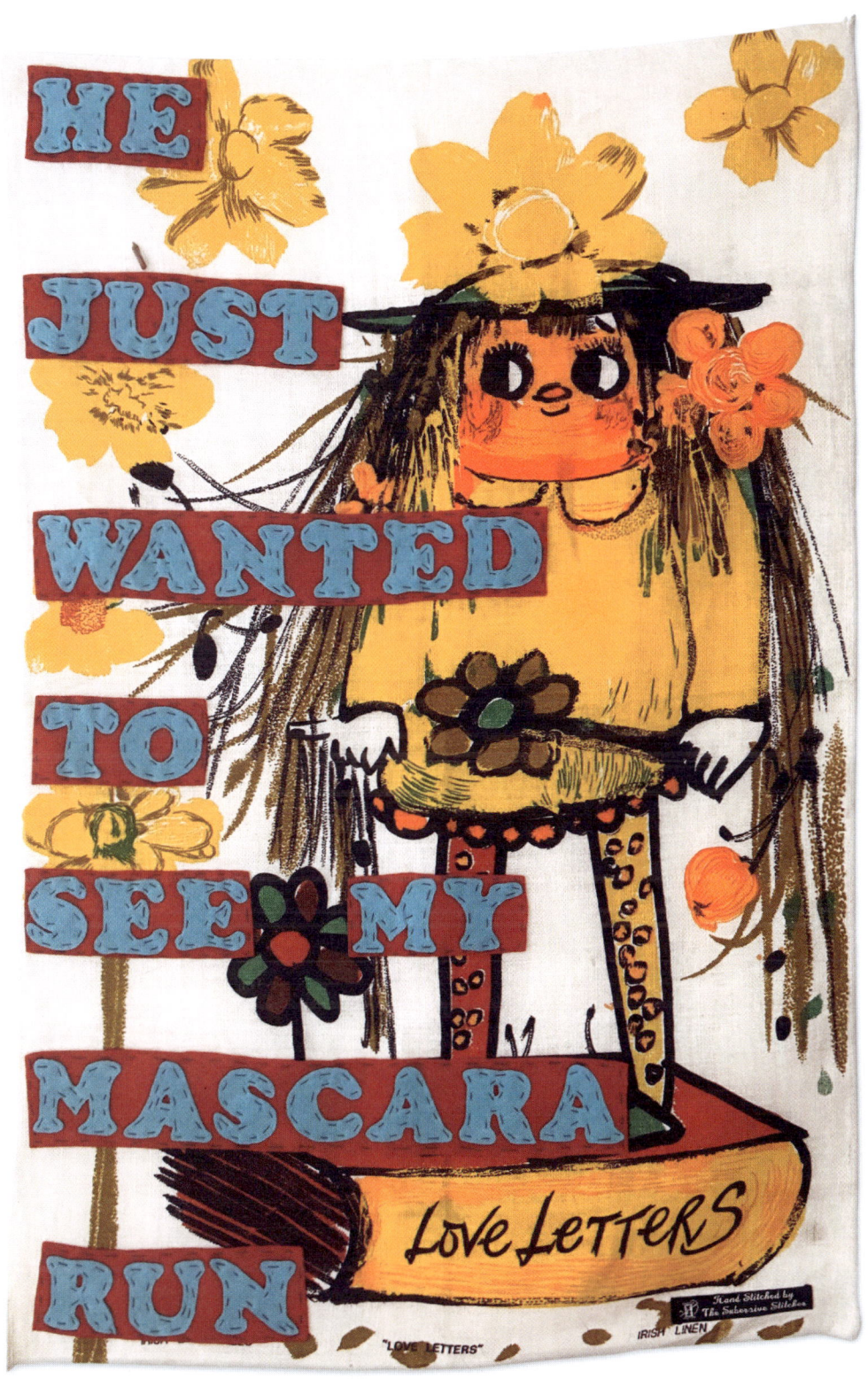

Provoke/Protect

Susie Vickery, a fine-art embroiderer, has worked with many minority women's groups throughout the world, developing community projects which explore issues through handicrafts, national dress and costume. In Mumbai, India, Vickery mentored and worked with ten local women on the Provoke/Protect project for the Dharavi Biennale in 2014 to create a collection of decorated saris in response to the horrific gang rape and murder of 'Nirbhaya' in South Delhi, December 2012. 'Nirbhaya' means 'fearless one' in Hindi. In accordance with Indian law, this was the pseudonym assigned to Jyoti Singh, the victim of this shocking and fatal act of sexual violence, before her name was officially released to the media.

The bespoke saris were boldly and colourfully adorned with protective symbols, such as traffic lights and horseshoes, and appliquéd slogans, notably 'Lock up the rapist, not the woman', '1000 Volts Shakti' and 'Stop Rape'. As the women stitched these powerful artworks together, they discussed issues around the prevention of violence towards women with experts on gender-based violence, and 'unpicked that old statement *she asked for it*'.

OPPOSITE

Provoke/Protect: Stop Rape (2013)

Anjali Amma

Recycled saris, appliqué, embroidery.

OVERLEAF, LEFT

Provoke/Protect: Keep Out (2013)

Usha Kharatmal

Recycled saris, appliqué, embroidery.

OVERLEAF, RIGHT

Provoke/Protect: Don't Touch Me (2013)

Nirmala Panjabi

Recycled saris, appliqué, embroidery.

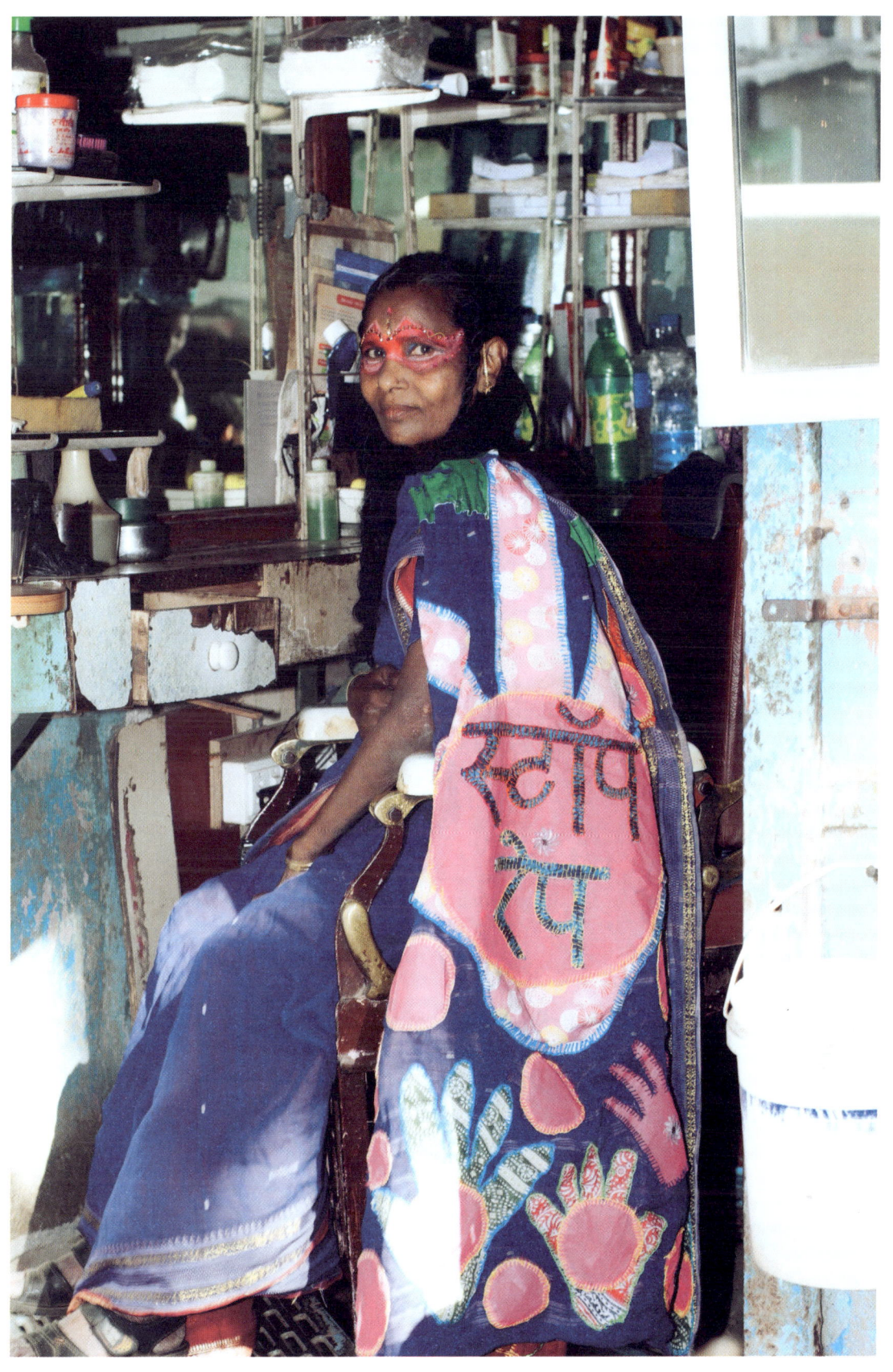

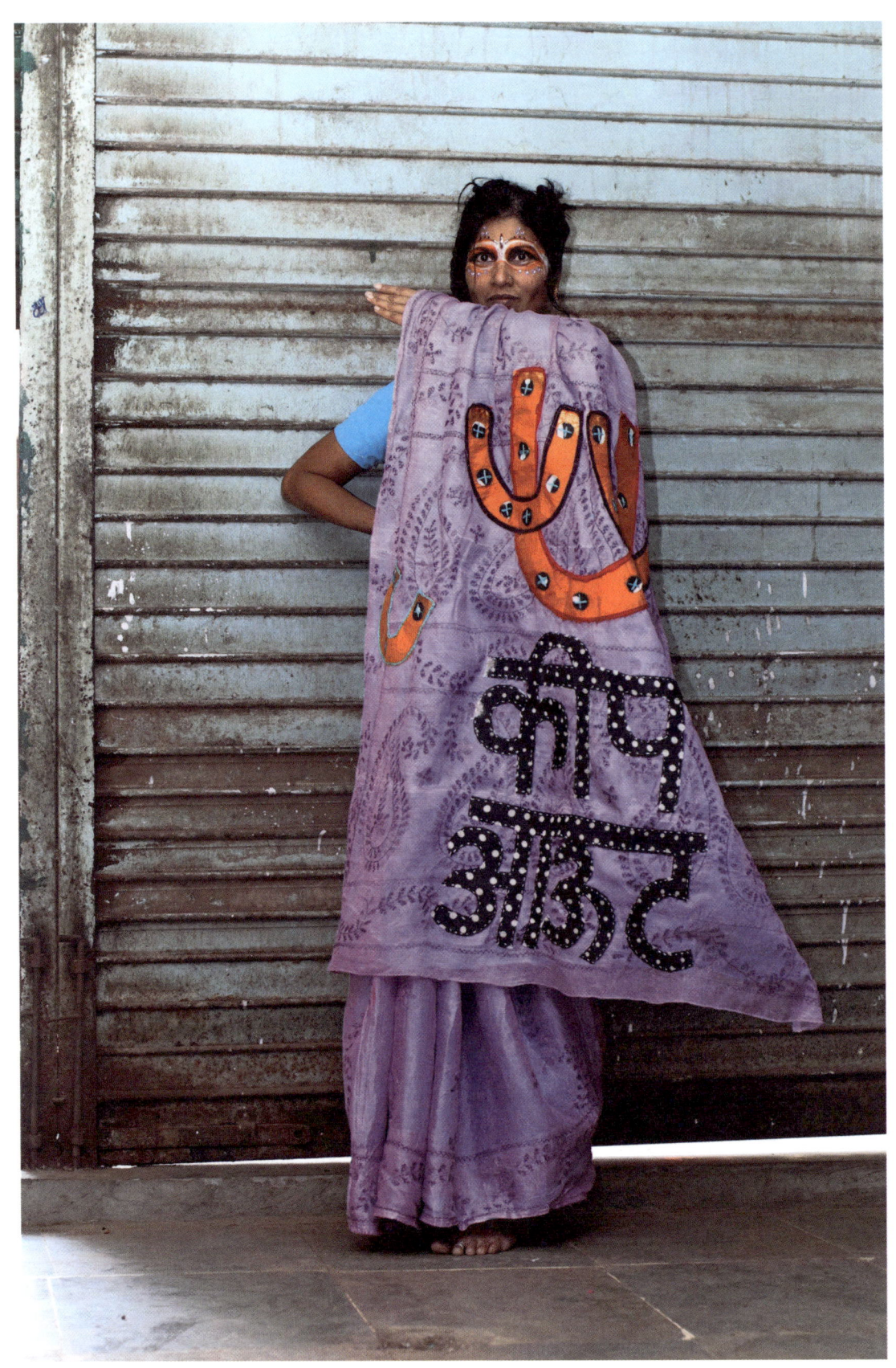

'AND STILL I RISE …'

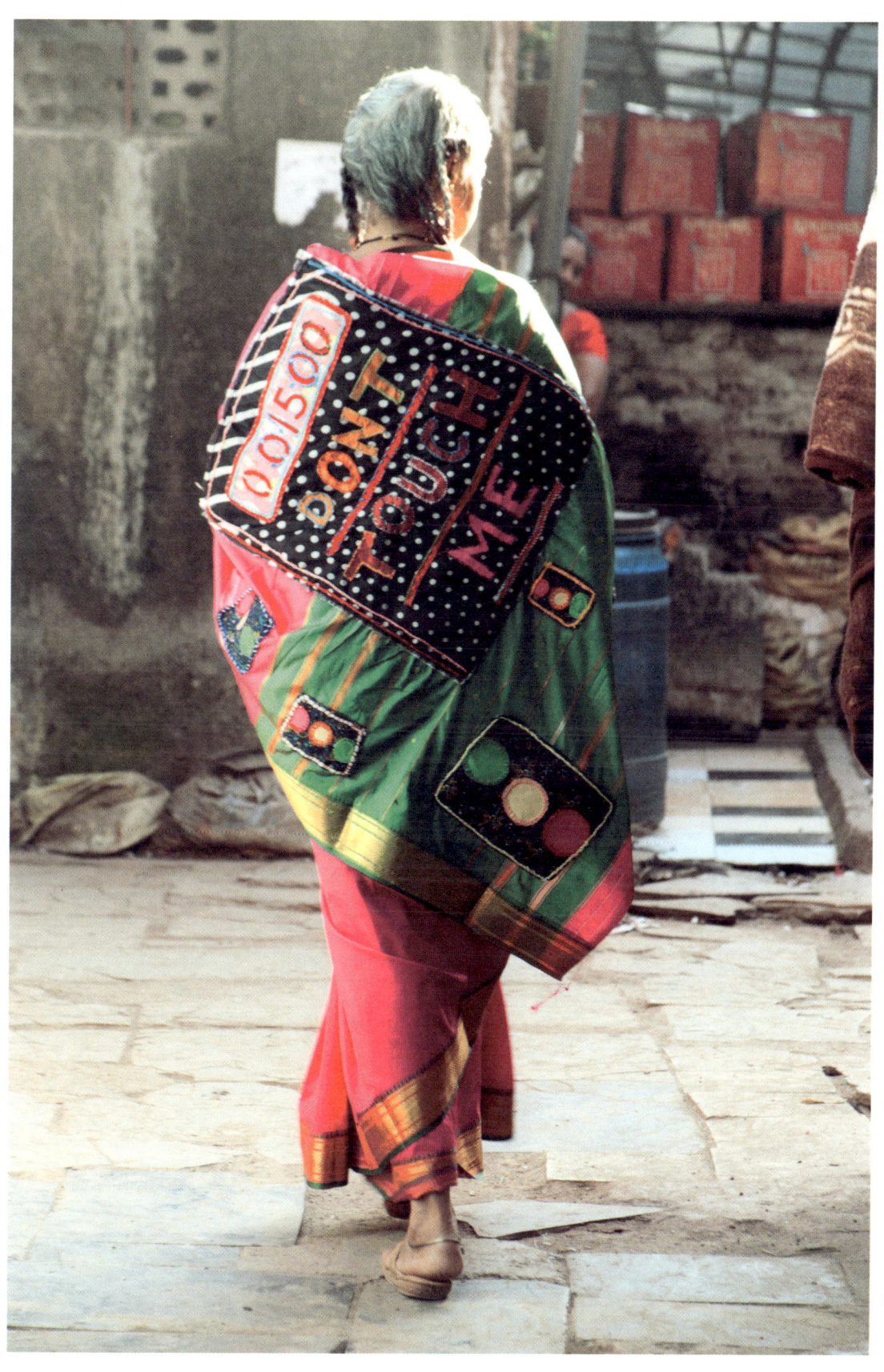

Abolish #522

In 2017, Mireille Honein, a Lebanese artist, came to international prominence when she created a textile installation of 30 wedding dresses that she dangled from nooses in palm trees on a Beirut seafront. Her ghostly bridal gowns were a metaphor for rape victims and survivors of sexual violence, and aimed to draw attention to a loophole in an archaic law dating from the 1940s. Article 522 in the Lebanese penal code exonerated a rapist from criminal punishment if he married his victim; supporters of the law claimed this would 'salvage the victim's honour'.

But with the support of Abaad, a local non-governmental organization, Lebanese women ferociously protested against this for decades, claiming that the loophole in the law was a violation of their human rights. After a change of government in 2016, activists ramped up their campaign and gathered in their hundreds, and the wedding dress became their symbolic costume of protest. The loophole was finally abolished in August 2017.

OPPOSITE, ABOVE

Women wearing wedding dresses and veils in protest of rape exonerations.

OPPOSITE, BELOW

Mireille Honein's installation of wedding dresses, each hung from a noose.

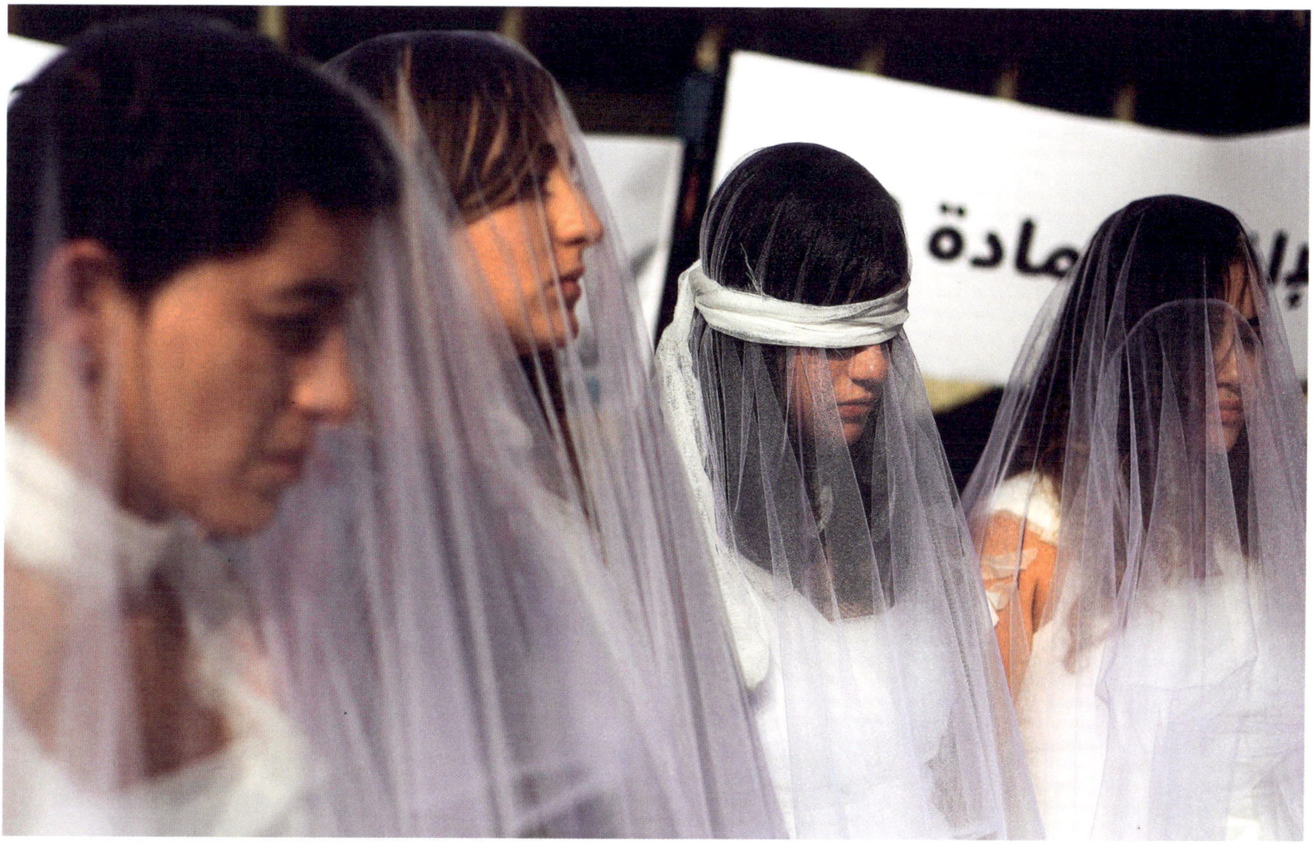

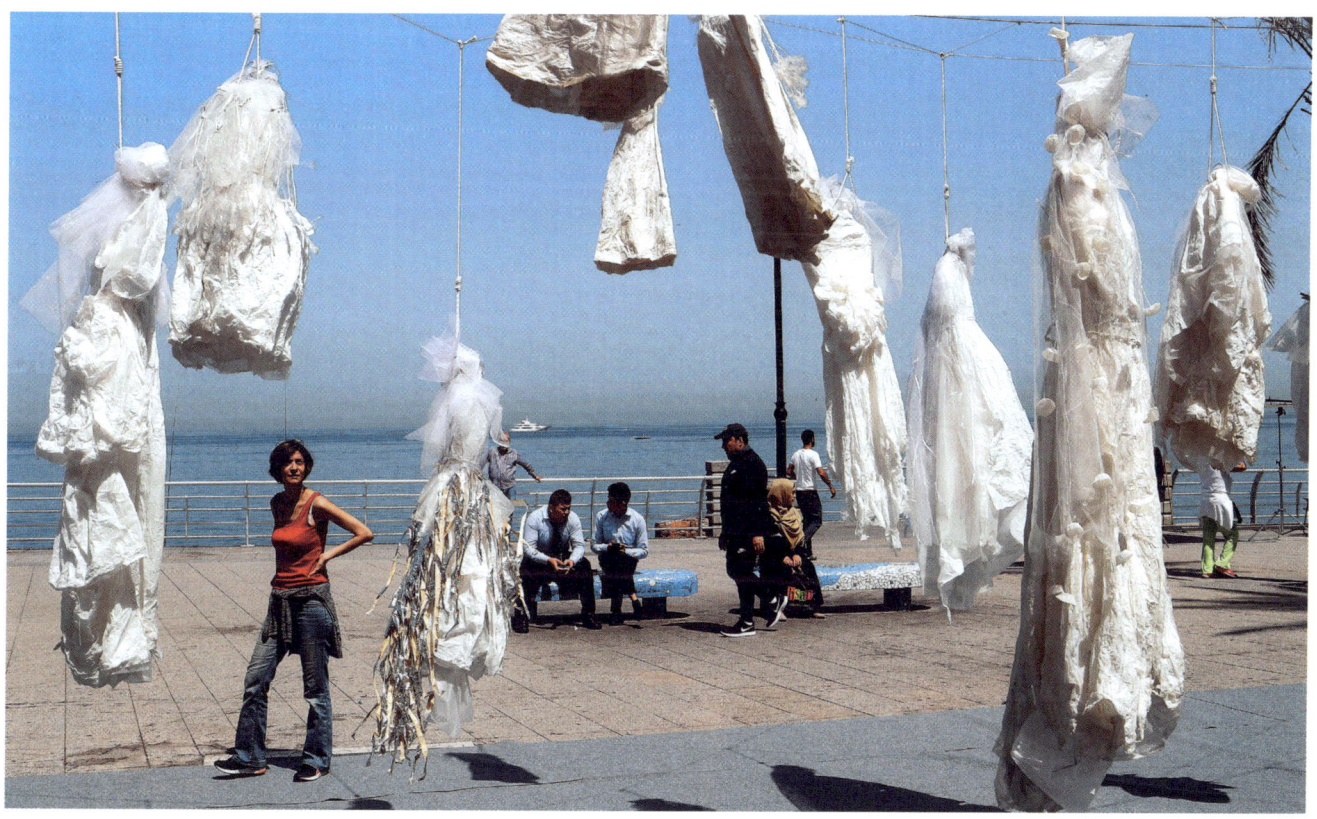

'AND STILL I RISE …'

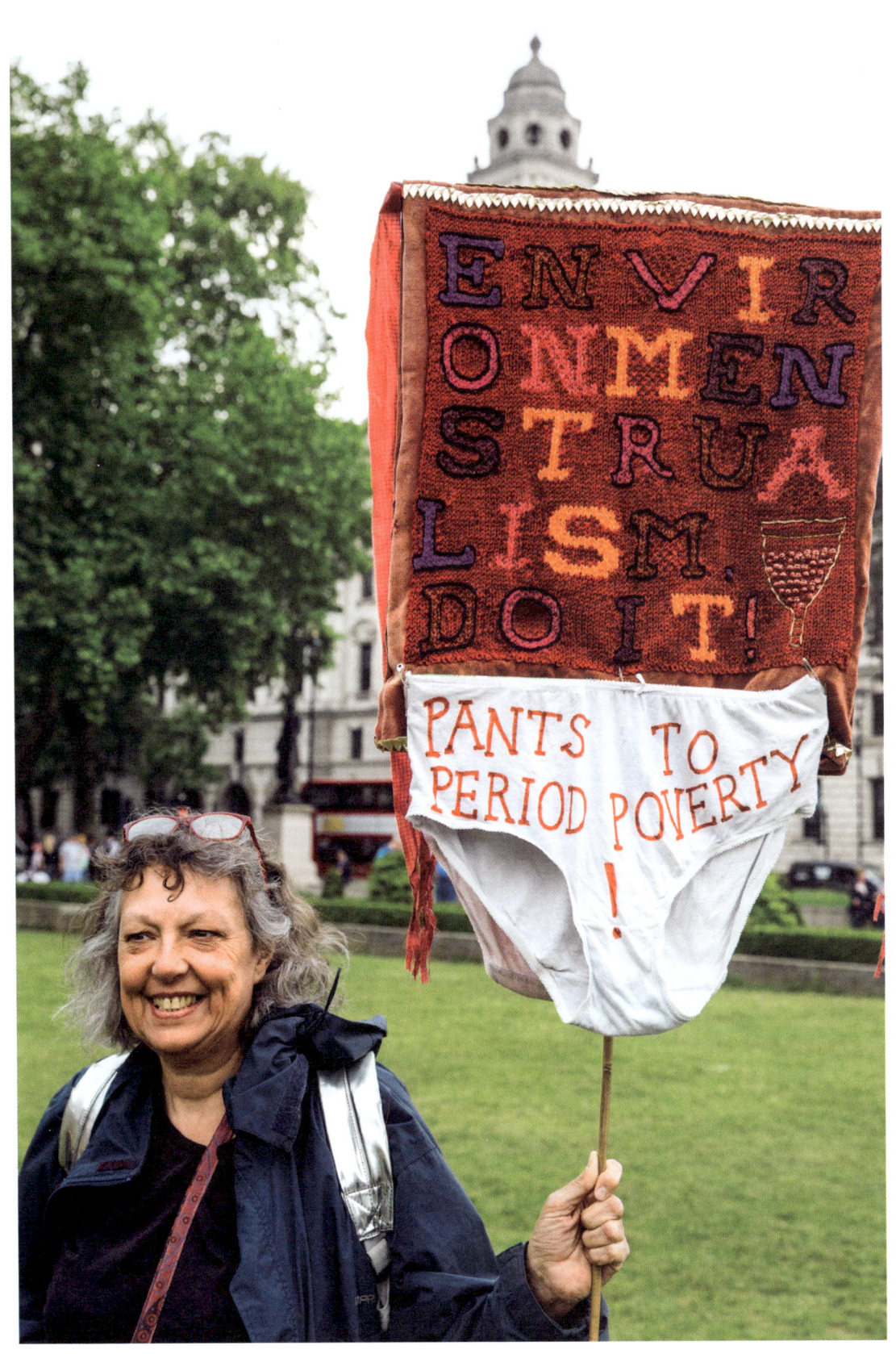

'AND STILL I RISE …'

Menstruation and Period Poverty

Menstruation is a fact of life, but there is much stigma and social taboo surrounding periods both culturally and globally. Periods are a natural and biological function, but a lack of understanding and ignorance about this can lead to embarrassment and period shaming. In addition, religious or cultural traditions can lead to those who are menstruating being banned from school, social activities, from touching holy books, having sex or even cooking because they are deemed to be 'unclean' or 'impure'. Enforced isolation can have an impact on a person's physical and mental welfare, and these practices exacerbate gender inequality at a societal level.

Period poverty is a serious issue throughout the world and a lack of access to clean and accessible bathrooms, safe and affordable period products, and support to manage menstruation effectively creates physical, social, economic and psychological barriers to those who have periods. To combat the stigma and taboo surrounding periods, there are many global organizations running educational programmes to normalize menstruation, empowering not only those who have periods, but their communities too.

Menstrual Artists

Several artists have used their menstrual blood to make intriguing and dignified artworks to bring attention to period poverty and to address period stigma.

In 2016–2017, Dr Bee Hughes documented the rhythm of their changes in bodily fluids in a textile installation in order to 'challenge menstrual norms'. They printed with their vulva onto linen every evening for six months to visually demonstrate 'a menstrual cycle that does not fit the normal descriptors provided by medical texts'.

Casey Jenkins has been described as a 'vaginal knitting' performance artist and is well known for their 'Casting Off My Womb' installation that they performed over 28 days at the Darwin Visual Arts Association, Australia, in 2013. During the process of this performance, they inserted white yarn into their vagina, knitted it as they pulled it out and observed the change of colour to red as it soaked up their menstrual blood. They wanted to demonstrate that periods are a normal part of life and nothing to be feared or disgusted by. Combining craft and performance, their work investigates themes around power structures, identity, feminism and gender.

Chilean artist Carina Ubeda collected her menstrual blood on scraps of cloth for five years and turned them into an art installation. The rags were used as sanitary products because she is allergic to pads, but rather than discarding them, she stitched around each bloody stain with words such as 'destroyed', 'discard' and 'production', then framed 90 of them in embroidery hoops alongside hanging apples, which symbolize ovulation. Many visitors found the abstract installation offensive, but one, Silvana Sáez, astutely remarked that: 'Male blood is celebrated for being brave, whilst ours is a shame. This won't change until we release our body as the first stage of political struggle, repression and male power.'

OPPOSITE

Casting Off My Womb (2013)

Casey Jenkins

28-day performance, DVAA.

OVERLEAF, LEFT

Cycle (2) (2017)

Bee Hughes

Body prints (acrylic on cotton). Approx. 1.5×1.5m (59×59in). Artist's collection. Photographed by Milos Simpraga.

OVERLEAF, RIGHT

Cycles (2016–7)

Bee Hughes

6 hand-stitched linen scrolls, menstrual fluid and acrylic paint, each scroll 20×300cm (8×118in), artist's collection. Photographed by Milos Simpraga. As exhibited at *Periodical* (2018), Being Human festival, Atrium Gallery, Liverpool School of Art & Design, 15–24 November 2018.

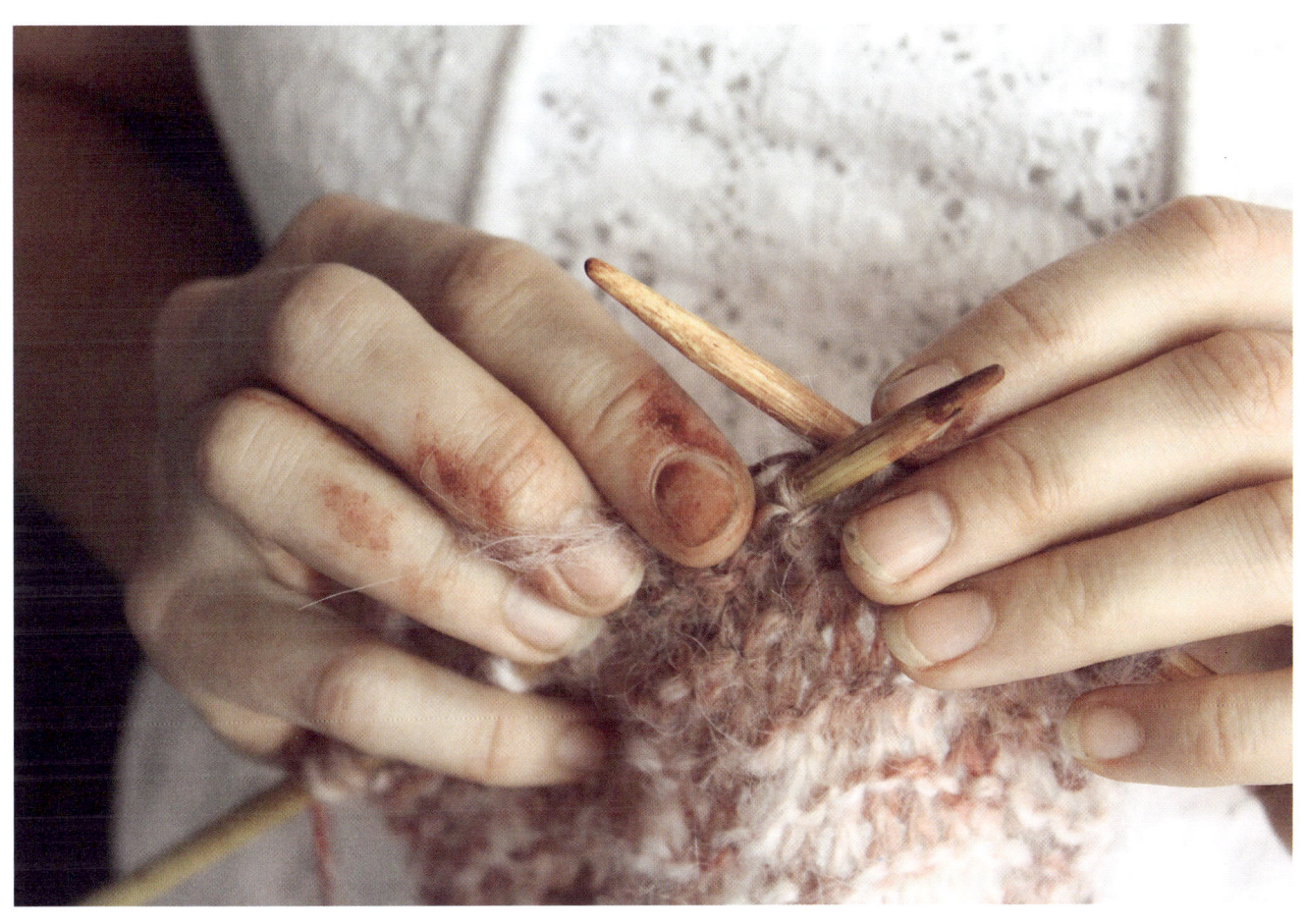

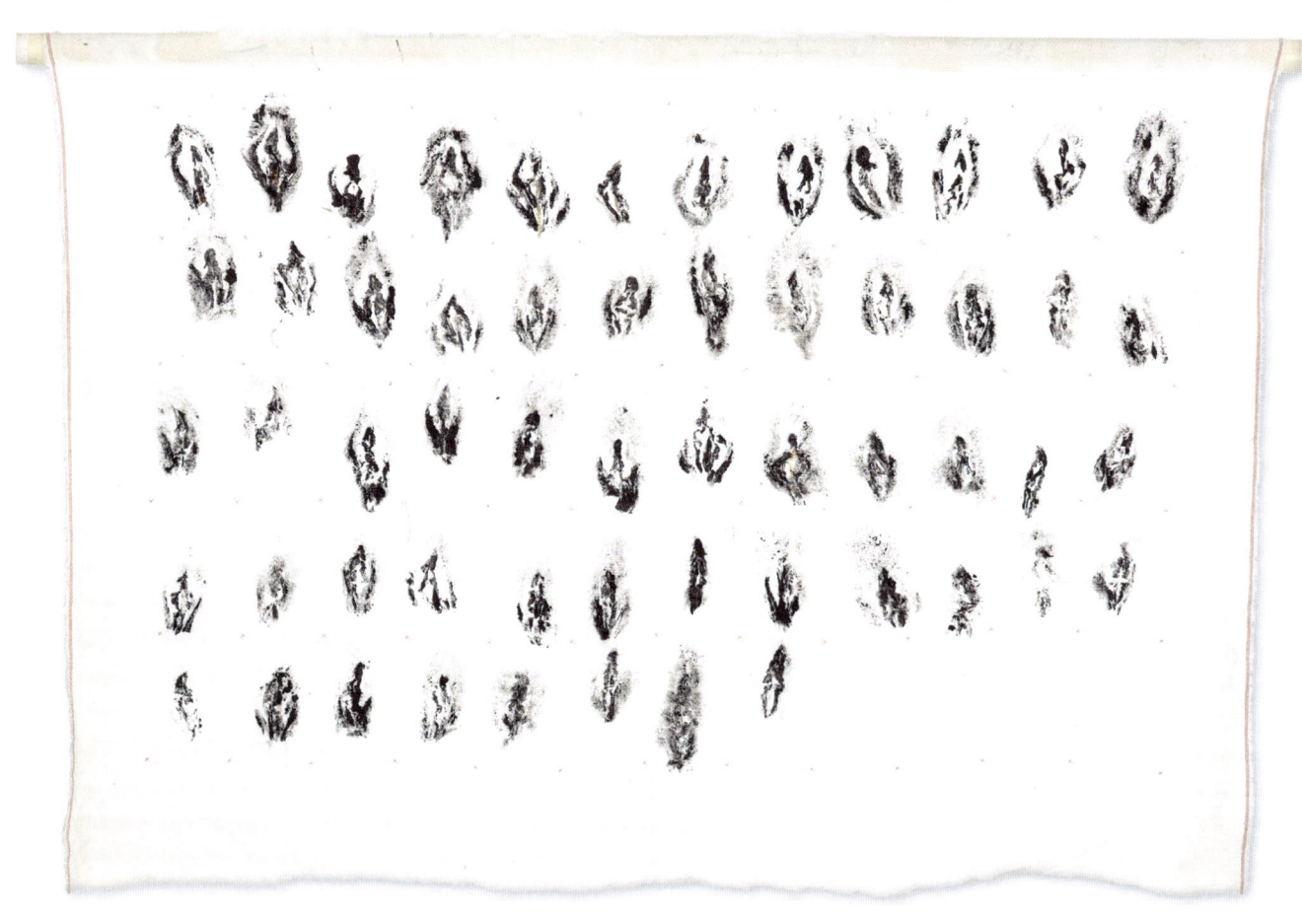

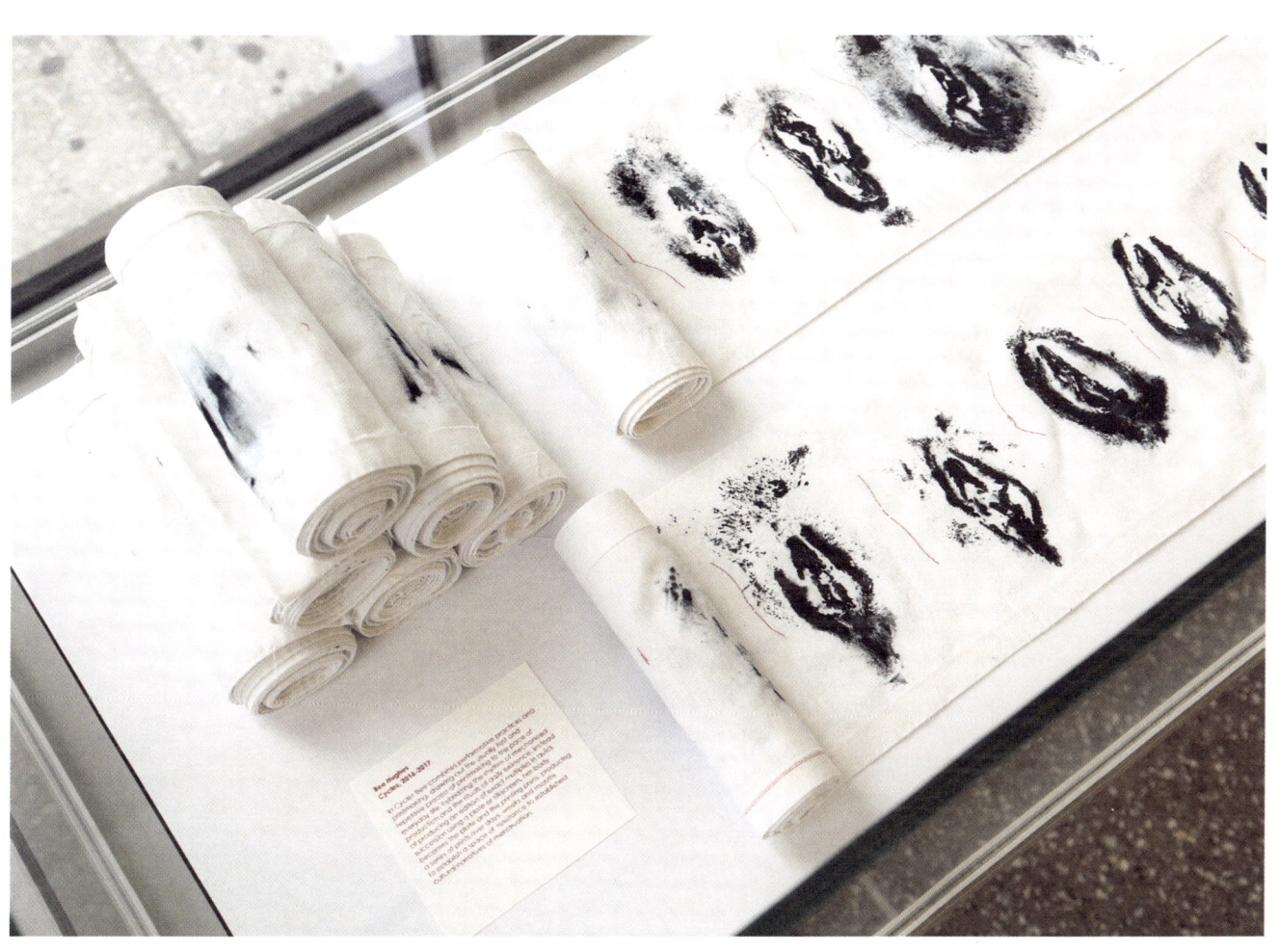

Abortion Rights

It is a fundamental human right for everyone to choose how to control their own fertility and have autonomy over their own body. But that doesn't happen for millions of people, especially those who face unwanted or unintended pregnancies. Deaths from unsafe abortions are preventable, and are highest in countries where abortion is criminalized or severely restricted, most often in lower-income groups.

Even when progress has been made, a different administration and anti-abortionists can reverse policies and laws. In the US, safe and legal abortion remained a constitutional right for all American women for nearly 50 years following the Roe vs Wade victory in 1973, until the Dobbs vs Jackson case overturned this ruling in 2022.

The abortion rights (or 'pro-choice') movement fights to break down barriers so that abortion is affordable, safe, legally available and destigmatized. An elective abortion without threat of intimidation, hostility, attack, arrest or any other repercussions should be the right for every pregnant person. Abortion is healthcare, and healthcare is a human right.

Artist and activist Viva Ruiz once asked the author and gay activist Sarah Schulman what advice she would give to 'someone wanting to make a difference'. The answer was: 'Be effective.' Ruiz, speaking during an interview with Aliza Shvarts in 2022 of her unapologetic, multi-platform art project, Thank God for Abortion (2015–present), said that 'mixing Christian iconography with themes of abortion and joy was immediately effective'. She aims to 'shift the dialogue about abortion away from a conversation about "sin" and morality and toward a conversation centred around the liberation and support of marginalized people.'

BELOW

Hands Off (2022)

Alexandra Dewez

60x60cm (23.6x23.6in). Hand embroidery on vintage French linen, stitched in response to the reversal of the Roe vs Wade decision.

OPPOSITE

Thank God for Abortion (2019)

Viva Ruiz

The Vatican, Rome.

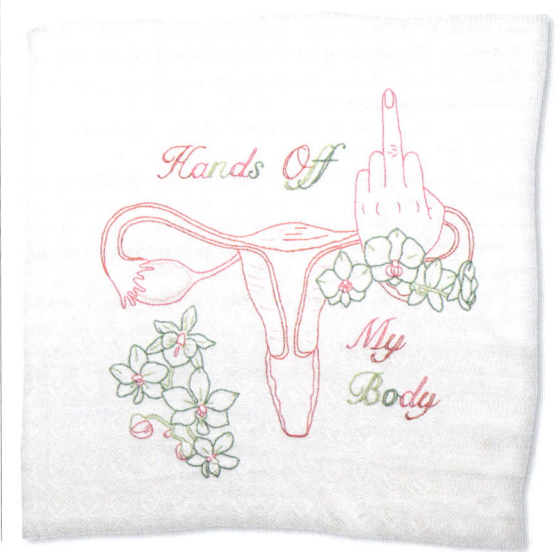

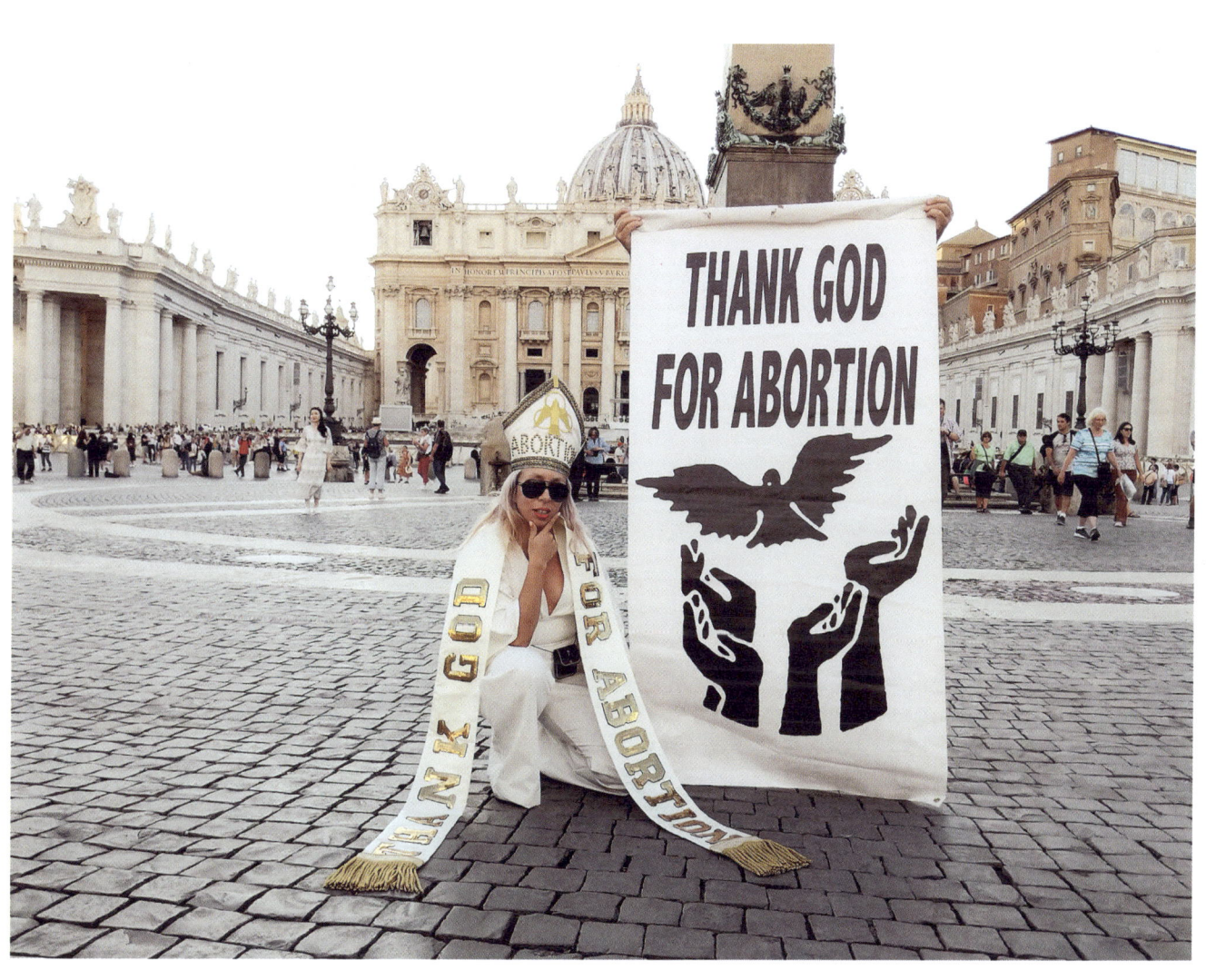

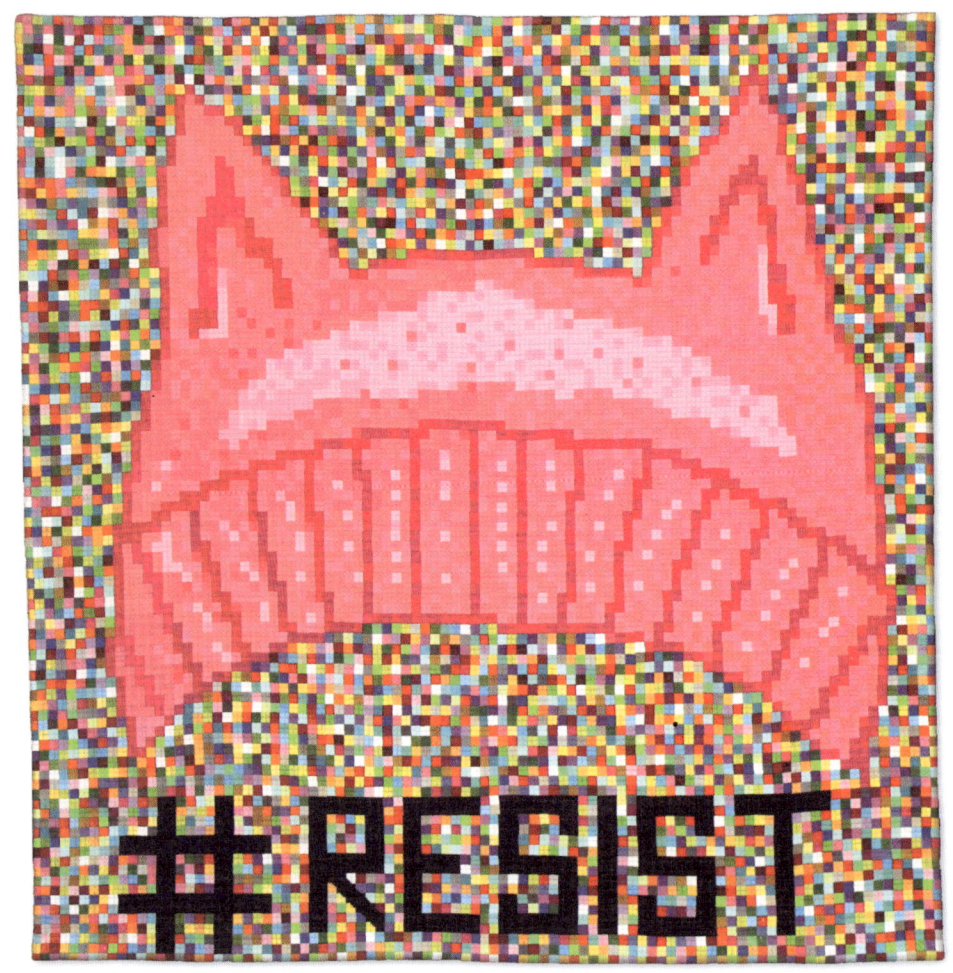

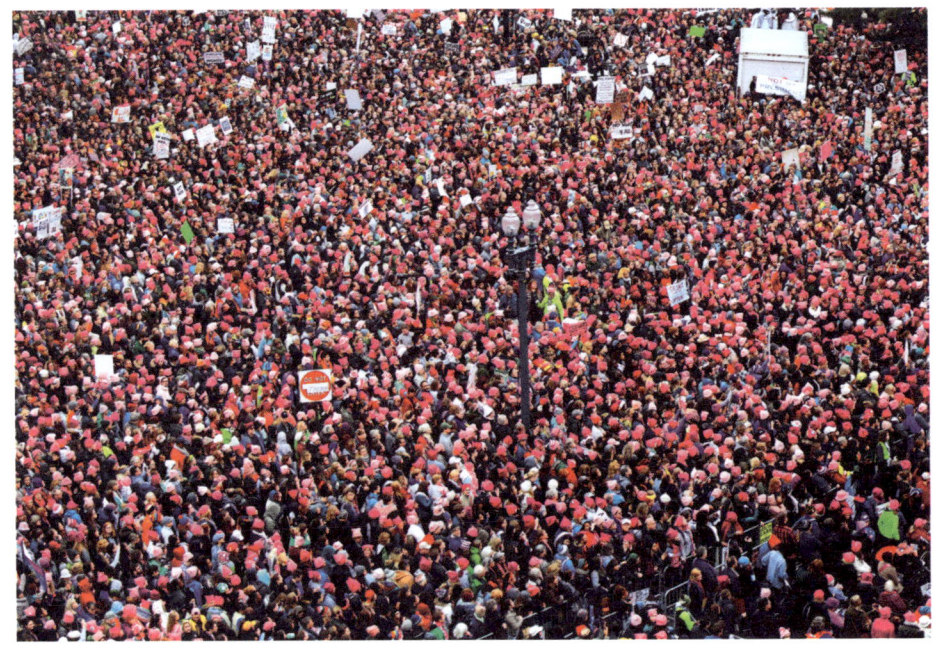

'AND STILL I RISE ...'

The Pussyhat

OPPOSITE, ABOVE

Women's March 2017: By the Numbers (2017)

Kathy York

122x122cm (48x48in). This quilt is made from 9216 half inch squares. Each square represents 325 people – it honours the 3 million people who marched globally on 21 January 2017.

OPPOSITE, BELOW

Pussyhats at the Women's March.

In November 2016 the Pussyhat Project was founded by screenwriter Krista Suh and artist/designer Jayna Zweiman. Whilst attending crochet classes together at Little Knittery, their local yarn store, and discussing their passion for women's issues, they came up with a plan to create a 'sea of pink hats' at the Women's March on 21 January 2017 – a worldwide protest arranged the day after the inauguration of Donald Trump as US president. The hats would not only keep heads warm in winter, but would be a visual symbol of feminism and solidarity, uniting everyone against misogyny through a common garment, whether or not they could physically attend a march.

Kat Coyle from Little Knittery designed the Pussyhat and launched the knitting pattern globally; it was an instant success and has become an iconic protest textile that symbolizes solidarity and resistance, and the power of collective activism.

The name Pussyhat was chosen as a protest 'against vulgar comments Trump made about the freedom he felt to grab women's genitals, to de-stigmatize the word "pussy" and transform it into one of empowerment'. People all over the world started making pink Pussyhats in a mass movement of political activism, and millions were knitted and worn on the Women's March by anti-Trump protestors around the world on all seven continents. A Pussyhat knitted by Zweiman and worn on the march is now in the collection at the Victoria & Albert Museum in London.

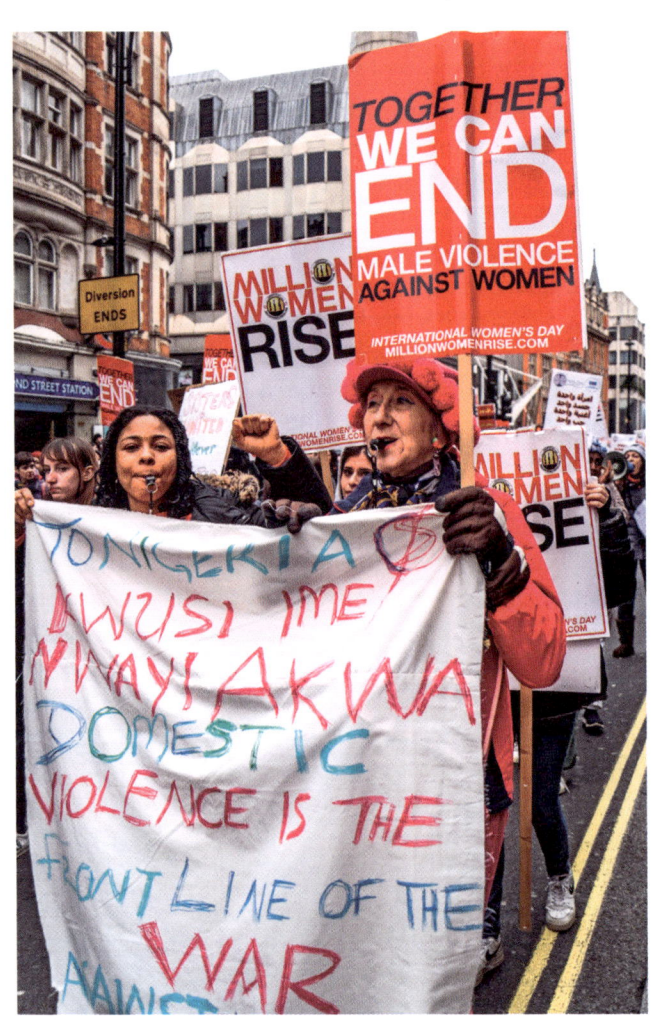

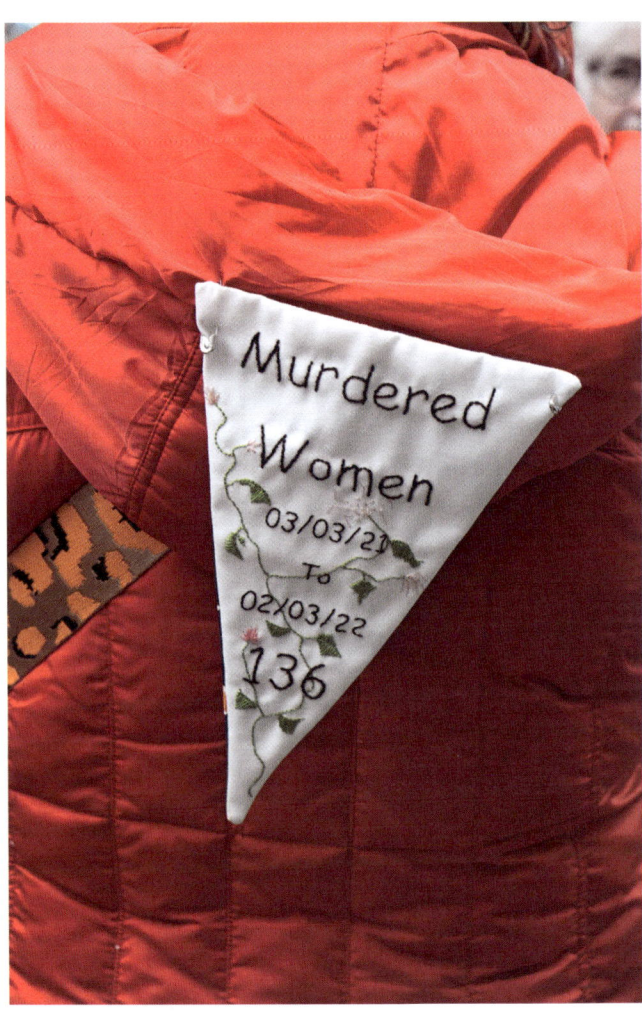

'AND STILL I RISE …'

International Women's Day

OPPOSITE, LEFT

International Women's Day march.

OPPOSITE, RIGHT

Embroidered cloth protesting violence against women.

International Women's Day (IWD) has been universally celebrated on 8 March since 1917, but previously by different nations on different dates. The earliest recording of a 'Woman's Day' being celebrated was in New York on 28 February 1909 by the Socialist Party of America, instigated by Theresa Malkiel. The idea spread to Europe and more than one million people in Denmark, Germany, Switzerland and Austria-Hungary marched for suffrage and equality on 19 March 1911.

On 8 March 1917, women textile workers in Petrograd (now St Petersburg) began a strike and a demonstration demanding 'Bread and Peace'. They called for an end to food shortages, World War I and Tsarism. Their actions sparked the March Revolution, the first of two Russian Revolutions that year, and Leon Trotsky later wrote that 'we did not imagine that this "Women's Day" would inaugurate the revolution'.

Remaining a predominantly communist holiday until the late 1960s, the day was claimed by feminist activists as a day to protest and be heard, and was marked by the UN for the first time in 1975.

IWD remains one of protest, and Million Women Rise (MWR), a grassroots collective founded by Sabrina Qureshi in 2007, organize a women-only rally in London every year to demonstrate against male violence against women, which MWR calls a 'global pandemic'. Hundreds of women from different nationalities come together each year, bringing along their creatively embroidered banners, pennants and flags.

Although IWD is not a public holiday in many countries, throughout the world the day is still observed, celebrated and used as an opportunity to highlight issues of injustice, as well as to celebrate women and their achievements and to show solidarity to other comrades fighting for emancipation. It is also a day to challenge and make laws, and on IWD 2024, France celebrated as guaranteed abortions became constitutional law, and six couples sued the Japanese government for the right to have different last names from their spouse.

THE ADVANTAGES
OF BEING
A WOMAN ARTIST:

Working without the pressure of success
Not having to be in shows with men
Having an escape from the art world in your 4 free-lance jobs
Knowing your career might pick up after you're eighty
Being reassured that whatever kind of art you make it will be labeled feminine
Not being stuck in a tenured teaching position
Seeing your ideas live on in the work of others
Having the opportunity to choose between career and motherhood
Not having to choke on those big cigars or paint in Italian suits
Having more time to work when your mate dumps you for someone younger
Being included in revised versions of art history
Not having to undergo the embarrassment of being called a genius
Getting your picture in the art magazines wearing a gorilla suit

GUERRILLA GIRLS

LOQI

'HER'Story

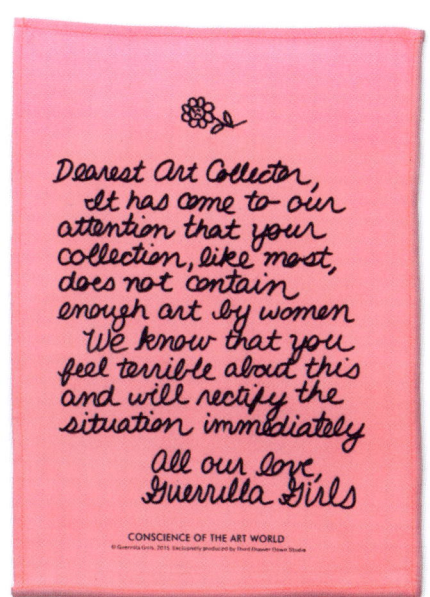

The omission of women from *'his'tory* is an issue that has been taken up by many feminists and activists to redress the balance of patriarchal archives and discriminatory systems.

The Guerrilla Girls, a group of anonymous activists from New York, believe in an intersectional feminism that fights for the human rights for all people. Formed in 1985, they aim to challenge gender and ethnic biases, particularly in the art world, to reveal 'the understory, the subtext, the overlooked and the downright unfair'.

The group's high-profile protests, which take place wearing gorilla masks to focus on the issues rather than their own identities, have included poster and billboard campaigns, interventions and exhibitions. Across their posters and textile banners they list stark statistics and display bold visuals challenging prejudiced and sexist practices that uphold biased corrupt systems. They especially target art galleries which under-represent women artists across every genre in favour of white men, representing the history of wealth and power, not the diversity of art.

Their 2024 'Manifesta' is a declaration of the group's continuing mission to expose inequality, challenge stereotypes and advocate for the inclusion of women and artists of colour.

Whilst many protest textiles are made quickly from everyday materials for immediate use, there are many others that have taken more consideration and a greater length of time to realize. Some of these protest textiles are works of fine art, installations and gallery exhibits. Judy Chicago's 'The Dinner Party' is one such example, taking five years to construct by more than 400 volunteer researchers, makers and embroiderers.

Now permanently housed in the Brooklyn Museum, this seminal feminist artwork commemorates 39 important women from history (some mythical) with an elaborate table-setting for each around a large triangular table.

The guest place-settings feature a table runner embroidered with each woman's name and symbolic references to her artistic and intellectual accomplishments. On top of each placemat is a sculptural ceramic plate, inspired by sensual vulva and butterfly shapes and forms, beside a ceramic chalice and cutlery. A further 999 names of notable women are inscribed on the base of the installation as a testament to the history of women.

Chicago's primary aim in creating 'The Dinner Party' was to protest against the omission of women from mainstream historical and artistic narratives, and to give visibility to women who had made significant contributions to their fields but had been marginalized or ignored by a patriarchal system.

'The Dinner Party' has become an iconic installation, a celebration of women's creativity and accomplishments, including those in the realm of textile art. It not only honours important and significant individuals, but is a metaphor for women – recognizing them rising and progressing throughout civilization and forever in search of gender equality.

BELOW

The Dinner Party
(1974–9)

Judy Chicago

Place setting for Sacajawea (c. 1787–1812); number 28 in Wing III of the artwork – from the American to the Women's Revolution – symbolizing the exploitation of Native Americans by Europeans.

OPPOSITE

The Dinner Party
(1974–9)

Judy Chicago

Two views of The Dinner Party from the Brooklyn Museum, New York, showing all three wings of the triangular artwork with its 39 place settings and the 999 notable women from history inscribed on the floor.

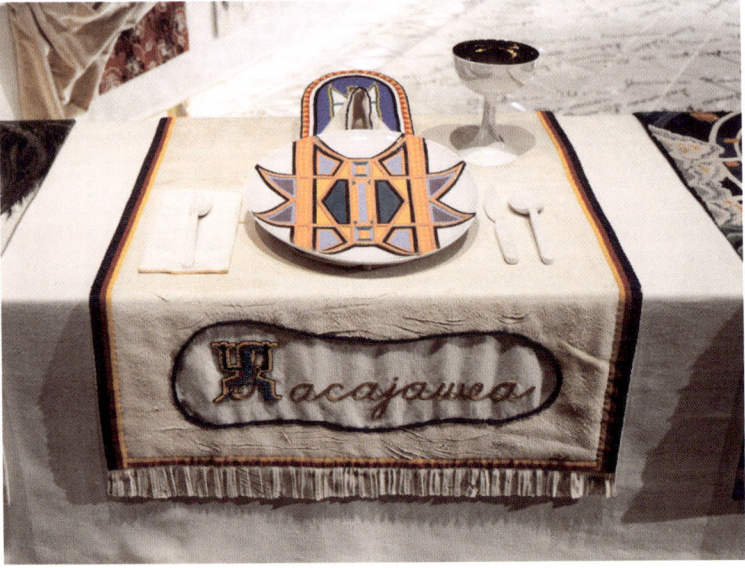

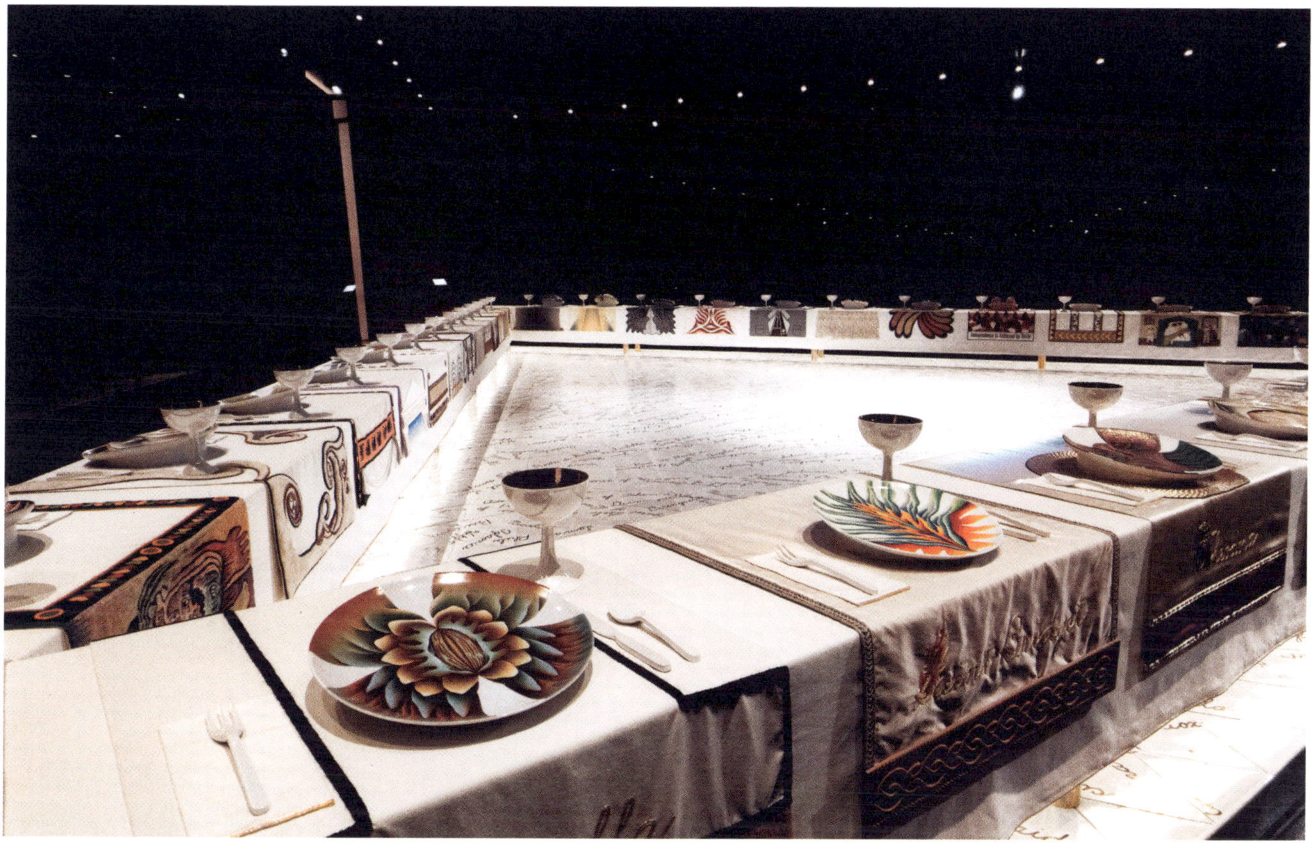

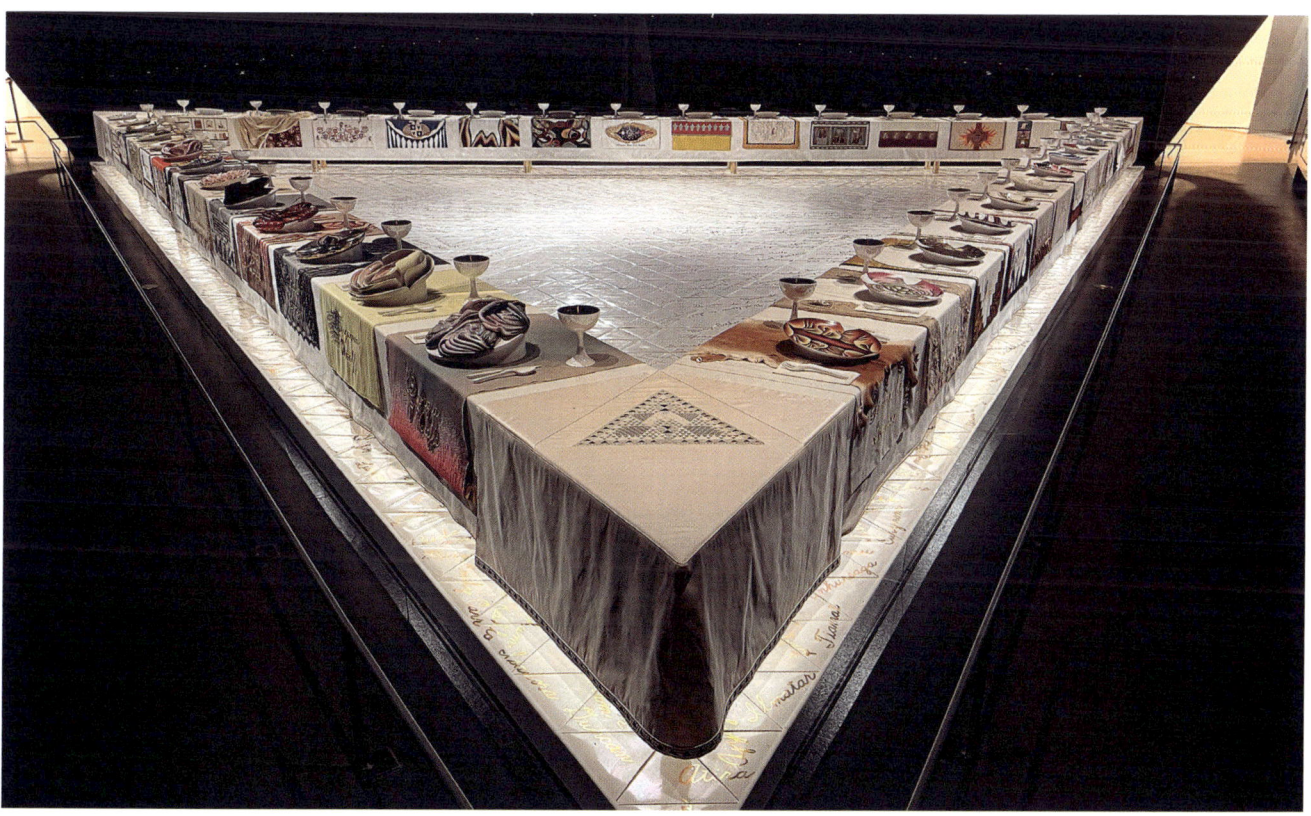

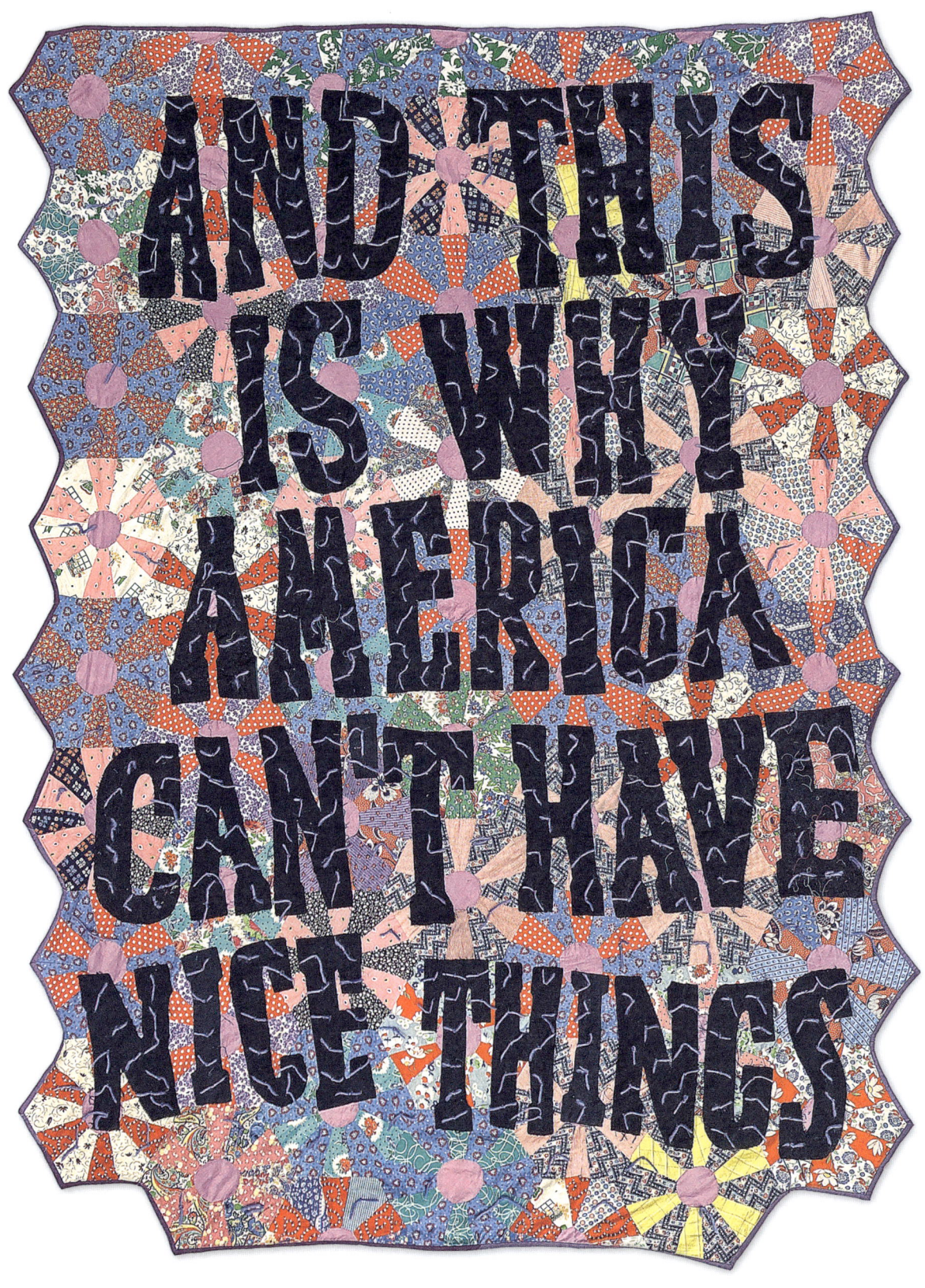

IDENTITY

IDENTITY

'If the system cripples you, you must cripple the system.' VINCE LAWS

OPPOSITE

Nice Things (2018)

Zak Foster

203×152cm (80×60in)
approx. Made from
reclaimed textiles.

Identity is a complex concept, and how we identify or describe ourselves is determined by a multitude of factors. Whilst the genetics we inherit biologically shape and predetermine some aspects of our identity and physical characteristics, other factors are influenced by our environment and the social and cultural contexts in which we live. Identity is fluid and dynamic.

During our upbringing, our opportunities, attitudes and behaviour are shaped by many influences, including the family, culture and class we are born into; the beliefs and values of those around us; and laws, traditions and social norms. All these can both bind us and divide us. Identity is both personal and collective.

These factors intertwine and shift, creating an ever-evolving self that reflects our individual experiences and the collective frameworks that surround us. Our identity is a unique reflection of our personal interactions and our encounters in the broader society we navigate.

US-based Zak Foster is a self-taught quilter who explores the 'great human questions through the lens of textiles'. Predominantly made from upcycled and repurposed fabrics, Foster's improvised quilts tell stories that challenge and engage. His pieces are infused with current social and political issues which explore intersections of identity, heritage, justice, solidarity and freedom. Foster's quilt opposite is a personal critique of American systemic flaws and the historical and biased narratives surrounding the country's culture, society and political structures (see also page 131).

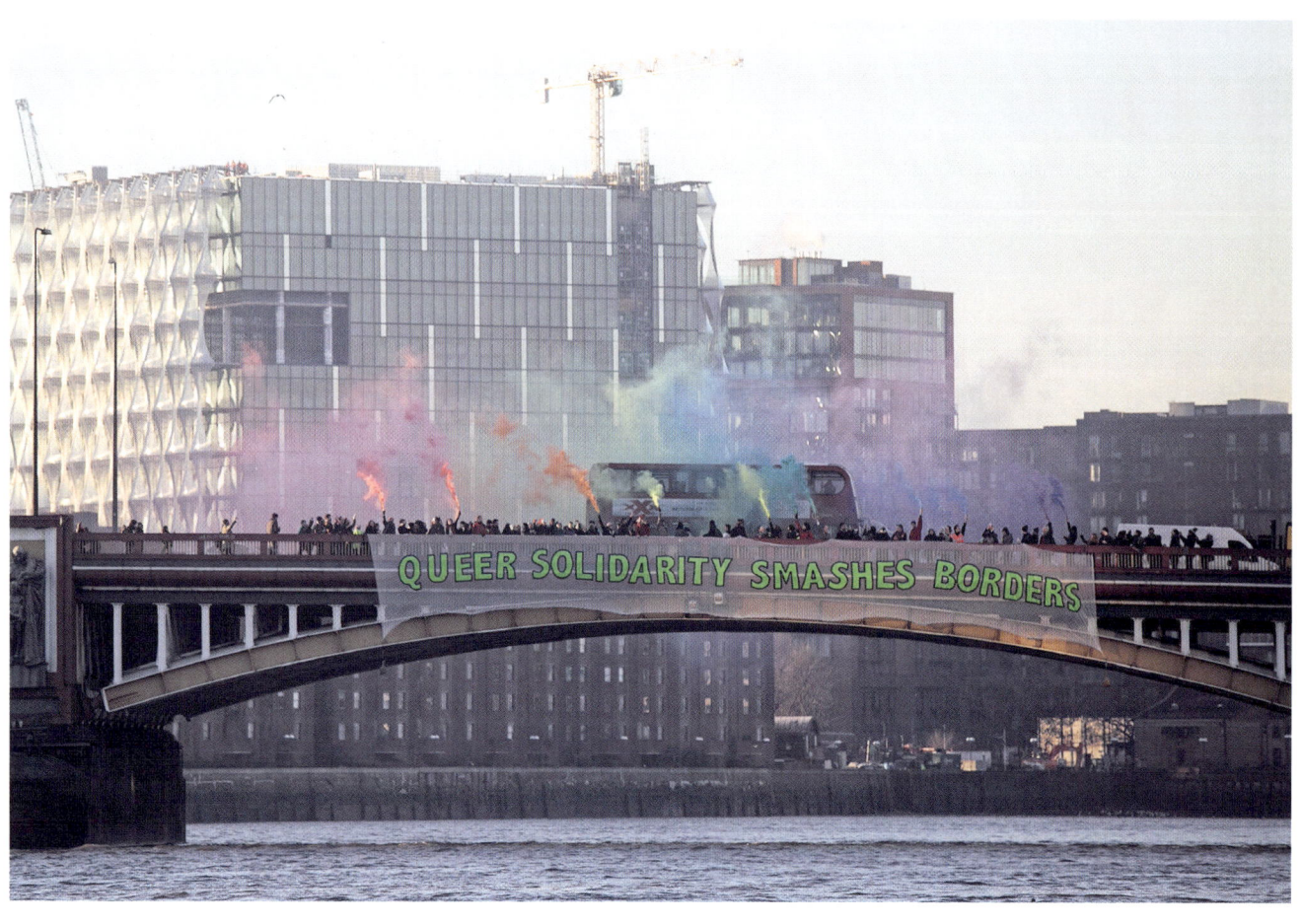

IDENTITY

Intersectionality

OPPOSITE

A Queer Solidarity banner on Vauxhall Bridge, London. On 20 January 2017 over 50 groups across the United Kingdom dropped banners from bridges as an act of defiance against Trump's inauguration. The groups, who form the 'Bridges not Walls' movement, staged their demonstration to show support for people in the USA and beyond fearing the consequences of Trump's election.

Intersectionality, a critical concept introduced by the academic and civil rights advocate Kimberlé Crenshaw in 1989, is a framework for understanding overlapping forms of oppression and how aspects of our social identities, such as gender, sexuality, class, race, and disability, intersect and compound to create unique experiences of discrimination and/or privilege. This concept is crucial for recognizing that social issues and injustices cannot be fully addressed by focusing on one single or isolated aspect of identity.

Intersectionality emphasizes the importance of inclusive approaches in education, policymaking, activism and social justice to ensure that the needs and voices of all affected groups are considered. It promotes a deeper understanding of diversity, inclusivity and the complexity of social inequalities, to achieve effective outcomes.

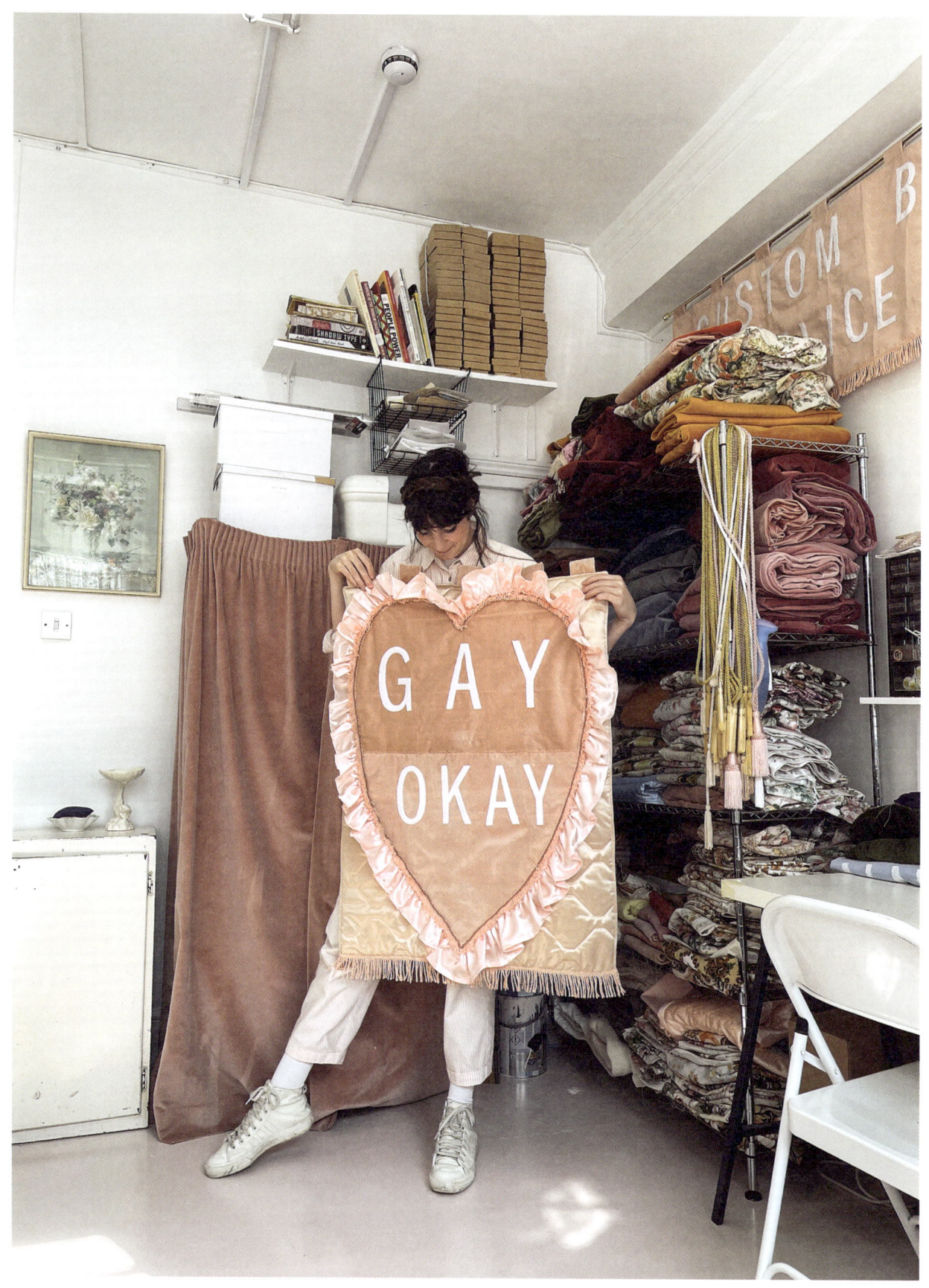

Gender and Sexuality

In the West, gender and biological sex have historically been assumed to be the same thing and to be something that is both binary and fixed at birth. This, however, is not culturally universal, as different Indigenous peoples have had other ways of viewing sex and gender. These cultures and forms of social organization were often suppressed under European colonialism.

Attitudes and beliefs about sex and gender are now changing in Europe and elsewhere. Today there are increasing opportunities for people, in some countries, to legally declare their gender as they wish, including outside their gender binary. For individuals to be recognized and addressed as they themselves identify is a major shift in cultural attitudes that creates a more diverse, inclusive and equitable world for us all.

Whilst gender identity is about who we are, sexuality is about our feelings and behaviours influenced by our patterns of attraction, or sexual orientation, which can overlap and intertwine with other aspects of our identities. Defining ourselves can, therefore, be complex.

The acronym LGBTQIA+ represents different facets of the lesbian, gay, bisexual, transgender, queer or questioning, intersex and asexual communities. The '+' encompasses those of other sexual and gender identities such as pansexuality and gender fluidity.

Language is deeply connected to identity, and an inclusive shift to use the gender-neutral pronouns, such as they/them, and gender-neutral descriptions (for example 'partner') positively avoids perpetuating stereotypes and biases.

Alice Gabb, a British lettering artsist, activist and banner maker, uses language and text in her bespoke banners and hangings to highlight issues of identity and protest. Her banners are made from vintage fabrics and are inspired by 'the incredibly rich history of peace campaigning, secret societies and social justice movements within the UK'.

Pride and Protest

The Stonewall uprising in Greenwich Village, New York City, in 1969 sparked a mass movement of lesbian and gay activists around the globe, and was the catalyst for uniting hundreds of thousands of activists in the fight for equal rights. The first official Pride march was held on the first anniversary of the Stonewall riots in New York City on 28 June 1970.

In the aftermath of the riots, campaigners felt the need to develop a recognizable emblem to represent the LGBTQIA+ community's diversity, and to unite their struggle for inclusion, acceptance and gender equality. What eventually emerged was one of the most iconic and familiar protest textiles: the Rainbow Pride flag – a universal symbol of LGBTQIA+ pride, visibility, diversity and celebration.

Designed by artist Gilbert Baker and two collaborators, Lynn Segerblom (aka Faerie Argyle Rainbow) and James McNamara, and a group of volunteer activists, the first Rainbow Pride flag design debuted on 25 June 1978 at the Gay Freedom Day Parade, San Francisco. Two identical flags were made for the event, constructed from different-coloured hand-dyed fabrics, hand-stitched together in eight horizontal stripes.

The colours of the stripes were significant, and each had its own symbolic meaning: pink represented sexuality, red represented life, orange represented healing, yellow represented sunlight, green represented nature, turquoise represented magic and art, indigo represented serenity and harmony, and violet represented spirit.

Demand for the flag increased, particularly after the assassination of the politician and gay rights activist Harvey Milk in San Francisco in November 1978, but this first design proved difficult to mass-produce as the hot pink and turquoise colours were hard to match in the production process. These practical restrictions led to the flag being streamlined to incorporate just six standard colours, rather than the original eight, and this redesign quickly became the most familiar and universally recognized Pride flag.

By the mid-1990s the Rainbow Pride flag was firmly established as the emblem for LGBTQIA+ pride communities, and remains one of the most visually recognizable and enduring symbols of hope, liberation, diversity and unity.

OPPOSITE, ABOVE

Gilbert Baker sewing a Pride flag.

OPPOSITE, BELOW

Harvey Milk celebrates his election as a San Francisco Supervisor on election night, 8 November 1977.

OVERLEAF

Adaptations of the Pride flag.

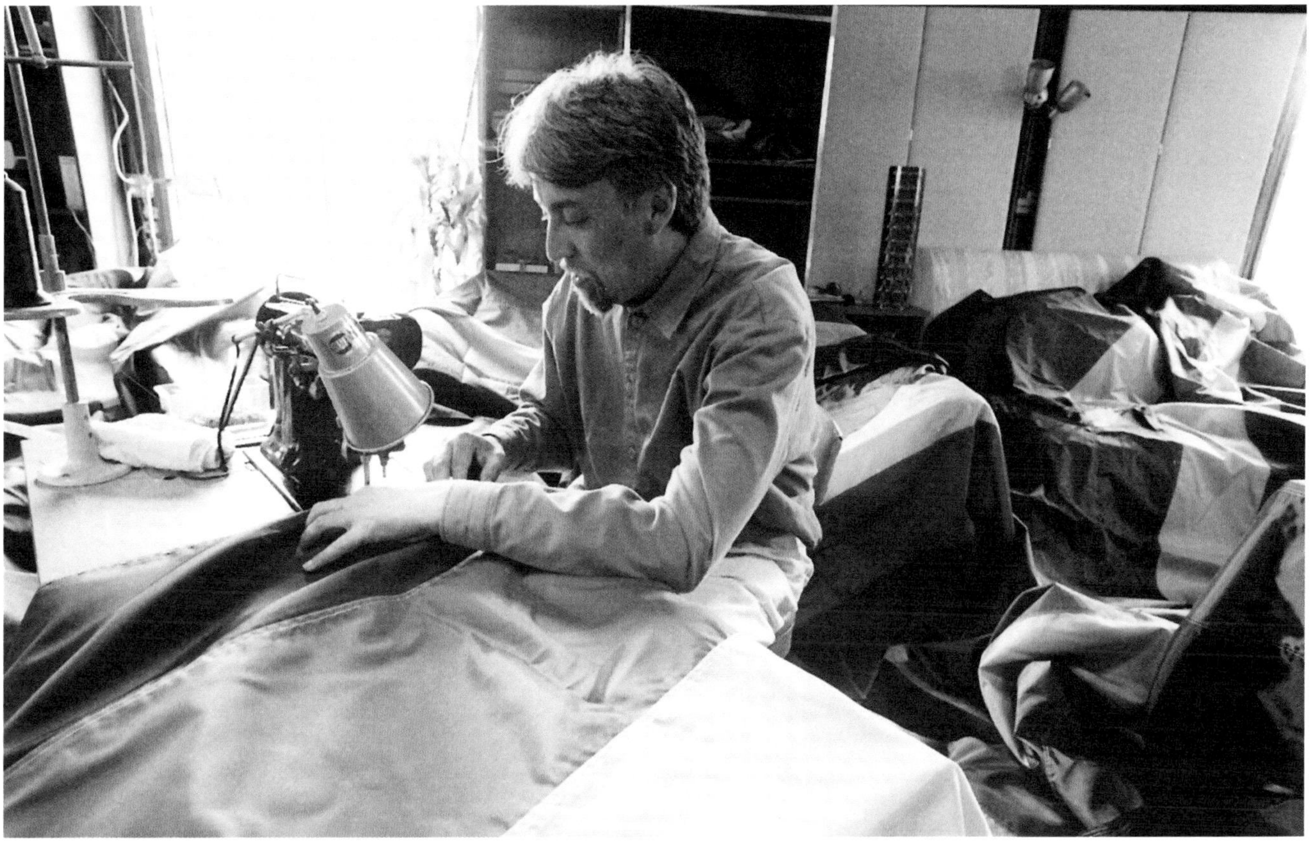

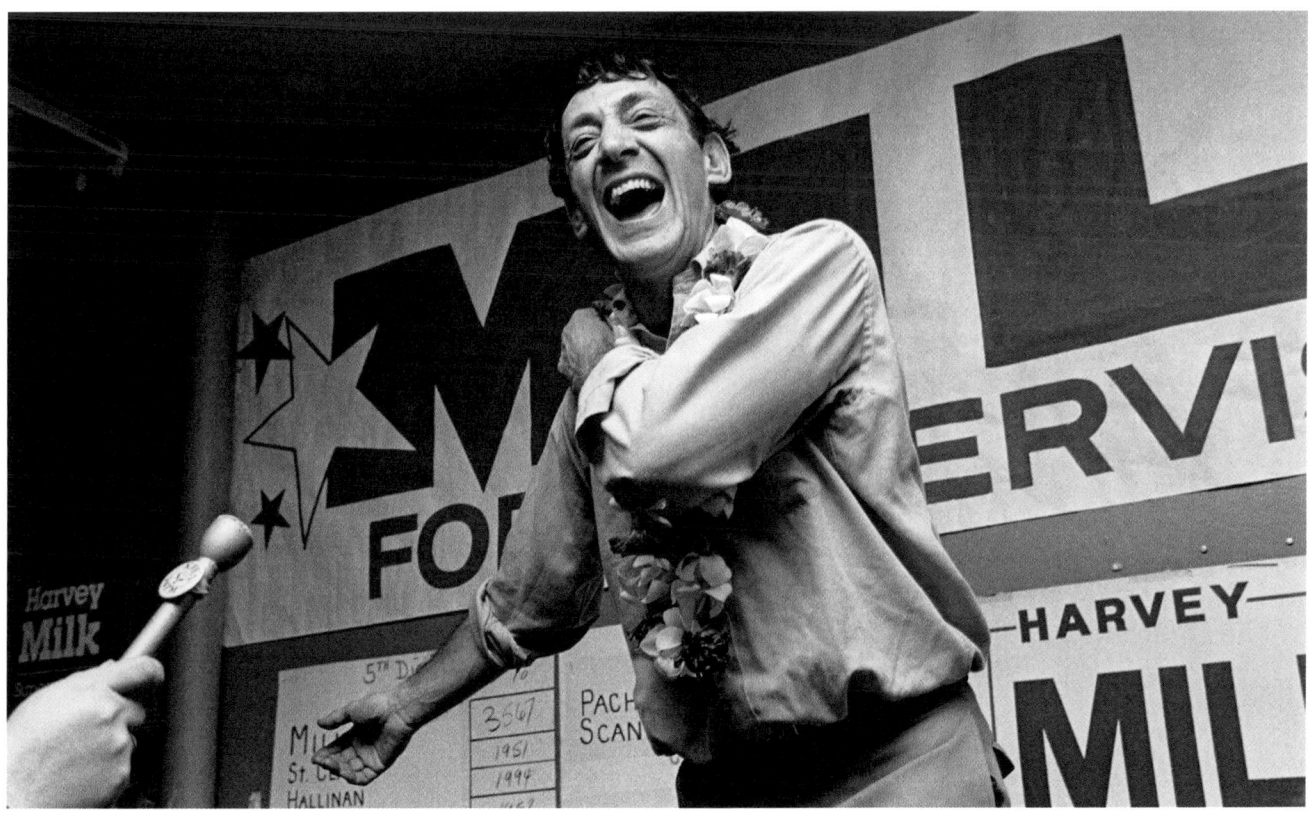

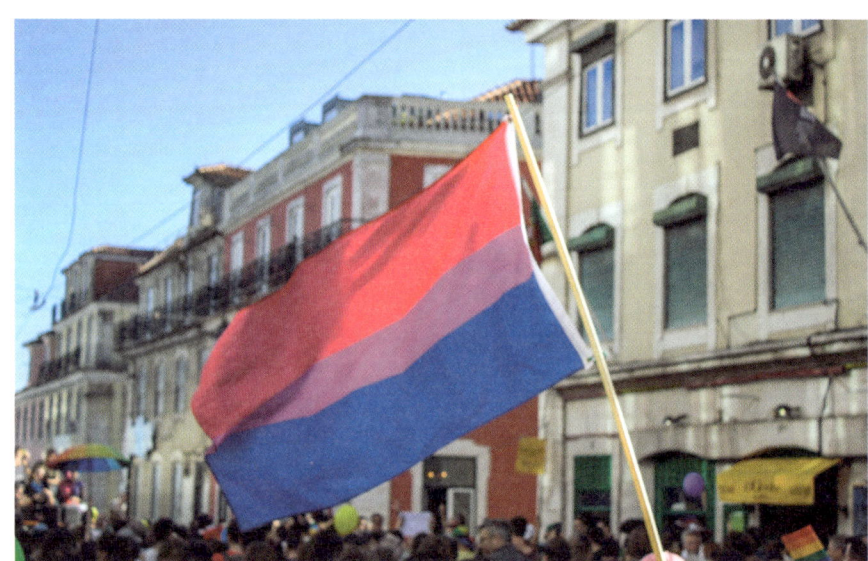

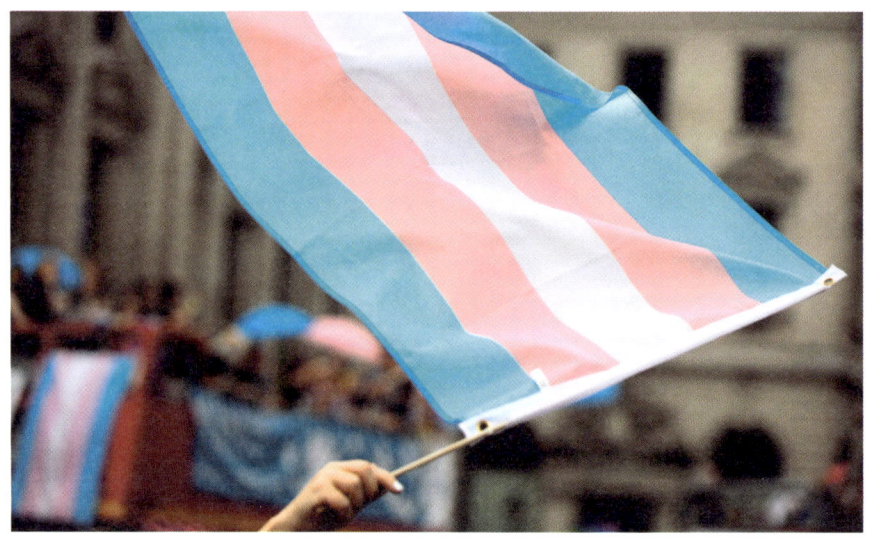

IDENTITY

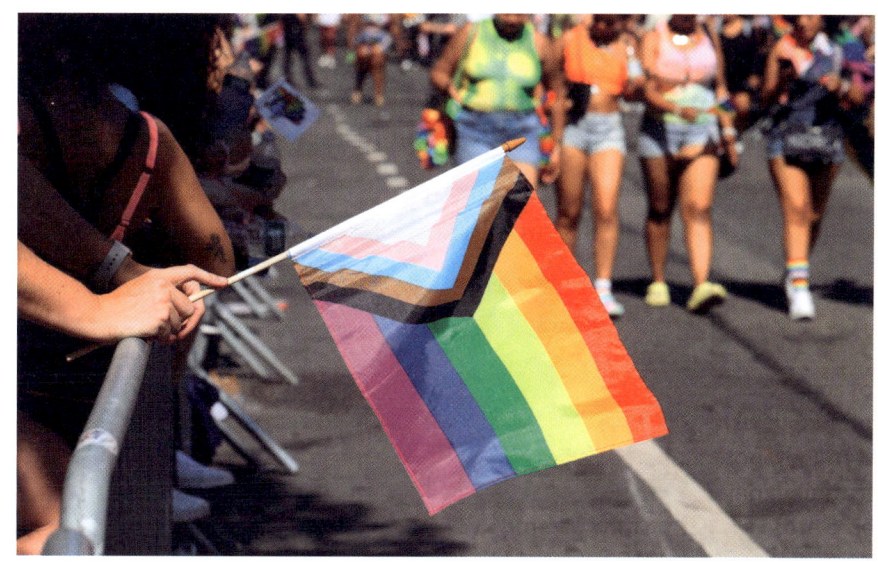

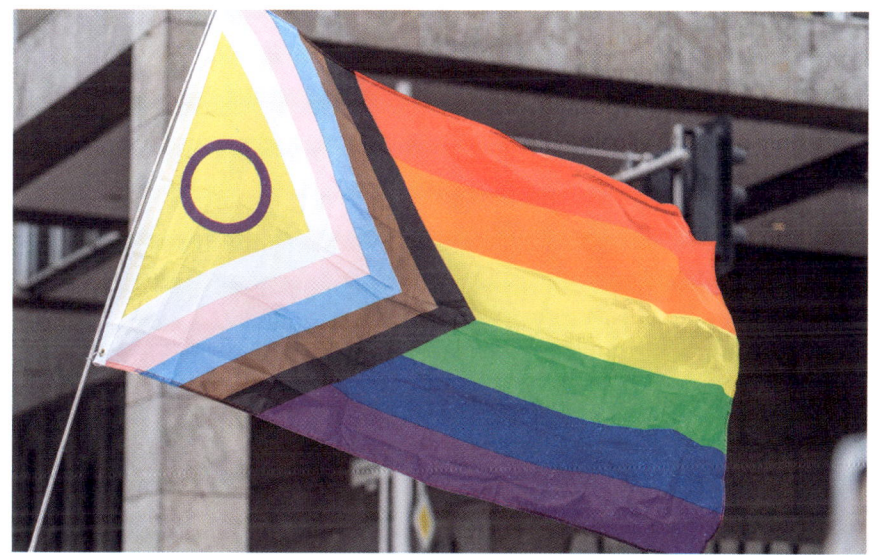

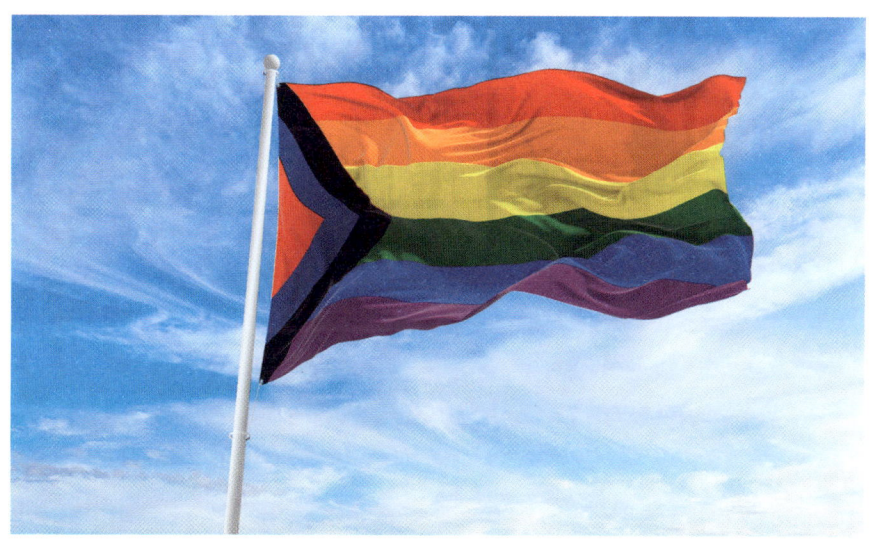

Since the widespread adoption of the Rainbow Pride flag, several other distinct variations have been designed, such as the Bisexual Pride flag (Michael Page, 1998), the Transgender Pride flag (Monica Helms, 1999), and the Gender Queer Pride flag (Marilyn Roxie, 2011).

Although the Pride flag has seen many adaptations, there have recently been a number of significant redesigns.

Gilbert Baker redesigned his original Rainbow flag in 2017, adding a lavender strip to symbolize the spirit and diversity of LGBTQIA+ people, and the Philadelphia Pride flag was debuted the same year, with the addition of black and brown stripes to symbolize queer communities of colour.

Three new Pride flags were introduced in 2018. Whilst each design still retains the six original rainbow stripes, they all celebrate the diversity of the LGBTQIA+ community by introducing new perspectives and calling for a more inclusive society globally.

Julia Feliz, a Puerto Rican designer, created the New Pride flag, which incorporates the pink, white and blue colours of the Trans Pride flag with brown and black diagonal stripes to emphasize the importance of trans people of colour within the queer rights movement.

Daniel Quasar, a non-binary American artist and designer, launched the Progress Pride flag. Their redesign adds a chevron that incorporates the colours of the Transgender Pride flag, as well as black and brown stripes to represent people of colour, those living with AIDS, and those no longer living, or living surrounded by stigma. The chevron points forward from the hoist to acknowledge progress, but indicates that progress towards inclusivity still needs to be made.

Moulee, an Indian activist, released his Social Justice Pride flag for the Chennai Queer LitFest. His redesign also includes a forward-pointing chevron that references elements of the Self-Respect Movement (in black), the anti-caste Ambedkarite movement (in blue) and leftist ideology (in red), emphasizing intersectionality and interconnected struggles within the Indian LGBTQIA+ community.

In 2021 Valentino Vecchietti of Intersex Equality Rights UK adapted Daniel Quasar's Progress Pride flag by adding the yellow triangle and purple circle from Morgan Carpenter's 2013 Intersex

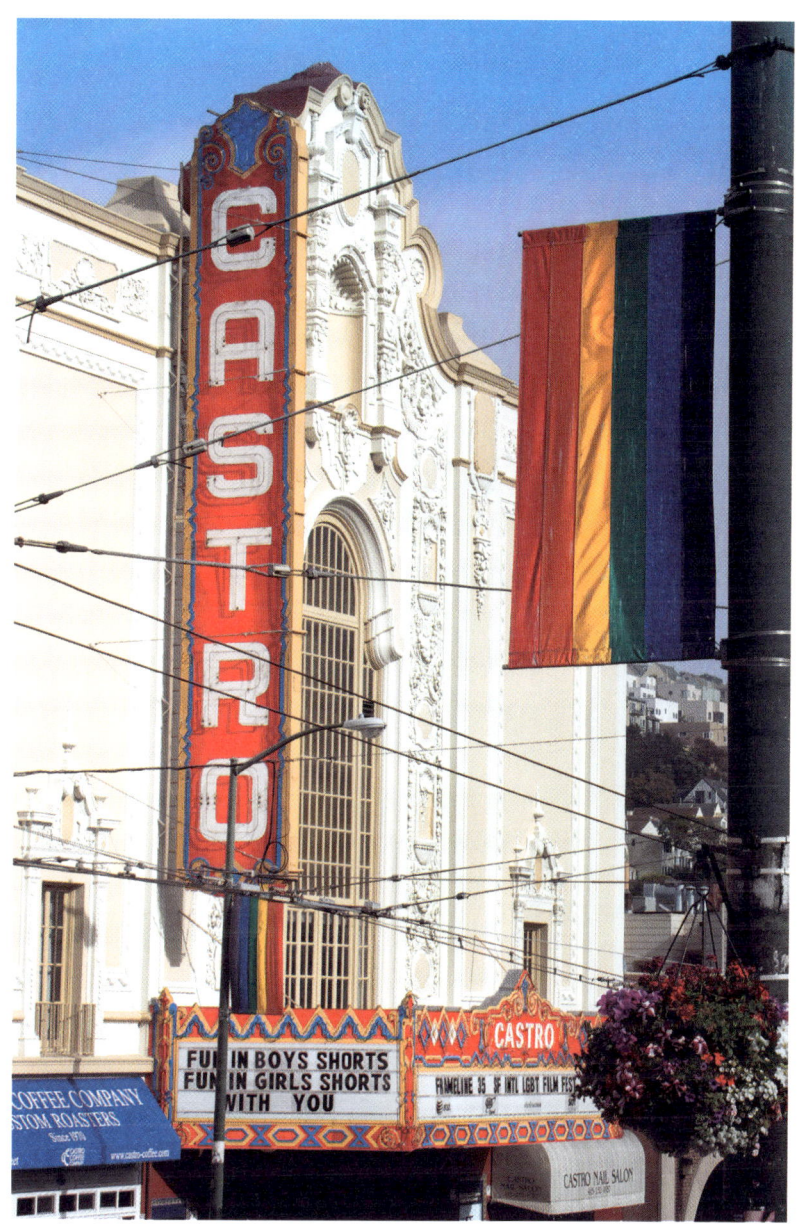

flag design to create the Intersex-Inclusive Progress Pride flag.

Although it's still illegal for it to be displayed in some countries, the Rainbow Pride flag, and all its variations, continues to stand as an international symbol of ongoing activism, and a powerful emblem of diversity. At MoMA in New York the Rainbow Pride flag was hung for the first time on 26 June 2015, the day the US Supreme Court reached its historic decision to legalize same-sex marriage in all states. The flag hangs permanently in the museum galleries as a commanding and evocative symbol of community, acceptance and love.

Class

The majority of societies organize their citizens into a social stratum, and where we fit into this hierarchy is predominantly determined by the wealth, privilege, status and social standing of our families or carers.

The organization of society according to a socioeconomic hierarchy is the basis for class, which is inseparable from economic inequality. Class can be used as a marker of identity to separate 'us' from 'them', the 'haves' from the 'have nots', but it can also be a source of pride for workers and their communities.

Trade Unions

Trade unions have a close history with the working class and the labour movement, and were established to protect the rights of workers, particularly those in low-paid manual or industrial jobs. Through collective bargaining, they advocate for fair wages, safe working conditions and an improvement in the quality of public services, and protests in the form of industrial action, such as strikes and work stoppages, are commonly organized.

During the Thatcher years in the UK (1979–90), there were many strikes as the government introduced privatization policies and measures of austerity that led to massive unemployment and economic inequality. One of the longest and most notable was the miners' strike between 1984 and 1985, led by the National Union of Mineworkers (NUM) against the National Coal Board after the announcement of the closure of 20 coal mines and the redundancy of 20,000 miners. The strike, the biggest industrial dispute in post-war Britain, was a bitter battle between the miners fighting for their livelihoods and the government reforming the coal industry, and undermining and weakening the trade union movement.

Mass protests in support of the 187,000 striking miners were frequent, and miners' wives organized collections of money and distributed food for striking families as they battled to survive hardship. Although the strikes were mostly peaceful, the confrontation at the Orgreave coking plant in Yorkshire in June 1984 marked a turning point as 6,000 police officers clashed violently with 5,000 flying pickets. Known as the Battle of Orgreave, eye witnesses report that riot and mounted

OPPOSITE

Thatcher's Thugs
(1984)

Thalia Campbell

177×119cm (70×47in).

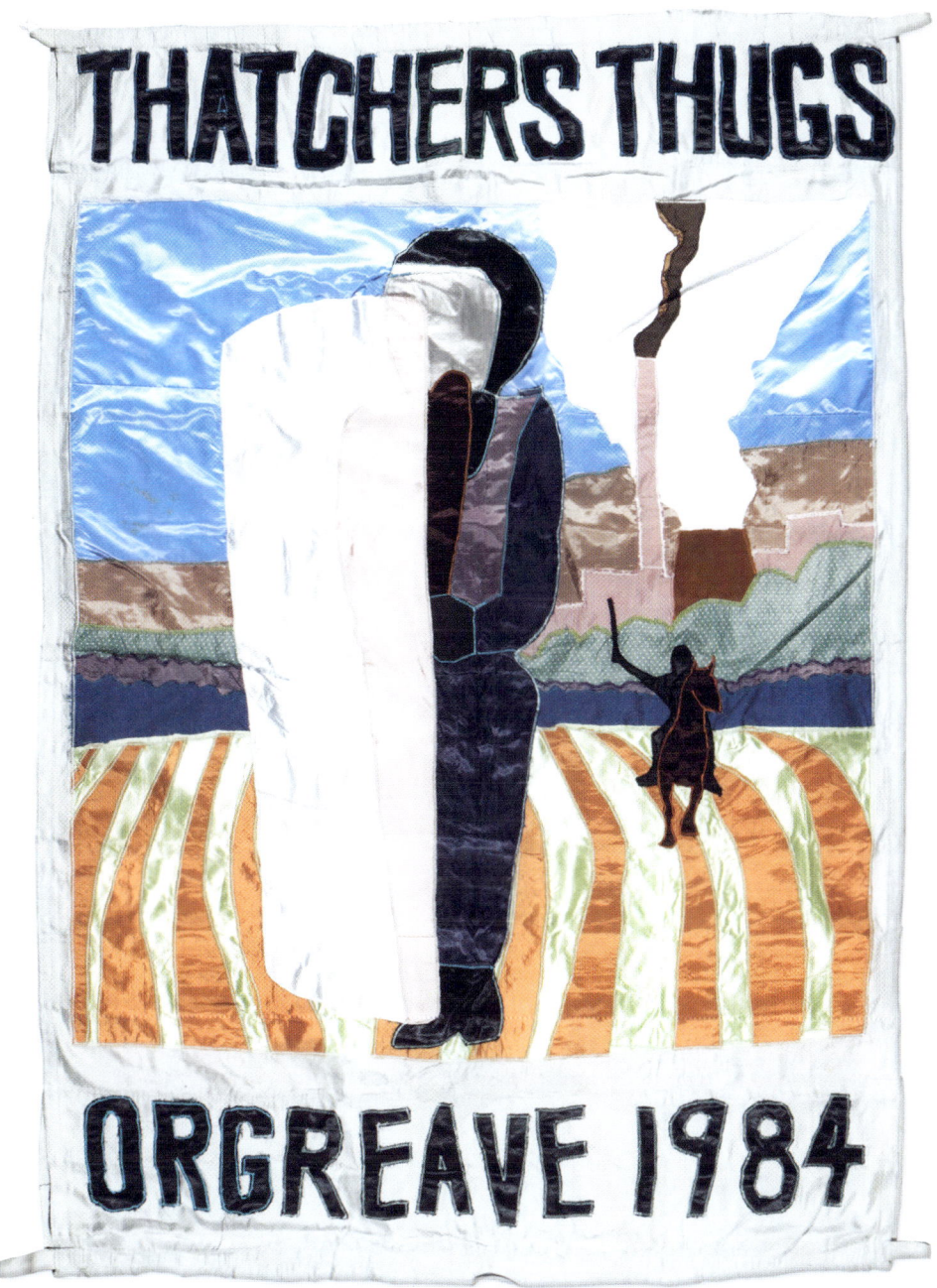

police charged at the defenceless miners with truncheons, brutally battering and trampling those in the way, and pursued those fleeing with riot squads, resulting in more than one hundred injuries.

The Orgreave Truth and Justice Campaign have not given up hope for a public enquiry.

Solidarity

Lesbians and Gays Support the Miners (LGSM) was founded in 1984 in solidarity with striking miners, and to raise money for them and their families. Their support, depicted in the film *Pride* (2014), was reciprocated when the NUM and Welsh mining communities marched with the LGSM at the head of London Pride in 1985.

Lesbians and Gays Support the Migrants is a queer activist group that builds on the philosophy of LGSM. Established in solidarity to say 'no one is illegal', it is another example of solidarity in action as one marginalized group supports another.

The Gay Liberation Front and the Black Panthers in the US also formed a strong alliance to protest against shared struggles of systematic oppression and discrimination. Huey P. Newton, an African American activist and founder of the Black Panther Party, urged a coalition between the two groups in his historic speech in 1970. His aim was to strengthen each other's causes by focusing on shared principles of justice and equality, exemplifying how solidarity can create a united front to significantly build bridges across movements and protests.

OPPOSITE

Lesbians and Gays Support the Miners banner.

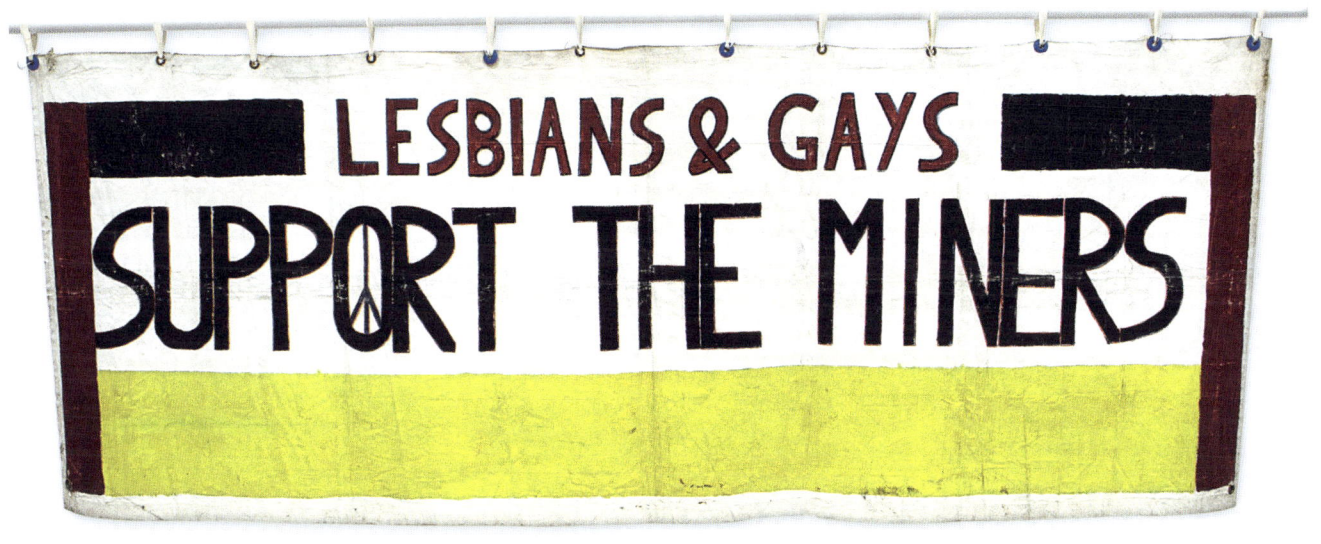

Race and Resistance

Race is a social construct that has been used to define, categorize and distinguish different populations and citizens throughout the world. It is used to divide and marginalize, establish hierarchies and exploit generations of people according to their heritage, skin colour and cultural identity. For many, race defines the lens through which they navigate the world, dictating how they are perceived and treated.

This construct of race has shaped societies and power structures for centuries. Governments, institutions, and individuals have used it as a tool to justify oppression, slavery, and systemic inequality. The embedding of racial distinctions into legal codes, social norms, and cultural narratives maintains a divide that perpetuates privilege for some whilst denying opportunity and dignity to others. The legacy of these practices still persists today, influencing everything from access to education and healthcare to perceptions of worth and belonging.

Challenging the construct of race, as an imposed historical framework, and addressing the deeply rooted structural forces that profoundly affect personal identities and lived experiences requires more than policy reforms; it calls for a deep reckoning of the cultural and psychological foundations of bias, as well as a collective commitment to justice and equity.

In her signature cloth paintings, US artist Dawn Williams Boyd explores issues of race and resistance and the enduring legacy of systemic racism in America. The textile artworks that form the 'The Sins of the Fathers' series are brutally honest illustrations of racial violence, injustice and resilience, graphically depicting the 'sins' and horrors of past generations, such as enslavement, segregation, lynchings and white supremacy. Her expressive textiles not only memorialize the victims of racial oppression, but also discuss the persisting structures of power that perpetuate inequality and injustice against Black American citizens.

OPPOSITE, ABOVE

Bad Blood: Tuskegee Syphilis Experiments – Macon County, AL 1932–1972 (2016)

Dawn Williams Boyd

135×173cm (53x68in). Assorted fabrics and cotton embroidery floss.

OPPOSITE, BELOW

Baptizing Our Children in a River of Blood (2017)

Dawn Williams Boyd

345×122cm (136×48in). Assorted fabrics and cotton embroidery floss.

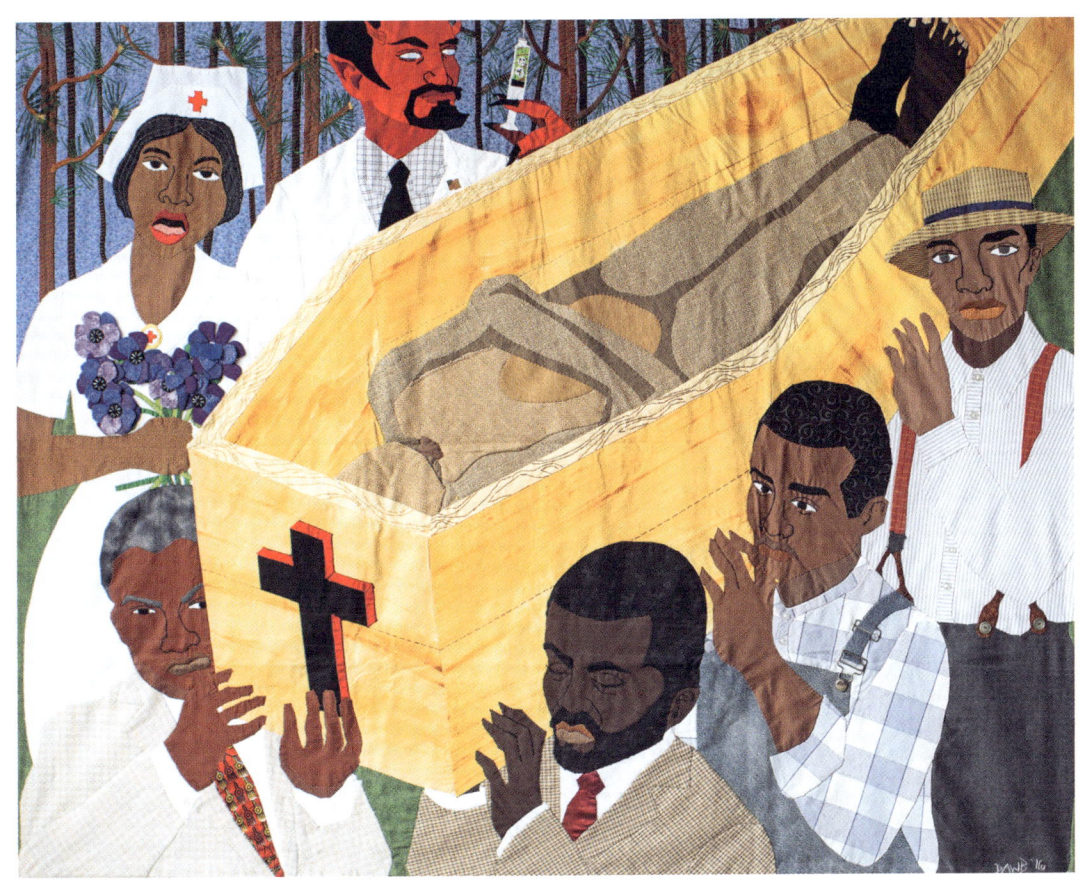

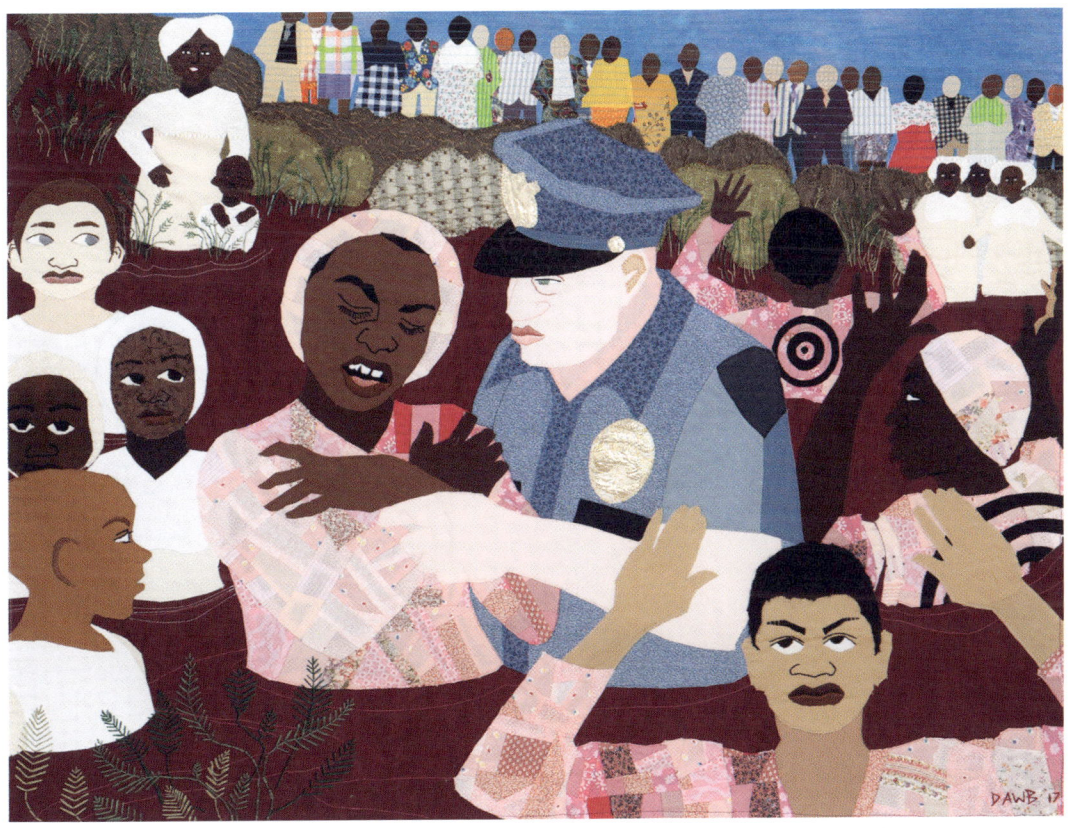

The American Civil Rights Movement

The American Civil Rights Movement (1954–68) was a pivotal era of social activism, and an important grassroots protest that transformed US laws and changed history. The aim of this mass movement was to end the inherent system of racial segregation and discrimination against African Americans, particularly in the southern states, by changing social and cultural norms, policies and legislation that prohibited equal rights.

Building on centuries of unrest and resistance, rooted in struggles to abolish slavery and oppose entrenched racial oppression, the successful Civil Rights Movement had a lasting impact, with notable reforms, dramatic legal victories and the introduction of the Civil Rights Act.

The National Association for the Advancement of Colored People

The National Association for the Advancement of Colored People (NAACP) was founded in 1909 and remains an active civil rights organization today. It was established following the race riot in Springfield, Illinois, in 1908, and the terrifying rise in mob lynchings of Black people. During the Civil Rights Movement, its members were at the forefront of the fight to overturn the 'Jim Crow' statute (which legalized racial segregation in the late 19th and early 20th centuries), and the disenfranchisement laws that prevented Black people from registering to vote.

In 1957 the NAACP played a crucial role in supporting nine teenage African American students to be the first to attend the all-white Central High School in Little Rock, Arkansas. Known as the 'Little Rock Nine', these students were testing the Brown vs Board of Education case, which ruled that segregation for Black and white students was unconstitutional and illegal. This ruling was the first milestone in the American Civil Rights Movement, and paved the way for further changes in legislation. The nine courageous students were finally allowed access into the school after President Eisenhower sent federal troops to enforce their entry. Despite continual harassment and threats, on 27 May 1958 Ernest Green became the first African American to graduate from Central High.

OPPOSITE, ABOVE

Banner used by the Oklahoma Federation of Colored Women's Clubs, c. 1924, silk (fibre), wood, paint.

OPPOSITE, BELOW

Flag announcing another lynching. 'A MAN WAS LYNCHED YESTERDAY,' is flown from the window of the NAACP headquarters on 69 Fifth Ave., New York City in 1936.

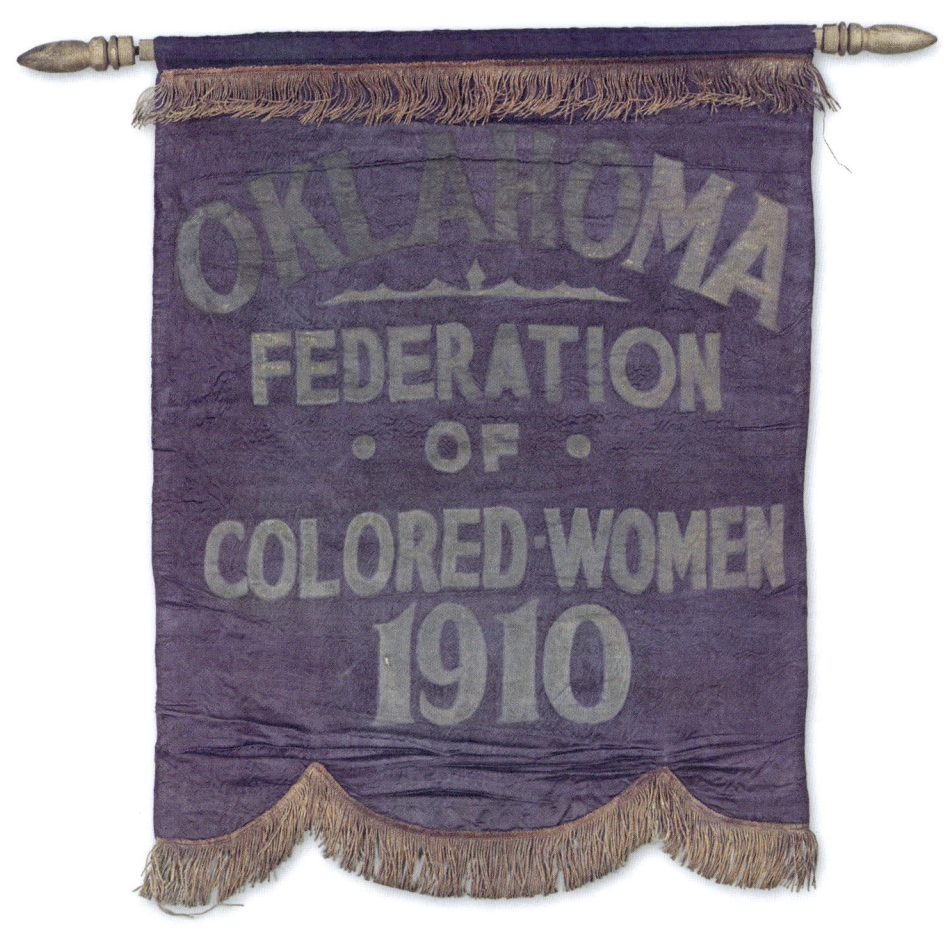

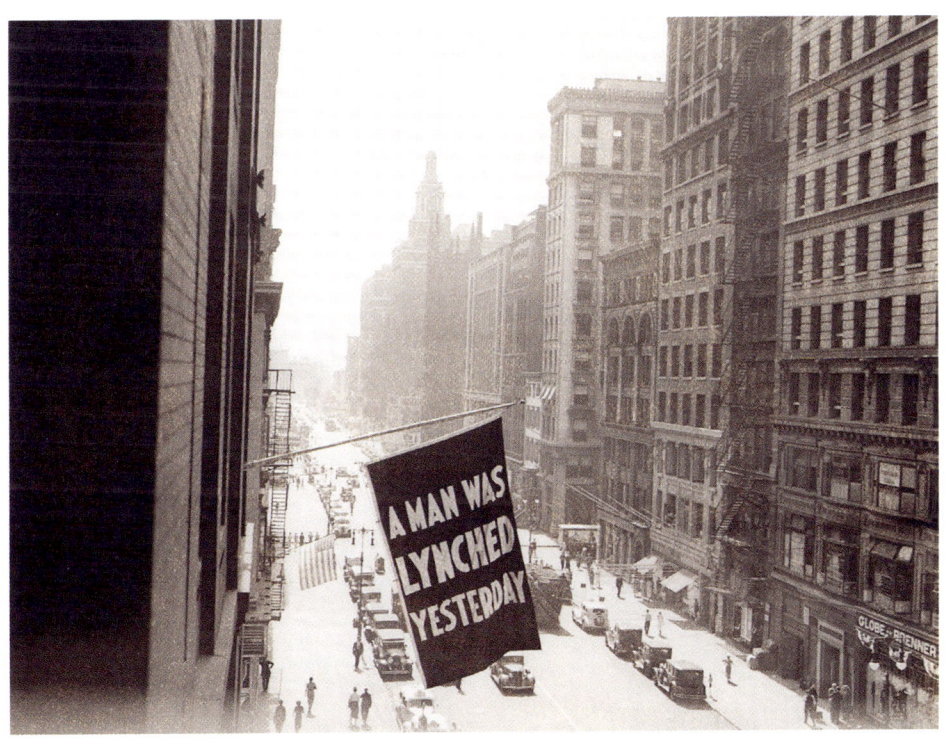

Rosa Parks and the Montgomery Bus Boycott

On 1 December 1955, Rosa Parks, an African American woman, refused to give up her bus seat to a white man in Montgomery, Alabama. She was legally sitting in the first row of the 'colored section', but when a white man could not find a seat in the 'white section', the bus driver ordered the commuters in Parks' row to stand. Three did, but Parks refused, not because she was tired on her commute home from work, but because she was 'tired of giving in'. This one-person protest against racial segregation on public transport went down in history as one of strength, courage and dignity.

Nine months earlier Claudette Colvin, an African American student, refused to give her seat to a white woman on a bus as the 'white section' became full. She said 'history kept me stuck to my seat. I felt the hand of Harriet Tubman pushing down on one shoulder and Sojourner Truth pushing down on the other'. Colvin was forcibly removed from the bus, arrested and faced charges including violating segregation laws. Her one person stand for justice did not go down in history like Rosa Parks' (her mentor) as she was an unmarried pregnant teenager during her trial, but she remains an important pioneering activist and hero of the Civil Rights Movement.

Parks was also arrested for her actions, and charged with violating segregation laws, but her non-violent direct action sparked a mass protest known as the Montgomery Bus Boycott, which instantly gained momentum with the Black population. The boycott ran from 5 December 1955 (the date of Parks' sentencing) until 20 December 1956, the day after a written court order, ruling that bus segregation was unconstitutional, arrived in Montgomery.

Parks had been a member of NAACP since 1943 and remained an activist all her life, tirelessly campaigning for the rights of Black people. After her protest she became known as 'the Mother of the Civil Rights Movement' and in 1999 was awarded the Congressional Gold Medal – the highest honour the US bestows on a civilian. After her death on 24 October 2005 she became the first woman in history to lie in honour at the US Capitol.

OPPOSITE, ABOVE

Rosa Parks memorial banner.

OPPOSITE, BELOW

Rosa Parks at a march at the South African Embassy protesting the country's racial policies.

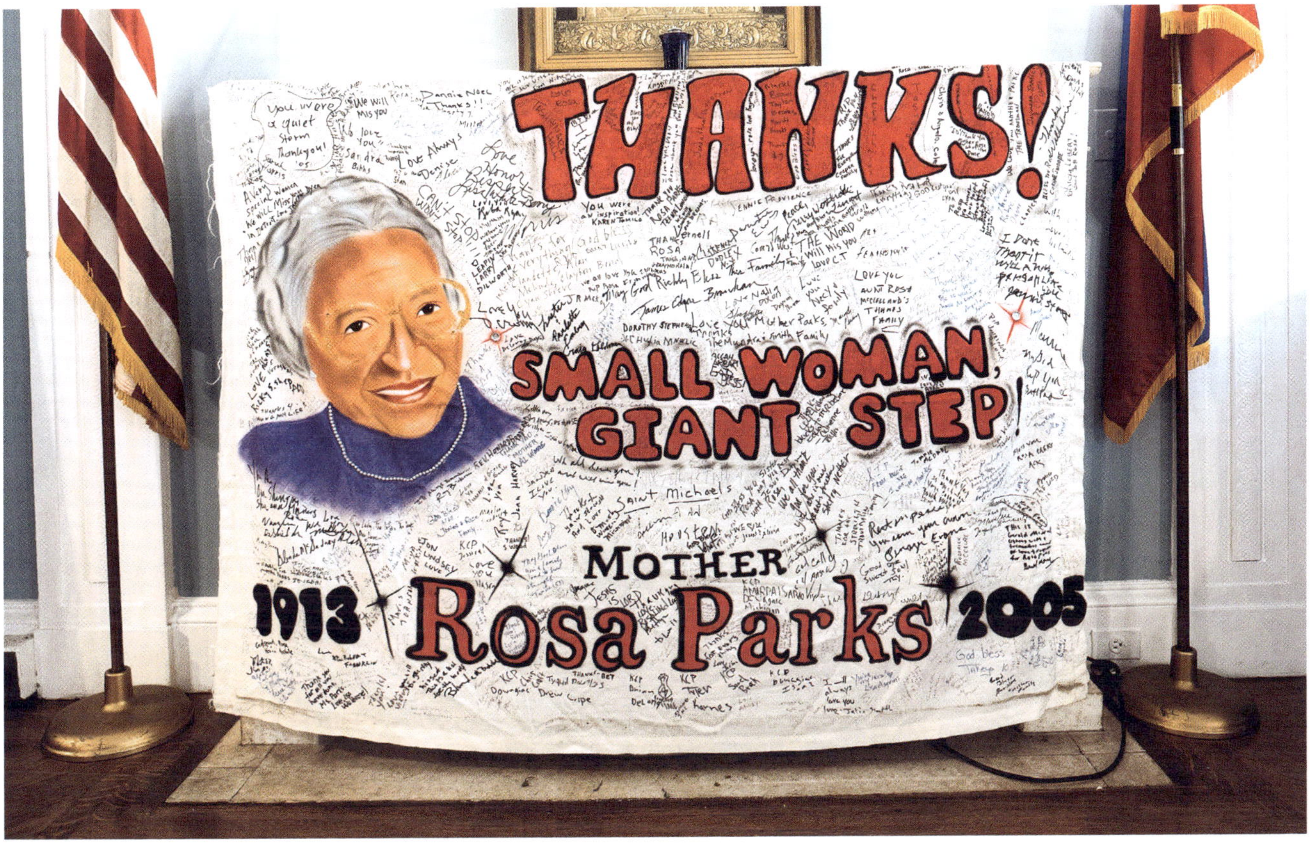

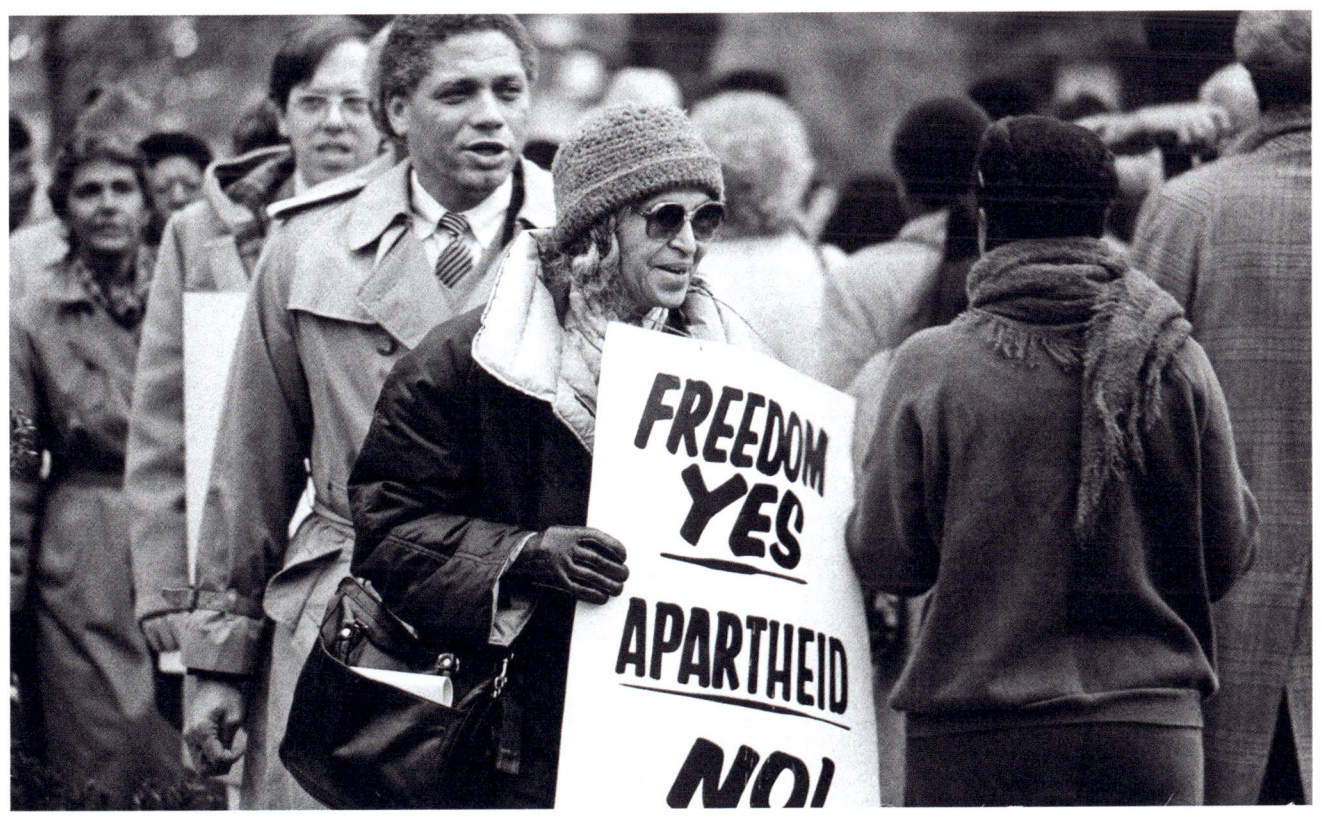

Reverend Dr Martin Luther King Jr and the Southern Christian Leadership Conference

Reverend Dr Martin Luther King Jr was a Baptist minister and activist who came to prominence as the leader and official spokesperson for the Montgomery Bus Boycott. His philosophy was to advocate for civil disobedience through non-violent resistance, and as a result he became a target of white supremacists who made several assassination attempts on him.

As the president of the Southern Christian Leadership Conference (SCLC), King travelled extensively giving lectures on civil rights and became a national figurehead in the American Civil Rights Movement. Along with other significant Black leaders of the American Civil Rights Movement, including Philip Randolph, Bayard Rustin, John Lewis, Whitney Young, James Farmer and Roy Wilkins, King was a central figure in organizing the historic March on Washington for Jobs and Freedom on 28 August 1963. This historic large-scale march was planned over a short timeline, but the original idea of Randolph's was conceived in the 1940s. It's estimated that up to 300,000 people attended this peaceful protest rally where King gave his rousing and iconic 'I Have a Dream' speech, sharing his vision of equality. King's 16-minute oration is one of the most famous speeches in history.

There were, of course, many other significant figures and organizations that played a major part in the fight for civil rights in the US, including Dorothy Height, Septima Poinsette Clark and Malcolm X, and their actions, and the protests of hundreds of thousands of citizens, led to the eventual signing of the Civil Rights Act of 1964, which King described as 'a second emancipation'. In the same year, King was awarded the Nobel Peace Prize for his significant commitment to the American Civil Rights Movement and his dedication to non-violent resistance to racial discrimination. He was assassinated in Memphis, Tennessee, on 4 April 1968.

OPPOSITE, ABOVE

Dr Martin Luther King Jr addressing a crowd at a protest in Chicago.

OPPOSITE, BELOW

Memorial banner for Dr Martin Luther King Jr's funeral procession, Atlanta, Georgia, 9 April 1968.

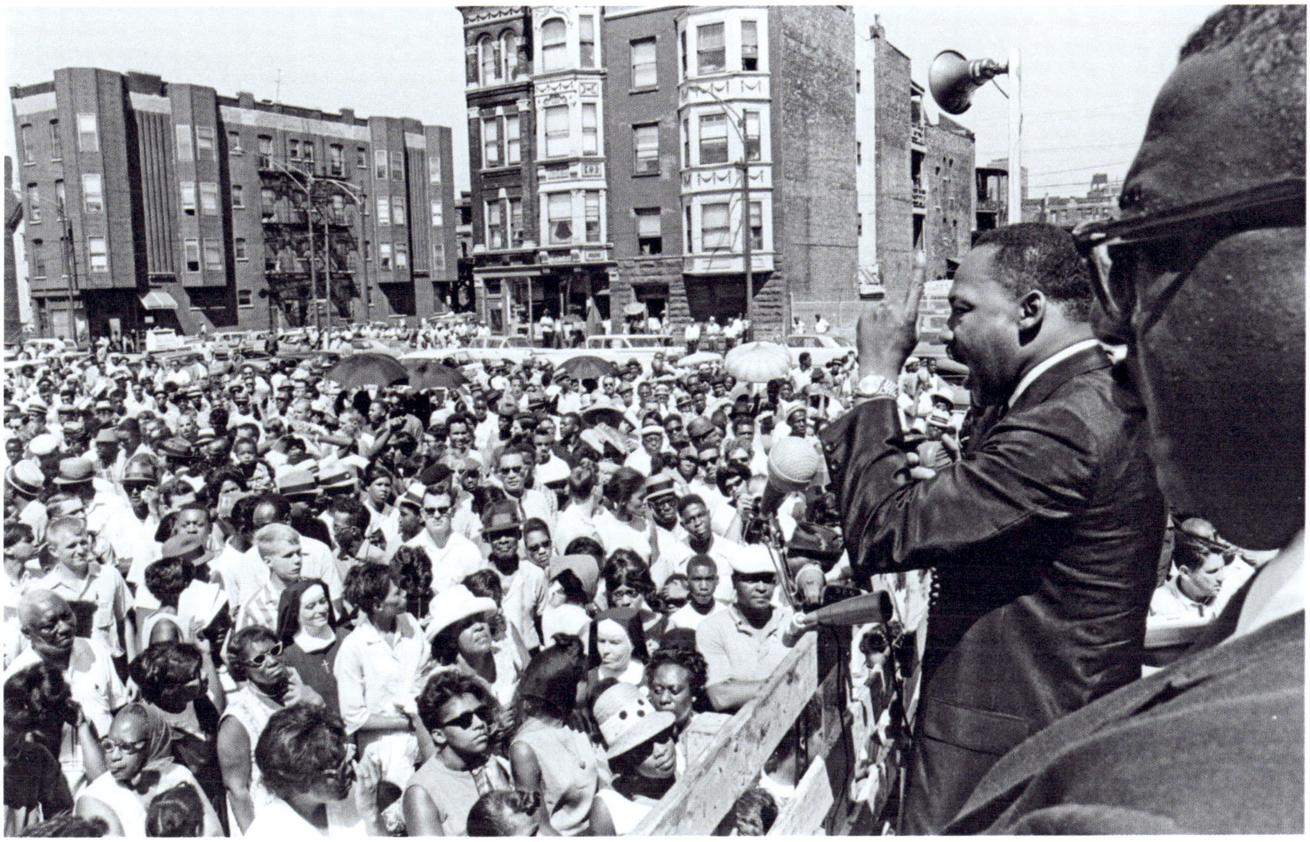

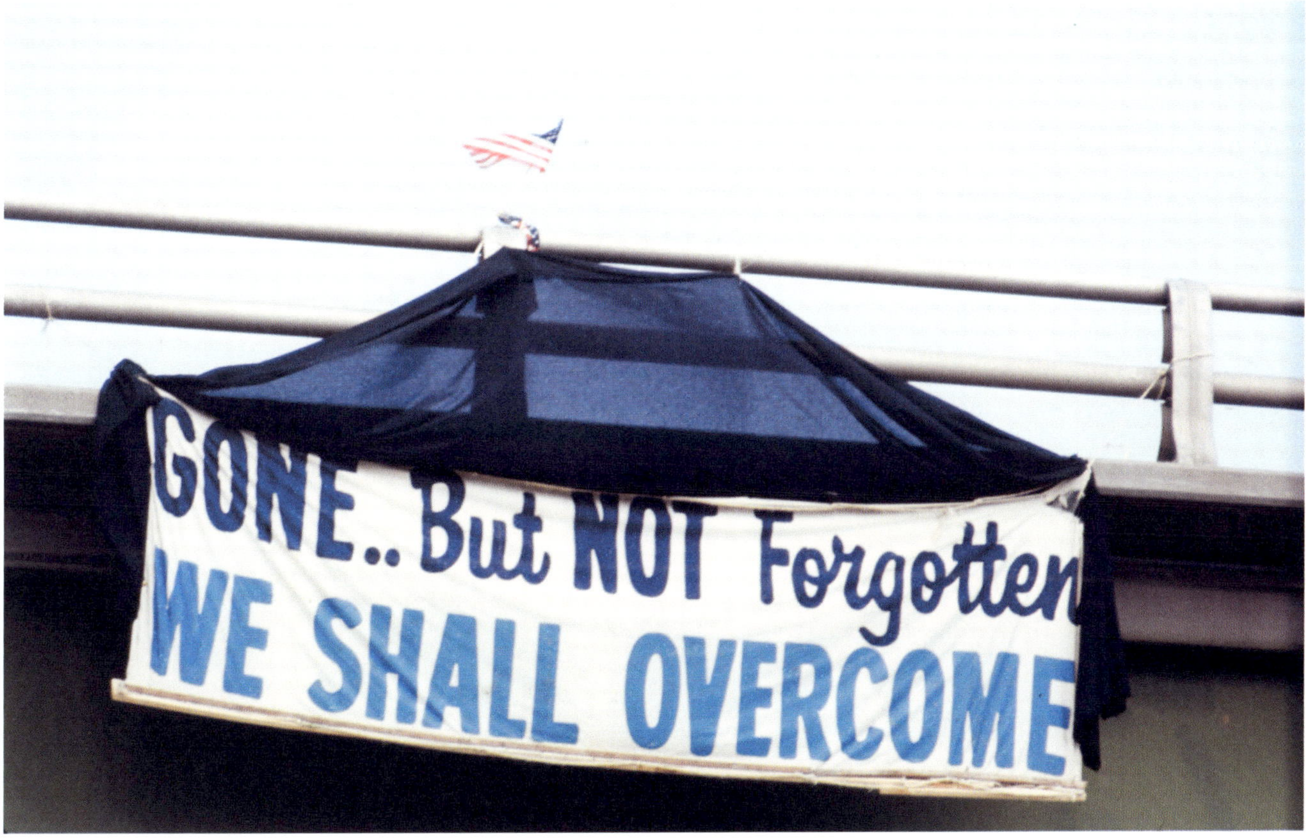

GONE.. But NOT Forgotten
WE SHALL OVERCOME

Police Brutality and Institutional Racism

Despite the introduction of the Civil Rights Act in 1964, deep prejudices, hostilities and ingrained racial stereotypical views remained in the US. Law-enforcement officers continued to discriminate and use excessive force, targeting African Americans in particular, as well as other people of colour, especially those on low incomes and the working class.

In the following decades, US police officers have unlawfully arrested, assaulted and even killed unarmed victims, either at the scene of arrest or later in police custody. Their actions have been the catalyst for many protests and violent race riots.

In the UK, there have also been many incidents of institutionalized racism resulting in protests and riots as long-standing hostilities between the police and the Black community reached a critical point. In 1981, discriminatory stop-and-search police practices triggered the Brixton Riots, and the death of Cynthia Jarrett, an Afro-Caribbean woman who died of heart failure during a police search at her home, led to violent clashes and the Tottenham (Broadwater Farm) Riots in 1985. Whilst policing the riots, a white police officer, Keith Blakelock, was murdered, which sent shockwaves throughout the nation.

The shooting of Mark Duggan in his community in Tottenham, by police officers in 2011, sparked riots in London and other UK cities, further highlighting issues of racial profiling and police brutality towards Black people.

The name of Stephen Lawrence, who was killed in an unprovoked racially motivated attack by a group of white youths in 1993, has been inextricably linked with police institutional racism ever since. The attack on the streets of London led to significant protests and a call for a reform of the police force. The subsequent Macpherson Report (1999) criticized the police and concluded that the investigation was 'marred by a combination of professional incompetence, institutional racism and a failure of leadership'.

Baroness Louise Casey was appointed by the former Commissioner of the Metropolitan Police Service to undertake an independent review into the standards of behaviour and the internal culture of the Metropolitan Police Service in 2022. Her findings, published in 2023, suggest that nothing has changed; she found the Met guilty of 'institutional racism, misogyny and homophobia'.

BELOW AND OPPOSITE

Freedom Seekers (USA) (2019)

Precious Lovell

The artist was inspired by Harriet Jacobs who was born enslaved in North Carolina. Writing in her autobiography, Jacobs said, 'When they told me my new-born babe was a girl, my heart was heavier than it had ever been before. Slavery is terrible for men; but it is far more terrible for women.' Lovell says that *Freedom Seekers* honours the many enslaved women in North Carolina, who risked life, limb and loss of loved ones to run towards freedom. (See also pages 104, 105.)

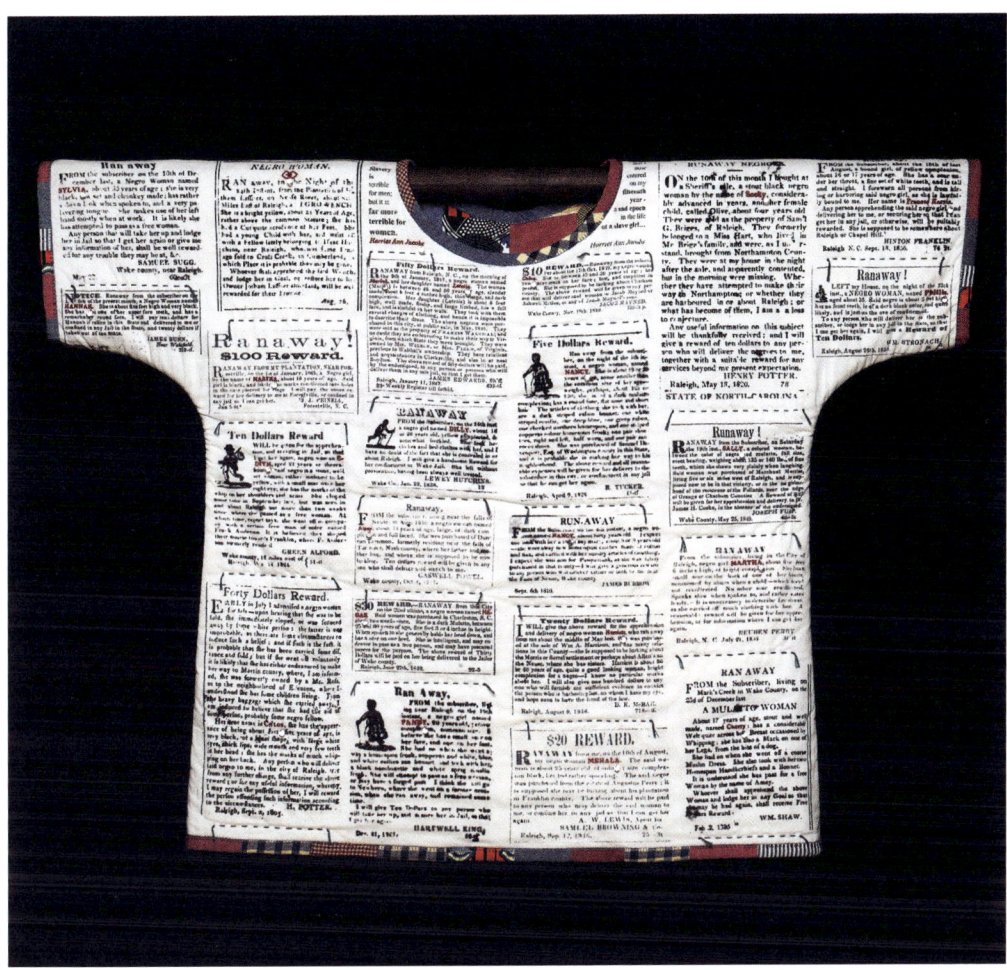

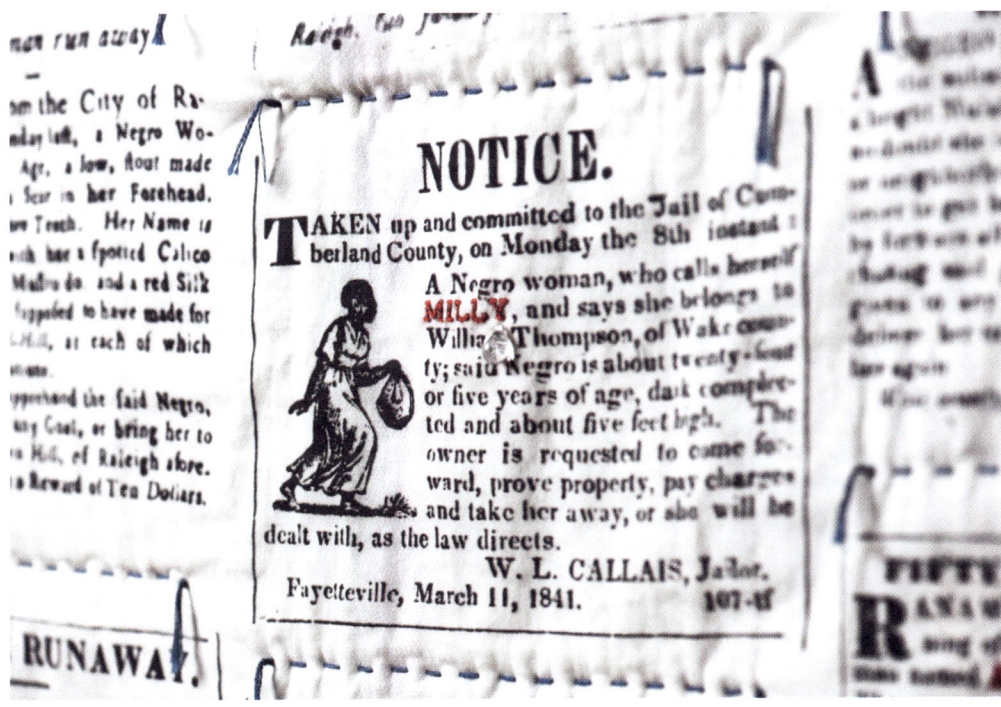

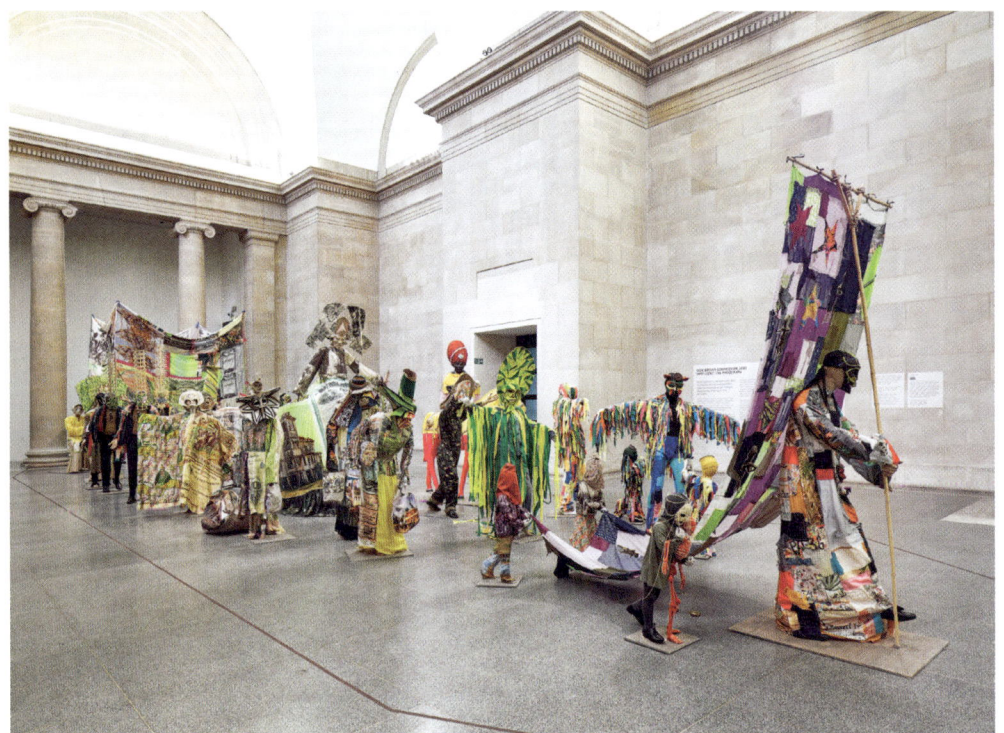

Many visual artists address the themes of police brutality, racism, misogyny and homophobia in their artworks, and also memorialize victims in permanent banners, textiles and installations, to remember both individuals and communities who have suffered. Their thought-provoking works initiate debates on social, political and cultural issues, many of which highlight and critique the power structures that perpetuate these historical and systemic inequalities.

One such artist, Hew Locke OBE, a Guyanese-British contemporary artist, investigates the intersections of many of these inequalities, and the power structures which uphold them. Locke's work addresses colonial legacies and the cultural symbolisms that societies adopt to assert identity. Locke explores themes of nationhood and empire through sculptures and installations, collages and mixed-media artworks. His questioning of the importance and presence of statues, which carry the weight of history, and boats as containers for refugees, treasure seekers or colonialists, are favoured recurring subjects.

'The Procession', commissioned by Tate Britain in 2021, consists of 150 life-sized figures, including horses and children. This installation, with textiles at its core, reflects upon a wide range of historical and contemporary issues such as colonialism, migration, cultural identity, revolution, slavery, emancipation and global warming, indirectly powerfully engaging the viewer to contemplate themes of resistance and oppression.

The Procession (2022)

Hew Locke

5×6×85m (197×236×3346in). Mixed media inc. cardboard, fabric, gluegun, PVA, plastic, fibreglass, wood, metal, resin, paint.

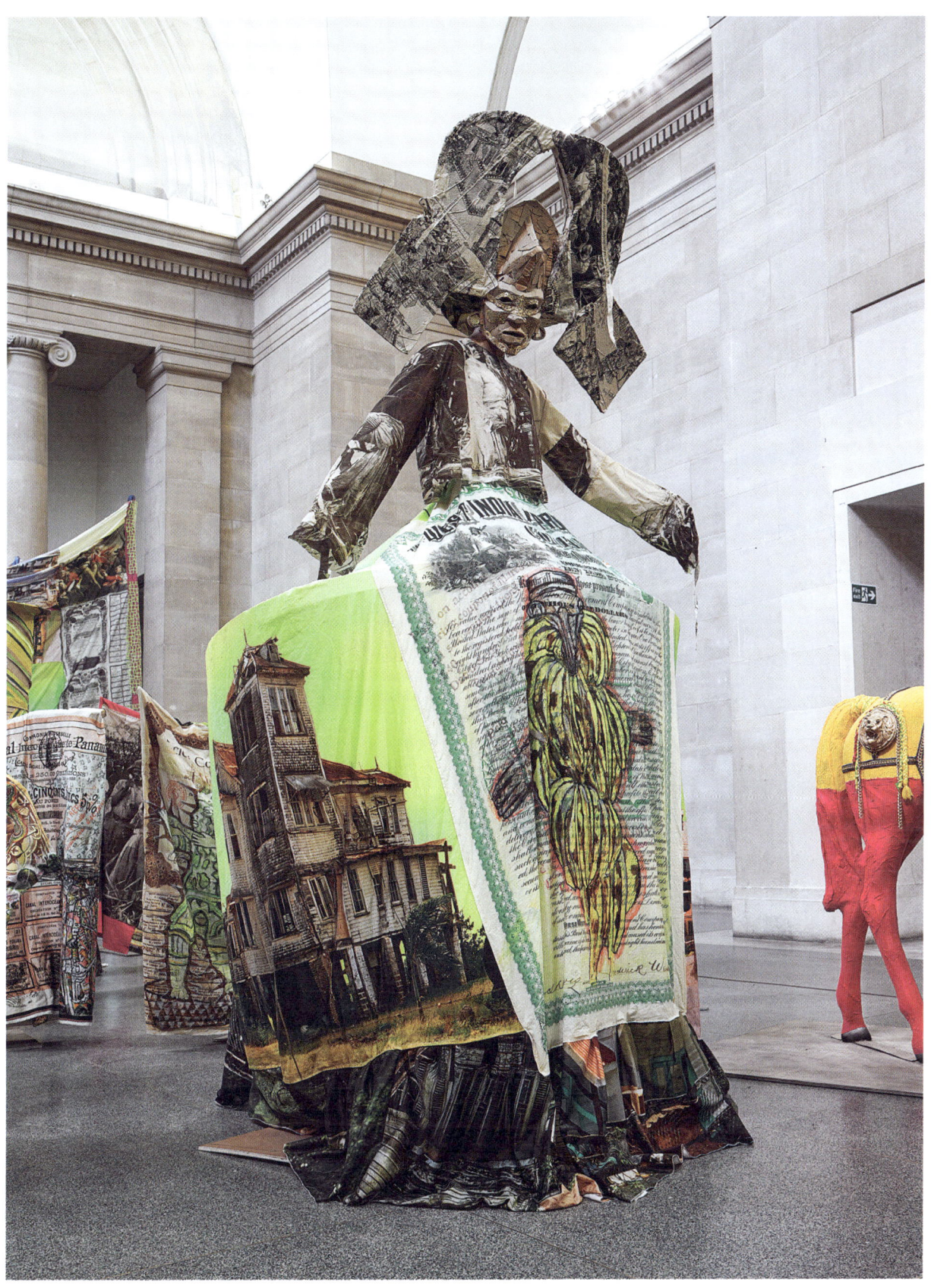

Untitled Flag
(2020)

Barbara Kruger

56×53.5cm (22×21
1/10in). Screenprinted
on cotton.

Kruger, an
American artist
and collagist,
has been at
the forefront of
conceptual and
feminist art for
decades, making
provocative work
that critiques
consumer culture,
patriarchal and
societal structures,
identity and
gender. Her
installations
of texts are
immersive and
iconic, reflecting
her training in
graphic design
and her interest
in the intersection
between art and
activism.

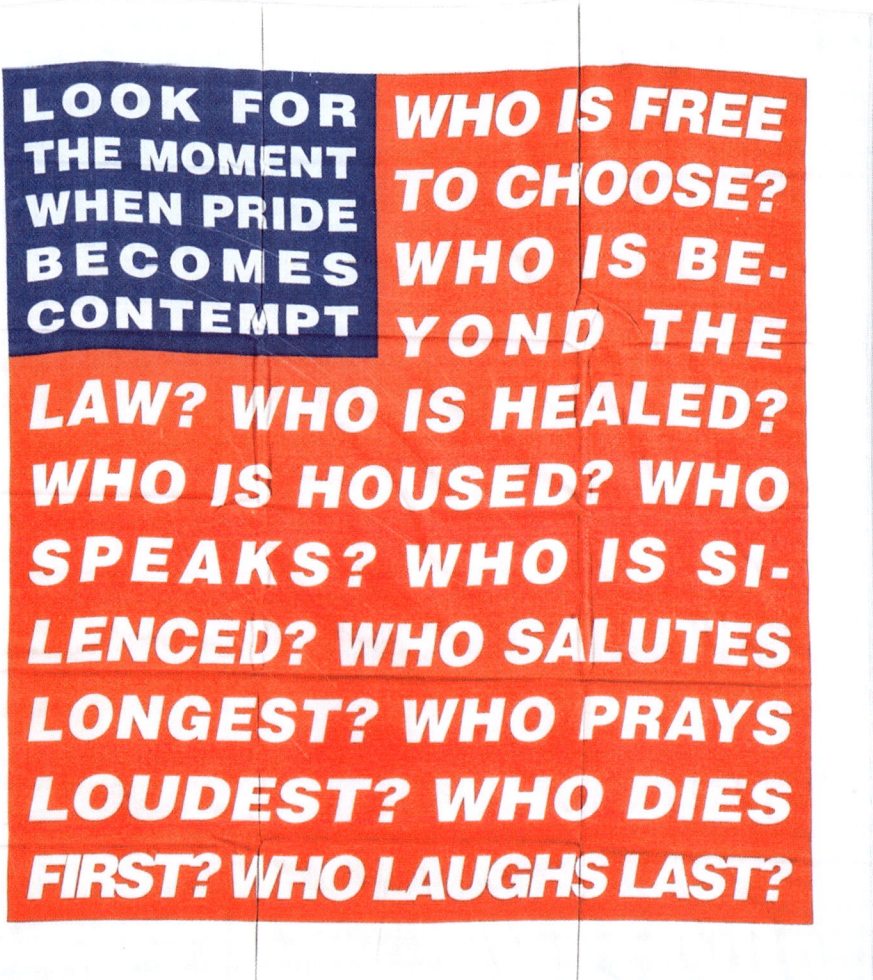

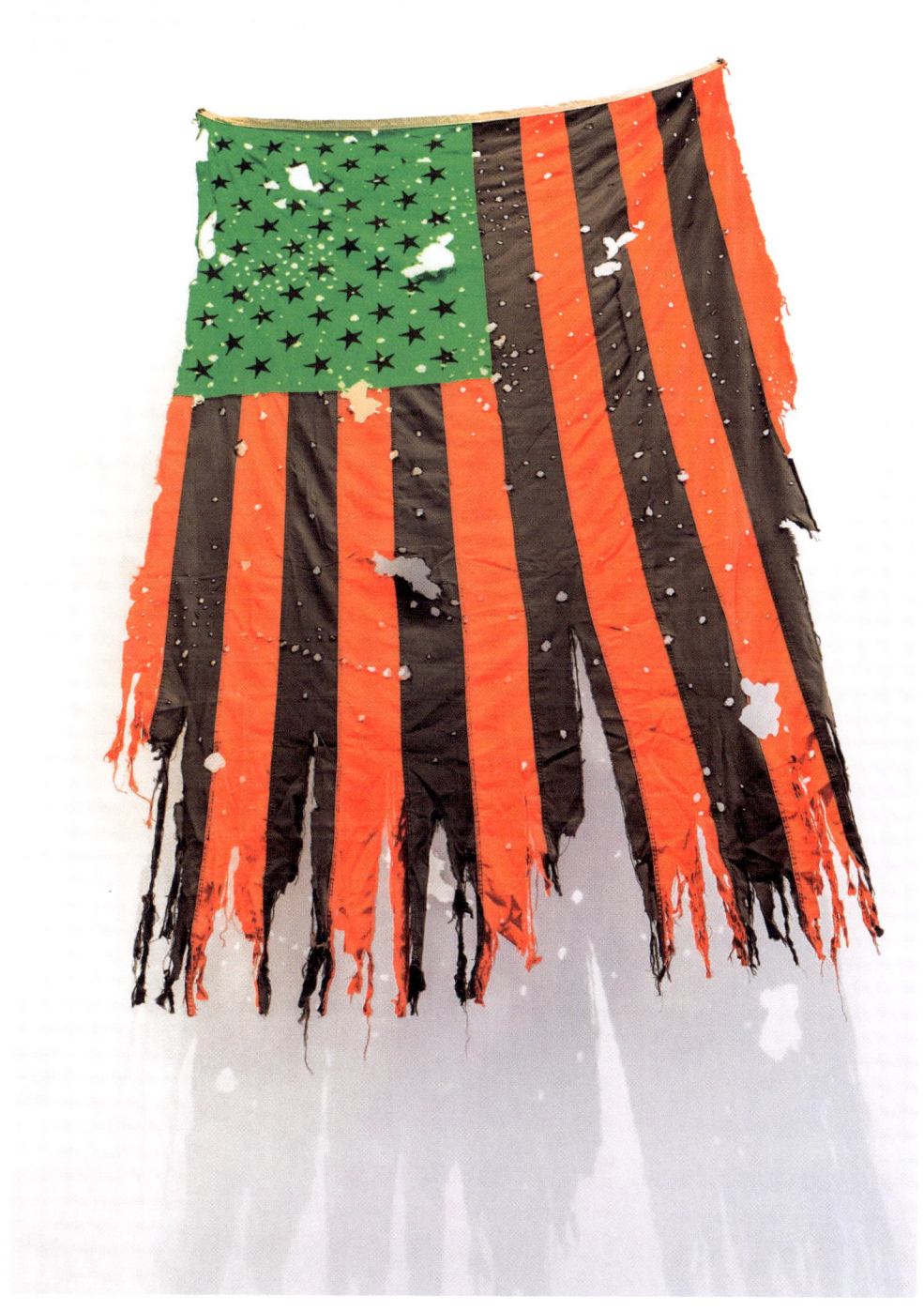

Oh Say Can You See (2017)

David Hammons

242.6×154cm
(95.5×60.75in). Cloth,
two metal grommets.

Hanging vertically,
torn and tattered,
Hammons'
version of the US
flag is radically
reappropriated
to reflect the true
history of America.
Black represents
the colour of skin;
red the blood of
African ancestors
and slaves; green
the abundance of
Africa and nature.
The holes and
tears represent
a fragmented
nation, wherein
Black Americans
are still oppressed
and violated. The
title of the artwork,
the first line of
the US anthem,
calls the viewer
to reflect on the
racial inequalities
and prejudices still
rife in American
society.

Black Lives Matter

The Black Lives Matter Global Network Foundation (BLMGNF) was formed in 2013 by three women – Alicia Garza, Patrisse Cullors and Opal Tometi, Black activists and human and civil rights campaigners – following the acquittal of Trayvon Martin's killer in Florida in 2012. Martin, an unarmed African American teenager, was shot by a white neighbourhood watch coordinator. Although the defendant pleaded his actions were in self-defence, others cited a racially motivated hate crime as his incentive to shoot.

BLMGNF's mission is to work 'inside and outside of the system to heal the past, reimagine the present, and invest in the future of Black lives through policy change, investment in our communities, and a commitment to arts and culture'.

The founders introduced the hashtag #BlackLivesMatter on social media in 2013 to highlight continuing police brutality and to raise awareness of several more deaths of Black people whilst in police custody, and a whole decentralized political and social movement has grown around it. Protests have taken many forms, including staged 'die-ins', strikes and 'taking the knee' during the playing of the US national anthem.

In the UK, Black Lives Matter (BLMUK), is an apolitical organisation operating within the global BLM Movement. Their social media platforms encourage people 'to kneel together for peace and unity, asserting Black Lives Matter'.

The advent of social media has brought protests to a global audience as they happen, but many historical protests are less well documented. One artist addressing this is Precious D Lovell, an artist of African descent who uses her creative practice to reclaim 'stories of the African Diaspora omitted from the traditional historical narrative'. Her 'Warrior Women of the African Diaspora' is a collection of war shirts that celebrate 'HER'Stories of courageous and defiant Black women. Of Harriet Tubman (see overleaf) Lovell says: 'as an enslaved girl and woman in Maryland, I believe that the future she dreamed of was in line with BLM and was one of TRUE liberation, where Black people live free from fear, oppression, poverty and inequality. She clearly understood overlapping forms of oppression and spent her entire life fighting the social injustices and inequalities of her time'.

OPPOSITE

Black Lives Matter protest textiles.

OVERLEAF

Harriet Tubman (USA) (2009)

Precious Lovell

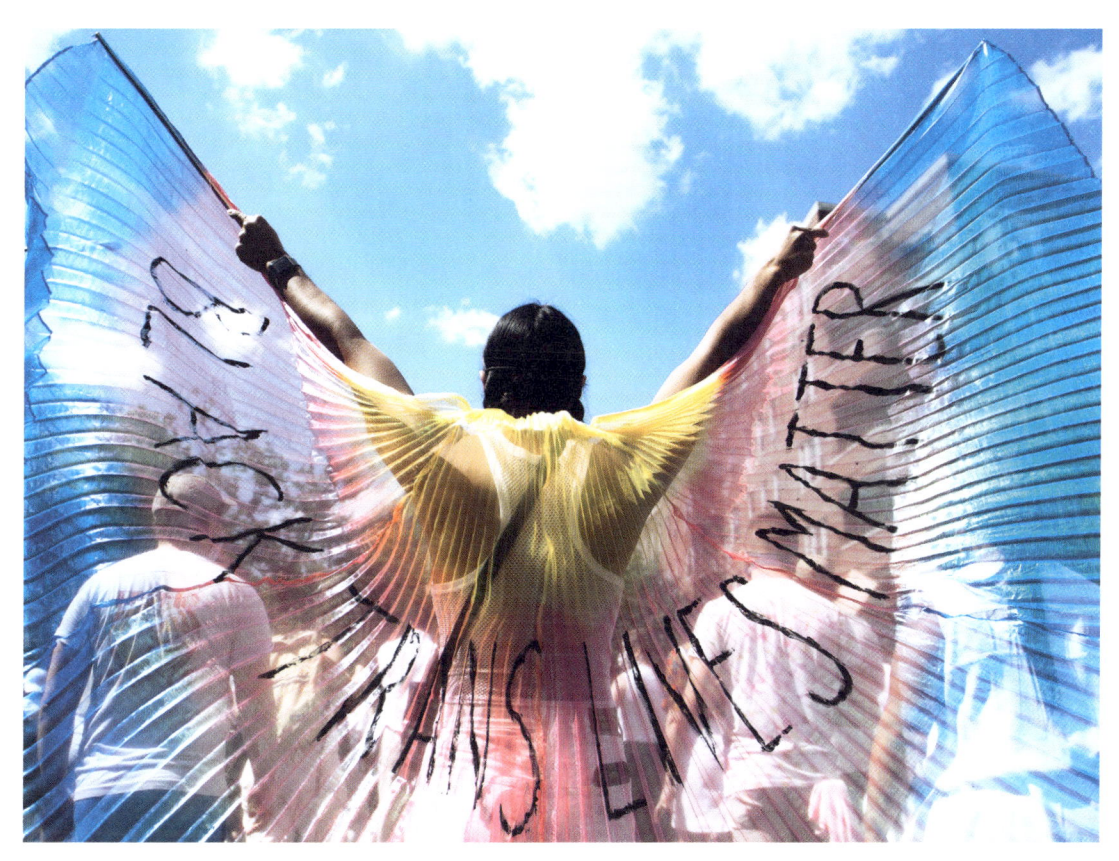

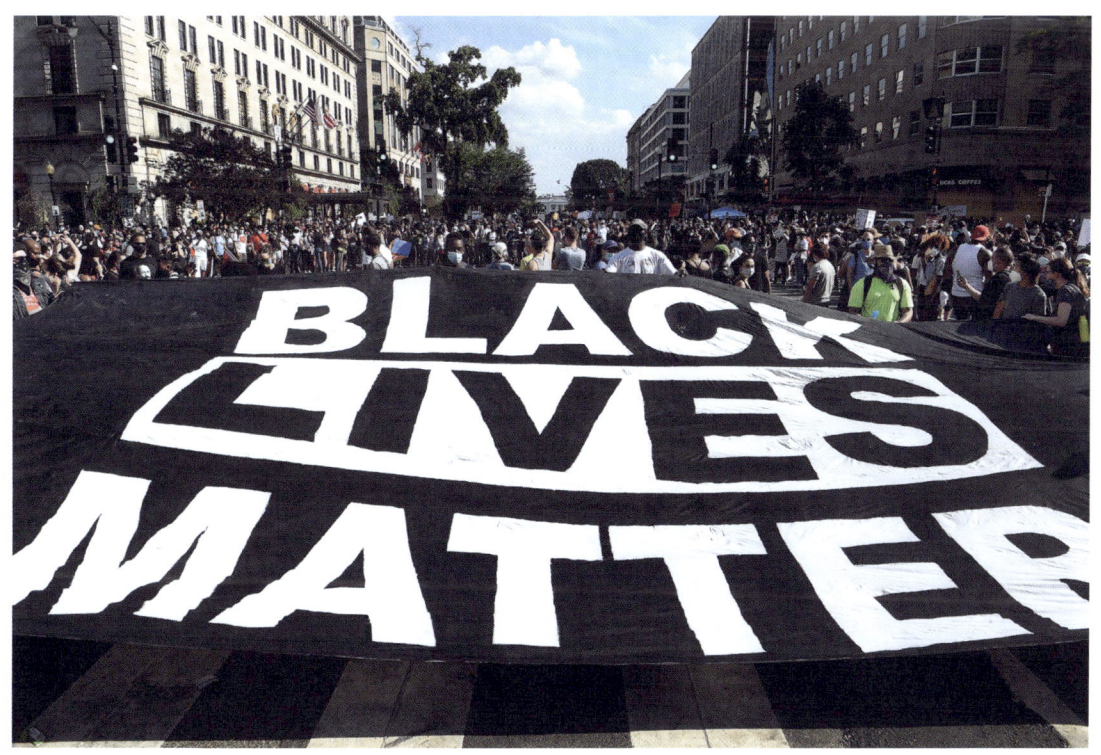

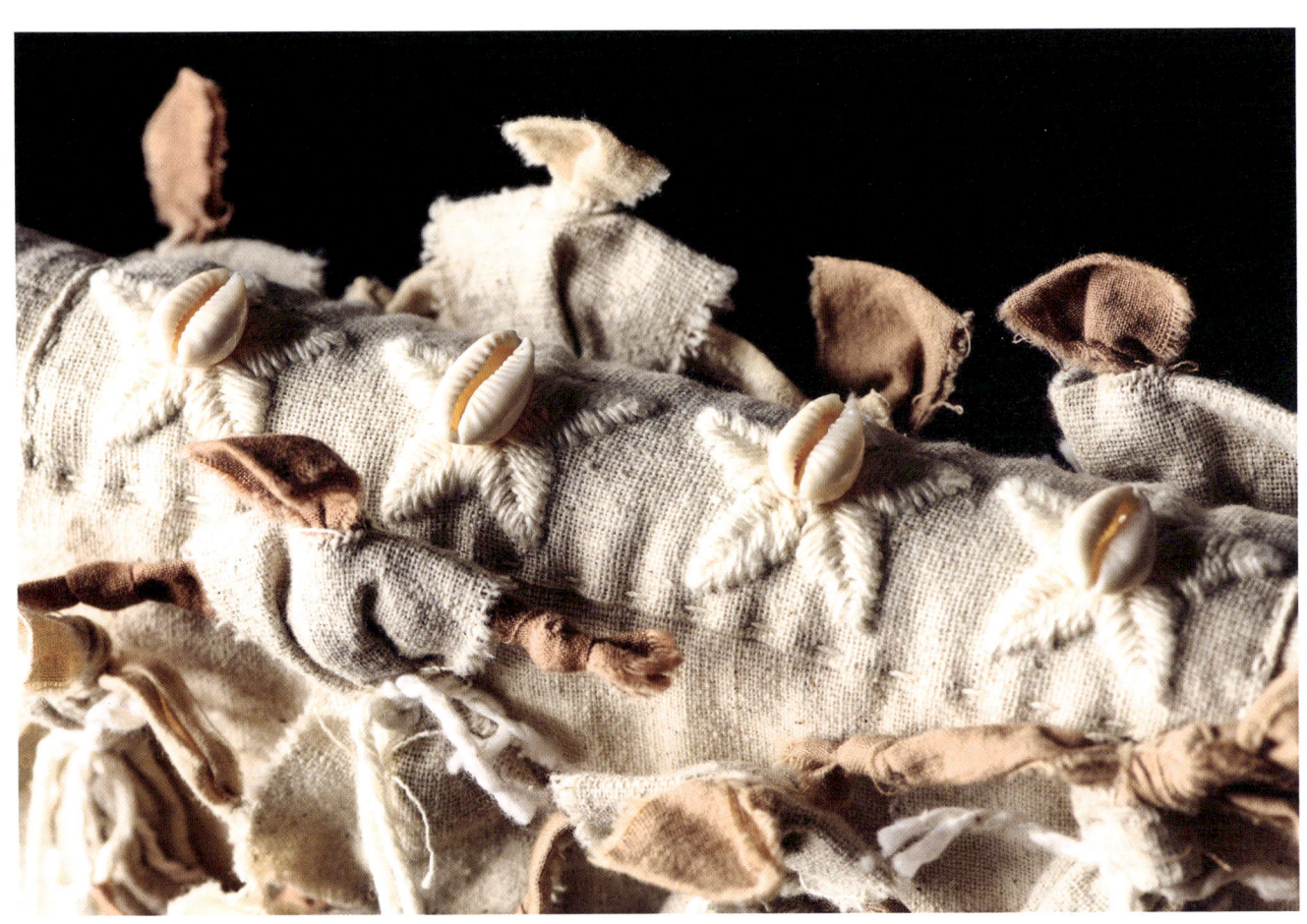

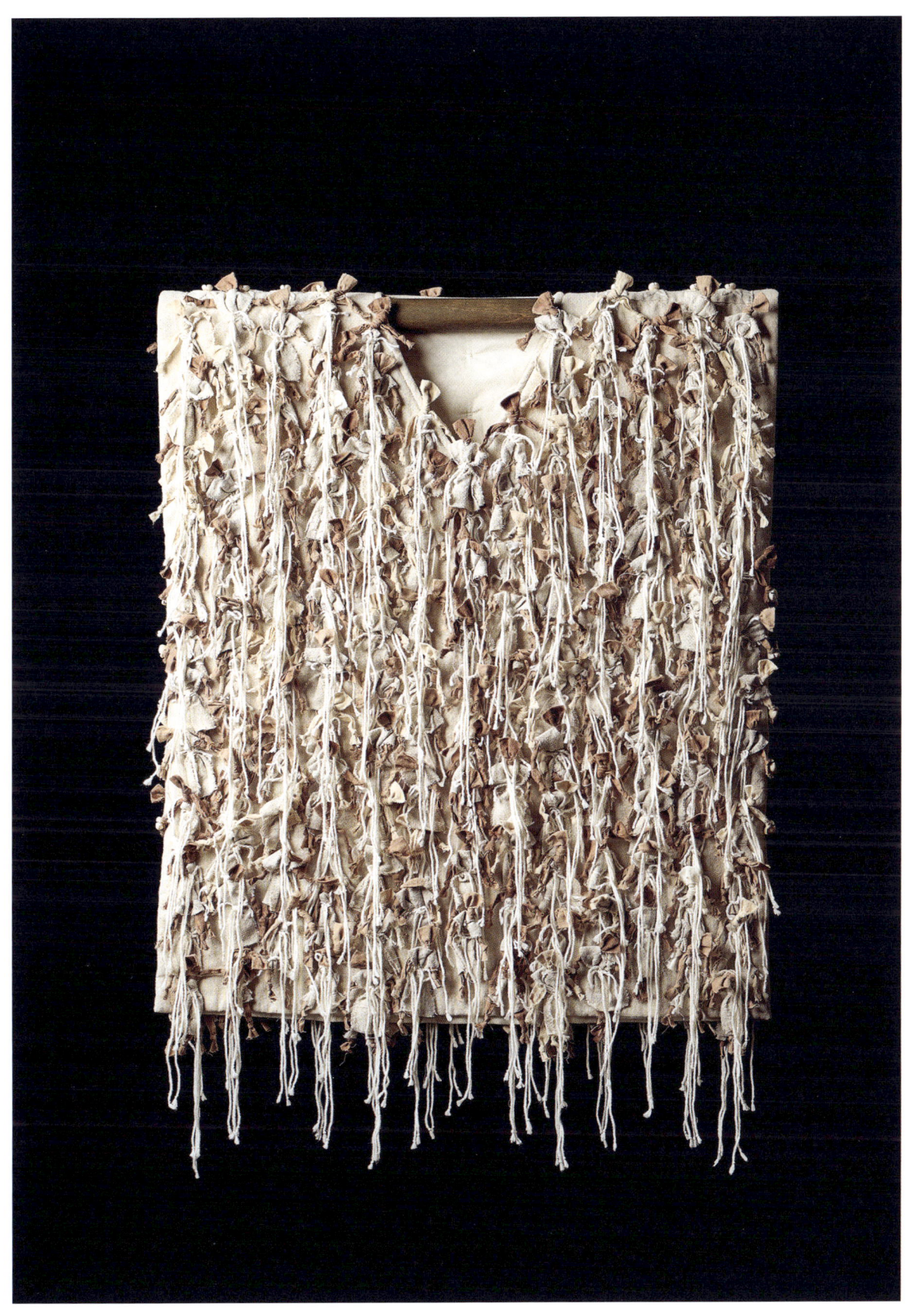

George Floyd

George Floyd, an unarmed 46-year-old African American, was murdered on the streets of Minneapolis on 25 May 2020 whilst handcuffed in police custody after being detained as a suspect of passing a forged banknote. When being restrained, his neck and back were knelt on for almost ten minutes by a white officer, and this led to Floyd's death by asphyxia.

Multiple witnesses tried to intervene, but they were held back by another officer. Several onlookers recorded the incident on mobile phones, images of which were uploaded to social media platforms, instantly sending shockwaves around the world. Angry protests and riots broke out throughout the US, and global citizens joined the BLM movement to express their anger at racial injustices in their own communities.

The law enforcement officer was found guilty of murdering George Floyd and was sentenced to more than 20 years in prison.

'I can't breathe' – George Floyd's dying words – became the slogan of the BLM movement.

Collective anger led to millions signing international petitions for justice, and statues and monuments representing a colonial past were torn down, including those of Christopher Columbus in Virginia, US, and Edward Colston in Bristol, UK.

OPPOSITE, ABOVE

Naomi Osaka wears a face mask featuring George Floyd's name at the US Open tennis championships in New York, 2020. Osaka's victory in the US Open helped raise the issue of racial injustice in the United States. Before each of her matches, she wore a face mask with the names of seven Black Americans who died as victims of racial violence.

OPPOSITE, BELOW

A day before Derek Chauvin, the officer convicted of murdering George Floyd, was put on trial protestors march through downtown Minneapolis to demand justice.

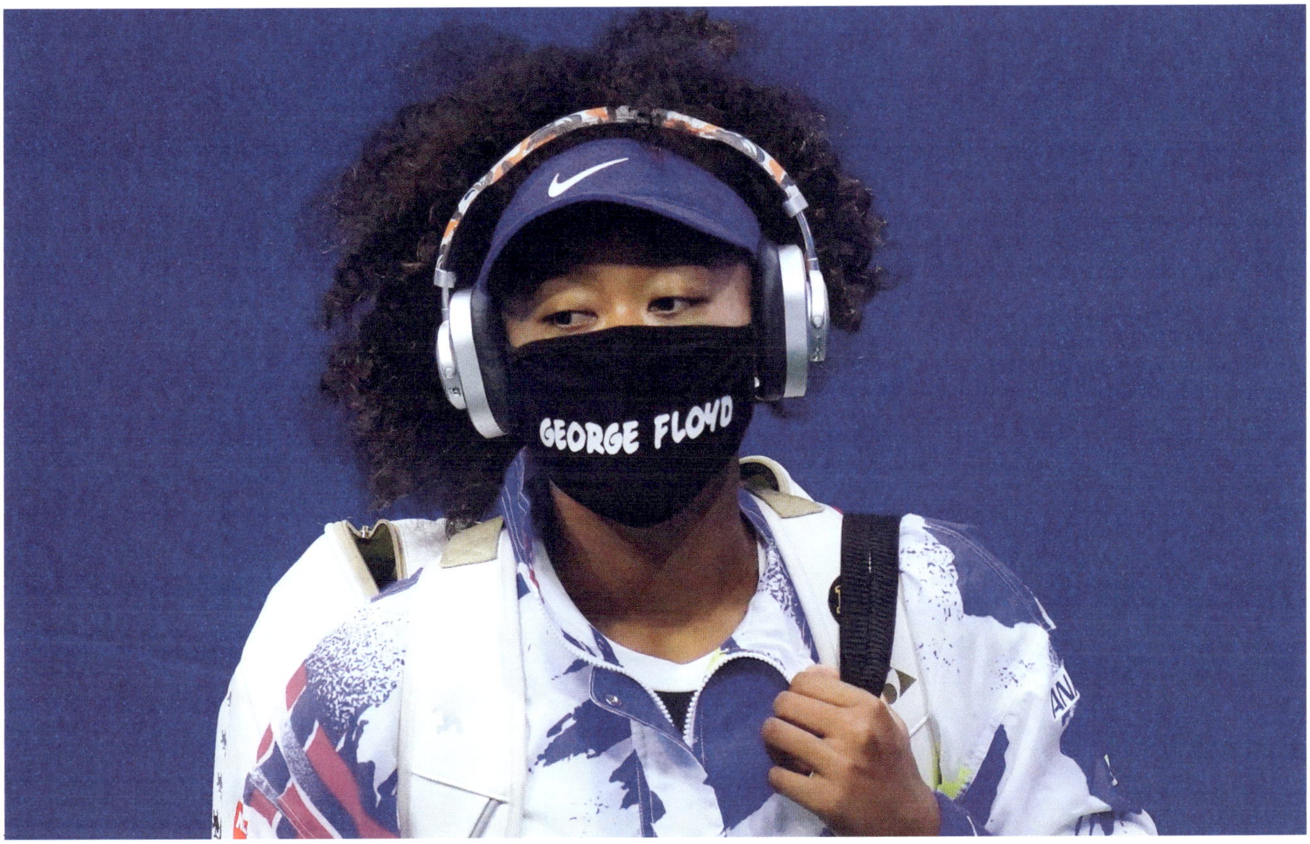

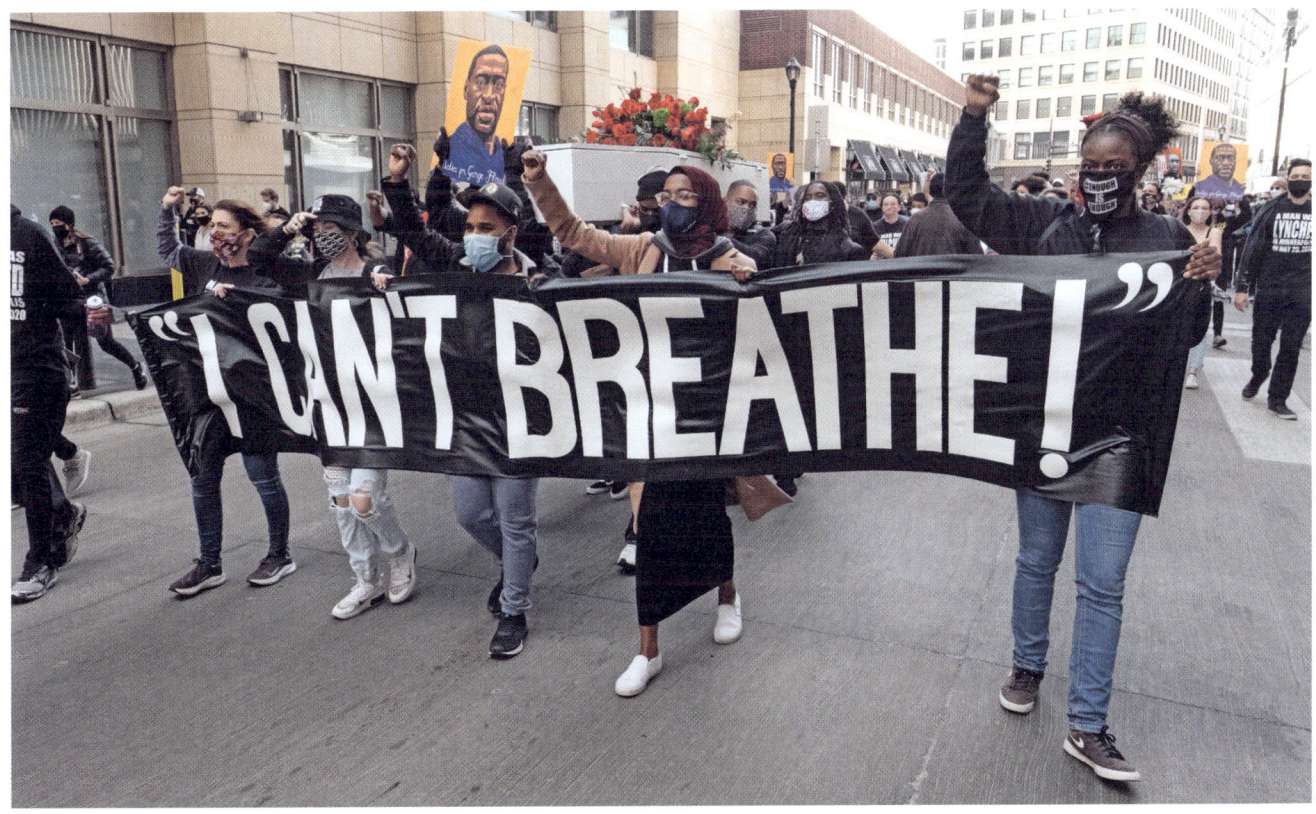

#SayHerName

The hashtag #SayHerName, coined by the African American Policy Forum (AAPF), sparked a social movement in 2015 after the death of Sandra Bland, a civil rights activist, who was found hanged in her cell after her arrest following a minor traffic incident.

The hashtag, used globally, spotlights Black women and girls who have been subjected to racist police brutality or murder whilst in custody. These victims of race-and-gender-based violence continue to be marginalized by police and their cases are often covered up by authorities. By saying her name, these Black women and girls are kept visible whilst families and loved ones seek justice.

In 2020 Breonna Taylor, a 26-year-old African American Black woman, was fatally shot by white police officers in Louisville, Kentucky, after they forced entry into her apartment in the early hours of the morning whilst she was sleeping. Her murder, coupled with the lack of immediate accountability for the officers involved (who raided the wrong address then falsely claimed she had no injuries on an incident report), ignited widespread protests against police violence and systemic racism.

Taylor became the focal point of the #SayHerName campaign, which demanded justice, transparency and change. In 2024 'Breonna's Law' was introduced; this national-level Act prohibits the controversial 'no-knock' search warrants, which police officers obtained for Taylor's apartment, to prevent future deadly raids.

More recently, the hashtag has been expanded to include women and girls from other races and ethnicities and other forms of violence, including familial murders and domestic violence, but its original and primary focus remains the same: to highlight and combat violence, police brutality and systemic injustices faced by Black women and girls.

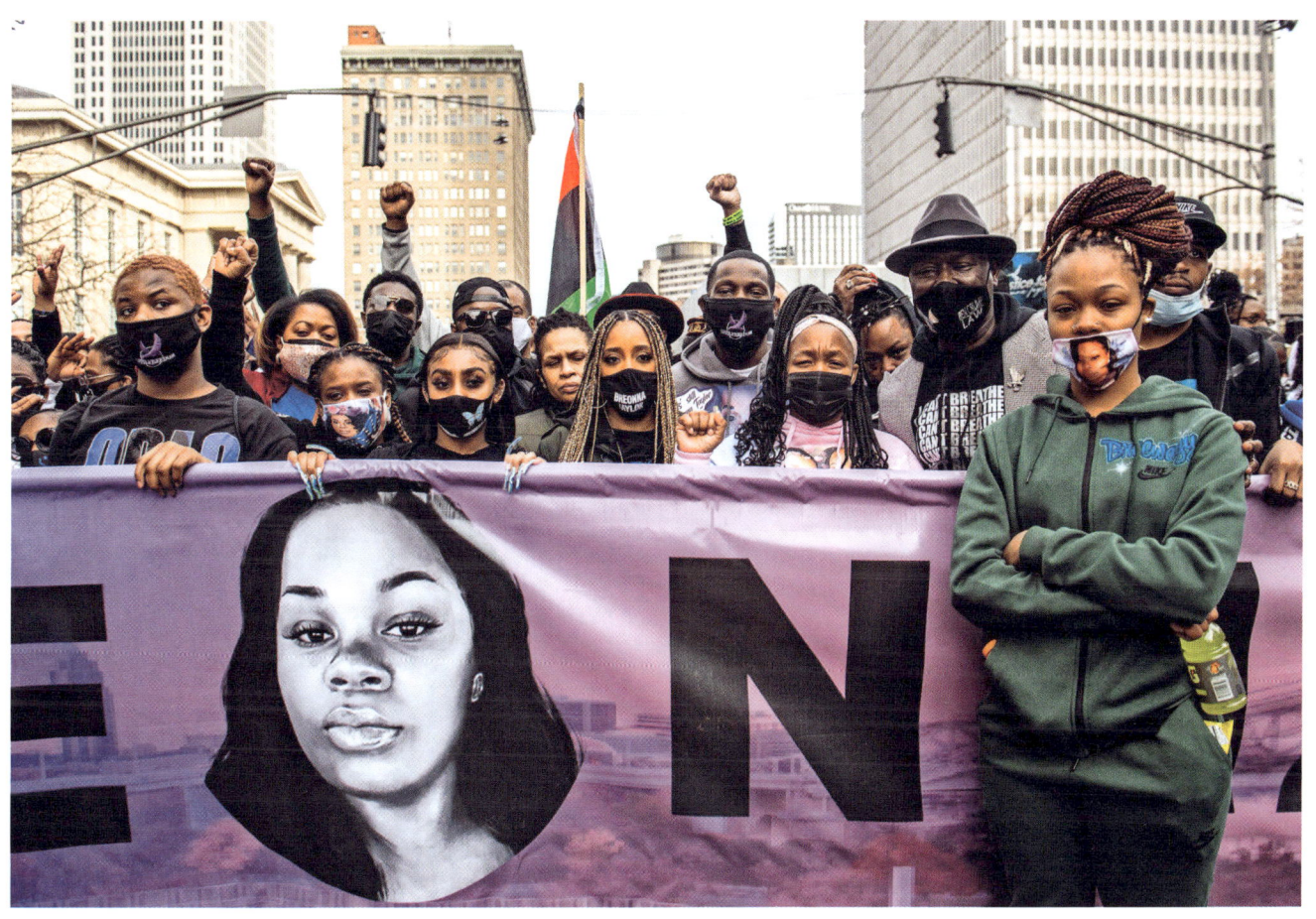

#WomanLifeFreedom

The slogan 'Woman, Life, Freedom' (Jin, Jiyan, Azadi) has its origins with the Kurdish Women's movement. It was traditionally used as a term of resistance against the persecution of women and their personal freedom under the oppressive regimes of Iran, Iraq, Syria and Turkey.

The phrase emerged as an international cry of protest in September 2022 after the brutal murder of 22-year-old Mahsa (Jina) Amini, who was tortured and beaten, then died of her injuries whilst in the custody of the morality police in Iran. According to the authorities, Jina, who was with her family at the time of arrest, and not described as an activist, allegedly violated the country's strict dress code for women by not wearing a hijab in accordance with government protocol.

Her death sparked a global protest. World leaders responded by condemning the police brutality and this gender-based murder as a crime against humanity. Women around the world, including high-profile celebrities and public figures, amplified the voices of Iranian women by symbolically cutting off chunks of their hair in solidarity.

In November 2024, Ahoo Daryaei, an Iranian student at Tehran's Science and Research University, fearlessly defied the morality police by removing her clothes and walking around the campus and streets in her underwear after being harassed for showing her hair in public and incorrectly wearing her hijab.

By disobeying the strict Islamic dress code and courageously discarding her clothing, Daryaei's actions resulted in arrest and detainment in a psychiatric hospital, and grave concerns for her safety, but her powerful statement of resistance will go down in history as a one-woman protest against an oppressive misogynistic regime which controls women's bodies.

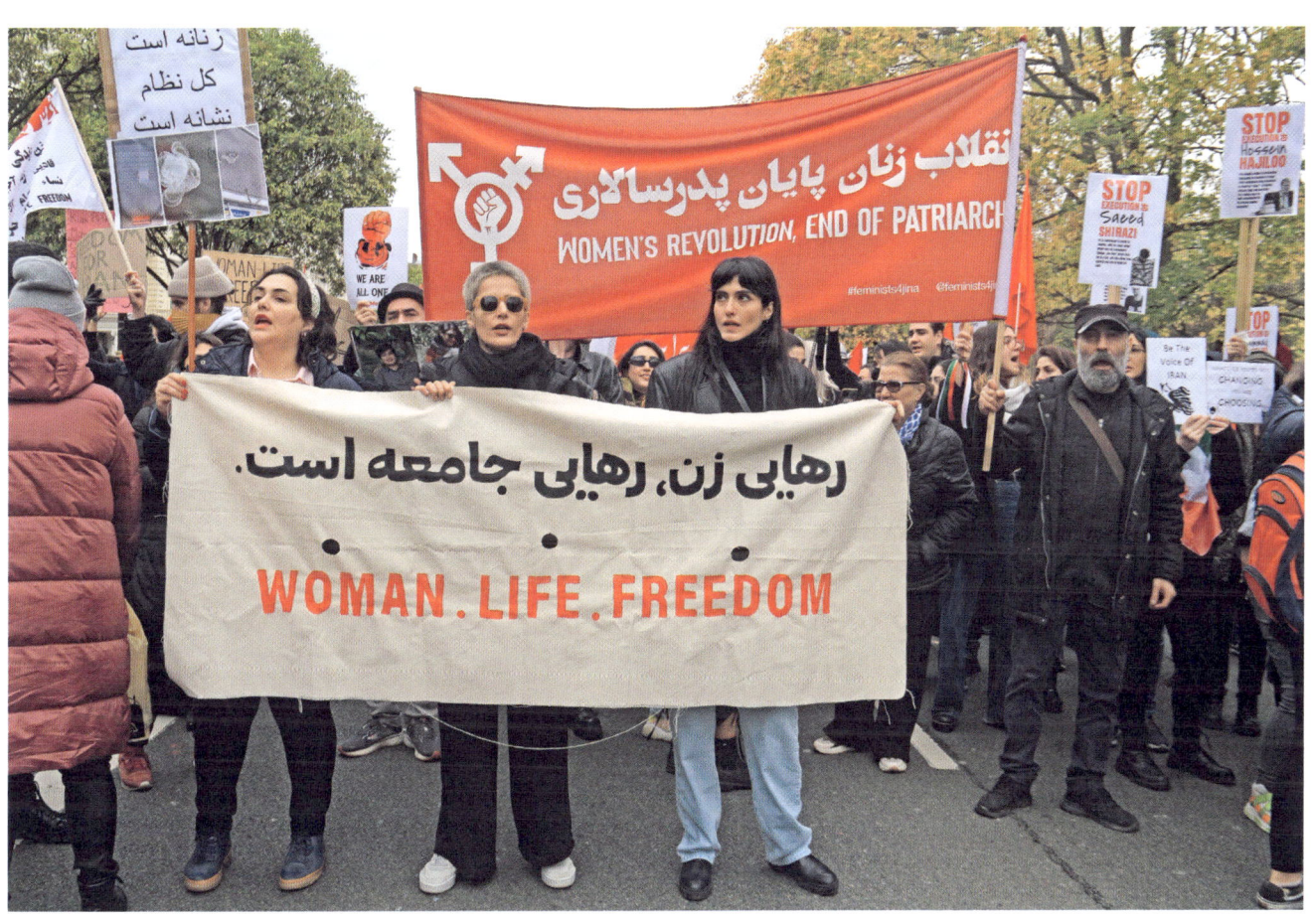

Disability

Disabled people are some of the most marginalized in society, and they face discrimination and stigma on a daily basis. Disabilities are diverse, as are the needs of disabled people, but society, and its infrastructure, is constructed to favour the able-bodied. This lack of inclusivity in societies results in those with disabilities encountering unnecessary challenges that can severely affect their ability to integrate in society, leading to marginalization, isolation and exclusion.

Barriers to a full social and economic life can increase isolation and impact the self-esteem, sense of identity and mental health of disabled people. Stairs, narrow doorways and trip hazards are impossible to navigate without full mobility, and low income makes it difficult to provide increased medical or care expenses, leaving many disabled people trapped in a cycle of poverty.

But attitudinal barriers stemming from institutional ignorance, deep-rooted prejudices and a lack of knowledge can be the most difficult to overcome, and uninformed attitudes and entrenched stereotypical values remain a widespread issue. Campaigners argue that they should be involved in policy changes that affect them, and to support this the disability rights movement adopted the powerful slogan 'Nothing about us without us'.

British architect and activist Ed Hall has been making banners for more than 30 years. He has collaborated with many local and international campaign groups, trade unions and museums to create bespoke handmade, stitched and appliquéd banners for many causes. His artworks not only raise awareness of issues such as disability, racism and police brutality, but also call for justice, peace and solidarity.

BELOW

Disabled People Fight Back (2015)

Ed Hall

180×180cm (70.86×70.86in). Appliquéd cotton drill with centrepiece painted with fabric dyes.

This artwork was the result of an all-day workshop of disability groups which met at the People's History Museum, Manchester, UK.

OPPOSITE

DWP Resistance (2017–23)

Vince Laws

180×122cm (72×48in) approx. Recycled bedding spraypainted. Text edited from article by Mo Stewart in Welfare Weekly 2018 (see also page 29).

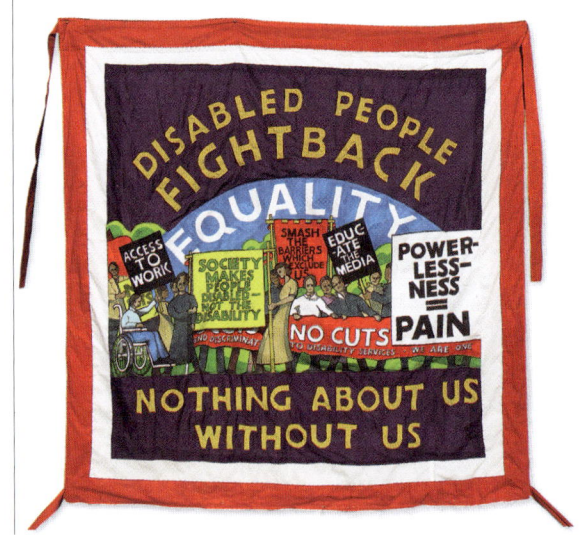

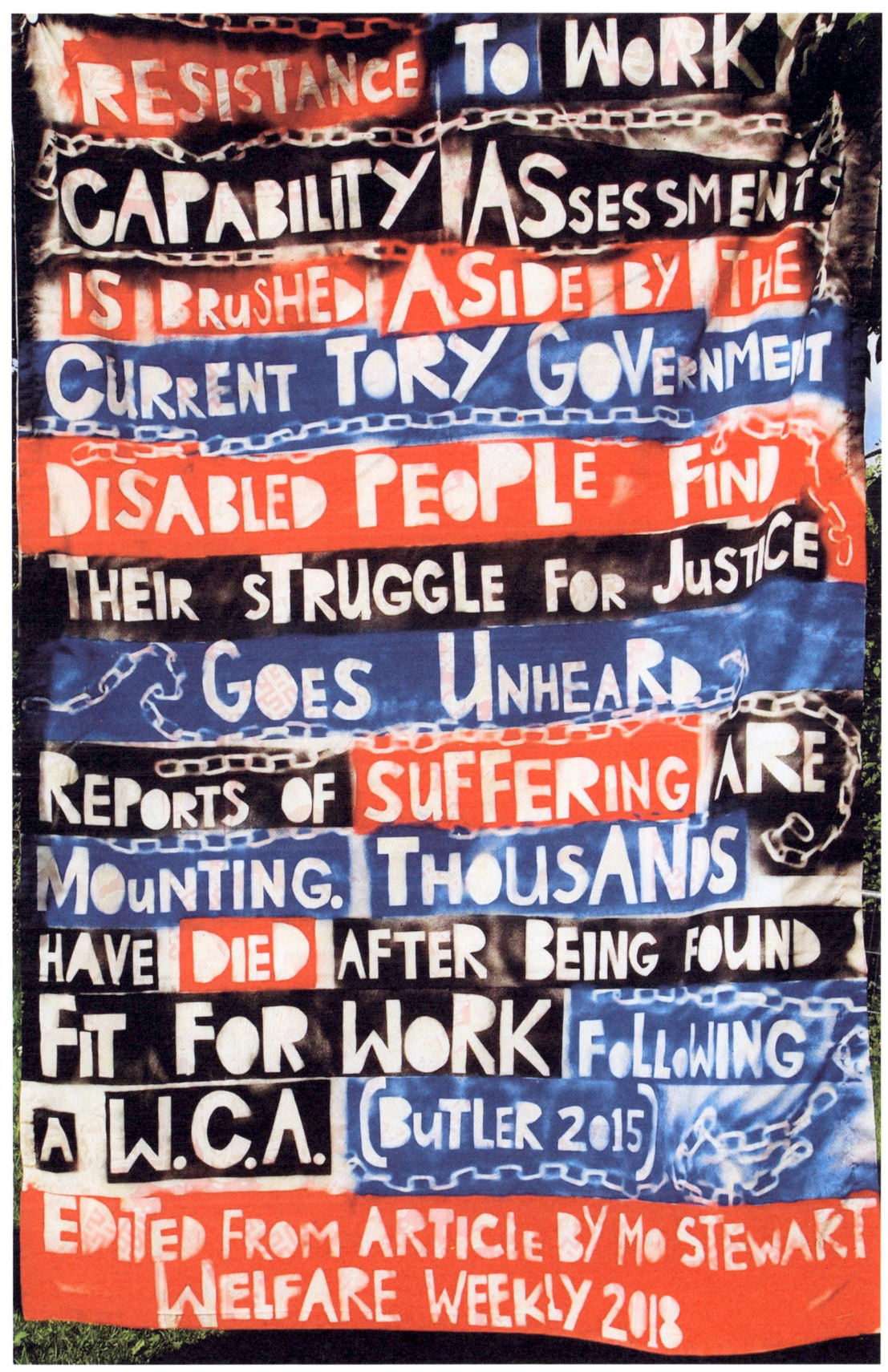

RESISTANCE TO WORK CAPABILITY ASSESSMENTS IS BRUSHED ASIDE BY THE CURRENT TORY GOVERNMENT DISABLED PEOPLE FIND THEIR STRUGGLE FOR JUSTICE GOES UNHEARD REPORTS OF SUFFERING ARE MOUNTING. THOUSANDS HAVE DIED AFTER BEING FOUND FIT FOR WORK FOLLOWING A W.C.A. (BUTLER 2015)

EDITED FROM ARTICLE BY MO STEWART WELFARE WEEKLY 2018

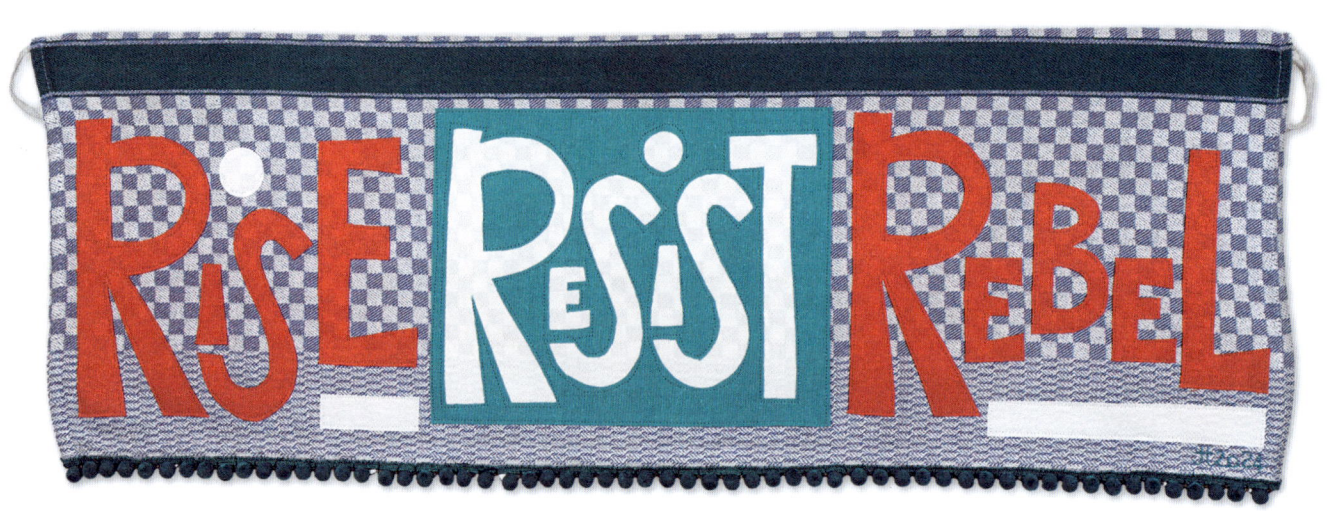

REBELS AGAINST REGIMES

REBELS AGAINST REGIMES

'Arpilleras became the language of resistance, testimony and protest for those who refused to be silenced.'

ROBERTA BACIC

The Universal Declaration of Human Rights (UDHR) was proclaimed by the United Nations General Assembly in Paris on 10 December 1948. Following the atrocities of World War II, it sets out the universal human rights to be protected, such as the right to life, equality, privacy, security, education, free speech, political and civil rights, and the right to be free from slavery and torture.

Whilst art has repeatedly been used as a propaganda tool by regimes to promote war, victims of conflicts and witnesses of atrocities have frequently turned to art as a tool to express, record and deflect their grief, anger and suffering, often in secret. Unlike textiles made quickly to respond to a sudden announcement of war, conflict textiles stitched during or after a war are personal and reflective. Designs and compositions have time to be considered, individually or collectively, and the making process may be facilitated by a textile artist or someone skilled in embroidery or trained in art therapy. By working with cloth and thread to visually portray and reflect upon situations that are too painful to speak about, voices are heard, a connection is made with others, and historical facts are recorded in the process. As outlined in many examples in this book, communal stitching can be therapeutic and healing in the aftermath of conflict or loss, and can help to build confidence and restore hope.

The Spanish Civil War

The Spanish Civil War is a conflict that has had a long-lasting influence on resistance movements throughout the 20th and 21st centuries. It began shortly after a coalition of nine anti-fascist, anarchist, socialist and republican groups won the general election in February 1936.

Five months after the election, an uprising of military junta executed a coup d'état and the Nationalists seized power, with General Francisco Franco as their leader. It was this overthrowing of the democratically elected Republican government which sparked the Spanish Civil War. Franco would rule Spain under a military dictatorship until his death in 1975.

Throughout the course of the war, the Nationalists received most of their backing and military support from two sources: Mussolini and the Italian fascists and Hitler and the Nazi Party. The Republicans were supported by the Soviet Union and Mexico, but key nations, including Britain, France and the United States, despite still recognizing the Republican government, chose not to intervene politically or militarily, expressing 'neutrality' for fear of a war potentially escalating to other states. France initiated a Non-Intervention Agreement in August 1936, which was signed by dozens of nations, including Italy and Germany, who subsequently blatantly violated this agreement.

The rise of fascism in Europe was opposed by many on the continent and throughout the world, and this led to the formation of the International Brigades in 1936. This paramilitary group consisted of 35,000–40,000 men and women soldiers from more than 80 countries; many Brigadistas enlisted from non-interventionist countries because they vehemently opposed fascism.

The International Brigades initially defended key Republican strongholds such as Madrid, which was besieged for two and a half years, led diversionary offensives such as in Segovia, and fought many significant bloody battles, for example in Jarama, Belchite and Ebro.

The fight against fascism by the International Brigades during the Spanish Civil War gained much attention from workers around the world. Spanish printers, trade unions, youth groups and government ministries produced iconic posters and publicity materials condemning the bombing of women and children

BELOW

A Spanish standard bearer of the British Battalion.

OPPOSITE

A gathering of members of the Catalan Pioneers, a Republican youth group, in Barcelona c. 1936.

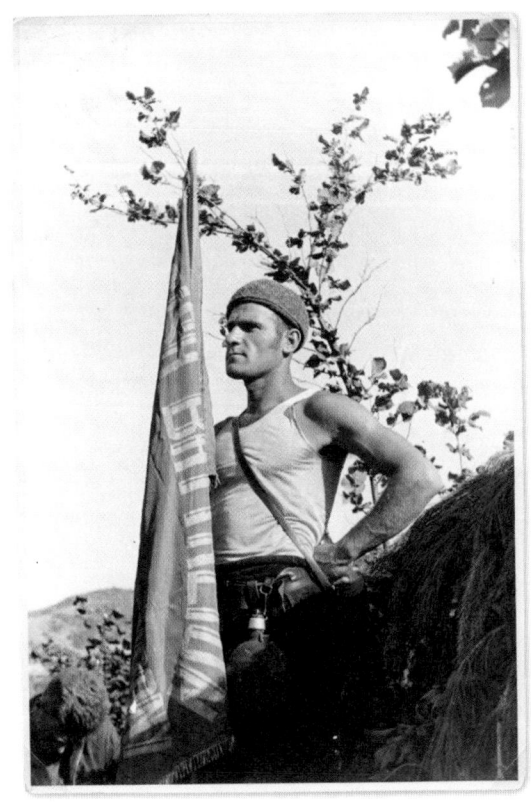

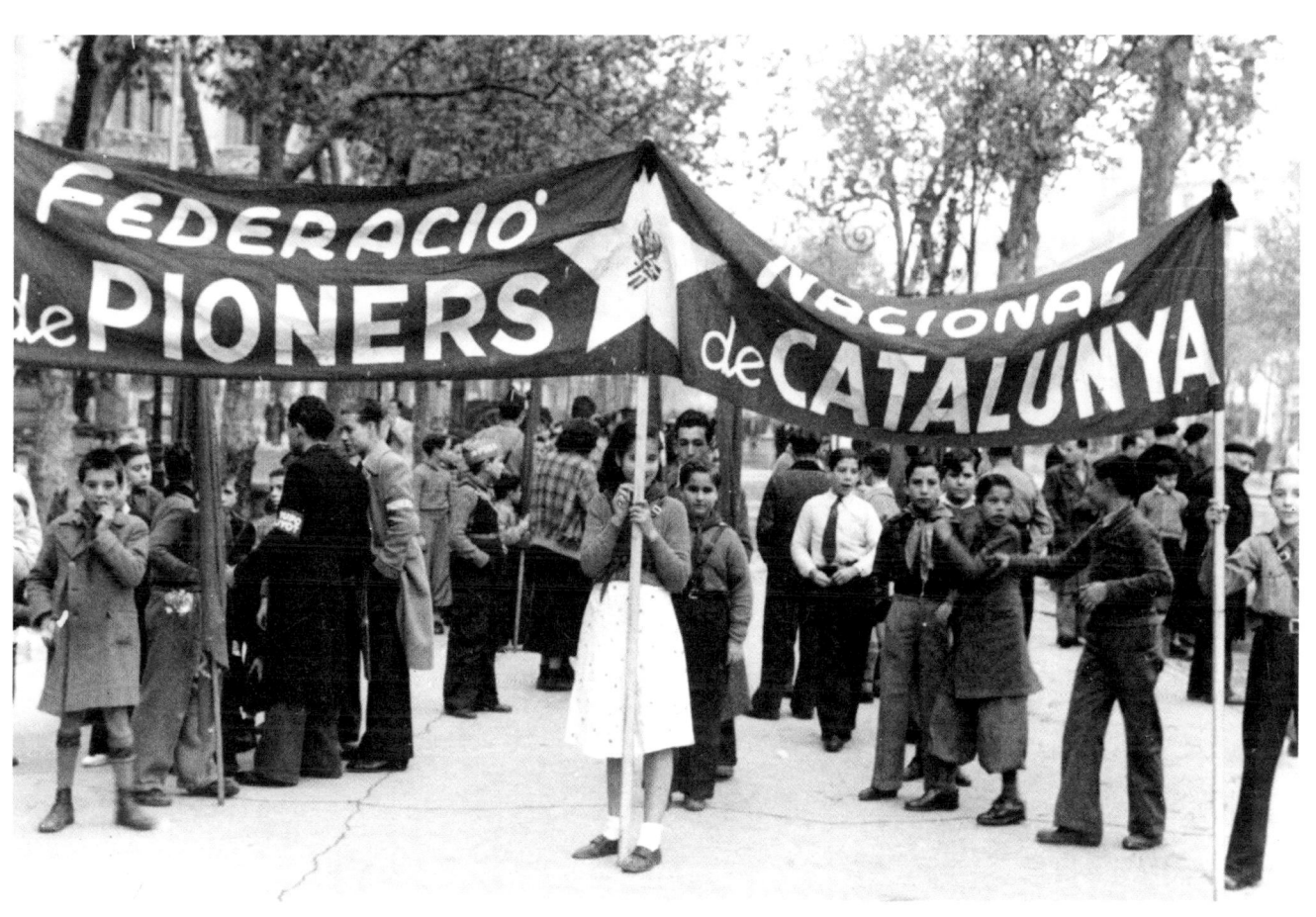

by the Nationalists, highlighting the threat of an invasion, and proclaiming the importance of unity.

Comrades from other countries responded and worked on local campaigns, which united voices and communities; they produced graphic banners calling for justice, and unequivocally summoning help and action, which was forthcoming. Aid was covertly sent in convoys to assist the International Brigades on the front lines in the form of money, food, transport and arms.

The banners shown to the right demonstrate the support of British printers for their Spanish comrades, asking for the British government to send arms to Spain. Despite repeated calls from many groups and unions, Britain remained non-interventionist throughout the Spanish Civil War.

The International Brigades disbanded in 1938 after being integrated into the Spanish Republican Army. It is estimated that around 10,000 Brigadistas lost their lives in the conflict. In the decades since, many countries have honoured and acknowledged the Brigadistas' contribution to the fight against fascism and their battle for workers' rights, democracy, moral truth and being 'on the right side of history'.

OPPOSITE, ABOVE

International Brigades Banner

Hammersmith Communist Party

186.5×215cm (73.4×84.6in). Graphite and paint on canvas.

OPPOSITE, BELOW

Arms and Justice for Spain Banner

Hammersmith Communist Party

186.8×200cm (73.5×78.7in). Graphite and paint on canvas.

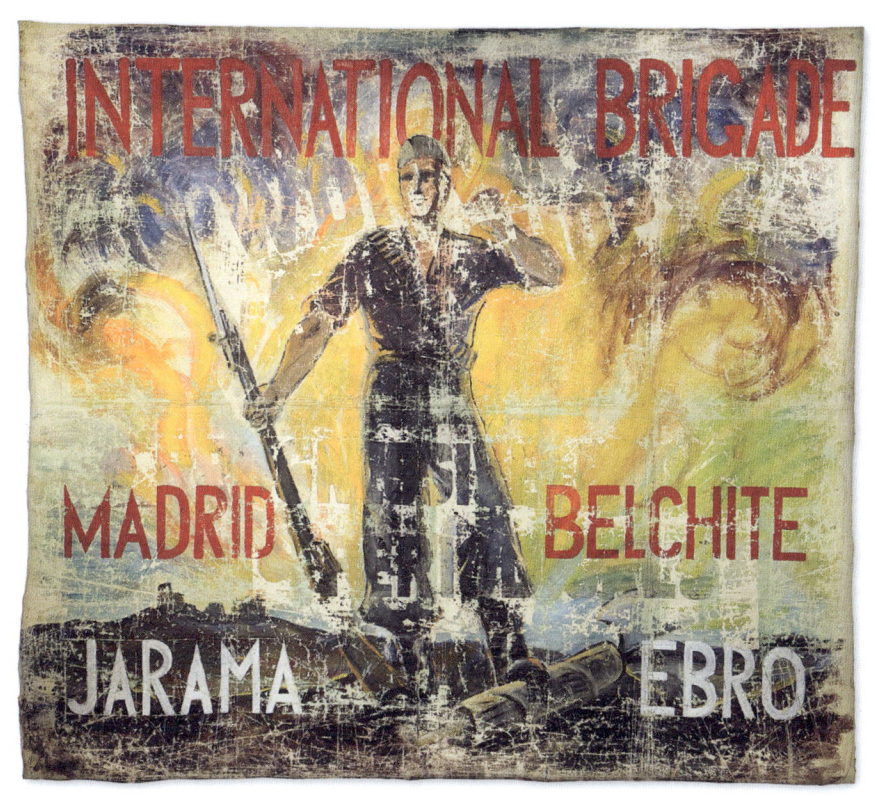

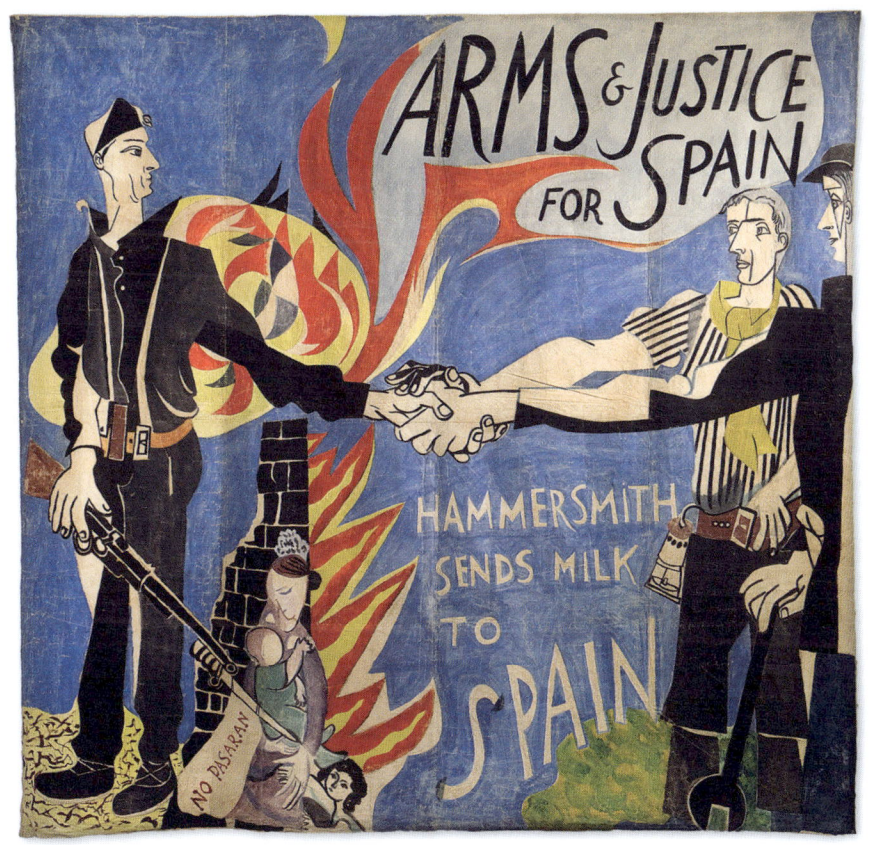

¡No Pasarán!

The slogan most frequently associated with the Spanish Civil War is *¡No Pasarán!* – 'they shall not pass' – adopted by the International Brigades during the siege of Madrid in 1936. Originally coined in World War I by the French (*On ne passe pas!*) at the Battle of Verdun in 1916, this slogan has since been used by many defiant fighters, activists and anti-fascists, including British trade unions, anarchists, British Jews and socialist groups in the Battle of Cable Street in the East End of London in 1936.

For more than a century *¡No Pasarán!* has been used as a slogan to defy dictatorships, for example by the Romanian Army in the Battle of Mărășești (1917), more recently in the Nicaraguan Revolution (1978–90), and today in the call for volunteer fighters by Ukraine following Russia's invasion.

¡No Pasarán! has also been used on textiles by individuals, including on banners, flags, artworks and T-shirts.

Famously, Nadezhda Tolokonnikova wore a T-shirt bearing this slogan at her trial in Moscow in August 2012. Tolokonnikova, along with Maria Alyokhina and Yekaterina Samutsevich – three political activists and performers from the Russian feminist punk group Pussy Riot – were on trial for 'hooliganism and motivated religious hatred' following a performance inside Moscow's Cathedral of Christ the Saviour in February 2012. After they were convicted and sentenced to two years' imprisonment, an appeal followed, whereafter Samutsevich was released on probation; the sentences of the others were upheld. Russia was heavily criticized over the trial and sentences, and human rights groups intervened. Eventually the State Duma, the lower house of the Federal Assembly of Russia, approved an amnesty and released the two prisoners.

In 2018, Clapton Community Football Club recognized the International Brigades when they launched their away strip in the colours of the Second Spanish Republic flag (red, yellow and purple), emblazoned with an embroidered *No Pasarán* slogan, and adorned with the three-pointed star of the International Brigades. The shirts became instantly popular, selling out in Spain immediately, and the team were praised for their anti-fascist message.

OPPOSITE, ABOVE

Two men hold flags of the Republic and the International Brigades during a demonstration for the rights of the victims of Francoism in Madrid, 2021.

OPPOSITE, BELOW

Clapton Community Football Club kit.

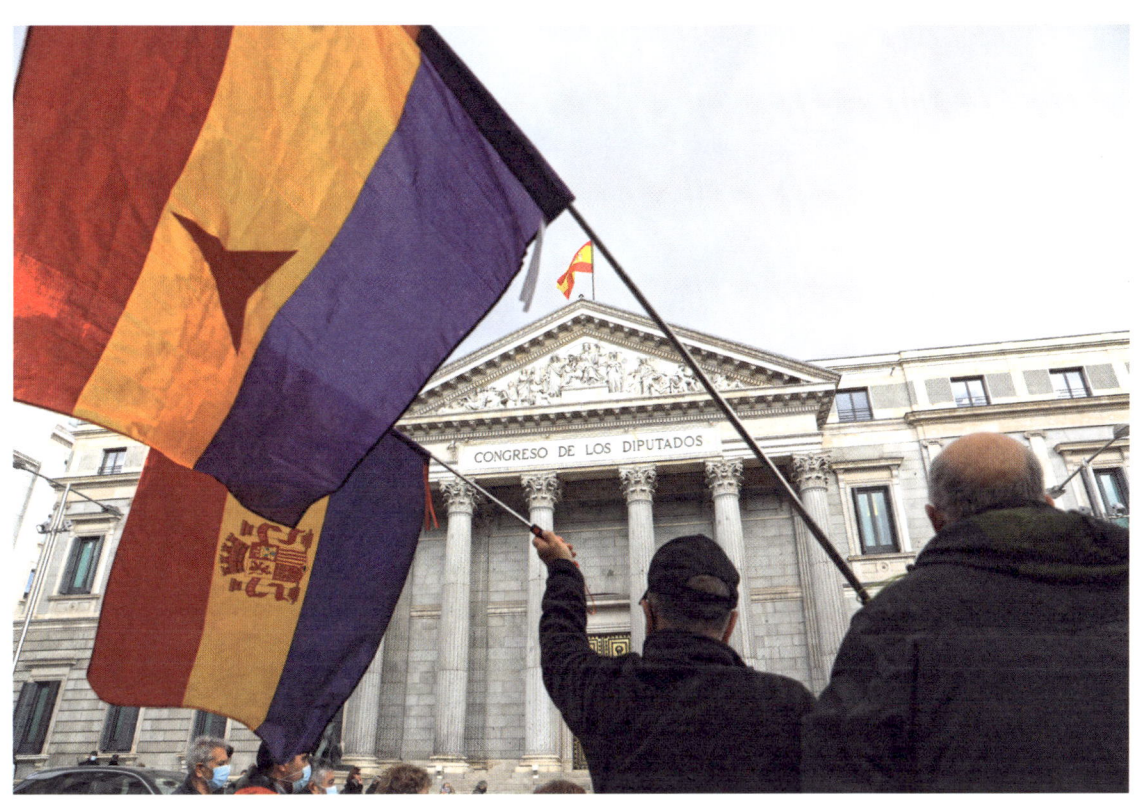

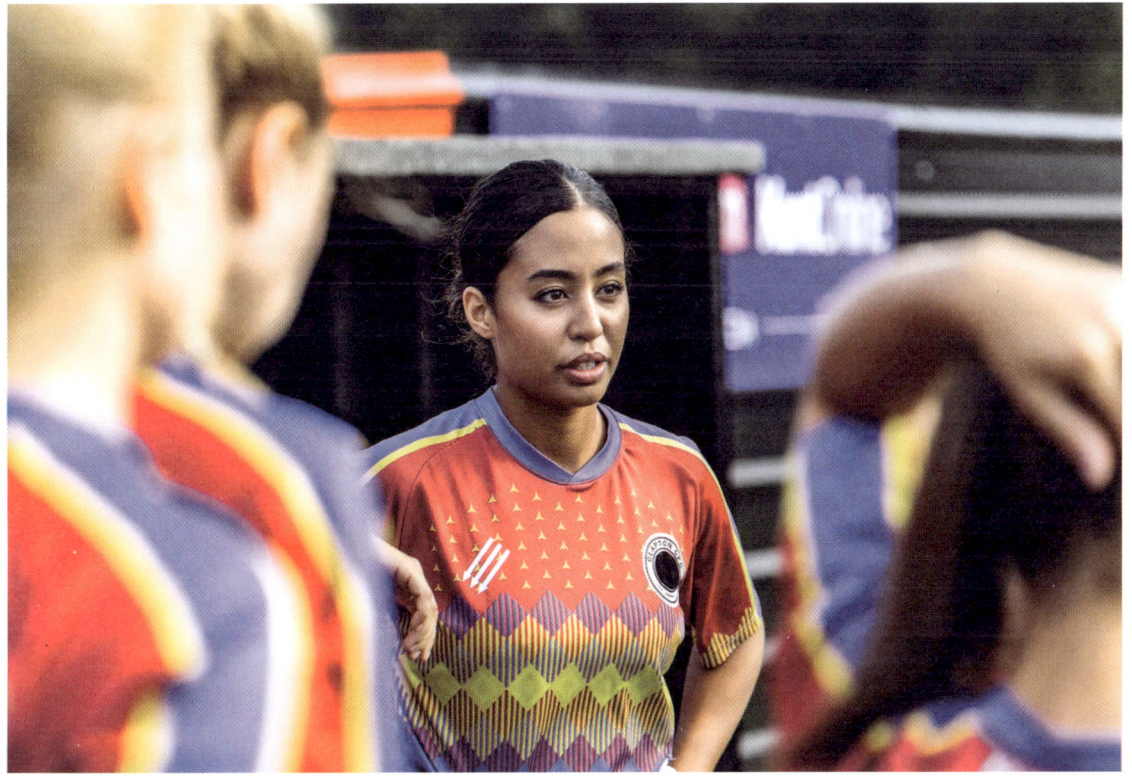

Apartheid

Apartheid was a policy of racial segregation and discrimination against Black, Coloured and Indian people in South Africa. It was introduced following the election of the white-supremacist National Party in 1948 and built on centuries of racial discrimination and exploitation under European colonialism and Dutch and British rule that placed Black Africans at the bottom of the racial hierarchy. Despite the UDHR having just declared that 'all human beings are born free and equal', in 1949 the South African government started enacting laws that made non-whites second-class citizens. Apartheid was finally abolished in the 1990s after decades of national and international resistance to the apartheid system.

The African National Congress

The African National Congress (ANC), founded in 1912, spearheaded the liberation movement and the struggle for freedom against institutional racism for Black people in South Africa. The ANC's flag, a horizontal tricolour in black, green and gold, was created to represent the people of South Africa, their land and its natural wealth, which were all controlled by the white minority.

Following the introduction of apartheid, the ANC led a campaign of defiance. In 1952, a mass protest of public disobedience took place when 'non-Europeans' entered townships without permission, or demanded service at 'whites only' counters, expecting to be arrested. It was hoped the *en masse* defiance would overwhelm the jails, judicial system and the government. Peaceful protestors were met with police brutality, and were beaten and shot. The campaign ended in 1953 to allow the resistance movement to regroup.

In the aftermath of the massacre of protesters at Sharpeville in 1960, the ANC shifted tactics, establishing Umkhonto we Sizwe (MK), the party's military wing. MK was founded by Nelson Mandela, who was in favour of taking up arms as 'freedom fighters' since the ANC's peaceful demonstrations were always met with force. He was arrested for militant activities in 1962 and sentenced to life in prison.

The internal struggle for a democratic and multiracial

OPPOSITE

A banner in support of Nelson Mandela is displayed at the funeral of nine people who were killed during the 28 August Gugulethu riots, 1985.

OVERLEAF, LEFT

A man displays a T-shirt in support of Nelson Mandela.

OVERLEAF, RIGHT

Nelson Mandela at an ANC election campaign rally, Paarl, Western Cape, 1994.

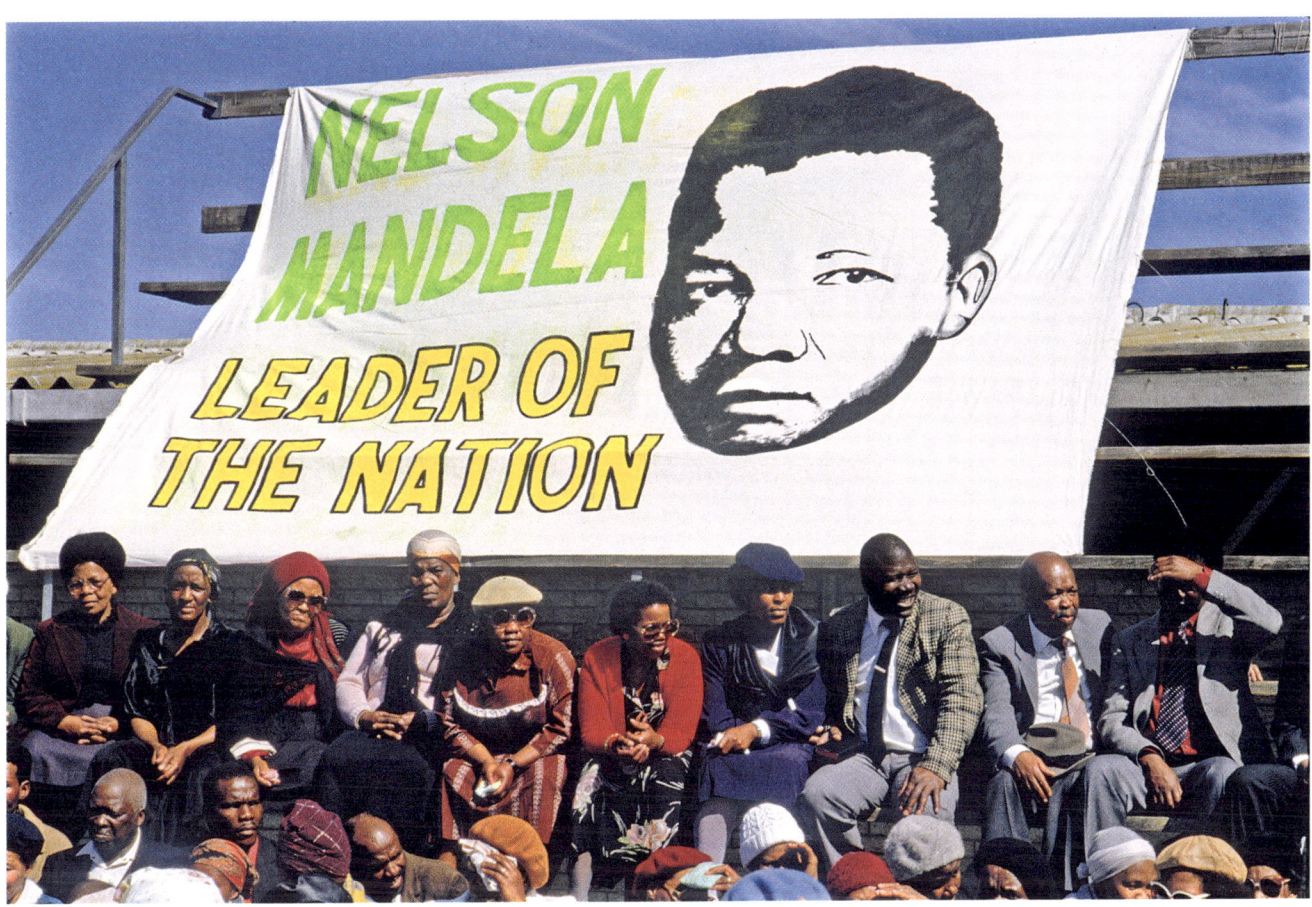

South African state also had international support, and countries responded to the continued police violence with economic sanctions and cultural boycotts.

Supporters throughout the world expressed their solidarity with the Black township of Soweto when in 1976 the police killed hundreds of protestors, many of whom were high-school students protesting against continued segregation and the compulsory teaching of Afrikaans in Black schools. As a result, thousands of youths joined the MK and the governing regime strengthened its military to repress 'revolutionaries'.

The apartheid system was eventually dismantled and a democratic South Africa was established in the 1990s when the ANC was finally legalized as a political party. After serving 27 years in jail, Nelson Mandela was released in 1990. His dedication to justice and equality remained constant throughout his incarceration and his dignity inspired the world. In 1994 Mandela, as leader of the ANC, was elected as the first president of a democratic South Africa following the country's first election with universal suffrage.

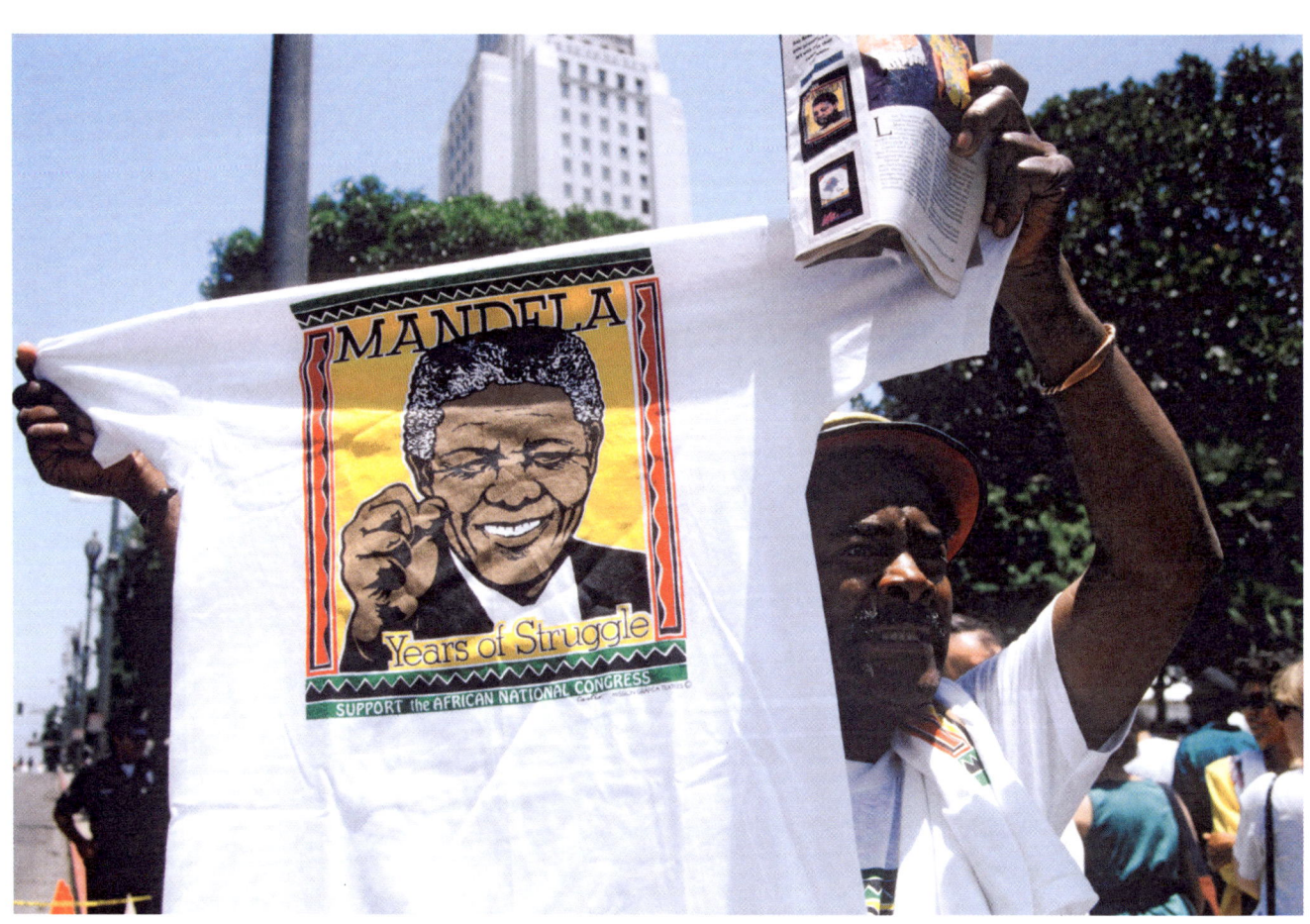

REBELS AGAINST REGIMES

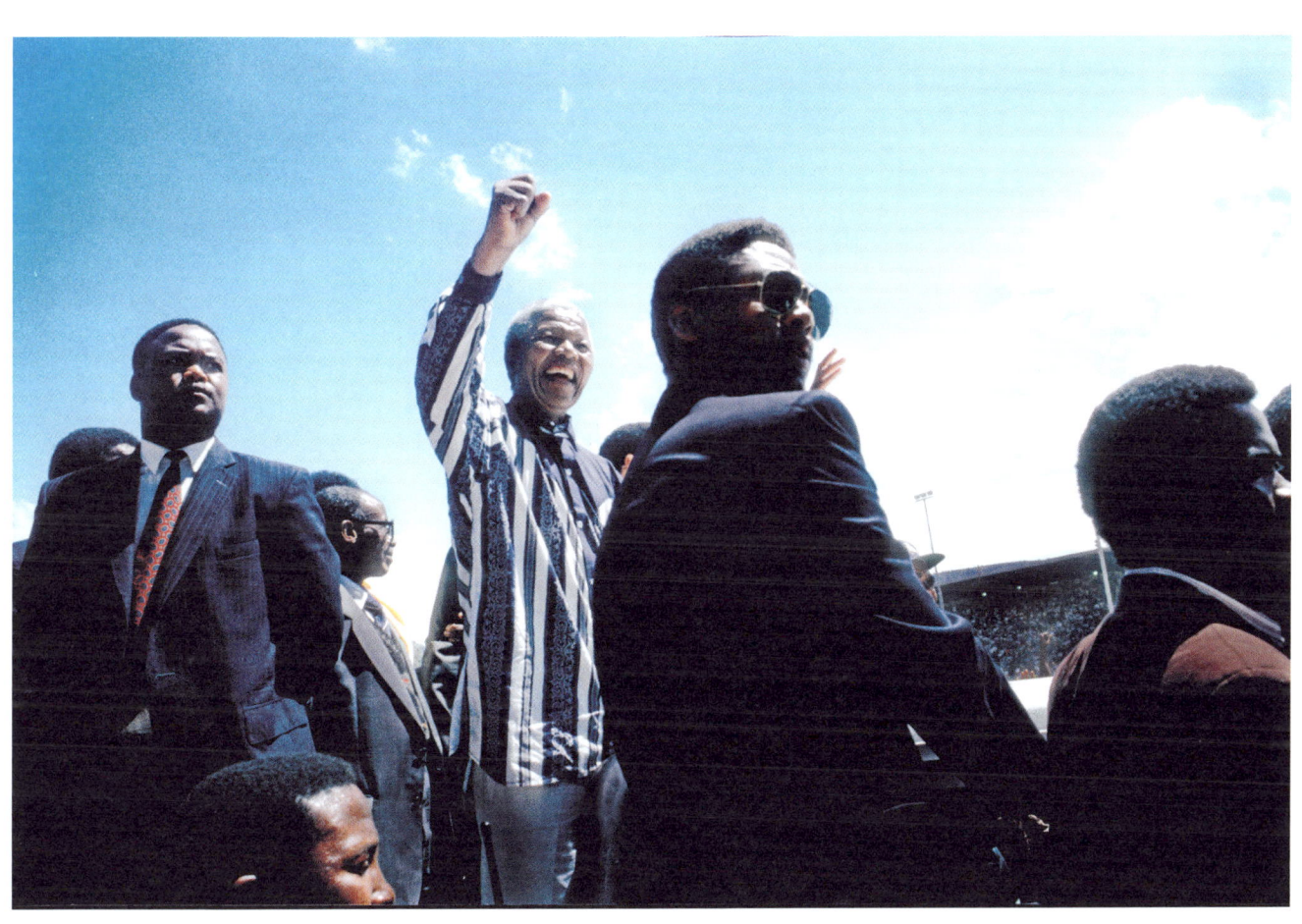

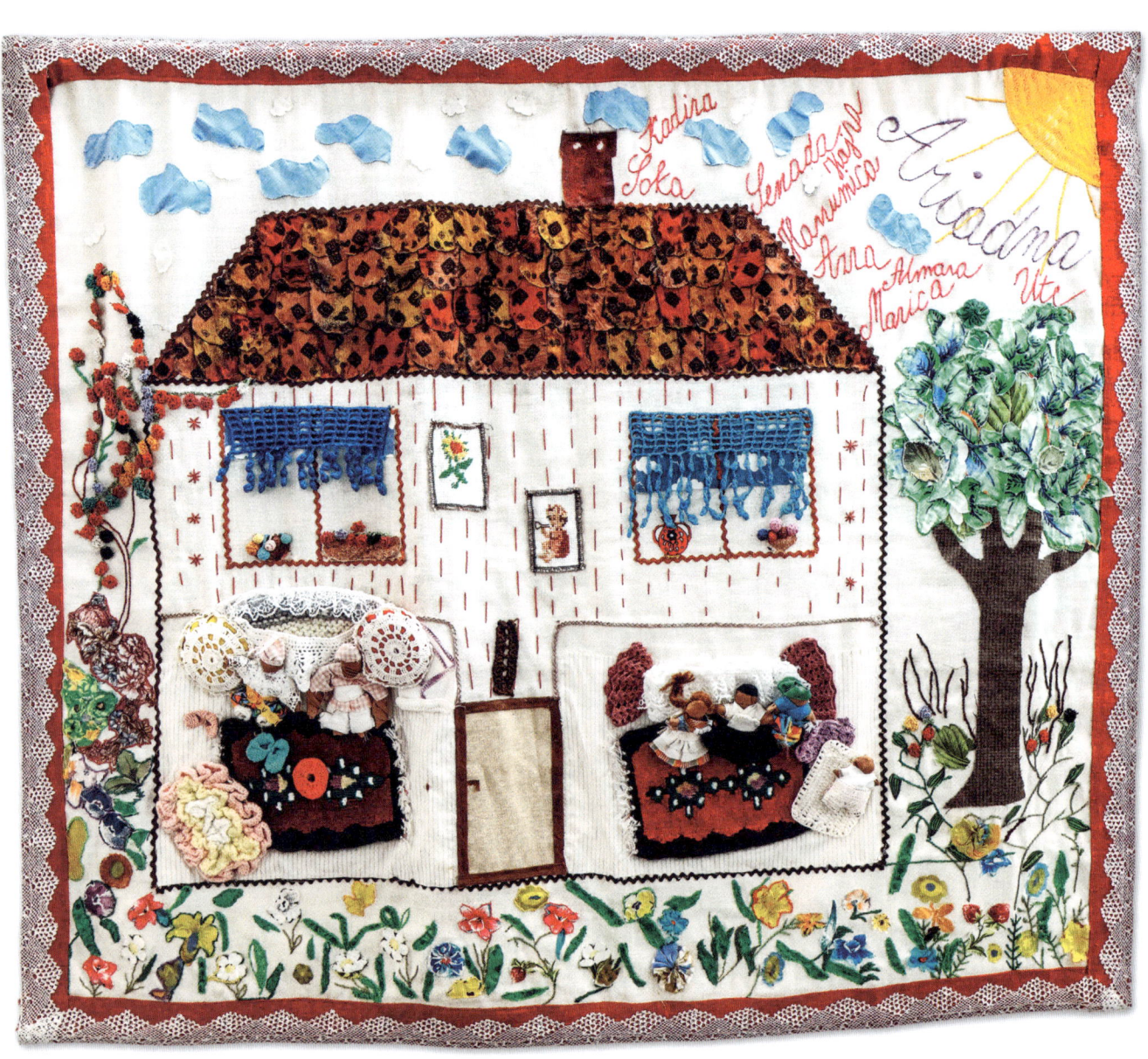

REBELS AGAINST REGIMES

Displacement

OPPOSITE

The House We Had to Leave, Quilt (1995)

'Art of survival', Frauen in der Einen Welt/ Women in One World Collection.

BELOW

Displacement (2014)

Women Knitting Dreams and Taste of Peace.

Forced movement of individuals, minority groups or whole populations have occurred during wars and conflicts for centuries. Internally displaced people (IDPs) remain within their country's borders having been forced to leave their homes. Refugees are forced to cross international borders due to conflict, persecution, ethnic cleansing or other war-related factors. They are often granted a special legal status under the 1951 Refugee Convention and its 1967 protocol.

Displacement can lead to the total devastation and disruption of communities, societies, economies and education systems. The conflict textile opposite is entitled 'The House we had to leave'. It was stitched in 1995 by a group of women from Rijeka in Croatia and refugee women from Bosnia at the Ariadna Project, founded in 1993 to support women who fled their homes in haste, leaving loved ones and abandoning all possessions and their familiar surroudings. Left with only their stitching skills and memories of home, the women created a textile story of the life they unwillingly left behind. During the making, the women experienced a sense of connection, and a sense of home and belonging. This quilt depicts old customs, traditions and happy times, as well as a colourful garden. The finished piece is a story in cloth that bombs cannot destroy.

The theme of displacement is obvious in the protest textile, pictured left, an arpillera made in Colombia in 2010 by 15 women who survived the massacre of Mampuján in March 2000 by the United Self-Defence Forces of Colombia (AUC). The AUC, a far-right paramilitary organization, was known for drug trafficking, kidnapping, extortion and the displacement of communities. The communities of Mampuján Viejo and nearby Las Brisas were invaded, accused of cooperating with insurgent guerillas and threatened with death if they didn't vacate their homes within 24 hours. This led to the displacement of 1,400 villagers.

Juana Alicia Ruiz, one of the women who worked on this protest textile, said at the time: 'Displacement in Colombia is like any typical displacement as it happens at times during night. It includes violent rape, burning of houses, having to leave behind belongings, houses and animals. The lady who is being carried on a hammock is a sick person, very old and who cannot walk. She is like the soul of the village.'

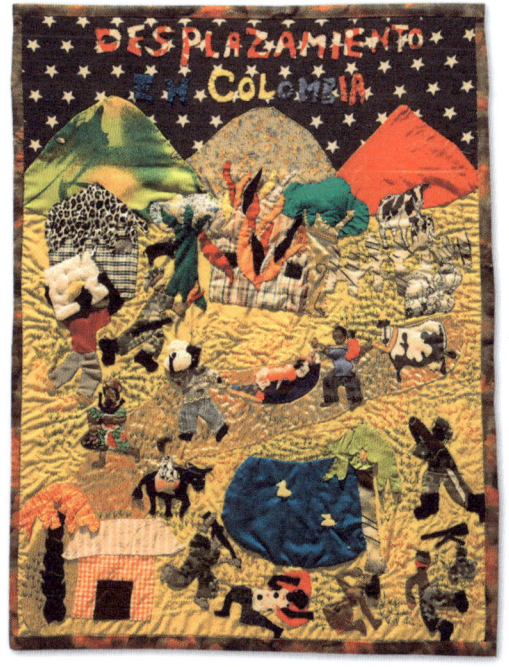

Enforced Disappearances

Despite the existence of the UDHR treaty to protect global citizens from arbitrary arrest, detention or exile, charities such as Amnesty International, an international non-governmental organization specifically set up to fight abuses of human rights, with the primary aim of bringing torturers to justice, are constantly called on to help investigate cases of 'enforced disappearances'.

In wars and conflicts, and in countries with dictatorships, military or emergency rule, enforced disappearances can be systematic and commonplace. Used as a tool of terror, the strategy is to spread a deep feeling of insecurity and fear in the population in order to repress or completely quash opposing religious, political or cultural views. Carried out by officials acting with state consent, the disappearances take the form of abductions and kidnappings, imprisonment (often in solitary confinement) and frequently torture or death.

The persistent threat of becoming 'disappeared' means that millions of people throughout the world live in constant fear of losing everything, from their voice to their life. The enforced disappeared are usually men, but activists, campaigners, investigative journalists, lawyers and defenders of human rights are particularly targeted.

It is usually women that lead the grassroots campaigns to seek answers, justice and reparation for their disappeared loved ones, and they not only experience intimidation and violence from the authorities, but are at a higher risk of being silenced or disappeared themselves. Protesting about enforced disappearances takes much courage and determination to stand up to the perpetrators of these crimes against humanity and violations of international law.

On 26 September 2014, 43 male students from a teaching college in Ayotzinapa, Southwest Mexico, were forcibly abducted whilst organizing an anniversary event to commemorate the 1968 Tlatelolco massacre in Mexico City. It is alleged that they were hijacked and kidnapped by local police officers from their convoy of buses after being intercepted in a roadblock. They were wrongly accused of organized drug crimes after being taken into custody, sparking one of Mexico's most infamous human rights cases. 'The Iguala kidnapping' led to widespread protests and international condemnation.

OPPOSITE AND OVERLEAF

43 FOR 43 (2016)

Zak Foster

Made from mixed fabrics.

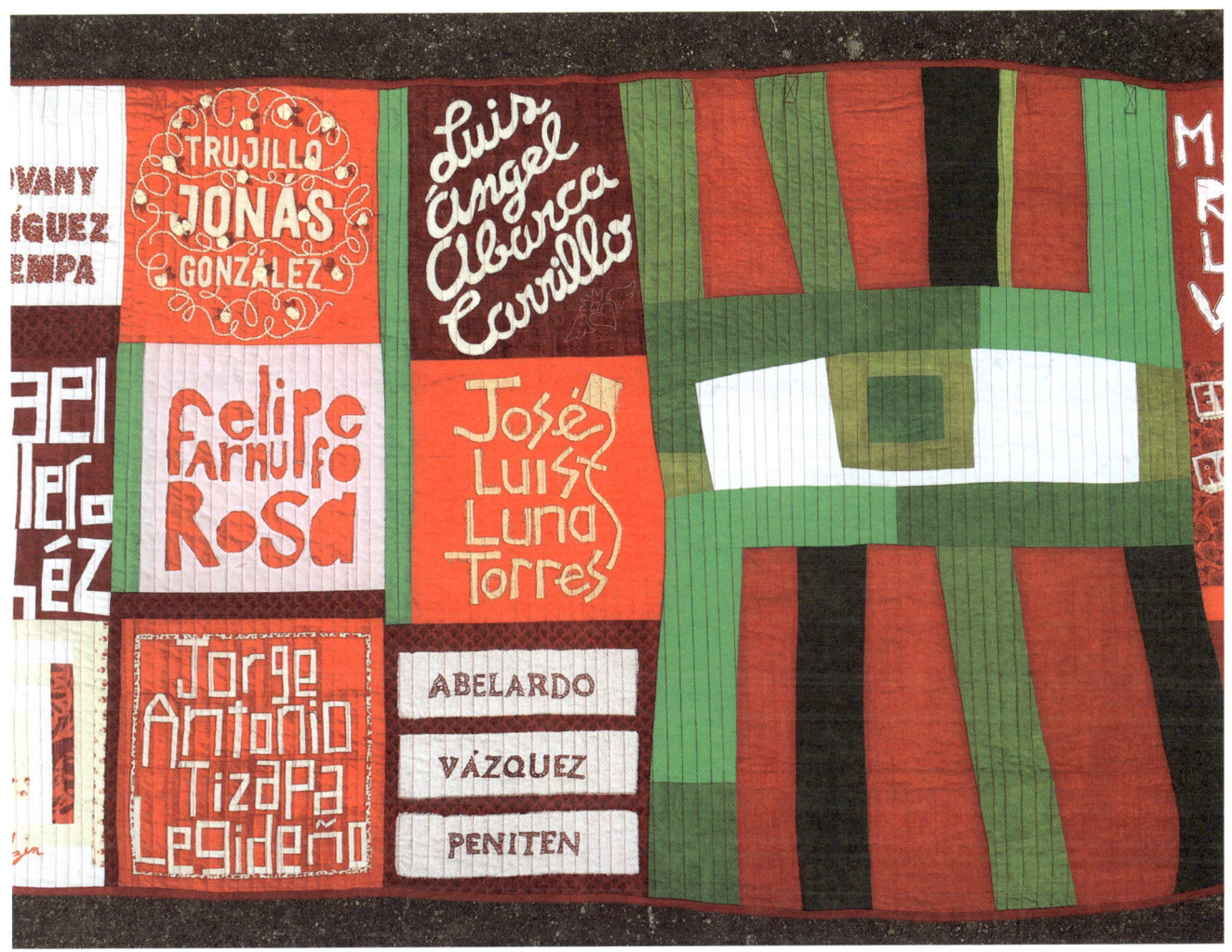

To date, only the remains of three of the students have been identified; the other 40 remain missing. Although there have been several arrests over the years, only two people have so far been imprisoned in connection with the students' enforced disappearances. Evidence points towards the Mexican military being implicated in their abduction and probable deaths.

Zak Foster's '43 for 43', above and overleaf, is a collaborative quilt project dedicated to the 43 missing students. It was made in 2016 as a protest banner by over 70 quilters and textile artists, assembled by Foster and delivered to the families in Ayotzinapa. The all-seeing eye forms the centrepiece around which the blocks dedicated to each student are arranged.

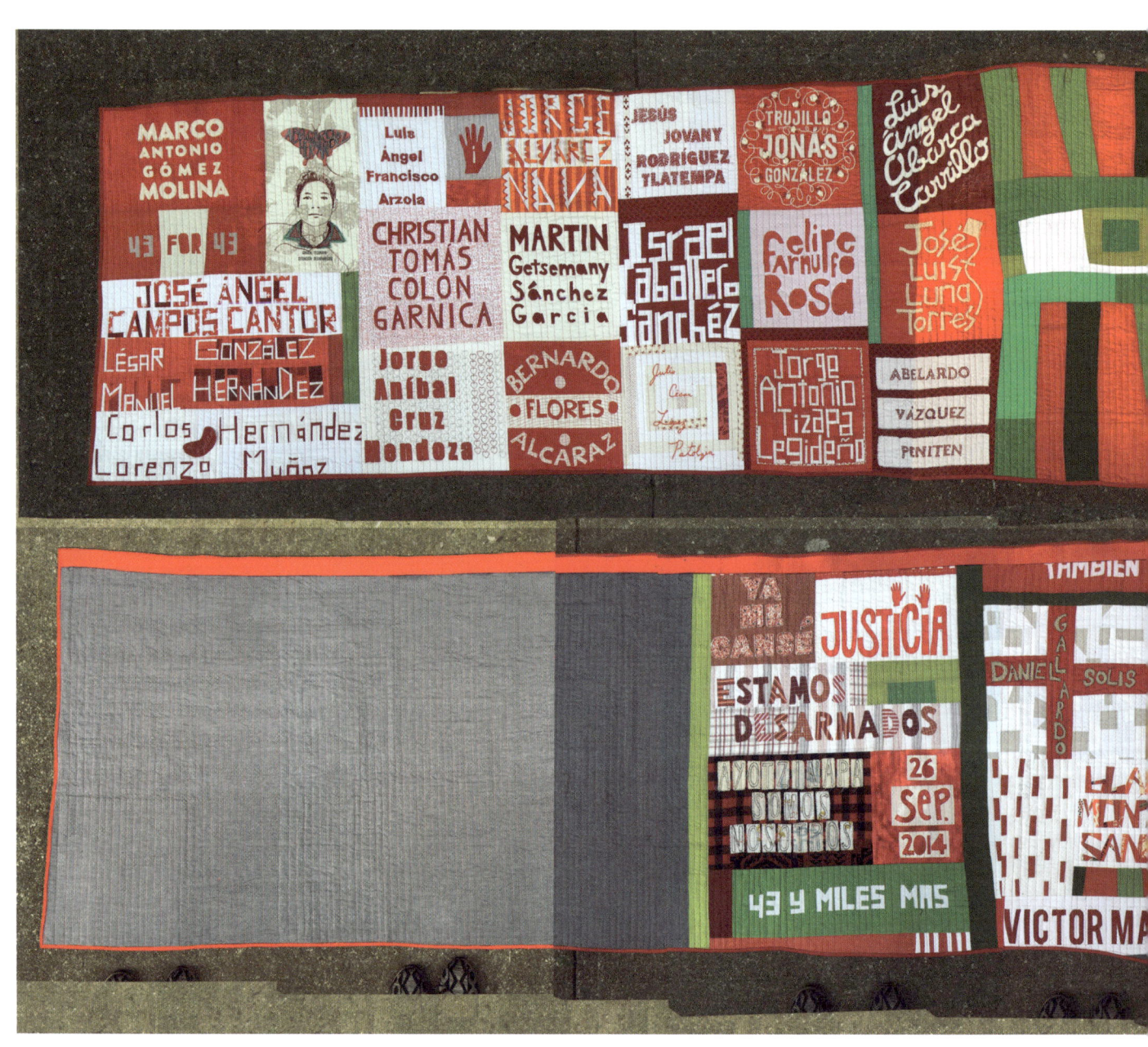

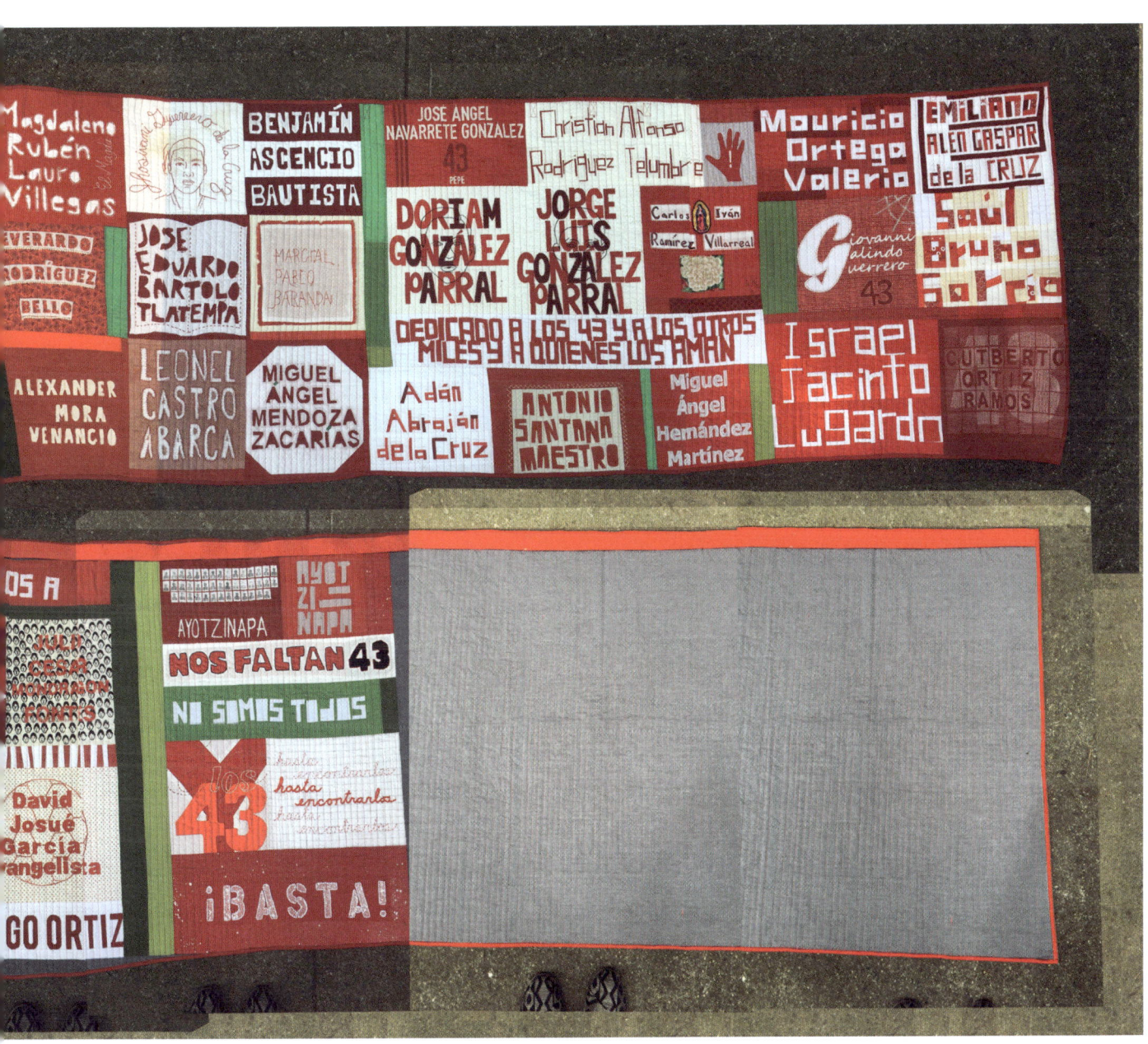

Arpilleras

Following the military coup in Chile on 11 September 1973, women began to protest against enforced disappearances through the medium of patched and embroidered textiles known as arpilleras. This traditional and distinct style of appliqué, a folk art established in the 1960s, became particularly popular during Augusto Pinochet's military dictatorship (1973–90) to highlight the plight of political prisoners and those who had involuntarily disappeared. Through coloured wools and stylized appliquéd motifs, stitched on a hessian (burlap) ground, these arpilleras portray narratives of fear, loss, struggle, oppression and suffering. Although they predominantly tell painful stories of those missing and voids left in lives, of hunger and poverty, many arpilleras also express hope, strength and solidarity, and depict the sun over the Andean mountains that, one day, will bring a new political dawn.

The women who commercially stitched arpilleras became known as *arpilleristas* and sewed alongside others in organized and regulated workshops (*talleres*). Their finished artworks were left unsigned to protect them, then smuggled abroad via the Vicaria de la Solidaridad, an ecumenical human rights group led by the Catholic Church in Santiago, who distributed the arpilleras internationally to disseminate testimonies and memories of what was taking place in Chile. Censorship and controls were often lax, as the stitched works were generally viewed as simple, harmless women's work, although Pinochet himself labelled them 'tapestries of defamation'. Known as the 'revolutionary banners of modern Chile', these subversive acts of collective resistance have since become a valued historic record of a repressive regime.

All profits from the sales went to the women who designed and stitched them. As most of the *arpilleristas* were wives, mothers and sisters of missing husbands, sons and brothers, this was their only source of income, as relatives of the enforced disappeared were banned from taking most jobs.

Very explicit scenes of torture and provocative words and slogans were banned from being part of the arpillera designs, as the workshop regulators thought the arpilleristas would be at greater risk of arrest if they were used. However, the appliquéd messages were strong, referencing recognizable symbols and well-established themes and Chilean landmarks, or common terms such as *¿Donde Están?'* (Where are they?). Designs often feature

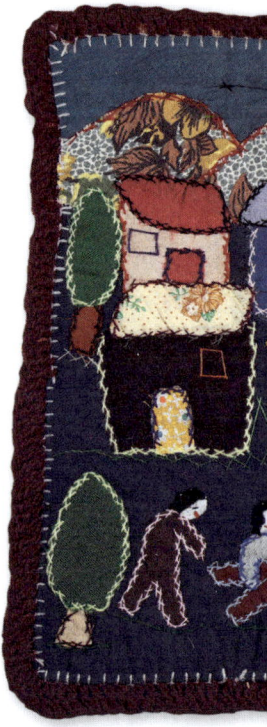

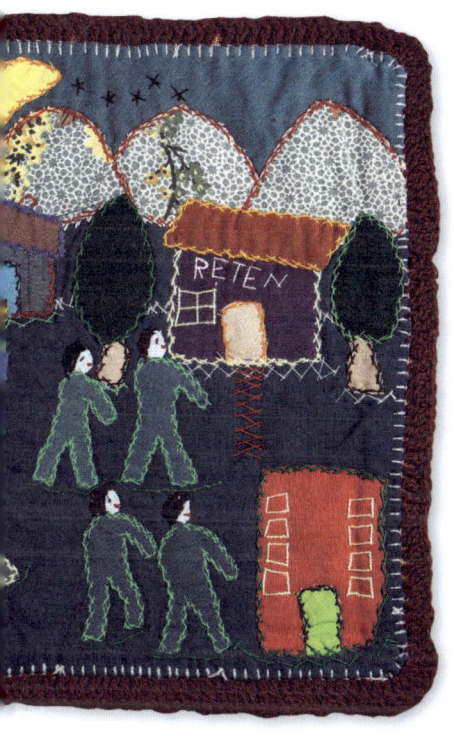

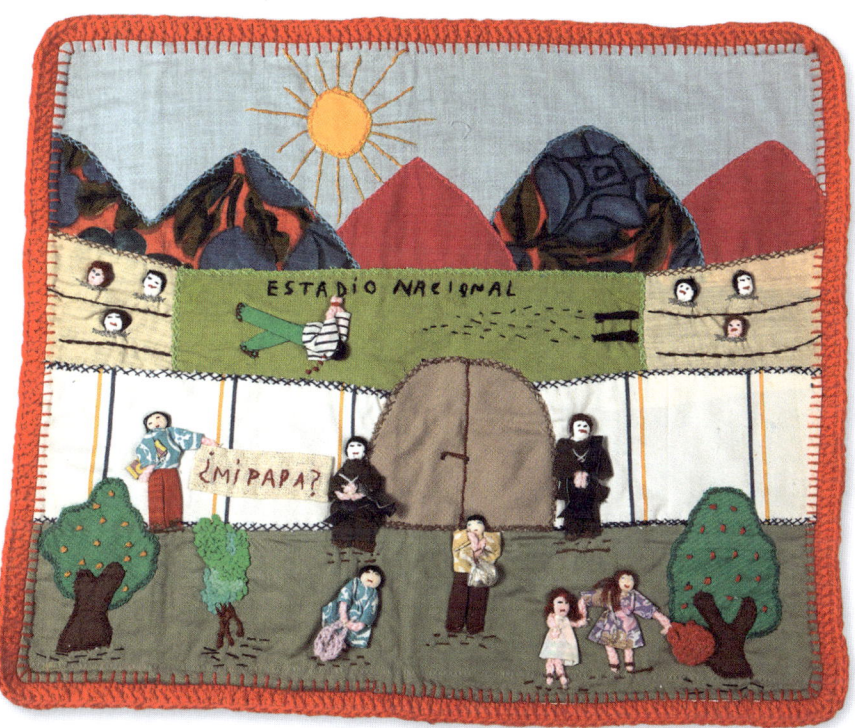

repetitive motifs and illustrate scenes of life at the time: children queuing for milk; groups of protesters illegally delivering leaflets or carrying banners; people praying for news of the disappeared; whilst the military look on, faceless in dark uniforms.

The art of making arpilleras has spread across the globe; interpreted as story cloths, they are still a common form of protest textile today, although the themes of protest are often rendered and visually communicated more graphically and dramatically, as contemporary artists are free to express their motives through this art form, unbound by rules and regulations.

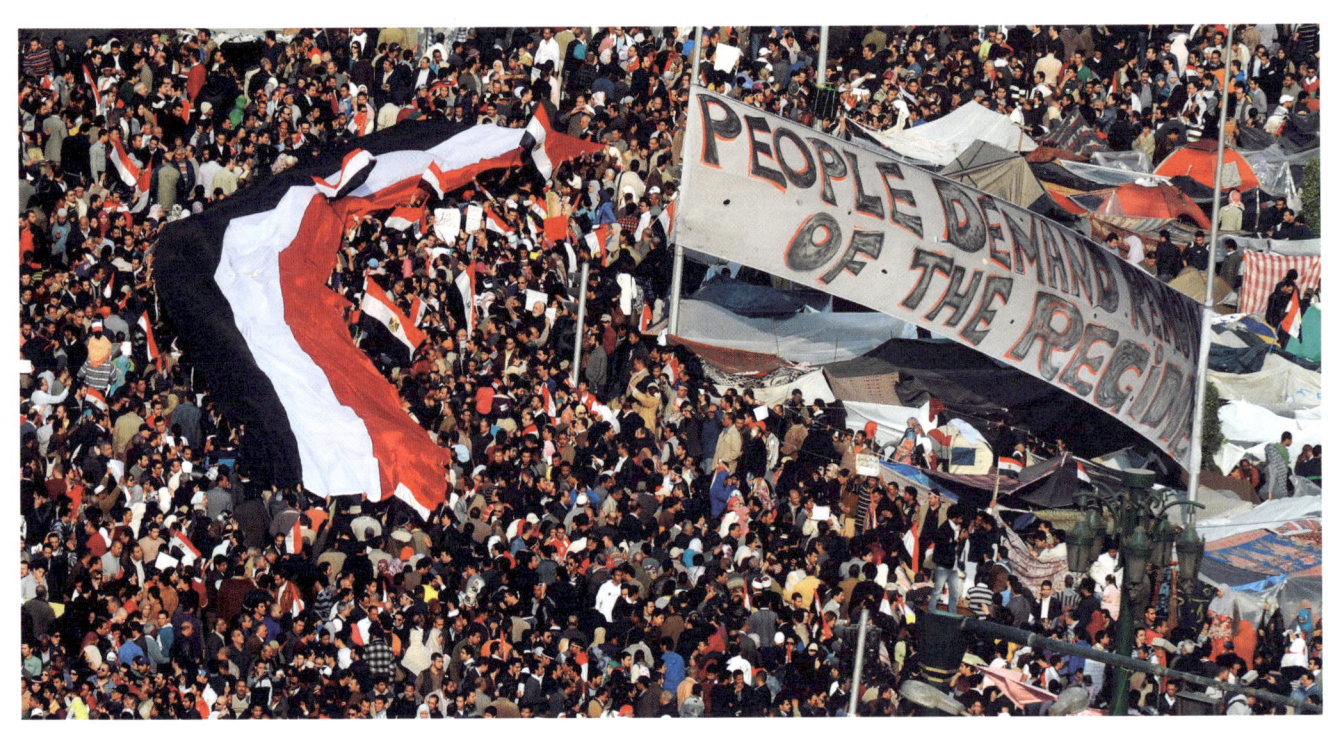

REBELS AGAINST REGIMES

The Arab Spring

OPPOSITE

People gather in
Tahrir Square in
Cairo on the 15th
day of continuous
protest against the
reign of President
Mubarak in Egypt,
8 February 2011.

The Arab Spring was a political revolution, beginning in late 2010, characterized by a series of pro-democracy uprisings that erupted across the Arab world, starting in Tunisia and quickly spreading to countries including Egypt, Bahrain, Libya, Syria and Yemen. The protests, driven by widespread dissatisfaction with authoritarian regimes, human rights violations, poverty, corruption and lack of political freedom, were originally peaceful, but turned violent and bloody when they were met with military force. Whilst the uprisings led to the overthrowing of some long-standing dictators, such as in Tunisia and Egypt, they also triggered violent conflicts and civil wars, most notably in Syria, Libya and Yemen. The Arab Spring resulted in much instability in some countries, but political reform in others.

The legacy of the Arab Spring marked a profound shift in the region, demonstrating the power of collective voices in challenging entrenched systems, and sparking ongoing debates about democracy, justice and the struggles for freedom and reform of human rights in the Arab world.

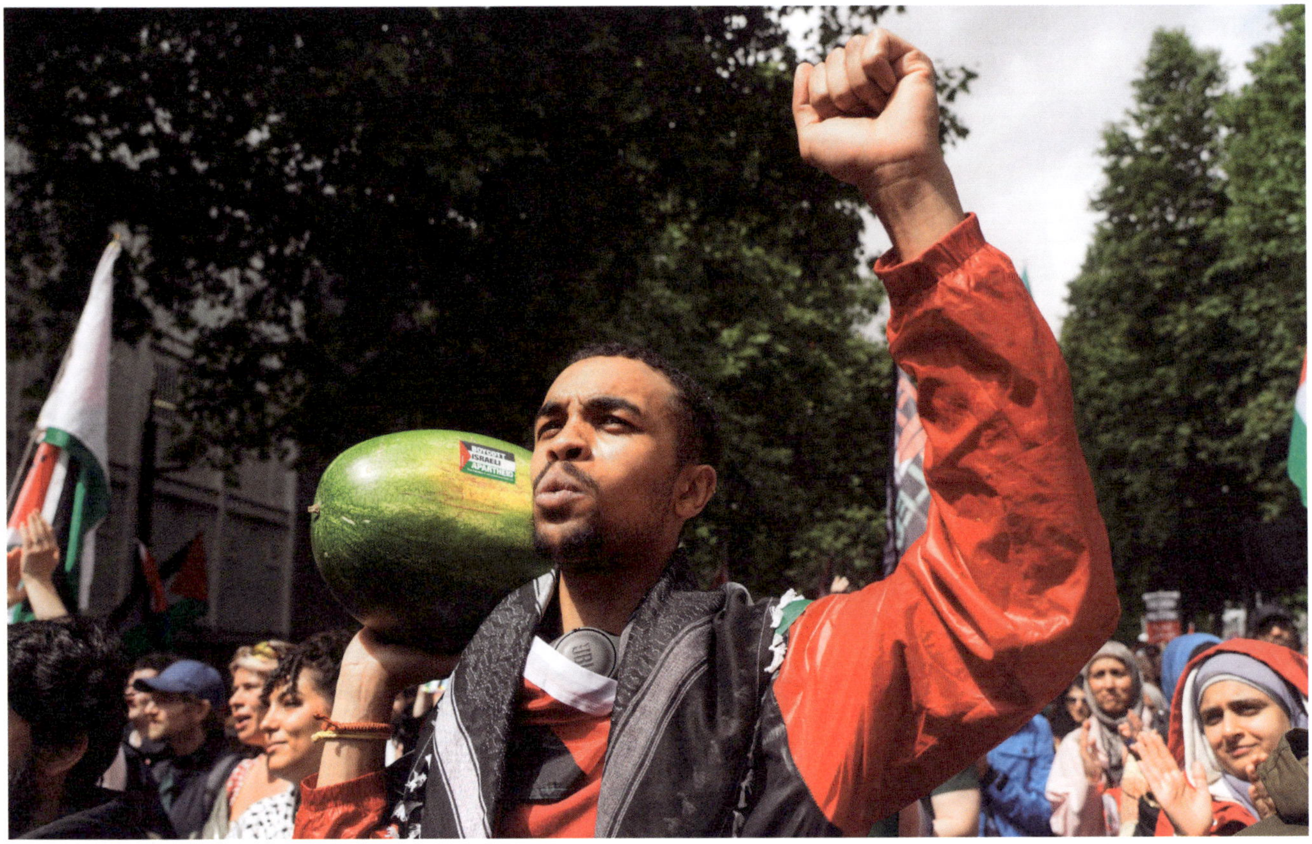

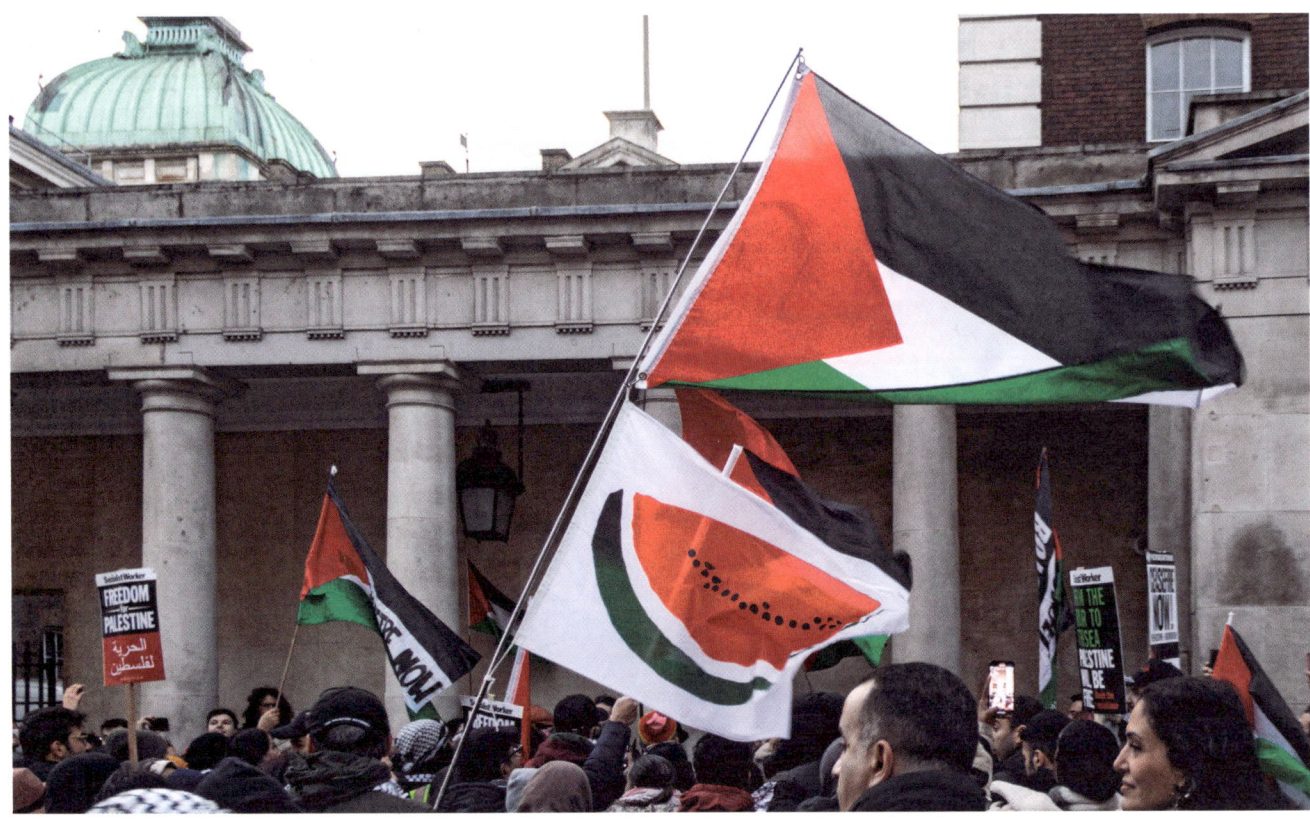

REBELS AGAINST REGIMES

The Watermelon

OPPOSITE, ABOVE

A man holds a watermelon, a symbol of solidarity with Palestine, during a march in London where tens of thousands took to the streets to ask the new UK government to demand an immediate and permanent ceasefire in Gaza, 6 July 2024.

OPPOSITE, BELOW

A flag featuring a watermelon is displayed alongside the Palestinian flag.

As well as slogans, powerful symbols of protest also emerge in times of conflict and repression. These symbols unite demonstrators and express, through simple and stylized imagery, solidarity and support for a particular campaign or struggle or resistance to a regime. One example of this is a slice of watermelon, which has become a symbol of Palestinian protest against the ongoing occupation of Gaza and the West Bank by Israel.

The flag of Palestine was unilaterally criminalized by the Israeli military forces following the 1967 Six Day War, and artists and protestors have been arrested over the years for violating this military order. Issam Badr, an artist arrested in 1981, was told not to make political art, or use the forbidden Palestinian flag colours of red, black, green and white, but to paint pictures of 'flowers' or 'nude figures'. He asked the arresting Israeli soldier, 'If I paint a flower with these colours what will you do?' The officer replied that the paintings would be confiscated: 'Even if you paint a watermelon, it will be confiscated.' So the idea for this well-recognized symbol of resistance and freedom ironically came from the oppressors, and the 'Watermelon Flag' (designed by Khaled Hourani) has been displayed and waved ever since at protests and exhibitions worldwide.

Although the ban on the Palestinian flag was lifted by Israel in 1993, after the signing of the Oslo Peace Accords, the flag and its colours are still targets of the Israeli authorities, who occasionally crack down on the display of the flag at public events and gatherings. During these crackdowns, images of watermelons emerge alongside the text 'This Is Not A Palestinian Flag' on banners and garments alike.

The watermelon, a staple food in the region, now strongly symbolizes Palestinian identity and the legacy of resistance to the prohibition of the Palestinian flag. In the fight for liberation, the Watermelon Flag has become particularly prominent on recent international marches and demonstrations against Israel's war on Gaza following the Hamas attack on southern Israel in October 2023.

We Stand With...

Tragically, many citizens of the world continue to experience the horror of war and all that it entails. When wars break out, and in times of military and political conflict, civilians are killed, orphaned, subjected to violence, kidnapped and tortured, raped, displaced, forced to migrate, separated from their families, and are victims of physical and psychological abuse and post-traumatic stress disorder (PTSD). Separated from loved ones and their known safe and familiar communities, victims of war often seek emergency safety, shelter, comfort and refuge, as they flee with few belongings.

During times of war and conflict, the use of flags can be ambiguous. Whilst each opposing 'side' may use their national flag to proclaim their own identity and express their loyalty, a nation's colours and flag can also be used as propaganda to galvanize patriotism, to invoke national pride and intimidate the opposition.

Conversely, flags and banners of those resisting are frequently waved in defiance to boost morale, to show solidarity and support, and to signify understanding and empathy with innocent civilians and those under threat.

Since Russia invaded Ukraine on 24 February 2022, the Ukrainian flag has become a familiar display in many windows and on buildings across Europe, as a protest against Putin's regime and as a visual symbol to say: 'We Stand With Ukraine'.

OPPOSITE

Gdansk, Poland. 16 February 2022. Protesters hold a banner reading 'Stand with Ukraine' during the demonstration at the Solidarity Square. The Ukrainian-Polish community of Gdansk gathered at the Solidarity Square for the territorial integrity and sovereignty of Ukraine in the face of the threat of an expansion of aggression by the Russian Federation.

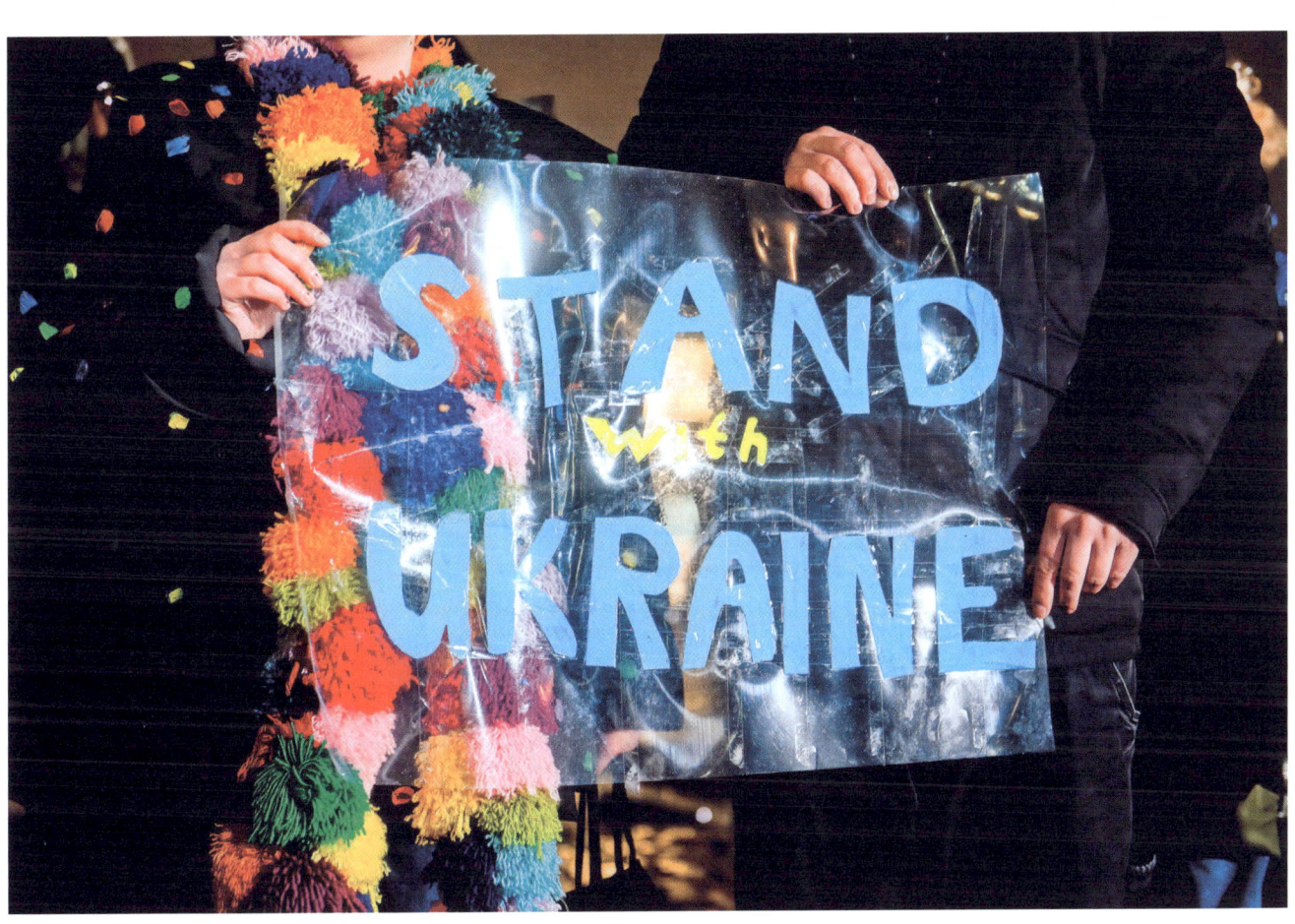

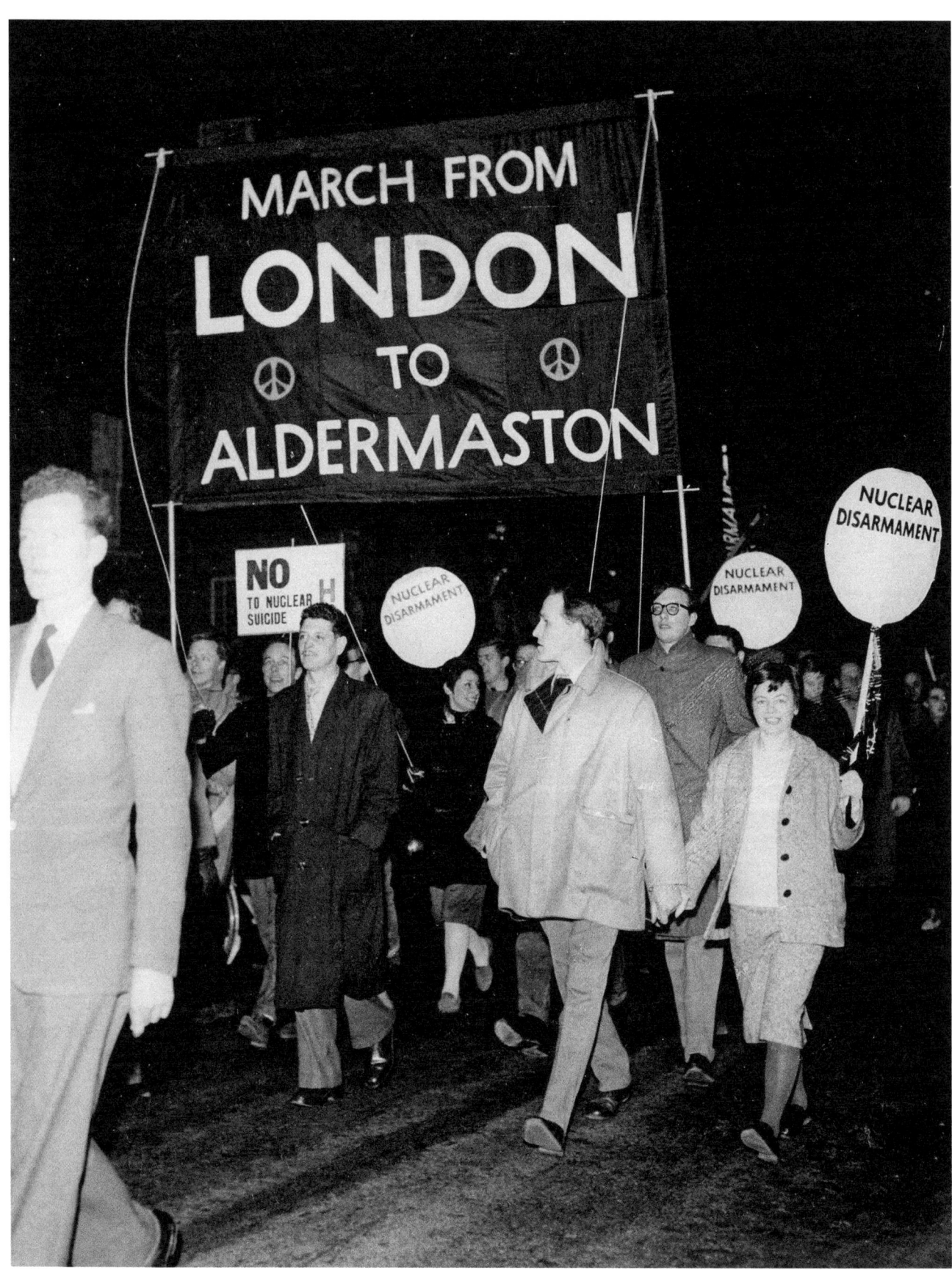

PEACE AND MOBILIZATION

OPPOSITE

Demonstrators marching against the continued development and testing of nuclear weapons through Hounslow, London, on 4 April 1958, en route to Aldermaston, the site of the atomic weapons development centre.

'I don't think there'll ever be a time when you don't need banners despite all this modern technology. They are like your standard – they show who you are and that you're proud and I think that we'll always sort of need that.'

THALIA CAMPBELL

For decades people have been marching for peace. In addition to anti-war demonstrations being against war and conflict, they also unite people from different nationalities, ages, genders, cultural, religious, economic and political backgrounds. Marches bring together those who want to make their voices heard; they often include survivors, victims and those protesting for the first time. As well as a desire for an absence of war, being pro-peace reflects a wish to live in a world without a dominant culture of violence, guns and nuclear weapons.

The voices of peace activists form a powerful reminder that peace is not just a stand against war, but a call for a world built on understanding and empathy, compassion and mutual respect, and one which reaffirms a collective commitment to a vision of shared humanity and harmony.

Anti-War

Following news of invasions, bombings, occupations and other atrocities, spontaneous protests, marches and vigils are common as individuals and communities unite to show their aversion to these political decisions. Many protestors carry makeshift placards and banners made quickly with limited resources such as bedsheets and spray paints. The text and images are simple and to the point: for example, 'Never Again' or 'Stop War, Stop Hate'. These textiles are temporary, being tied to buildings or public structures, then removed by police.

One particular slogan, 'Make Love Not War' (a prominent anti-war phrase that evolved from the 1960s demonstrations against the USA's involvement in the Vietnam War), has been tirelessly paraded on every anti-war demonstration since. It has taken on different formats, fonts and scales, and features on many types of wearable and non-wearable textiles.

Not In My Name

The biggest mobilization of protestors in recent years was against the then-imminent war in Iraq. On 15 February 2003, the world united for peace, and over 30 million people from more than 100 nations marched and protested. It became the biggest global demonstration in the history of political activism, and the *Guinness Book of Records* recorded a new entry as peace was globalized.

The most common slogans in the UK and US were: 'Don't Attack Iraq', 'Not In My Name' and the blood-spattered 'No' graphic designed by David Gentleman. Humour, too, was evident on banners and placards, with slogans such as 'Bliar' and 'Somewhere in Texas a village is missing its idiot'.

Despite international protests, Iraq was invaded in March 2003. The rationale for the invasion was based upon claims that Iraq had 'weapons of mass destruction' and that Saddam Hussein, the president of Iraq, had strong connections with al-Qaeda. Evidence to support these claims was never proven, but Hussein, the leader of a repressive totalitarian regime, was later convicted of crimes against humanity and executed in 2006. The Iraq War ended in 2011 when the last US troops withdrew.

BELOW

A 'Make Love Not War' appliqué patch (1970s) worn by Joan Baker, taken from the author's own collection.

OPPOSITE

A 'Not in My Name' T-shirt by Stop The War Coalition worn by the author on the protest march in Glasgow, 15 February 2013, against the imminent invasion of Iraq.

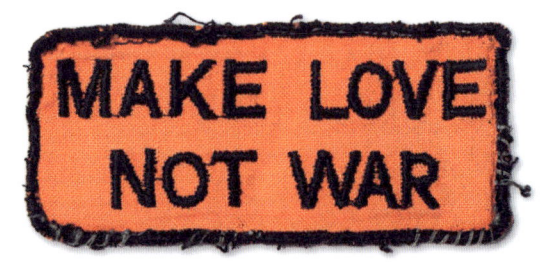

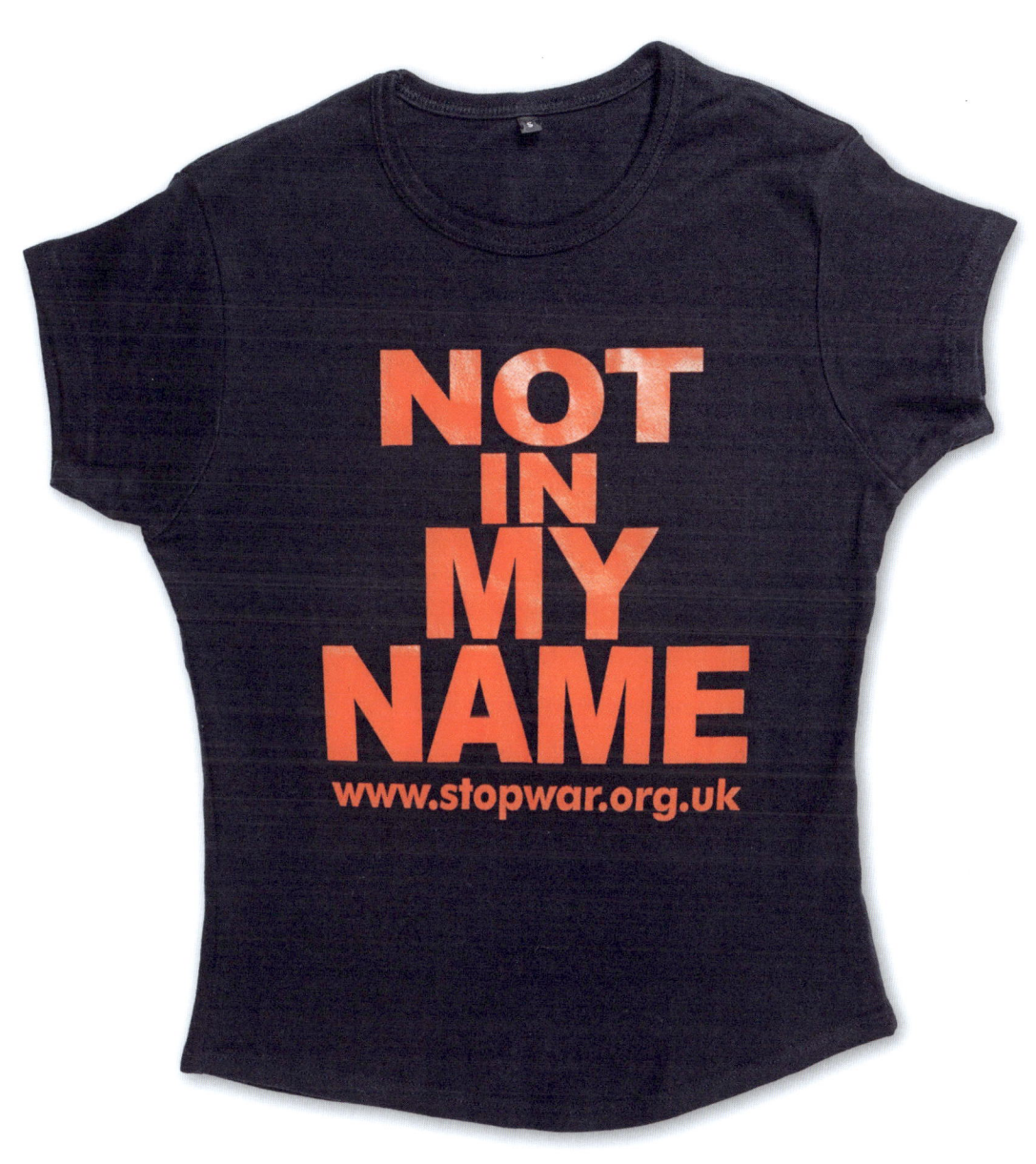

The Nuclear Arms Race and the Cold War

The first atomic bomb to be used as a weapon of war was dropped on 6 August 1945 by the United States, on the Japanese city of Hiroshima. The damage was indiscriminate and, although the actual number of deaths will never be known, it is estimated that more than 70,000 civilians died instantly. Three days later, the US dropped a second atomic bomb on Nagasaki, killing at least 40,000 people. It's estimated that thousands of other civilians died in the aftermath.

The dropping of these atomic bombs led to the end of World War II, but also to the dawn of a nuclear era. The two superpowers, the United States and the Soviet Union, began a nuclear arms race and the political rivalry and tension between them and their allies began a struggle for supremacy known as the Cold War.

In a speech in 1946, Winston Churchill, the former British prime minister, described how the Soviet Union had lowered an 'Iron Curtain' that divided Europe. He warned of Soviet expansion and requested a strengthening of the relationship between Britain and the US, and the importance of European unity.

On 1 March 1954, at Bikini Atoll in the Pacific Ocean, the US dropped their first experimental hydrogen bomb, which was 1,300 times more powerful than the atomic bomb dropped on Hiroshima. International condemnation followed, and peace activists initiated a movement to 'Ban the Bomb'.

OPPOSITE, ABOVE

Protestors display signs in German, French, English and Russian at a future rocket range near Milternberg, Germany, 2 April 1961.

OPPOSITE, BELOW

Hundreds of protestors join in circling the Ministry of Defence government building in London with a 'peace scarf' knitted by thousands of people for a rally against government plans to spend £100 billion replacing the Trident nuclear weapons system.

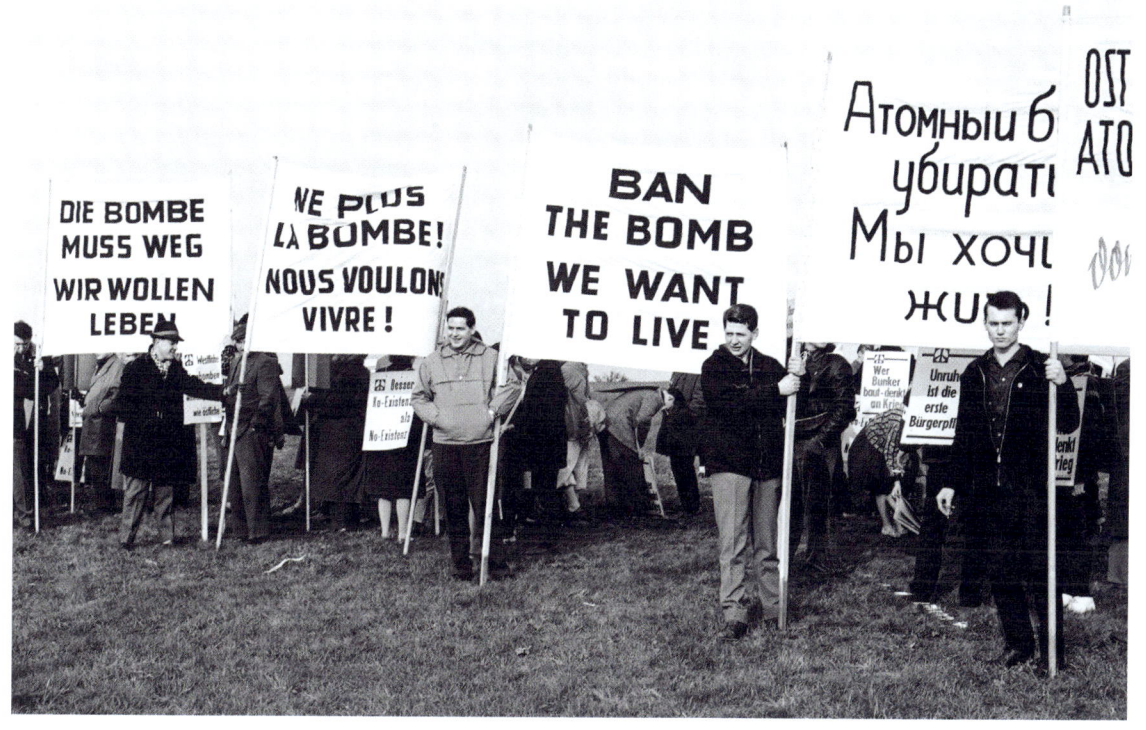

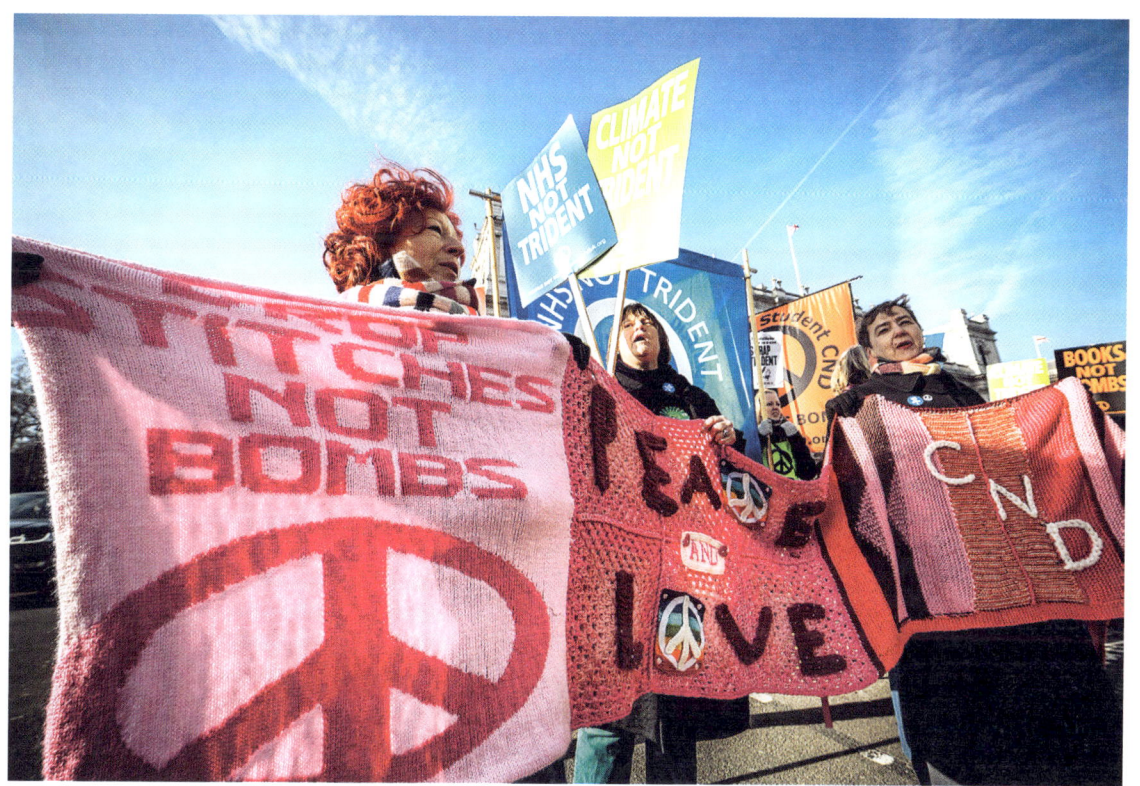

The Campaign for Nuclear Disarmament

Throughout the decades of nuclear testing, international concern rose over the effects of radioactive fallout and contamination, associated health risks, and the damage and long-lasting impact on the environment. Populations were concerned about the world being on the brink of a nuclear disaster, and anti-nuclear and anti-bomb campaigns and disarmament protests became increasingly common as the fear of this reality became acute.

The Campaign for Nuclear Disarmament (CND), a non-profit campaigning organization, was a conglomerate formed from many smaller 'Ban the Bomb' and other anti-war groups in London, and held its first public meeting in February 1958. It immediately attracted a large membership, and organized notable mass marches and protests. Lord Bertrand Russell, the world-renowned philosopher, became CND's first (and only) president. He previously published a manifesto in July 1955 appealing to capitalists and communists alike 'to renounce nuclear weapons' and for 'an abolition of war'. In its draft form, it had been endorsed and signed by Albert Einstein just before his death in April 1955. Russell split from CND in 1960 to found 'The Committee of 100', an anti-war group of 100 signatories, which believed that non-violent direct action (NVDA) was a more effective way to attract attention to the movement.

CND is still actively campaigning, maintaining the same objectives, and continues to take non-violent action to spearhead specific campaigns for nuclear disarmament and against cruise missiles, the abandonment of Trident (the UK's nuclear deterrent of submarines, weapons and warheads) and the cessation of wars – 'for peace and for planet'. In 2017, the International Campaign to Abolish Nuclear Weapons, of which CND is a member, won the Nobel Peace Prize.

OPPOSITE, LEFT

Protestors at an anti-nuclear protest in Glasgow, 4 April 2015.

OPPOSITE, RIGHT

Protestors march against the use of nuclear weapons in Parliament Square, London, 18 February 1961.

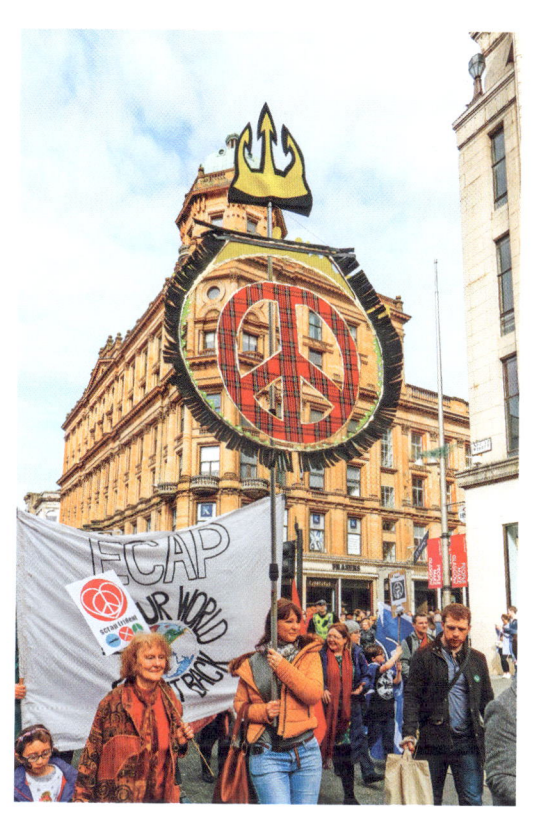

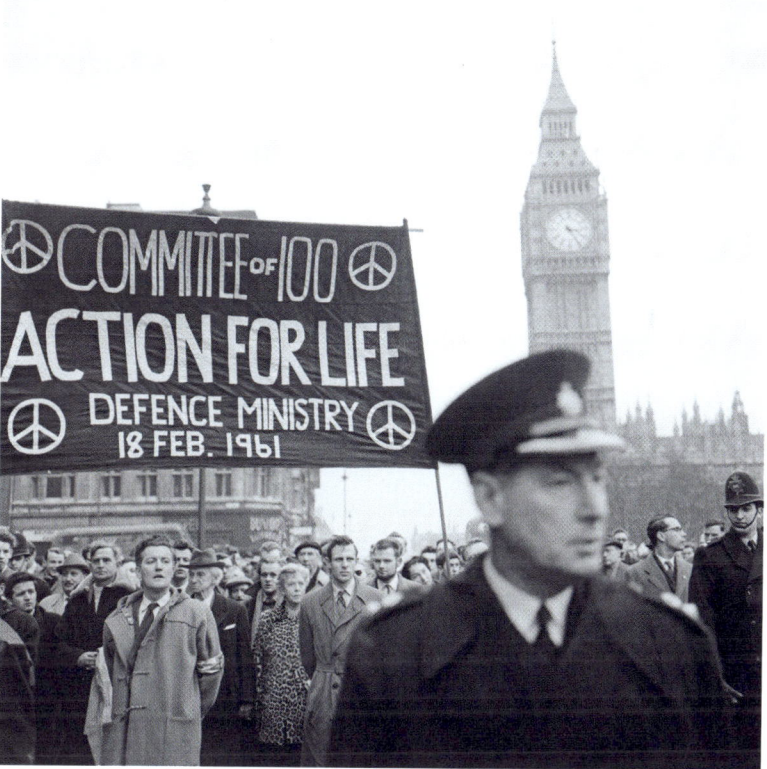

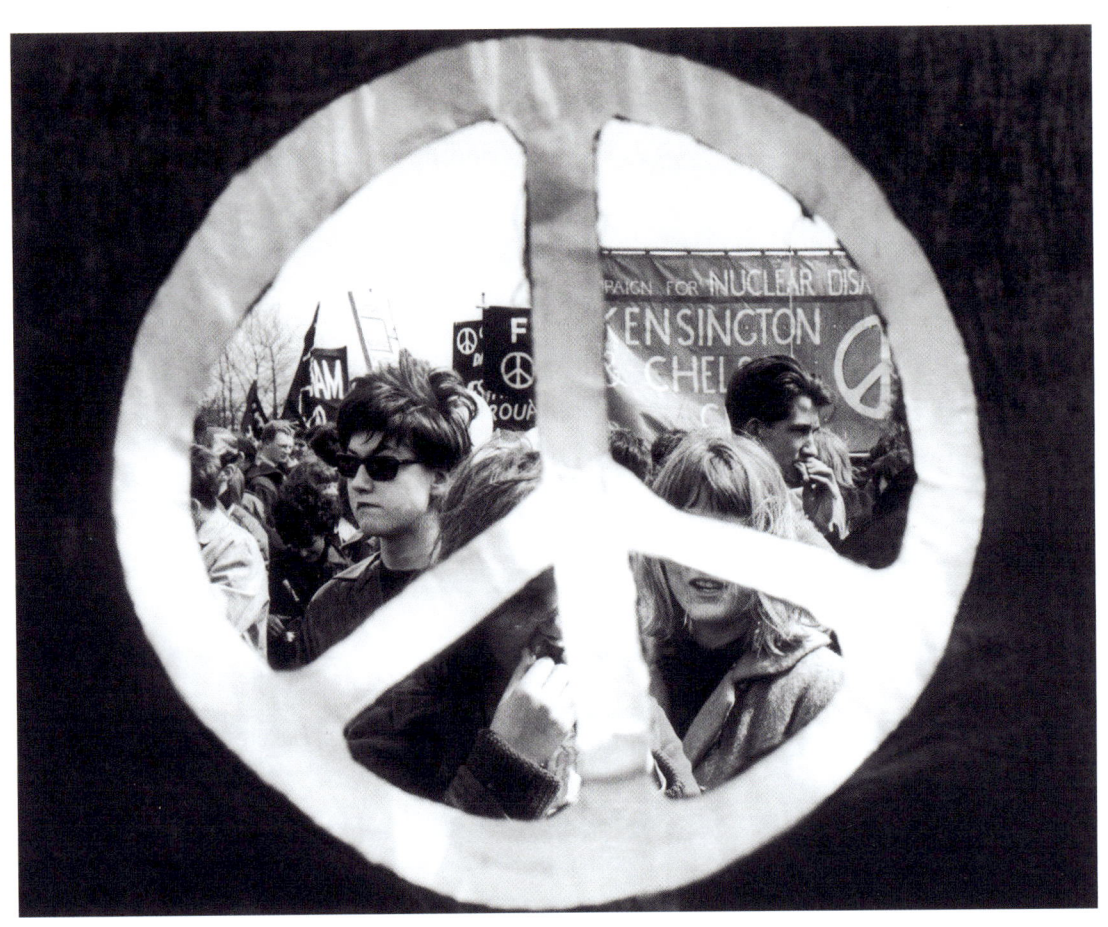

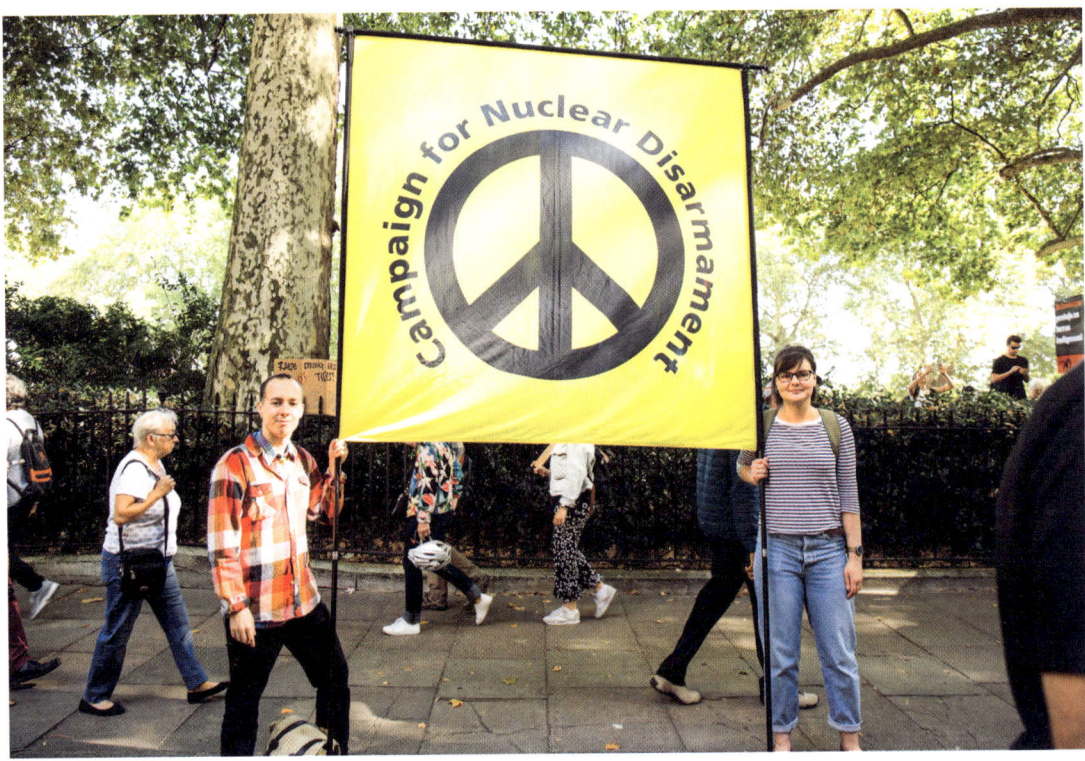

PEACE AND MOBILIZATION

OPPOSITE, ABOVE

Demonstrators on
an anti-nuclear
march from
Aldermaston to
London, 1963.

OPPOSITE, BELOW

CND protestors,
London.

A Symbol for Nuclear Disarmament

The nuclear disarmament symbol, often referred to internationally as the peace symbol, was designed in 1958 by Gerald Holtom, a graduate of the Royal College of Arts. He was a conscientious objector during World War II and remained a dedicated peace activist until his death in 1985.

The first public appearance of Holtom's iconic symbol was for the inaugural anti-nuclear protest march from London to Aldermaston, Berkshire, UK, where British nuclear weapons were manufactured. This historic march took place at Easter 1958 and was organized by the Direct Action Committee against Nuclear War – one of the smaller organizations that came together to form CND.

The symbol Holtom drew is the well-recognized three lines contained within a circle. The symbol was autobiographical: he drew himself in despair, hands pointing downwards, palms turned outwards, encircled. He simplified and stylized his design, and the semaphore letters of N and D (representing the desire for Nuclear Disarmament) are depicted within the circle. Holtom's design is not subject to copyright, as he wanted everyone to spread the message of peace behind it. This logo is one of the most ubiquitously used on protest textiles around the world, universally signifying peace, activism and solidarity.

Greenham Common Women's Peace Camp

In 1942, the Royal Air Force (RAF) of Great Britain opened a base at Greenham Common in Berkshire, UK. This was a major airfield during World War II, used by the United States Air Force, and during the Cold War it became a base for the deployment of nuclear cruise missiles.

In September 1981, Greenham Common came to international attention as 36 courageous women protestors chained themselves to the airfield fences in a protest against the arrival of 96 cruise missiles. Deciding that the original protest and makeshift camp (which started with a small protest march from Cardiff) needed to be extended, the women began to set up a long-term peace camp outside the perimeter fences of the airfield, with a station at each of the nine gates named after colours. Initially established by the Welsh group Women for Life on Earth, the camp grew, and from February 1982 became a women-only permanent protest with women from all generations and different walks of life involved. The protest camp became internationally known and was an embarrassment to successive governments until it closed in 2000.

Several imaginative non-violent direct action strategies were adopted during the time of the peace camp, including silent vigils, blockades and pickets to stop the movement of cruise missiles, human chains around the perimeter fences, and singing to keep up morale. The 'Embrace the Base' event on 12 December 1982 inspired many protestors globally. More than 30,000 women joined hands to form a human chain around the 14.5km (9mi) perimeter fence in the largest women-led protest since the fight for women's suffrage. One year later, more than 50,000 women repeated the action to demonstrate against the nuclear warheads that had recently arrived, in an event they called 'Reflect the Base', during which they held up mirrors as a symbolic invitation for the military to reflect upon its actions.

Many of the women were mothers and expressed their desire for a nuclear-free future for their children. Base fences were often breached or cut down as the women invaded the male-dominated military space.

The women were resilient and although it was a space for political protest, they also created a space for solidarity, compassion, refuge and creativity. During the 19-year history of the protest, thousands of arrests were made and several evictions

OPPOSITE

Greenham Common Women's Peace Camp (1981)

Thalia Campbell

114×163cm (44.8×64.1in).

Thalia Campbell, a well-known British activist and artist, was one of the original founders of Greenham Common Women's Peace Camp, and walked with the Women for Life on Earth from Wales to establish the camp in 1981. Her handmade banners, often collaborative, recorded names, actions and other camp memories. They have become a permanent and symbolic record and reminder of women's resistance to war and violence.

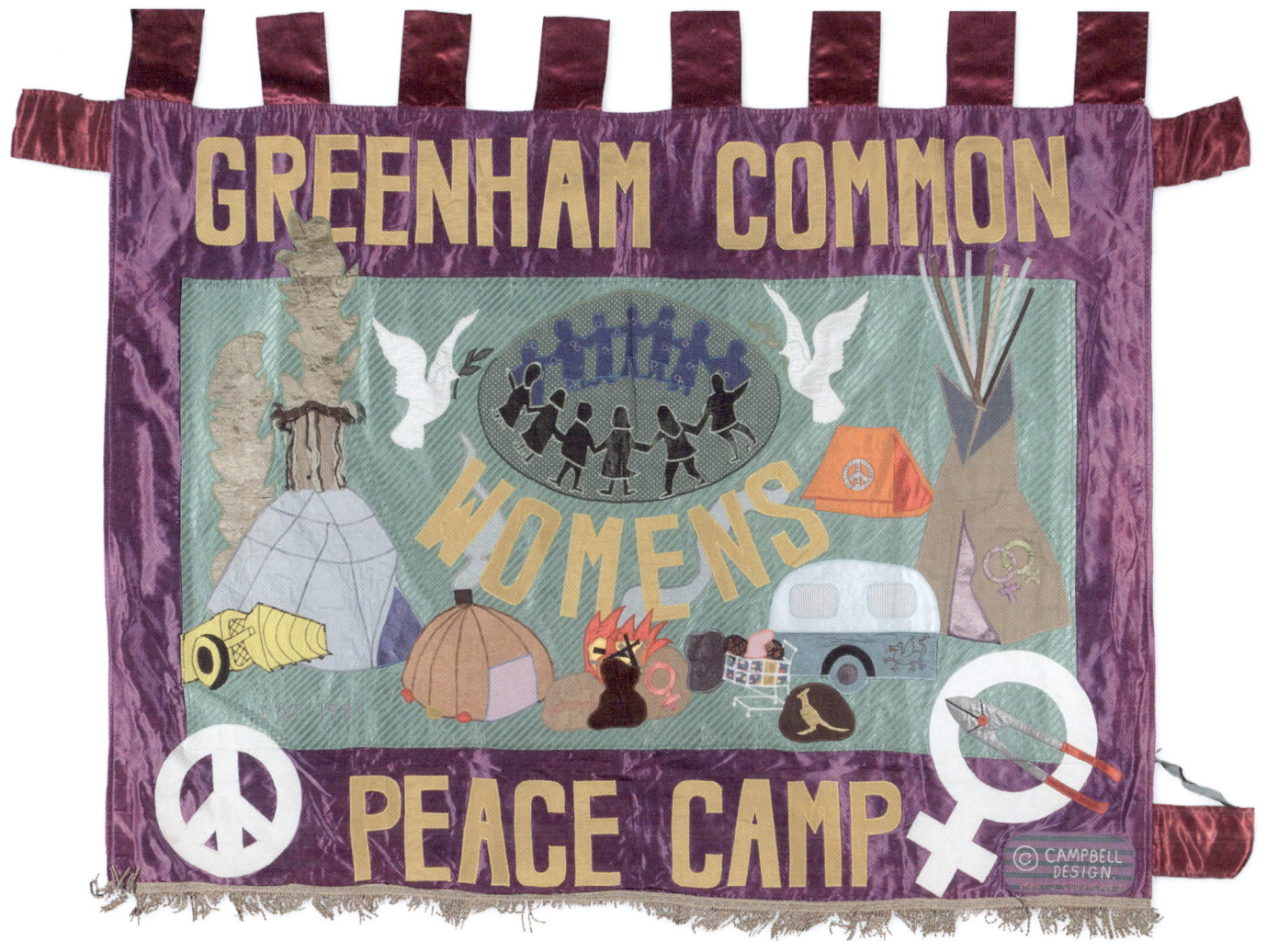

(then re-establishments) of the camp took place. Many locals opposed to the protest camp proclaimed themselves 'pro-defence', and carried out frightening attacks on the women; the police and bailiffs were also frequently brutal.

In a triumphant victory for the protestors, bylaws enacted by the British government in 1985 to prevent trespassers on the base were subsequently deemed unlawful by the House of Lords five years later.

The last cruise missiles were moved off-site in 1991 and the US Air Force vacated the site in September 1992, a momentous moment for the Greenham Common Women's Protest Camp. The perimeter fences were finally dismantled and removed in 2000, and the camp closed on 5 September, exactly 19 years to the day of its inception. The Greenham Common Peace Garden opened in 2002 as a permanent memorial, and the base was eventually bought back from the Ministry of Defence. Greenham Common, once again, belongs to the people of Newbury.

Anti-Gun Campaigns in the United States

Although many nations have permitted their citizens to bear arms throughout history, in the US today it is a constitutional right under the Second Amendment to own a gun, and approximately 43 per cent of households possess at least one firearm.

Predictably, high gun ownership and a legal right to bear arms leads to increased gun-related crimes, but as gun culture is part of American identity, and gun laws vary from state to state, implementing and enforcing laws on restricting weapons can be complicated.

OPPOSITE

Protestors at the March For Our Lives event in Orlando, Florida.

Mass Shootings

Mass shootings in the US are on the rise. Some of the most horrific have taken place in schools and were perpetrated by young men, often without a conclusive motive.

Columbine High, in Colorado, was a mass shooting in a US school, when in 1999 two twelfth-grade boys massacred 12 students, one teacher, and injured 24 others on a murderous rampage before killing themselves. Columbine has infamously inspired other copycat massacres such as those at Sandy Hook Elementary School in Newtown, Robb Elementary School in Uvalde and Marjory Stoneman Douglas High School in Parkland.

Other mass shootings have taken place in recreational venues where people had gathered together for enjoyment or worship: for example, at a country music festival in Las Vegas, the Aurora movie theatre in Colorado, the Pulse nightclub in Orlando and the First Baptist Church in Sutherland Springs, Texas. Devastatingly, the list goes on and the names of these venues become seared in our memories, forever linked to horrific atrocities. These atrocities put into context why so many survivors of gun crimes and campaign groups are lobbying for stricter regulations and tighter control of weapons.

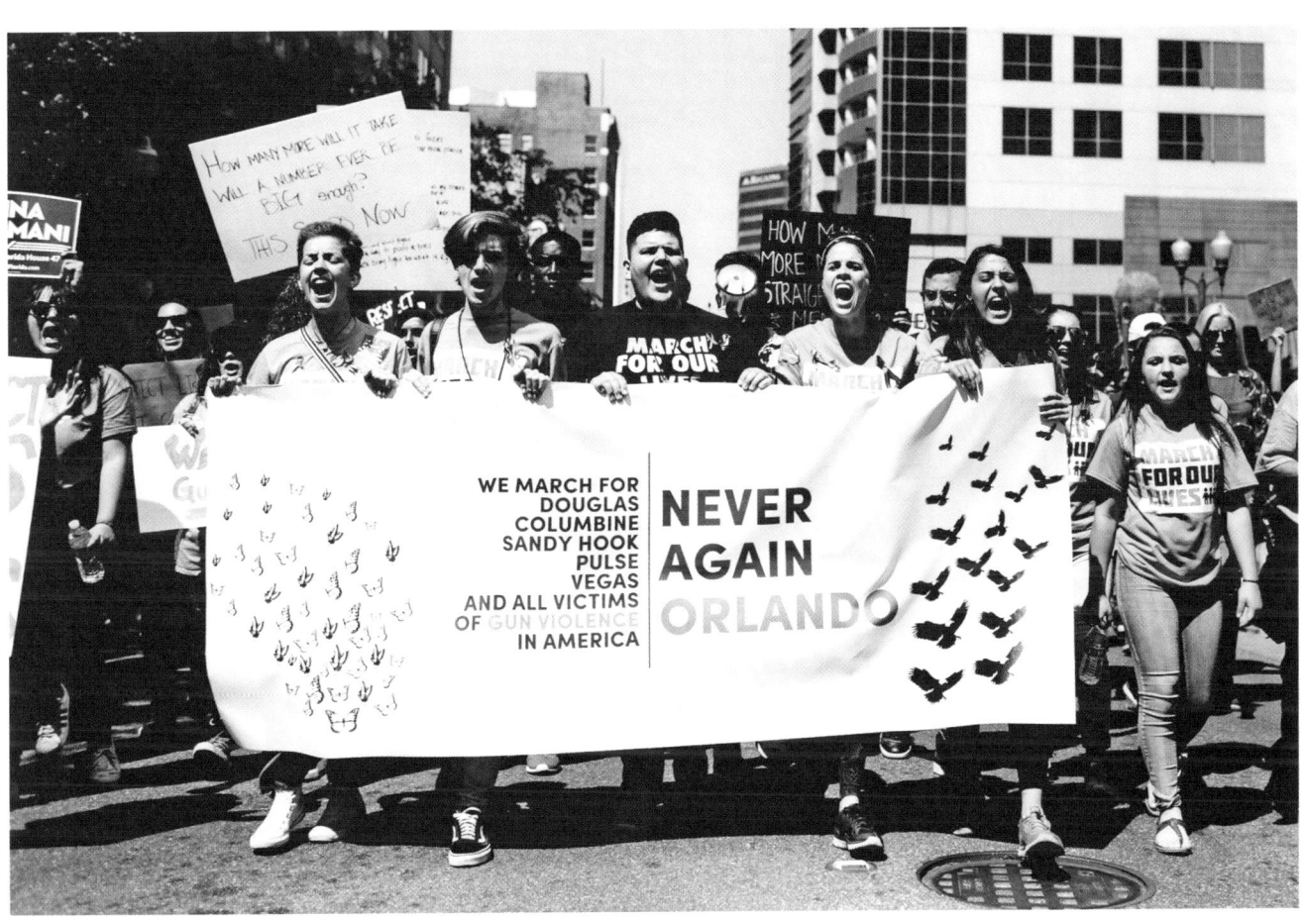

Gun Control and Legislation

The deadliest mass shooting in UK history (which left 16 children and one teacher dead and another 15 injured) was carried out in 1996 by a 43-year-old man at a primary school in Dunblane, UK. Within a year of this massacre the UK government passed legislation to enact stricter gun laws, and there have been no school shootings in the UK since.

The same has not happened in the US, but as deaths from gun crimes continue to rise there, the movement to stop it has too, as many individuals and organizations tirelessly campaign for stricter legislation to end gun violence. Some are outlined below.

OPPOSITE

Protestors with a 'Disarm Hate' sign at the Gay Pride Parade in New York, 2016.

Sandy Hook Promise

This non-profit organization, whose motto is 'turning tragedy into transformation', was founded after the Sandy Hook Elementary School tragedy by the loved ones of victims. Their programme 'Know the Signs' equips students and teachers with resources to look for warning signs of violence, such as a change in mental-health status, withdrawing socially, 'bragging about access to weapons' and 'making direct threats' about an attack.

Brady

Brady: United Against Gun Violence (Brady), is named after Jim Brady, who was shot in the head in the assassination attempt on President Reagan in 1981. He survived the attack, after which he and his wife Sarah relentlessly lobbied for a common-sense approach to control gun violence. Led mainly by survivors of gun violence, Brady aims to close loopholes in laws, and to shift attitudes and change the culture of how guns and weapons are perceived, similar to the way in which behaviours and understanding towards smoking and drink-driving has changed over time.

This bipartisan organization is at the forefront of holding the gun industry to account in the courts and working at a local, state and federal level towards gun reform. Originally established in 1974 as the National Council to Control Handguns, Brady's mission is 'to free America from gun violence', which they claim

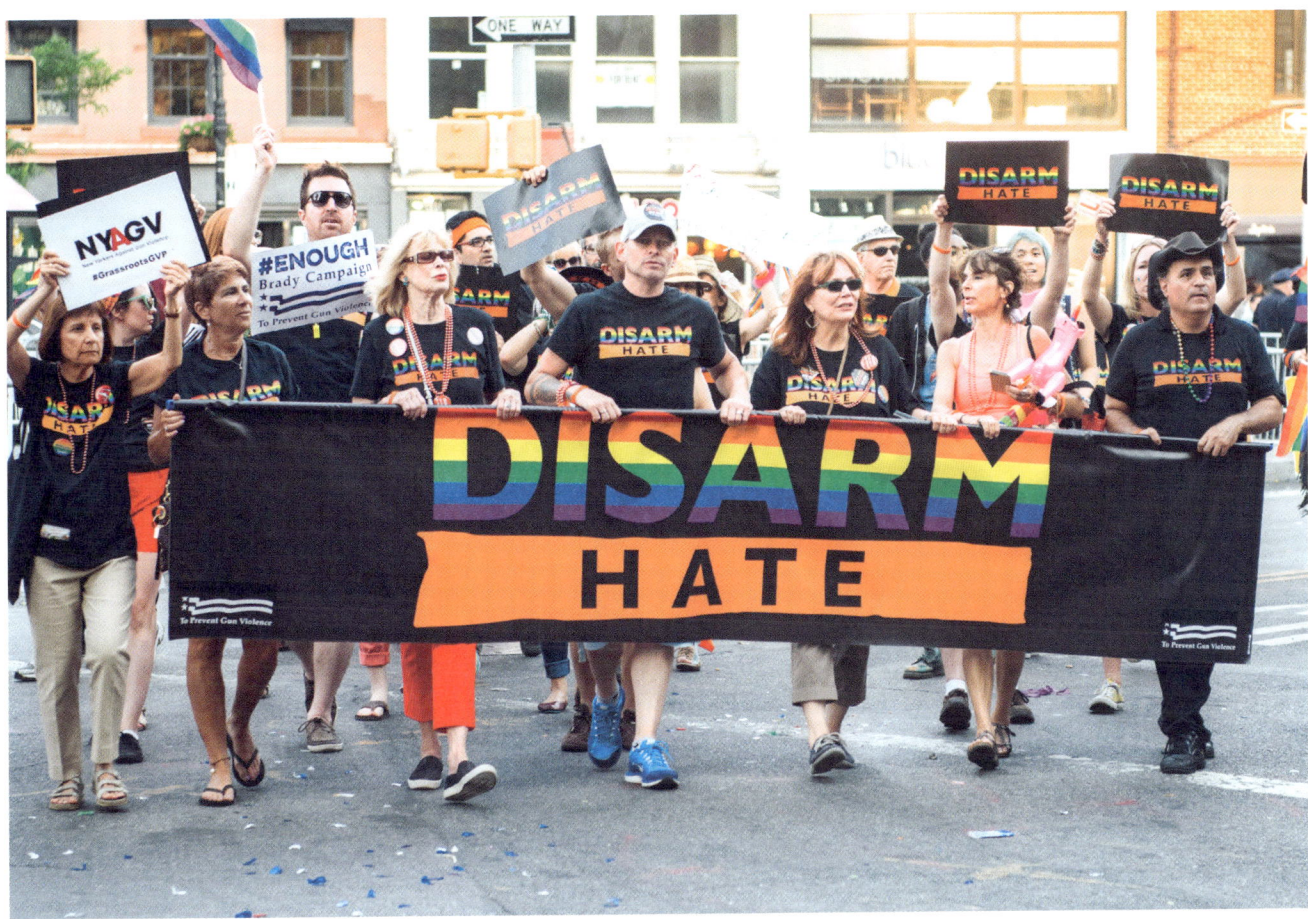

'is a uniquely American epidemic'. The Brady Handgun Violence Prevention Act, commonly known as the Brady Bill, was finally enacted in 1993. This tightened background checks and waiting periods to purchase firearms. The organization has worked with several presidential administrations, strongly endorsing the Bipartisan Safer Communities Act signed by Joe Biden in 2022, and welcoming the establishment of a White House Office on Gun Violence Prevention in 2023.

Everytown

Everytown for Gun Safety (Everytown) was formed in 2013 when two groups, Moms Demand Action for Gun Sense and Mayors Against Illegal Guns, joined forces; it is the largest grassroots group fighting against gun violence in the US.

Everytown acknowledges that guns combined with hate are a lethal combination; they support the Disarm Hate Act, which would prohibit people convicted of hate crimes owning a firearm. Everytown also campaigns to raise awareness around this issue, calling for the act to become federal law and working to prevent hate-motivated violence against LGBTQIA+ young people, who are often led to suicidal thoughts as a consequence of being a victim of hate crimes.

Students Demand Action (SDA) are a group affiliated to Everytown and consist of young activists who are 'turning their outrage into action'. Originally established in 2018 as a pilot programme, in the aftermath of the mass shooting in Parkland, the group was launched as a national initiative and now has more than 600 groups across the US.

Wear Orange

The Wear Orange campaign is a movement that was started by the friends and family of Hadiya Pendleton, a 15-year-old girl who was fatally shot by an 18-year-old boy in Harsh Park, Chicago, in 2013 in a case of mistaken identity. After her death, Pendleton's family started an annual 'Wear Orange for Peace Party', a campaign to build a more peaceful future by tackling the problem of gun violence. Orange was chosen as the colour to wear because it was Pendleton's favourite colour, which symbolizes happiness and strength, and is used as a highly visible colour for protection.

Wear Orange's website states that 'firearms are the leading cause of death for children and teens in the US' and that 'by participating in Wear Orange [...] we will organize, advocate and rally for safer communities'.

Protestors at the annual Wear Orange Day to end gun violence march from Manhattan to Brooklyn, New York.

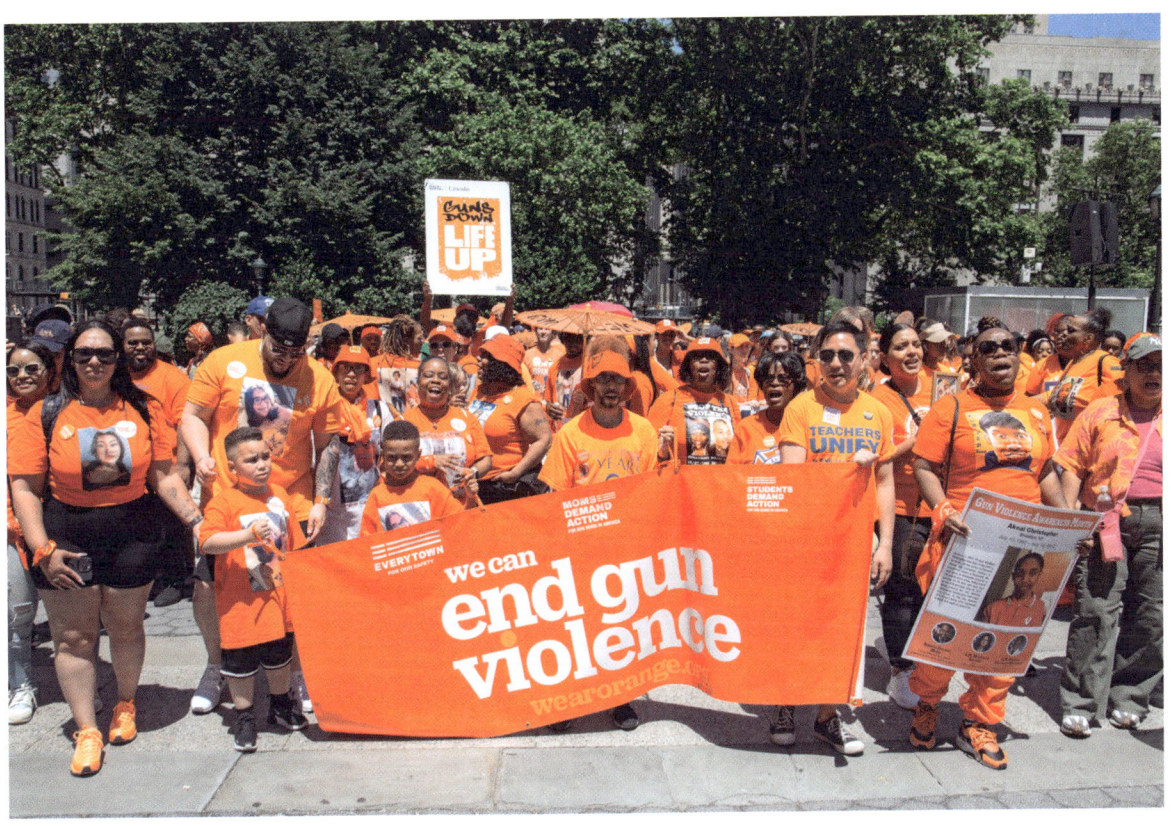

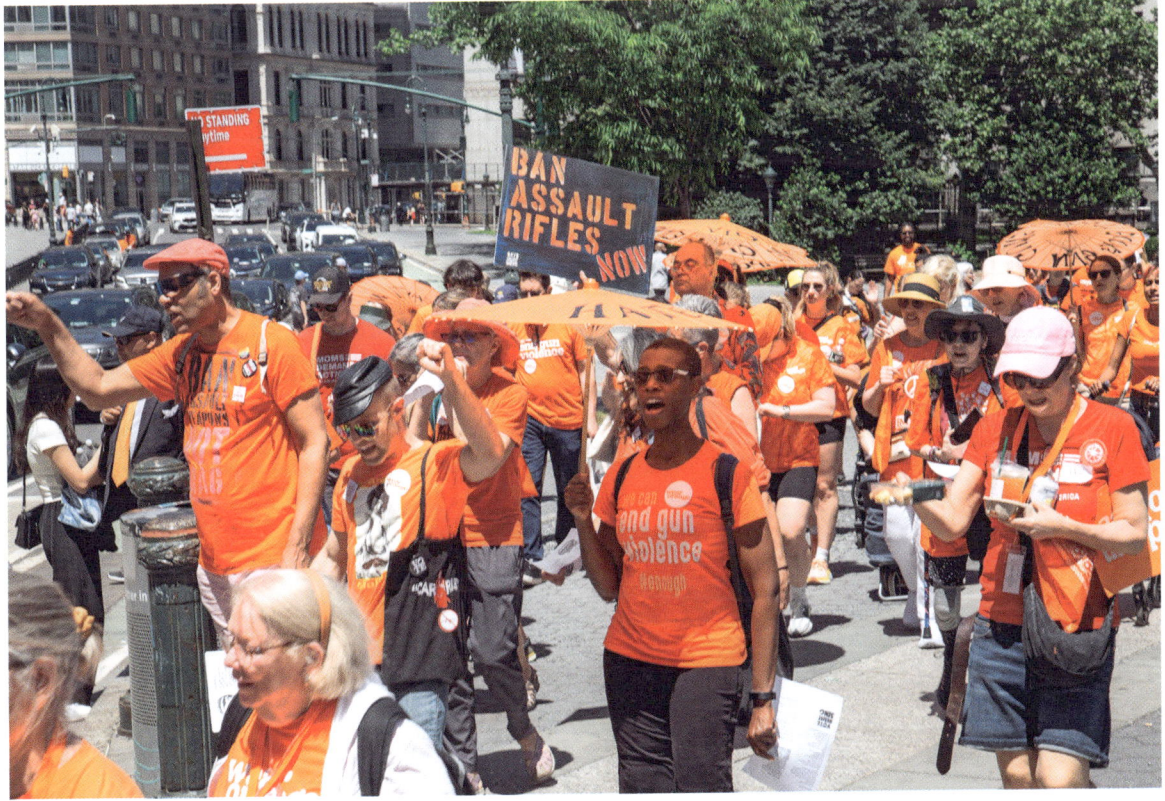

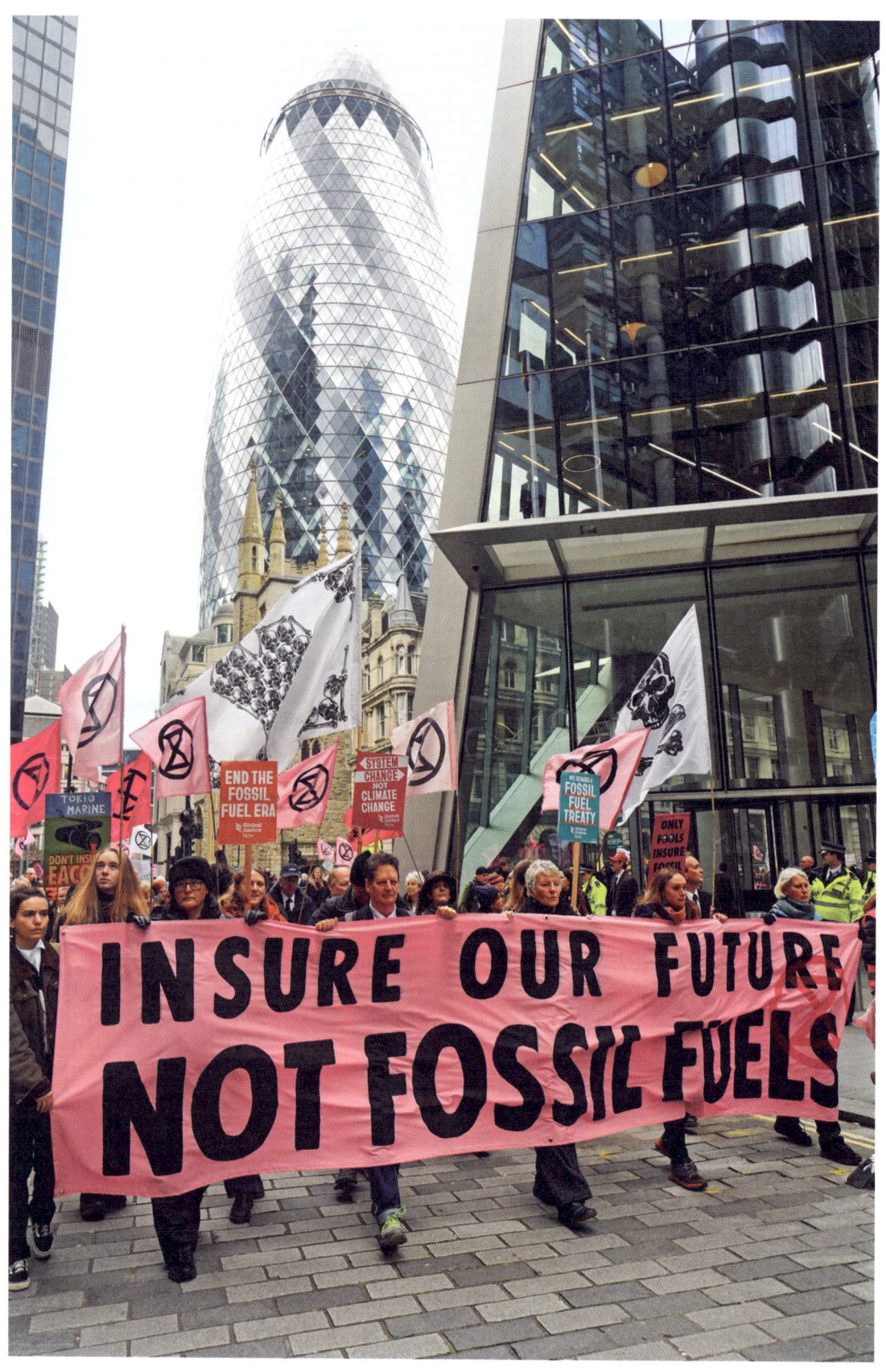

RESISTANCE FOR EXISTENCE

RESISTANCE FOR EXISTENCE

'I use performance to disrupt systems of power. In a context of planetary catastrophe, I'm committed to the potential of art to intervene; to challenge dominant structures and propose alternatives to an absurd status quo.'

JEREMY HUTCHISON

To exist we need resources. To thrive we need resources that are healthy, flourishing and free from pollution. But we are facing a climate crisis because we are destroying, degrading and depleting our environment as we exploit valuable natural resources and pollute our planet with toxic waste.

By burning fossil fuels, obliterating our forests and using industrial farming processes and fertilizers on a monumental scale, we are creating unprecedented levels of greenhouse-gas emissions and destroying ecosystems. This is causing rapid, severe and permanent changes in our global climate patterns.

Our actions affect livelihoods, food security, water availability and the balance of natural ecosystems, particularly for vulnerable communities who bear the brunt of extreme weather and resource scarcity. Addressing this crisis demands urgent and collective action to preserve the delicate systems that sustain life on earth.

Climate Change

Rising temperatures are leading to heatwaves, altered weather patterns and the melting of glaciers and polar ice, known as global warming. As a consequence, sea levels are rising, threatening the displacement and relocation of people. The acidification in our oceans from higher CO_2 levels is killing marine life. Infrastructure and human lives are in danger as the frequency and intensity of hurricanes, floods, droughts and wildfires increase. In turn this disrupts and destroys ecosystems and habitats, and endangers species, some of which are on the brink of extinction. Our air quality is impacted, water sources and food crops are contaminated, and we are losing biodiversity and habitable land. Every action has a profound knock-on effect.

All this is driven by consumer demand and corporate greed; the UN states, 'We are using the equivalent of 1.6 Earths to maintain our current way of life, and ecosystems cannot keep up with our demands.'

To combat climate change, we need to: transition to renewable energy programmes and keep fossil fuels in the ground; preserve and conserve rainforests, oceans, wetlands and natural habitats; implement sustainable transport, agricultural practices and energy-efficient homes; and lower our carbon footprints by making 'greener' lifestyle choices.

We have a climate emergency. We need to make smarter decisions, and we need to act now. Activists are responding, and the climate change movement is growing, but there needs to be more commitment from lawmakers in order to bring our planet back from the Anthropocene extinction we are creating.

OPPOSITE

Act Now (2024)

Brenda Jane Sanders

52×52cm (20.47×20.47in). Pieced and appliquéd with scraps of upcycled cotton fabrics, quilted.

The artist made this piece in response to our greed for instant gratification and useless things in a beautiful world. She questions what will be left for our children if we are not careful? (See also page 40.)

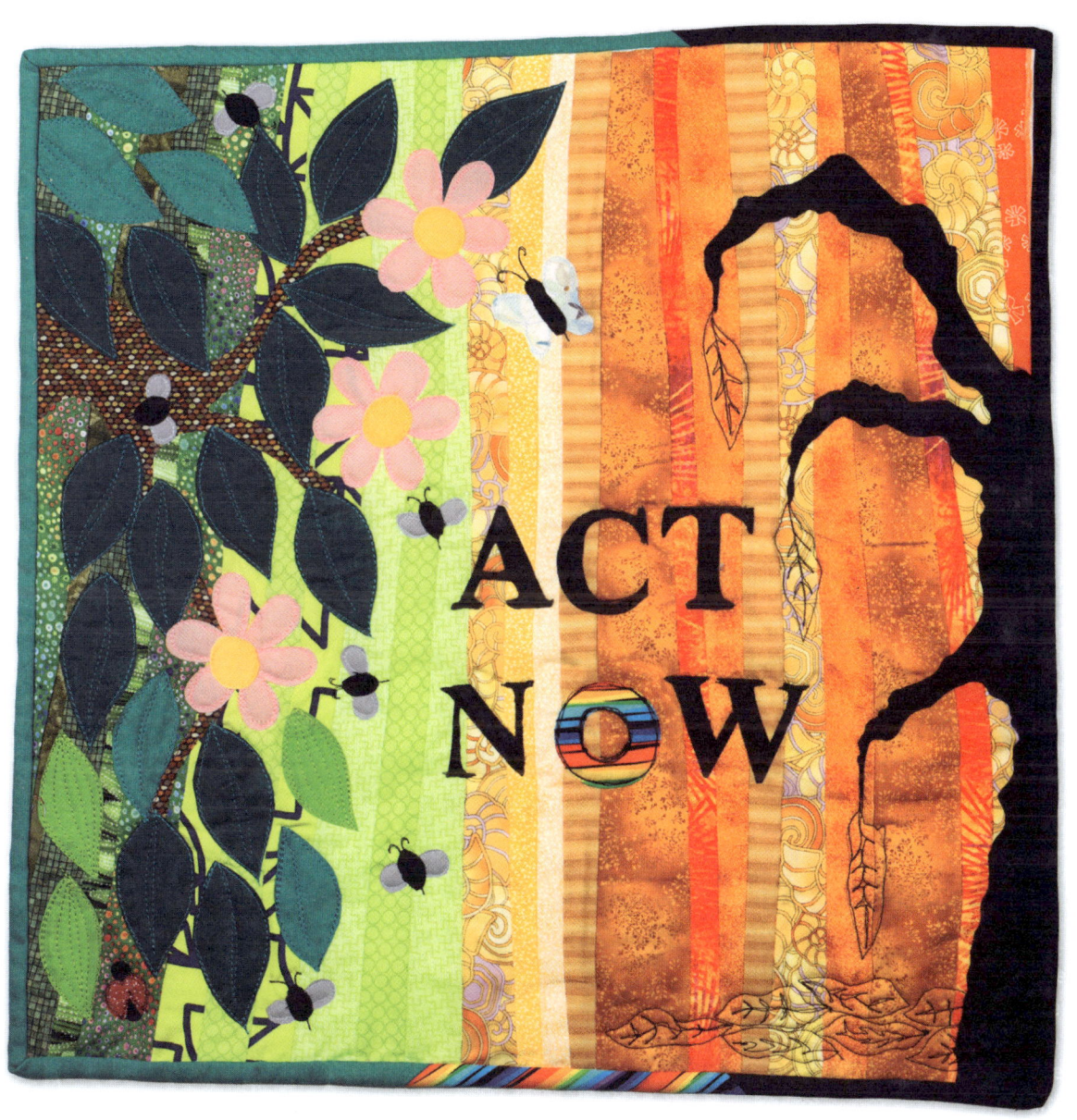

The Paris Agreement

The Paris Agreement, an international treaty signed by 195 parties in 2015, was a huge and important commitment towards reducing greenhouse-gas emissions and implementing long-term plans to combat climate change collectively, and is the most significant global climate agreement to date. It was built on previous legislation – the Montreal Protocol (1987) and the Kyoto Protocol (2005) – and is reviewed every five years.

The 26th session of the Conference of the Parties (COP 26) was held in Glasgow, UK, in November 2021, and negotiations led to the adoption of the Glasgow Climate Pact, committing to further reduce greenhouse-gas emissions and accelerate efforts to 'phase down' coal. The Paris Agreement was reaffirmed, to limit the global temperature rise 'well below 2°C above pre-industrial levels and pursuing efforts to limit this to 1.5°C'. In addition, more than one hundred countries pledged their commitment to ending deforestation by 2030. Although this progress for climate justice is a step in the right direction, many regarded this as a diluted outcome, as UN experts declare, 'The world is massively off track to limit global warming to 1.5°C.'

Greenpeace

Founded in 1971 by a group of activists who set sail in a boat called Phyllis Cormack – later renamed the Greenpeace by those on board – to try to stop a US nuclear weapons test off the coast of Alaska, the organization has grown in stature and has become a global movement. Its vision is for 'a greener, healthier and more peaceful planet, one that can sustain life for generations to come'.

Greenpeace is an organization at the forefront of educating and mobilizing the public on the urgency of climate change, calling for collective action, through peaceful protest, to pressurize multinational businesses to reduce emissions and to lobby governments towards making policy changes at such a 'pivotal point in human history'.

Greenpeace's skill-based activists are trained in 'Nonviolent Direct Action and Boat, Climbing or Kayak' practices. Many have

OPPOSITE

Greenpeace activists occupy the roof of Parliament to demand politicians pay more attention to climate change, 11 October 2009.

OVERLEAF

Activists in kayaks raise a banner reading 'sHellNo.org Arctic Drilling = Climate Chaos' as Shell's Polar Pioneer drill platform moves across Elliott Bay into the Port of Seattle where Shell is preparing its drilling equipment for oil exploration in the Alaskan Arctic.

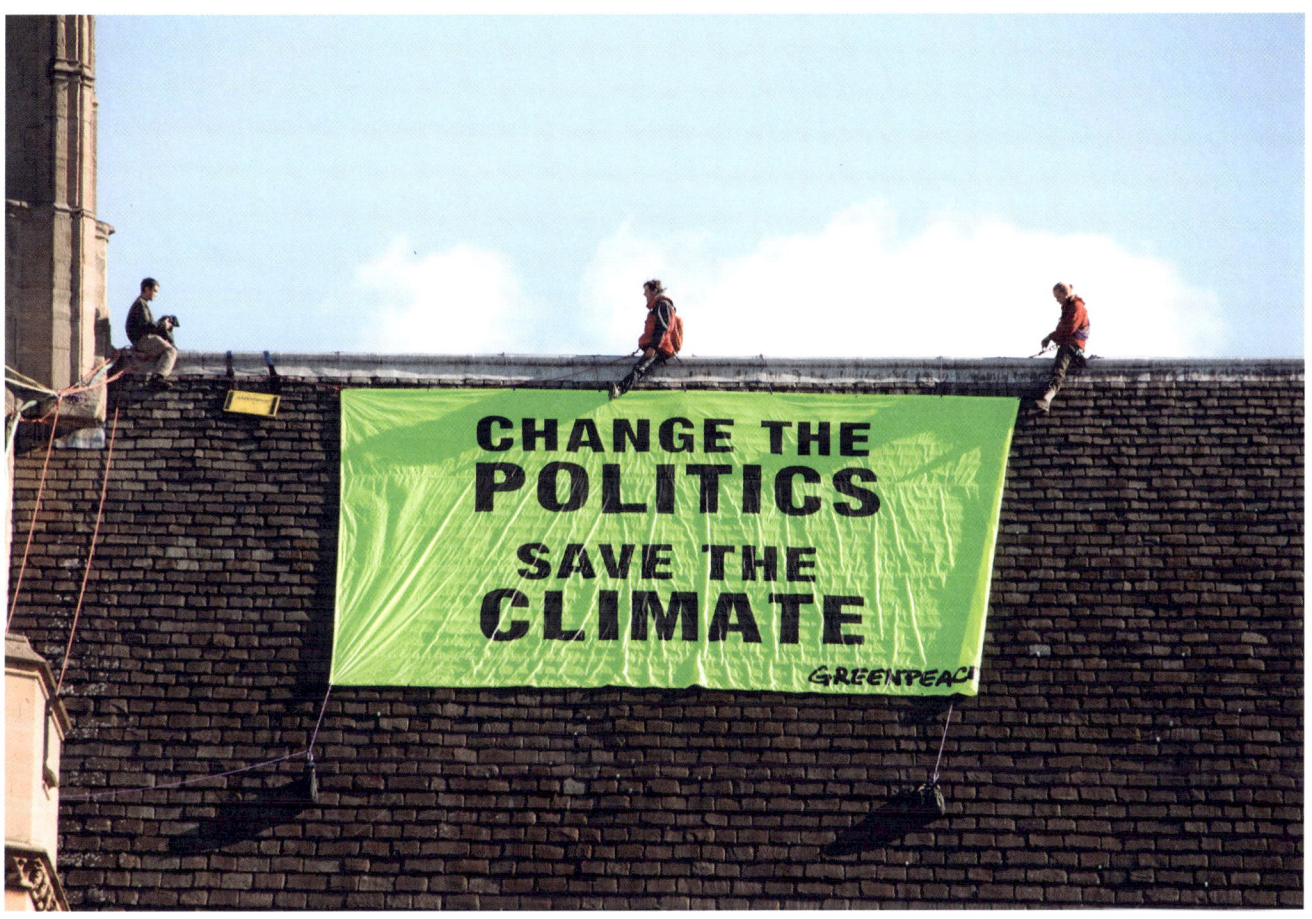

gained worldwide attention with their high-profile, tactically planned demonstrations as they work to investigate, document and expose the causes of environmental disasters and destruction, often placing themselves on famous buildings, exposed rooftops, industrial machinery or in the middle of forests or oceans. Their banners are durable, large and uncompromising – not just to gain attention, but to endure the weather or harsh conditions they are placed in.

Greenpeace often targets the fossil fuel industries and food conglomerates with their direct-action campaigns, carrying out demonstrations in dangerous territories and conditions, in order to prevent the acceleration of the climate emergency. In 2015 their successful campaign to stop Shell drilling for oil in the Arctic was a triumph.

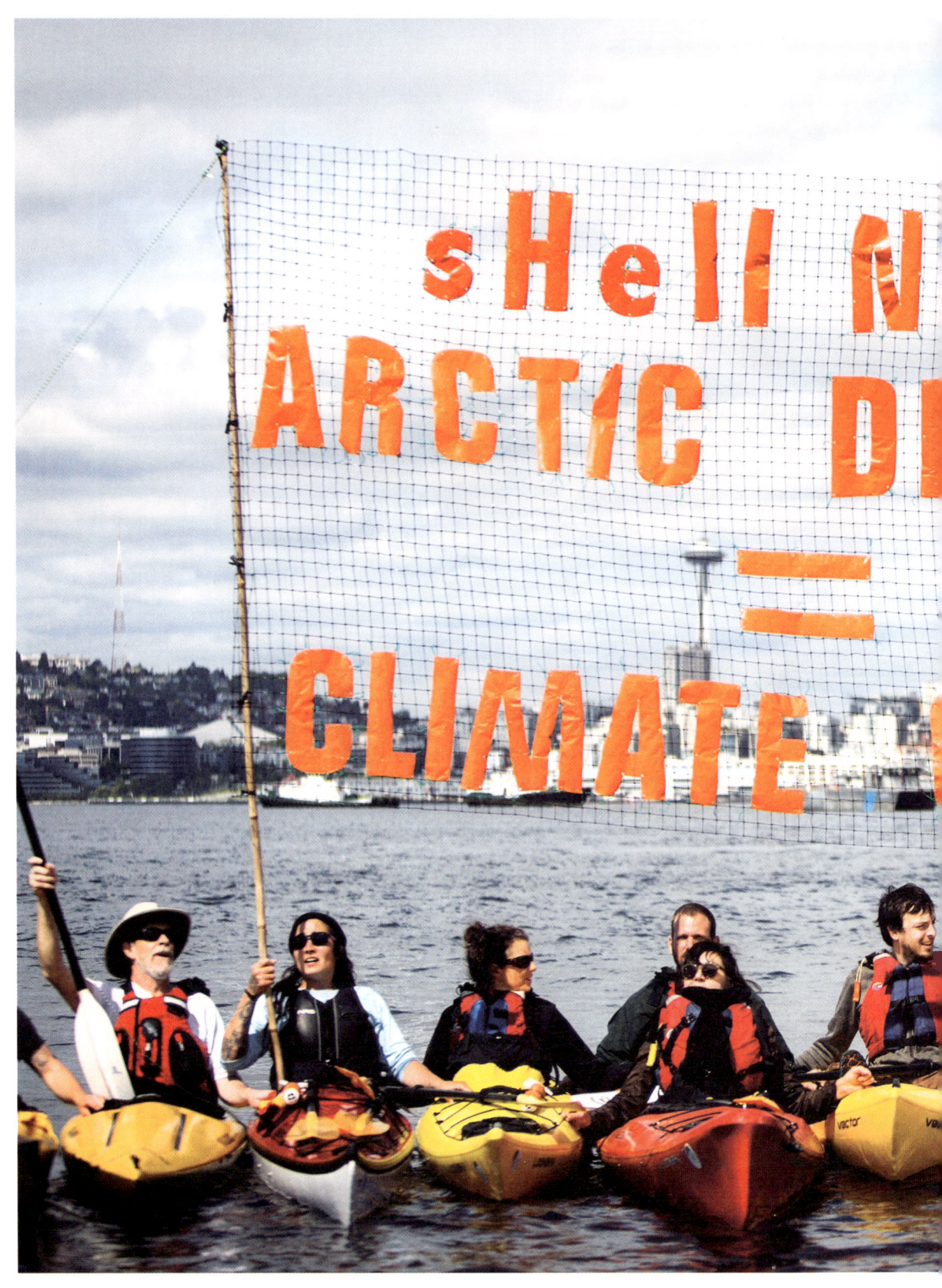

RESISTANCE FOR EXISTENCE

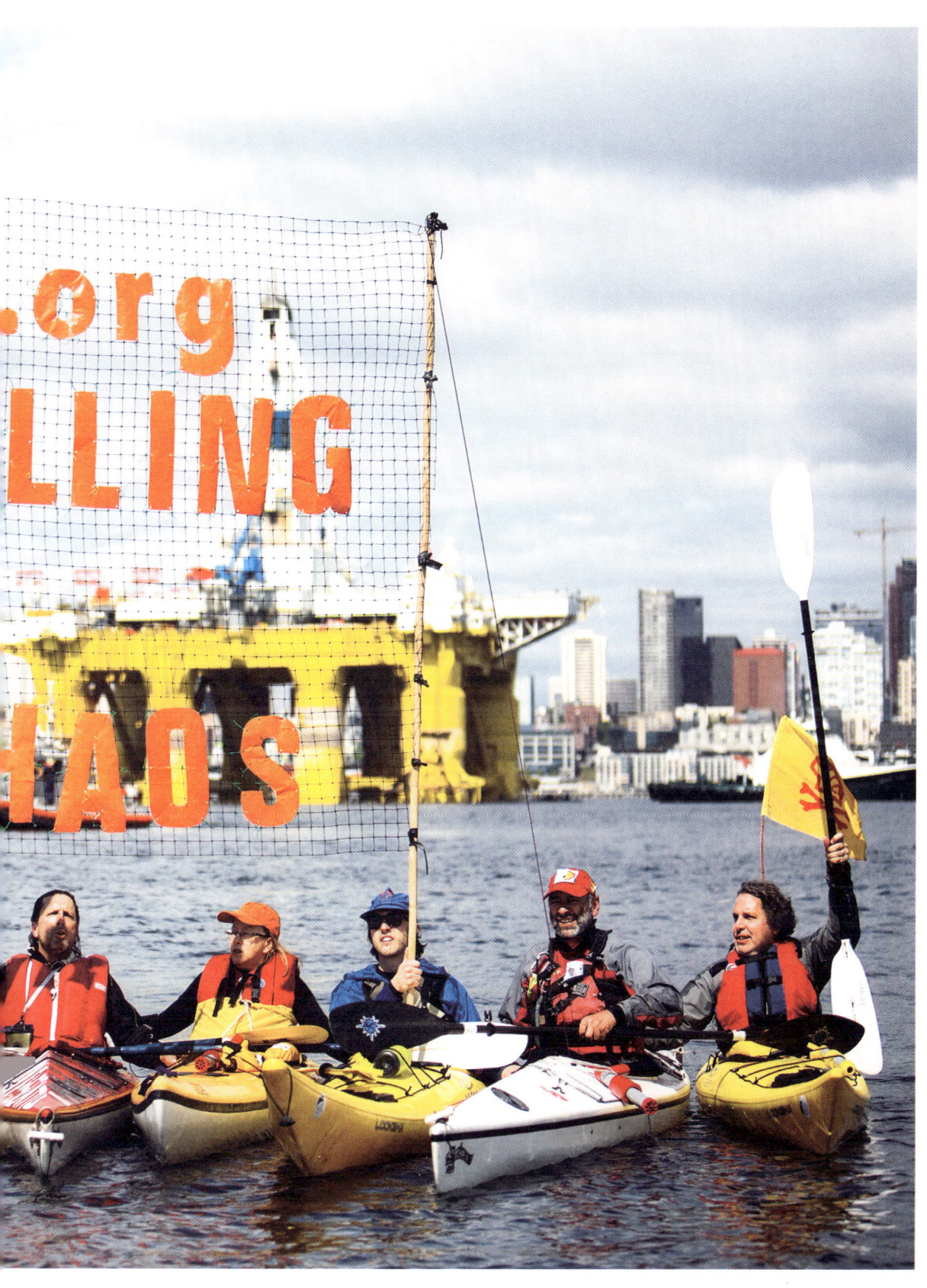

Fossil Fuels

Coal, crude oil, natural gas and petroleum products are fossil fuels, which are non-renewable energy sources. As they are naturally formed from plant and animal matter from millions of years ago, they have a high carbon content. When burned, fossil fuels emit carbon dioxide causing greenhouse-gas emissions and global warming. Although the burning of fossil fuels is the main driver of the climate crisis, the processes of their extraction, such as mining, drilling and fracking, also take an enormous toll on our environment. These processes destroy ecosystems and wildlife habitats, pollute waterways with toxic run-off, decimate ancient and natural landscapes irreparably, pollute air with particulate matter and contribute to ocean acidification. Fossil fuels need to be kept in the ground.

Sacred Stone Camp

In April 2016, the Standing Rock Sioux Tribe (SRST) defended their Indigenous land rights against the Dakota Access Pipeline (DAPL) construction from their Sacred Stone (protest) Camp, and brought to international attention the issues surrounding the destruction of their sacred sites and the detrimental impact on the environment, particularly where the pipeline traverses under Lake Oahe. A leak along the pipeline route would contaminate this water source, which is crucial for the reservation.

Although SRST were successful in halting operations and achieved some small victories in court, the underground pipeline went ahead and can transport up to 750,000 barrels of fracked crude oil per day from the Bakken oil fields, North Dakota, to Patoka, Illinois – a distance of 1,186km (1,172mi). The DAPL is still under scrutiny from SRST, and international environmentalists and ecologists.

OPPOSITE

Members of the Standing Rock Sioux Tribe march to a burial ground sacred site that was disturbed by bulldozers building the Dakota Access Pipeline (DAPL), 4 September 2016.

OVERLEAF

Indigenous people from numerous tribes attend a protest against the Dakota Access pipeline in Washington DC, 10 March 2017.

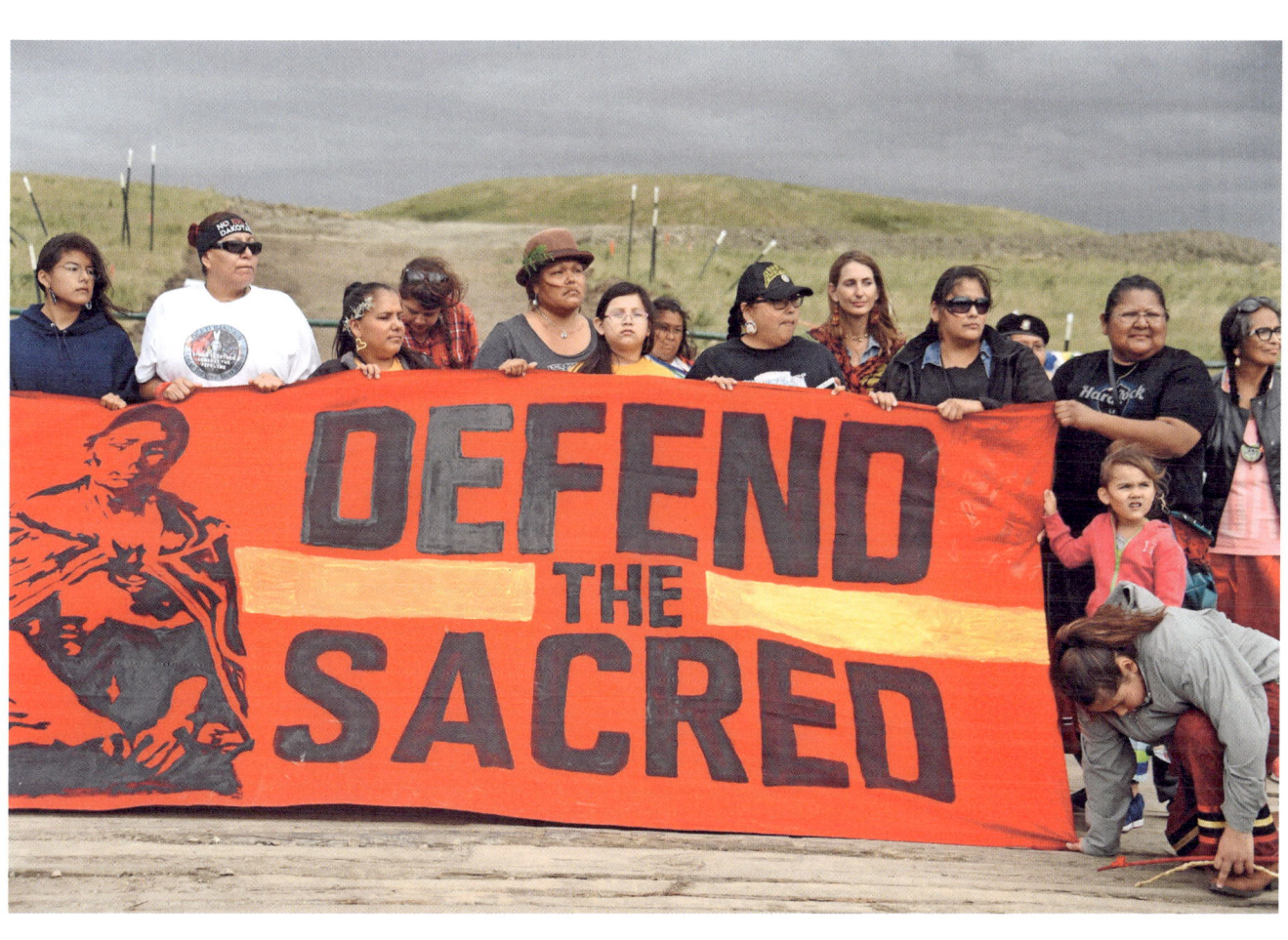

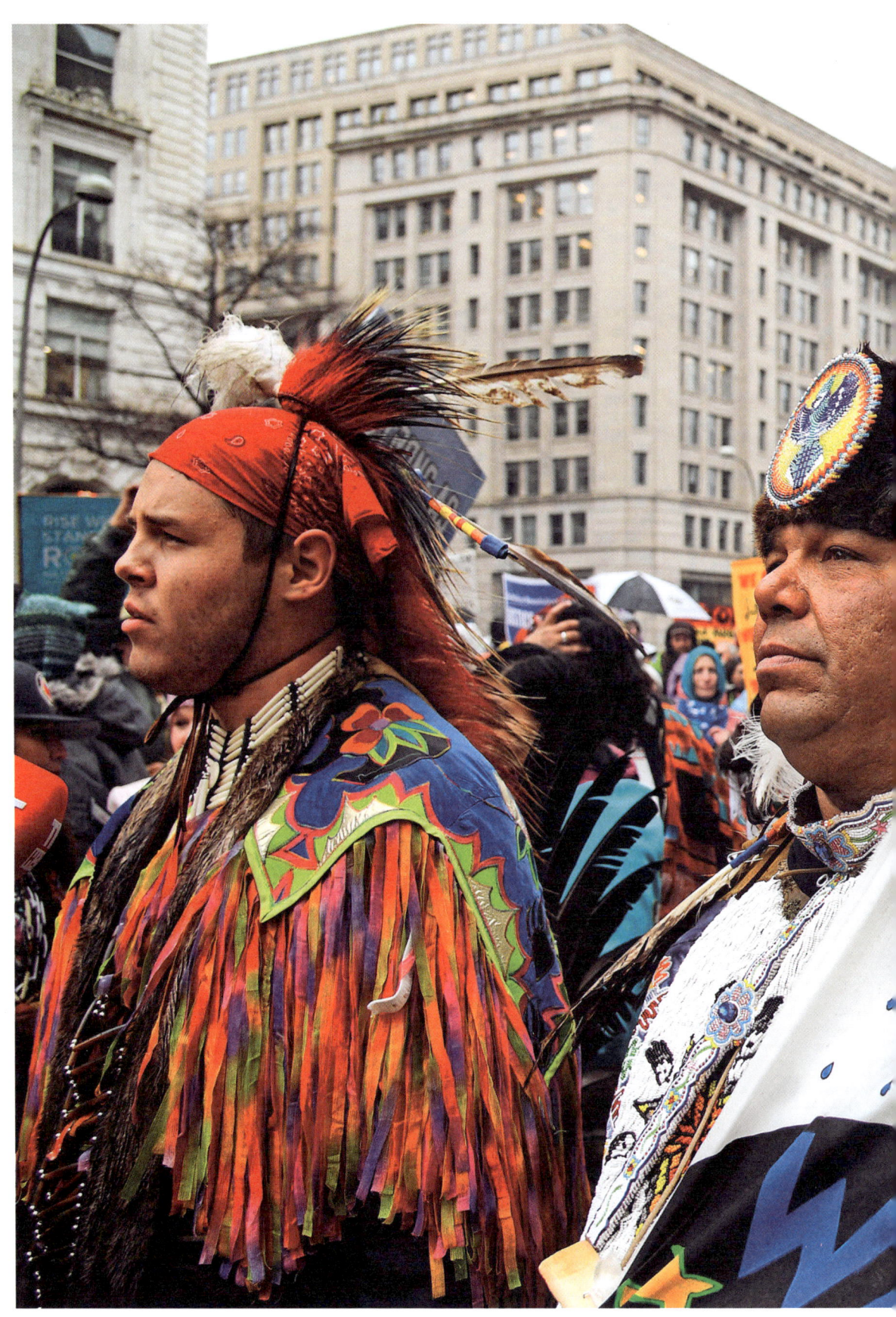

RESISTANCE FOR EXISTENCE

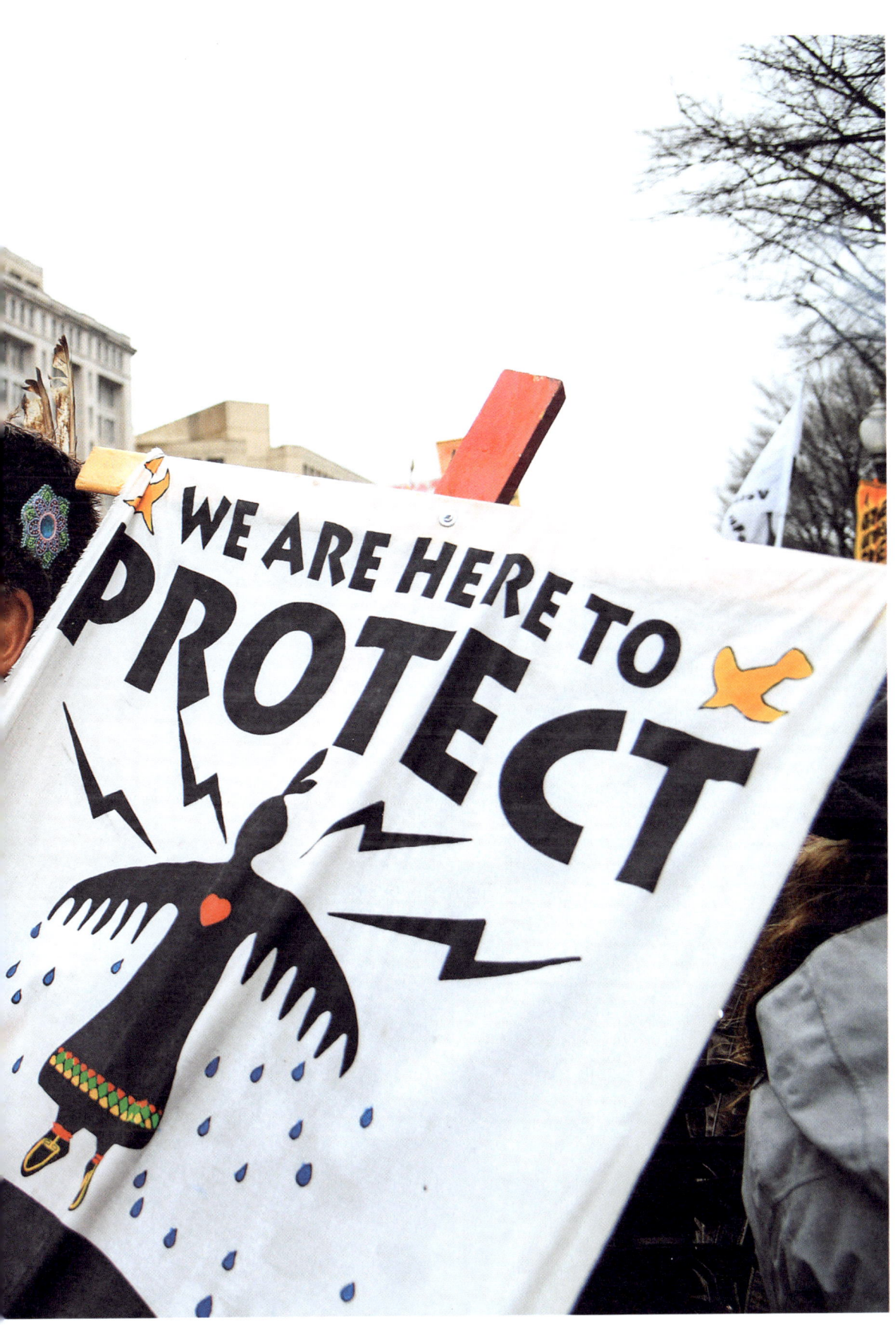

Campaign to Protect Pont Valley

For more than 40 years, residents in Pont Valley, County Durham, UK, faced the threat of a new opencast coal mine opening just 300m (330yd) from their houses. The public fought several successful campaigns and three High Court battles (in 1986, 2001 and 2011) against UK Coal to prevent this happening, but lost the fourth on appeal in 2015. The decision to grant mining rights was controversial, as the UK was on the verge of signing the Paris Agreement and UK Coal had gone bankrupt. But Banks Group bought UK Coal's permit, with a limited time frame to begin operations. To deter them from reaching this timeframe and to protect the valley from opencast mining, locals, assisted by experienced international activists, set up the Pont Valley Protection Camp (PVPC) in early March 2018, on the site of the proposed opencast area.

The protest camp drew much media attention during its defiant fight, and the international community watched developments as protestors held many peaceful demonstrations on the verge adjacent to the site and outside court hearings. When Banks Group started its operations in June 2018, the camp was relocated along the valley; activists continued their protest and carried out many acts of civil disobedience, such as blockades, lock-ons and sit-ins, some of which led to clashes with the police, arrests and evictions.

Protest textiles played a significant part in the campaign. Red ribbons and strips of fabric were frequently tied onto the abandoned public footpath signs and barricades, then replaced when they were removed, and many banners were painted, printed and stitched with stark messages about the environmental impact of opencast mining, and requests to stop it. The great crested newt was adopted as the logo of the campaign. This rare protected species was found onsite in the wetland habitat of the valley by site surveyors, including UK Coal, over a period of years, but Banks Groups denied the presence of the endangered newts and was accused of a committing a wildlife crime when they began mining.

Jane Gower, a local artist, painted a banner that was carried in the large procession at the Miners' Gala (known as the 'Big Meeting') in Durham on 14 July 2018. The Gala, celebrated annually, was established in 1871 as part of the miners' trade

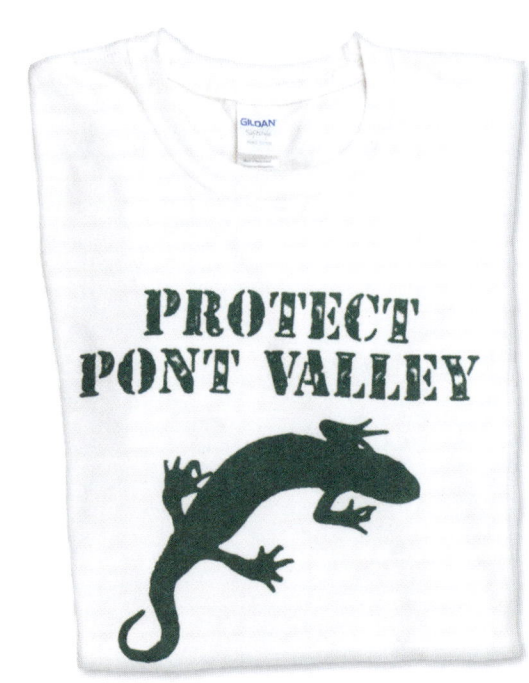

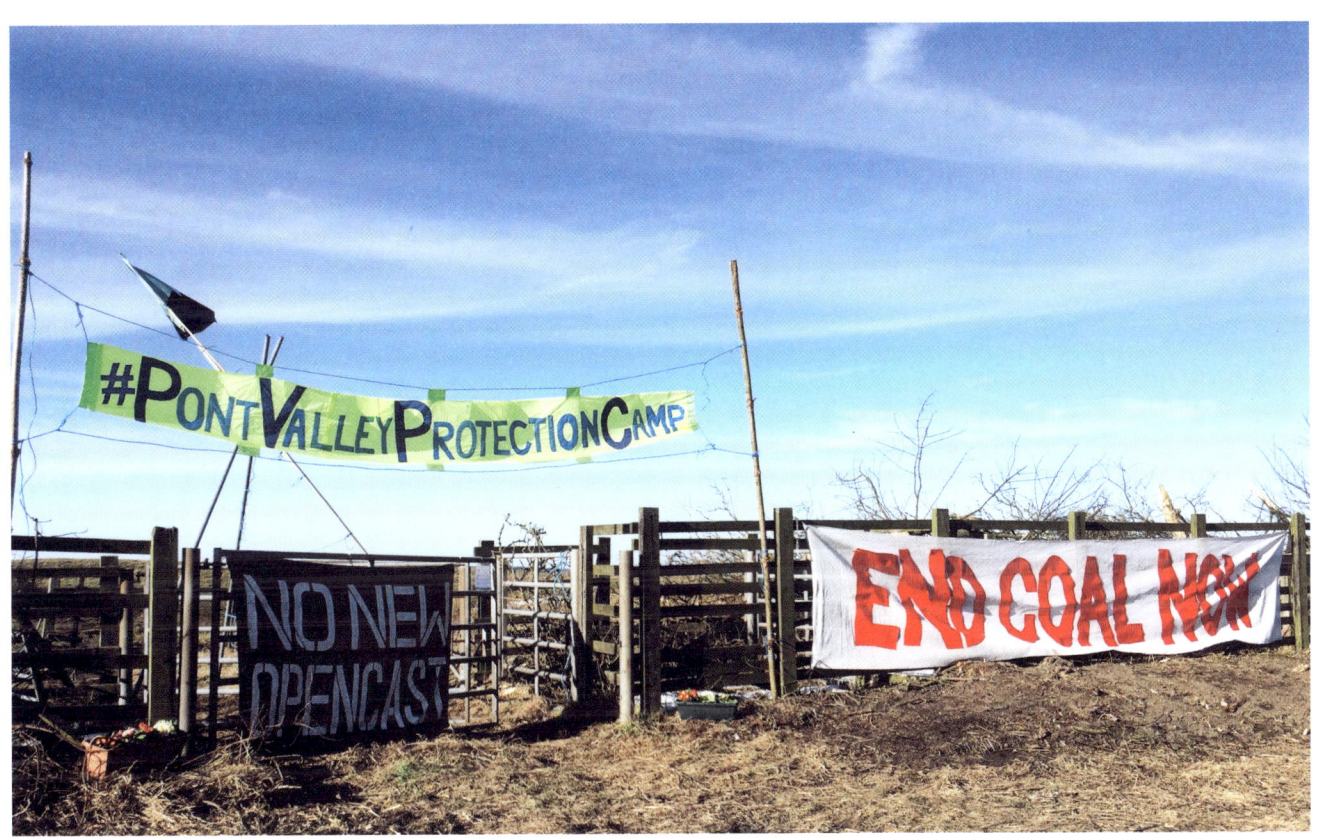

union movement. It was a triumph for the Campaign to Protect Pont Valley to be invited to join the parade, enabling them to display their anti-opencast banner alongside historical banners celebrating the working-class culture and history of deep mining in the area.

PVPC was finally dismantled late in the summer of 2018, but has become the subject of an award-winning film entitled *Finite: The Climate of Change*, which portrays an insider's view of defiance and direct action in the battle to stop climate change. Director Rich Felgate filmed the alliance that evolved between the activists protecting Pont Valley and those protecting the Hambach Forest in Germany.

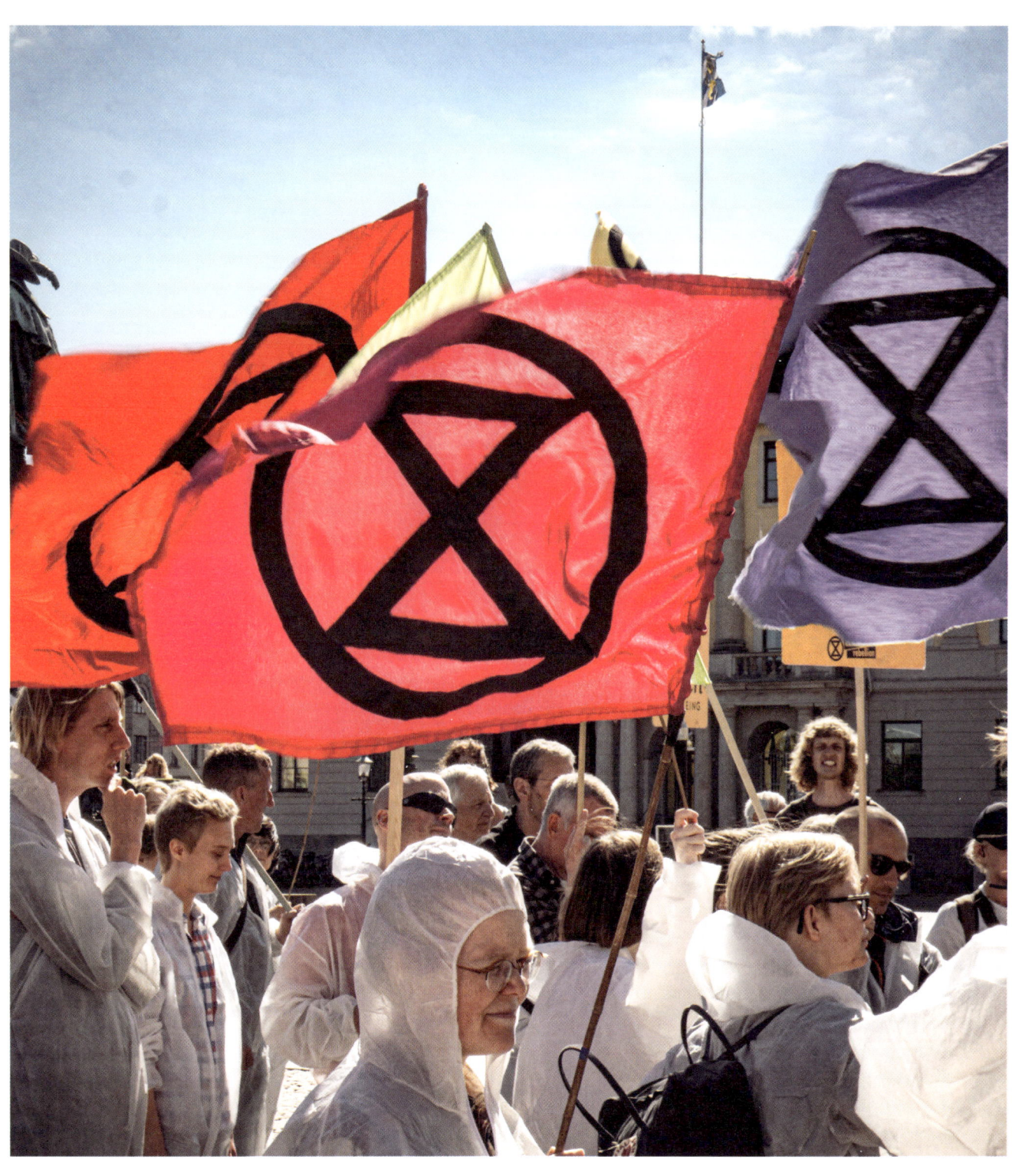

RESISTANCE FOR EXISTENCE

Extinction Rebellion

BELOW AND OPPOSITE

Extinction Rebellion march to challenge governments to address the climate emergency.

OVERLEAF

'Red rebels' from Extinction Rebellion gather in Trafalgar Square, to protest about the police ban on more than two XR members being together, 16 October 2019.

Extinction Rebellion (XR) is a non-partisan global movement that encourages non-violent direct action to challenge governments to act urgently and justly on the climate and ecological emergency. XR evolved from the campaign group Rising UP! and gained notoriety in October 2018 after a sit-in at Greenpeace's headquarters, urging their members to 'participate in mass disobedience as the only remaining alternative to avert the worst catastrophe'. On 31 October 2018, XR held a rally in Parliament Square where their 'Declaration of Rebellion' was proclaimed, and prominent environmentalists and activists, including Greta Thunberg (Swedish climate activist), Caroline Lucas (then a UK Member of Parliament for the Green Party) and George Monbiot (journalist and activist), gave speeches calling for climate action in support of XR's vision.

'Rebellion Day' was declared on 17 November 2018 where a coordinated action saw 6,000 people blockade major London bridges, disrupting traffic for hours; it was described by the *Guardian* as 'one of the biggest acts of civil disobedience in the UK in decades'. XR's grassroots campaign swiftly became a prominent international force, with an ever-growing membership.

Based on Doug Francisco's Invisible Circus troupe, and with his help, XR protesters have an army of performers known as the Red Rebel Brigade. They dress in scarlet robes, headdresses and veils and paint their faces white; the brilliant red signifies the blood of species. With slow and silent movements, they gather at protests to dramatically impress the importance and depth of non-violent direct action in the climate movement.

XR's logo is an encircled hourglass to symbolize time running out. This is seen on homemade flags and banners of different scales at every XR demonstration. The group continues to call for a rebellion 'against the systems that got us here' because 'our climate is changing faster than scientists predicted'.

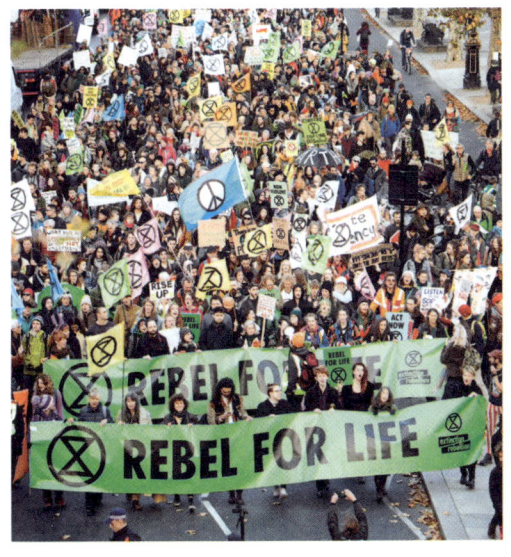

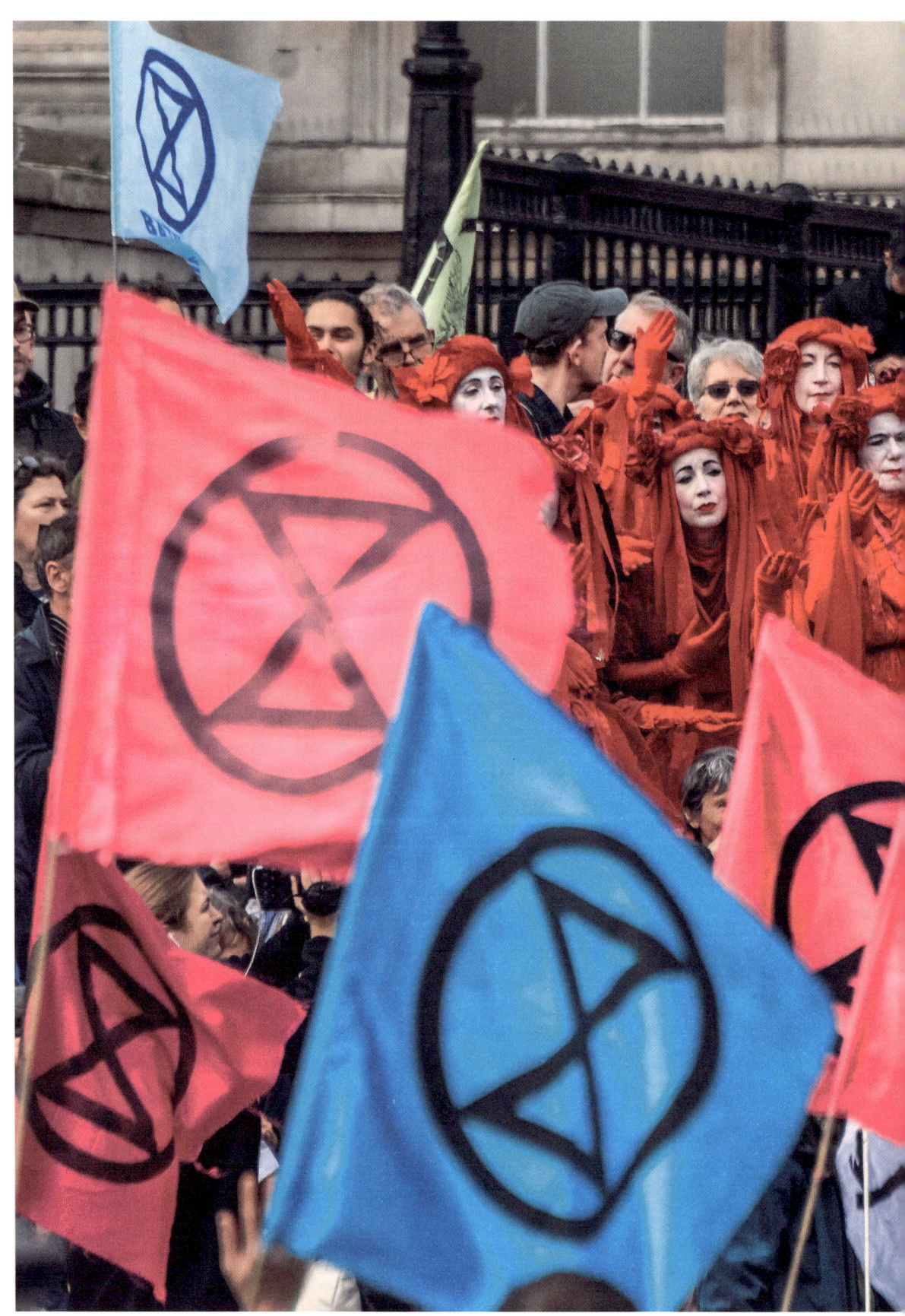

RESISTANCE FOR EXISTENCE

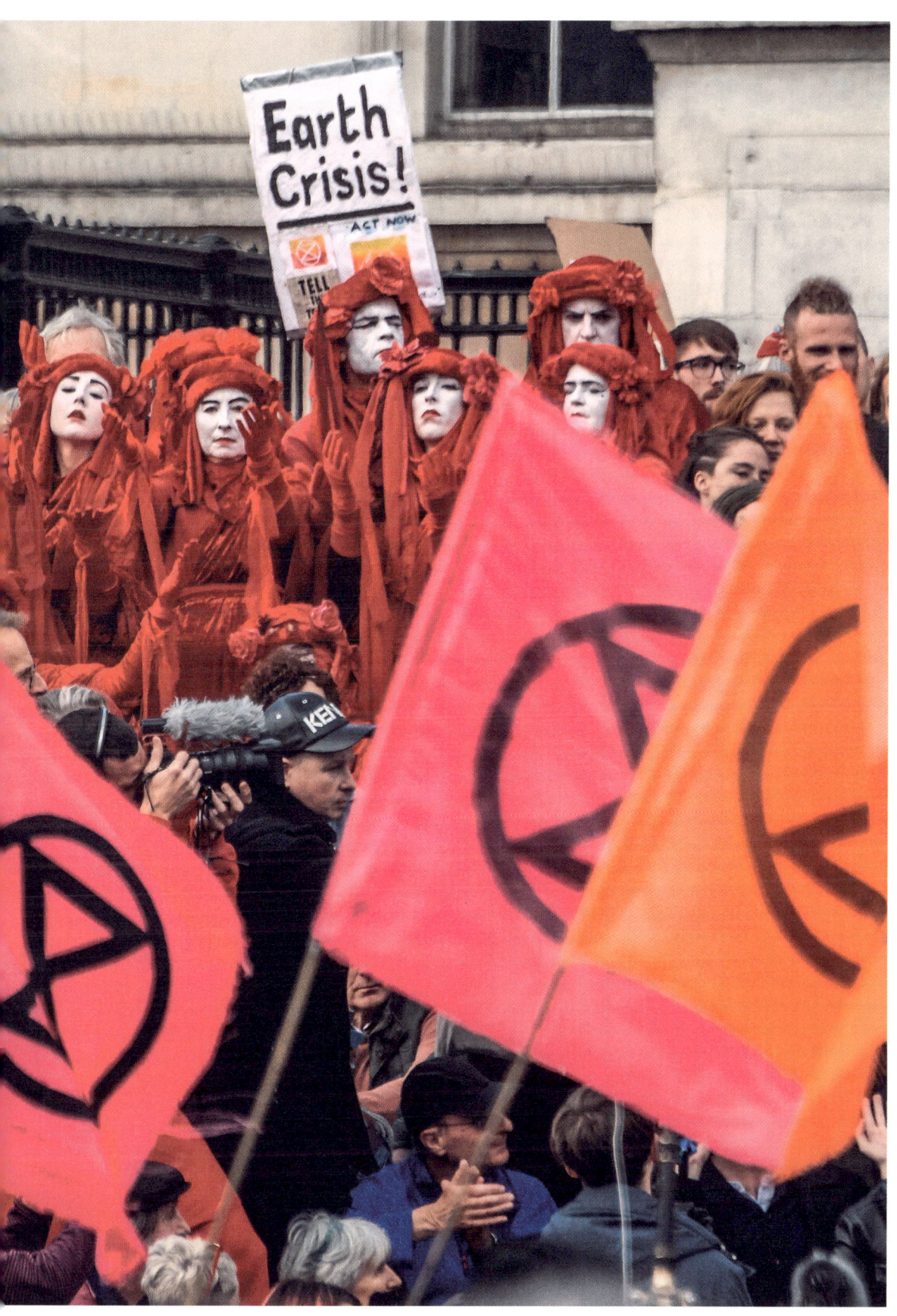

Just Stop Oil

Just Stop Oil (JSO), founded in 2022, are a UK-based environmental activist group whose aim is to highlight the issues of the climate emergency to prevent further fossil fuel extraction. JSO describe themselves as a 'non-violent resistance group', but the organization takes a bold direct-action approach, sometimes with controversial tactics, including vandalism. Their aim is to apply pressure on the UK government by banding together to form a revolution of civil resistance.

Their protests have been high profile and caused much disruption. For example, JSO protestors have slow-walked to create traffic jams, blockaded oil refineries and petrol stations, disrupted the 2022 British Grand Prix and other significant sporting events, interrupted West End theatre productions, glued themselves to famous artworks, and sprayed orange paint over significant buildings (the BBC, Scotland Yard, Harrods and the Bank of England) and monuments – most notably at Stonehenge in 2024 when three menhirs were vandalized. (The protestors actually used an orange cornflour mixture that would not permanently damage the stones.)

As with many radical groups, JSO have a visual identity. They have adopted a skull logo, but more recognizable and memorable is their adopted colour: orange. Orange stands for energy and drive, change and dissent. Orange is the colour of revolutions and unity, chosen by political movements and activists to bring attention to campaigns such as human rights violations, gun violence and ecological causes. From high-vis vests to cans of tomato soup, JSO uses the colour in many ways and many forms, including in a range of wearable textiles and banners.

Environmental Degradation

The extraction and burning of fossil fuels is a huge driver in the climate crisis, but our planet is also facing an unprecedented threat from the by-products of consumerism, particularly in the forms of waste and pollution, which contribute to the degradation of our environment. Our overfished oceans are filling with plastic waste and untreated sewage. Rivers are polluted with toxic waste from heavy metals, agricultural run-off and industrial discharges.

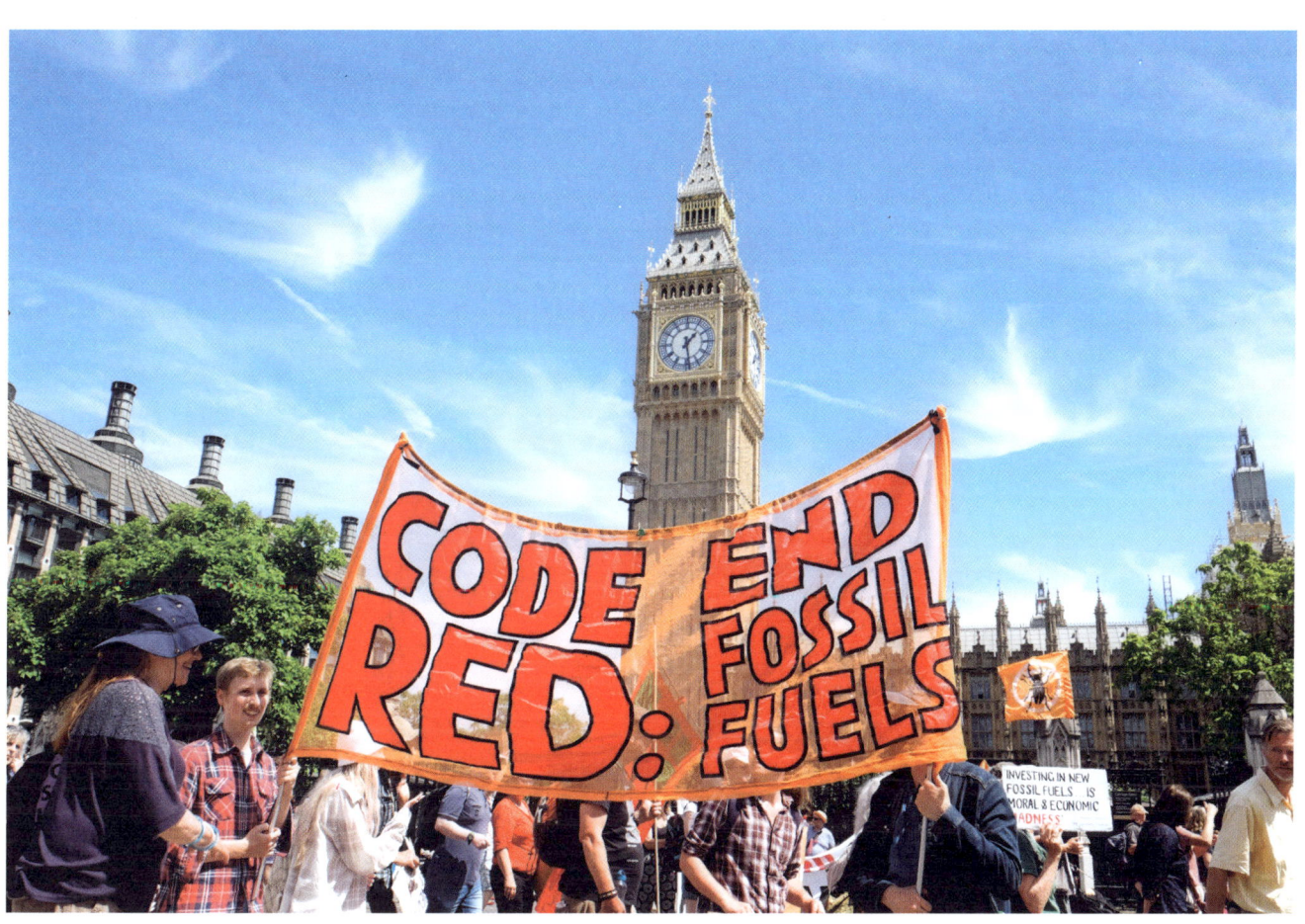

Deforestation, logging and mining practices are creating barren wastelands, soil erosion and irreversible environmental damage. And we are making mountains of hazardous waste that will not biodegrade.

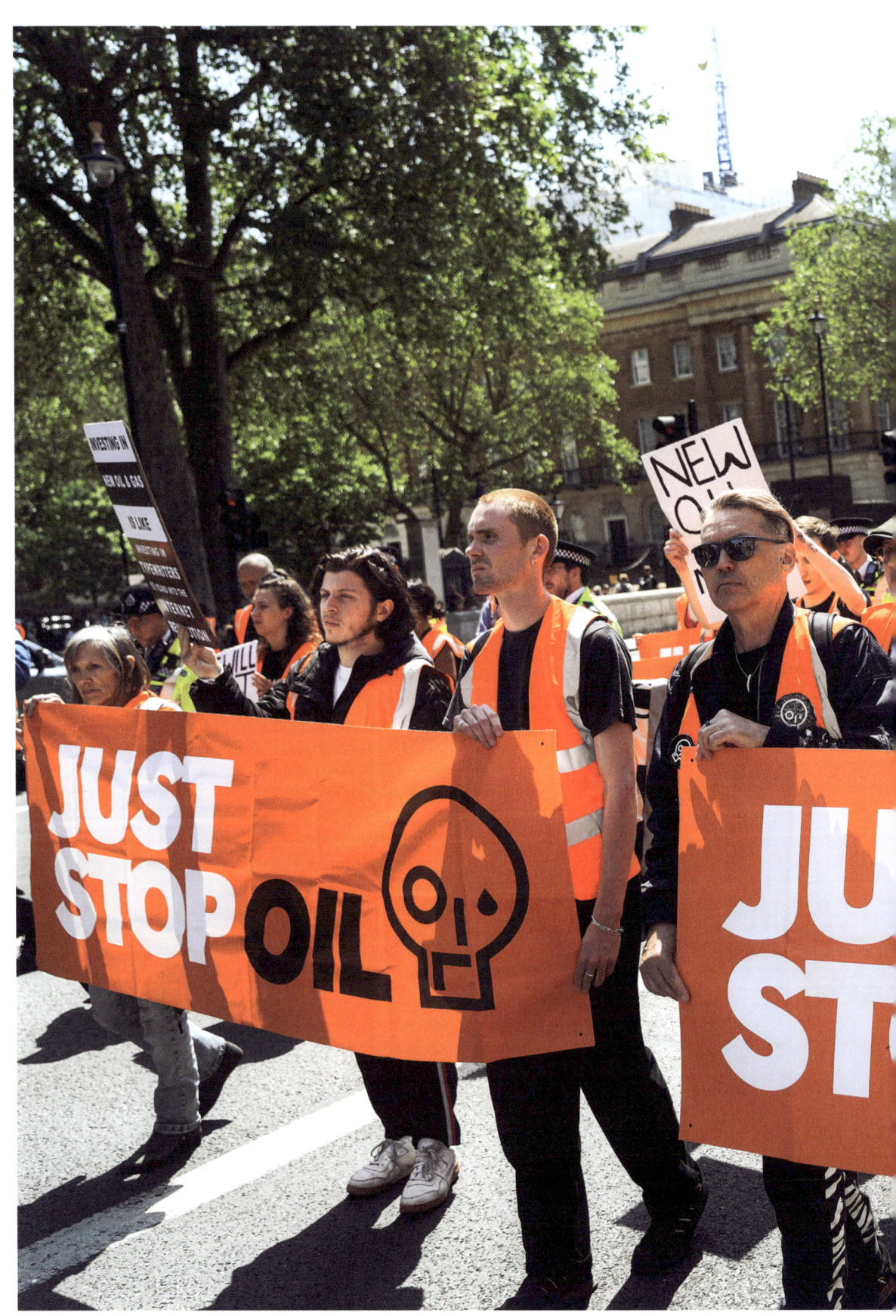

RESISTANCE FOR EXISTENCE

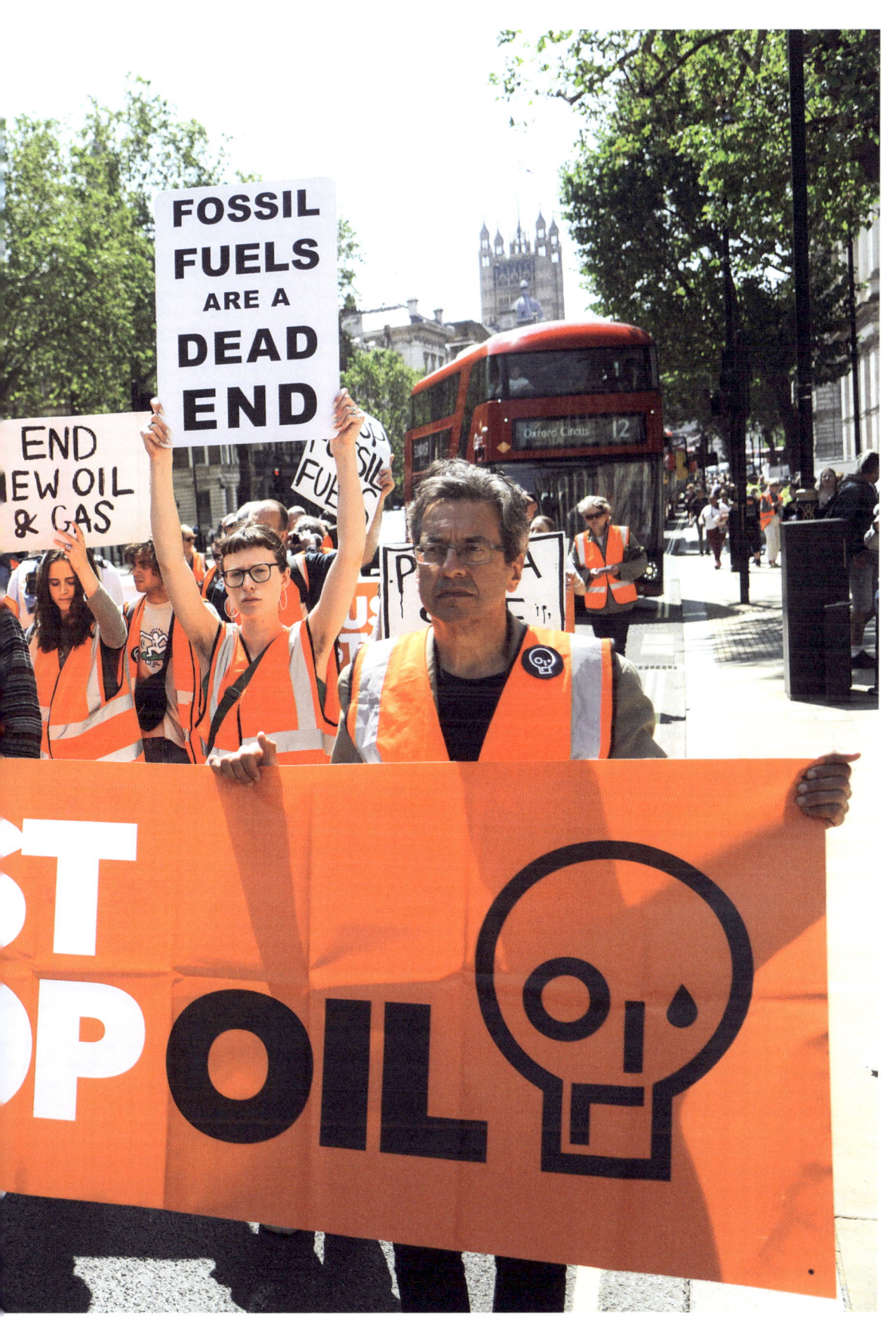

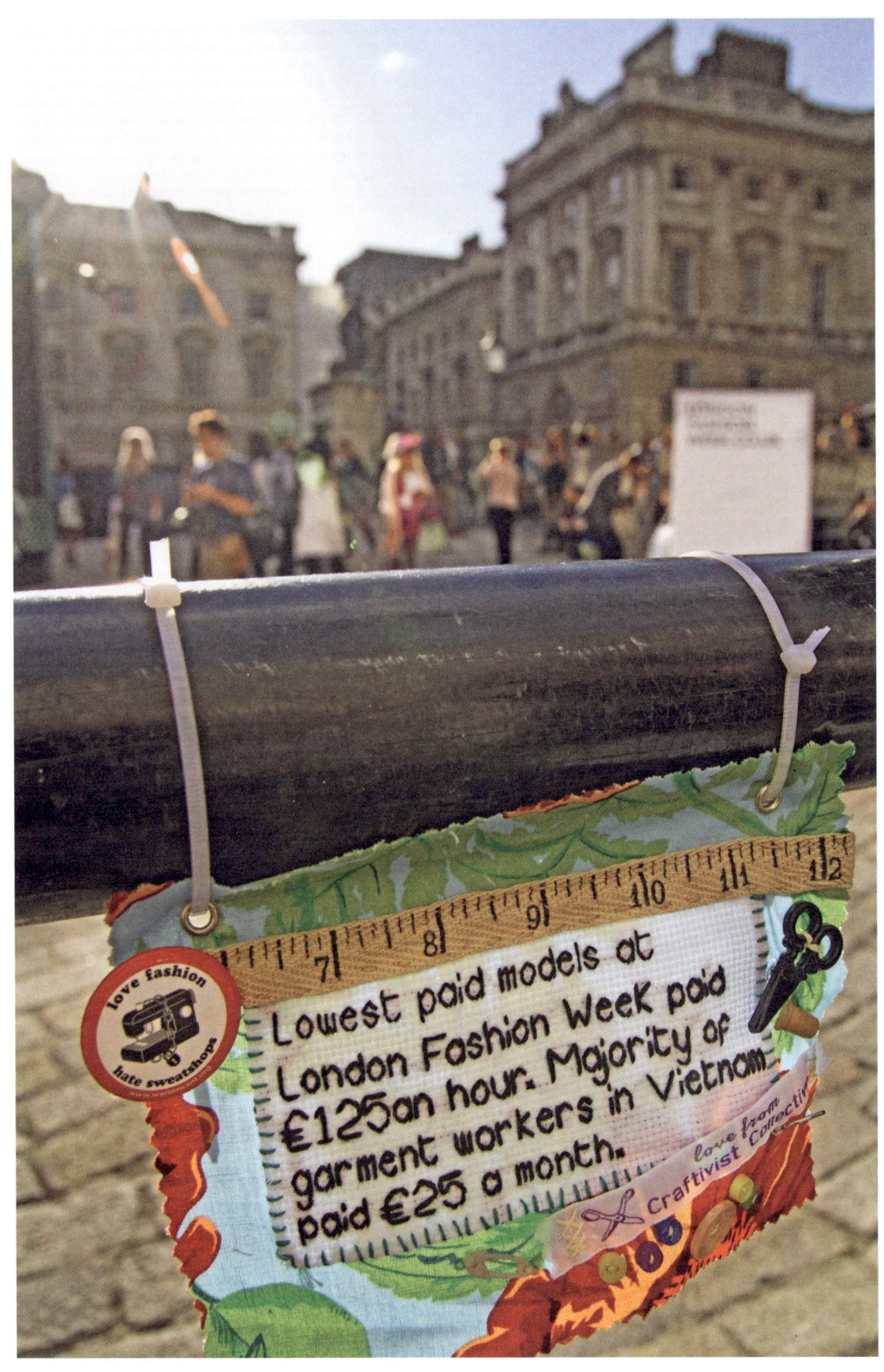

Lowest paid models at London Fashion Week paid €125 an hour. Majority of garment workers in Vietnam paid €25 a month.

love fashion hate sweatshops

love from Craftivist Collective

Fast Fashion

Because of its manufacturing processes, the fashion industry has a massive carbon footprint and contributes to approximately one tenth of the world's carbon emissions.

Every stage of production – from sourcing raw materials, preparing and producing fibres, and the dyeing, bleaching and finishing processes, to the assembly of garments – relies heavily on vast amounts of water and energy. The industry's water-intensive practices contribute to the planet's depleted resources and the contamination of water sources, which has a lasting effect on aquatic ecosystems. The UN states that textile dyeing is 'the second largest polluter of water globally'.

In addition, the production of synthetic fibres, such as polyester, nylon and acrylic, is fossil fuel based. Per wash load, these textiles shed thousands of microfibres – a significant amount of which bypass treatment systems and ultimately end up in our waterways.

As the fashion industry is under increased pressure to reduce its carbon footprint, 'greenwashing' is rife with token efforts and deceptive marketing practices being used to cover up unethically sourced materials and environmentally harmful practices. A garment might be labelled 'eco-friendly' or 'biodegradable', to tempt the consumer into buying a 'green' product, but these claims can be without substance and deliberately used to mislead.

Fast fashion is cheap, accessible and convenient. As demand has grown, and the mass-manufacturing production of apparel has been outsourced to the Global South (for example, China, Vietnam, India and Bangladesh) where labour is cheaper, and health and safety legislation is often not implemented, fashion retail companies have cut their costs whilst increasing production, and this has led to a vicious cycle of fast-fashion consumerism.

Garment industry workers are often subject to long hours, extremely low pay and few workers' rights. They often stitch on production lines in sweatshops in confined spaces, breathing air filled with toxic textile fibres and dust, and face the risk of their workspaces collapsing around them, as happened in the Rana Plaza factory in Bangladesh when 1,134 died in 2013.

In the aftermath of this tragedy, the International Accord (for health and safety in the textile and garment industry) was signed by hundreds of international brands and retailers pledging support for workplace safety programmes.

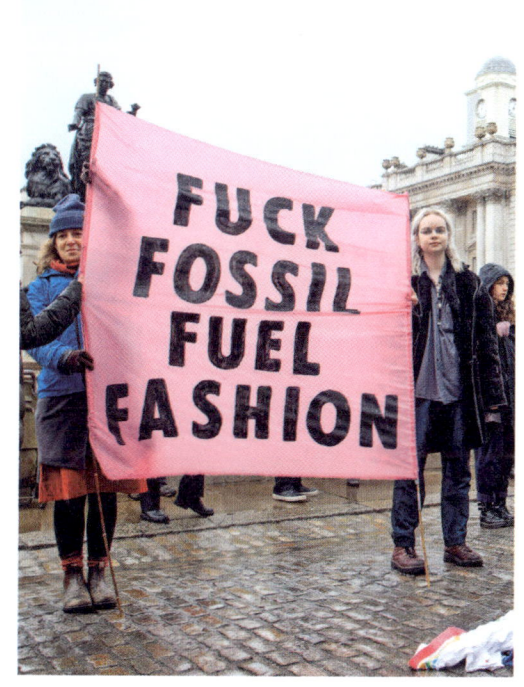

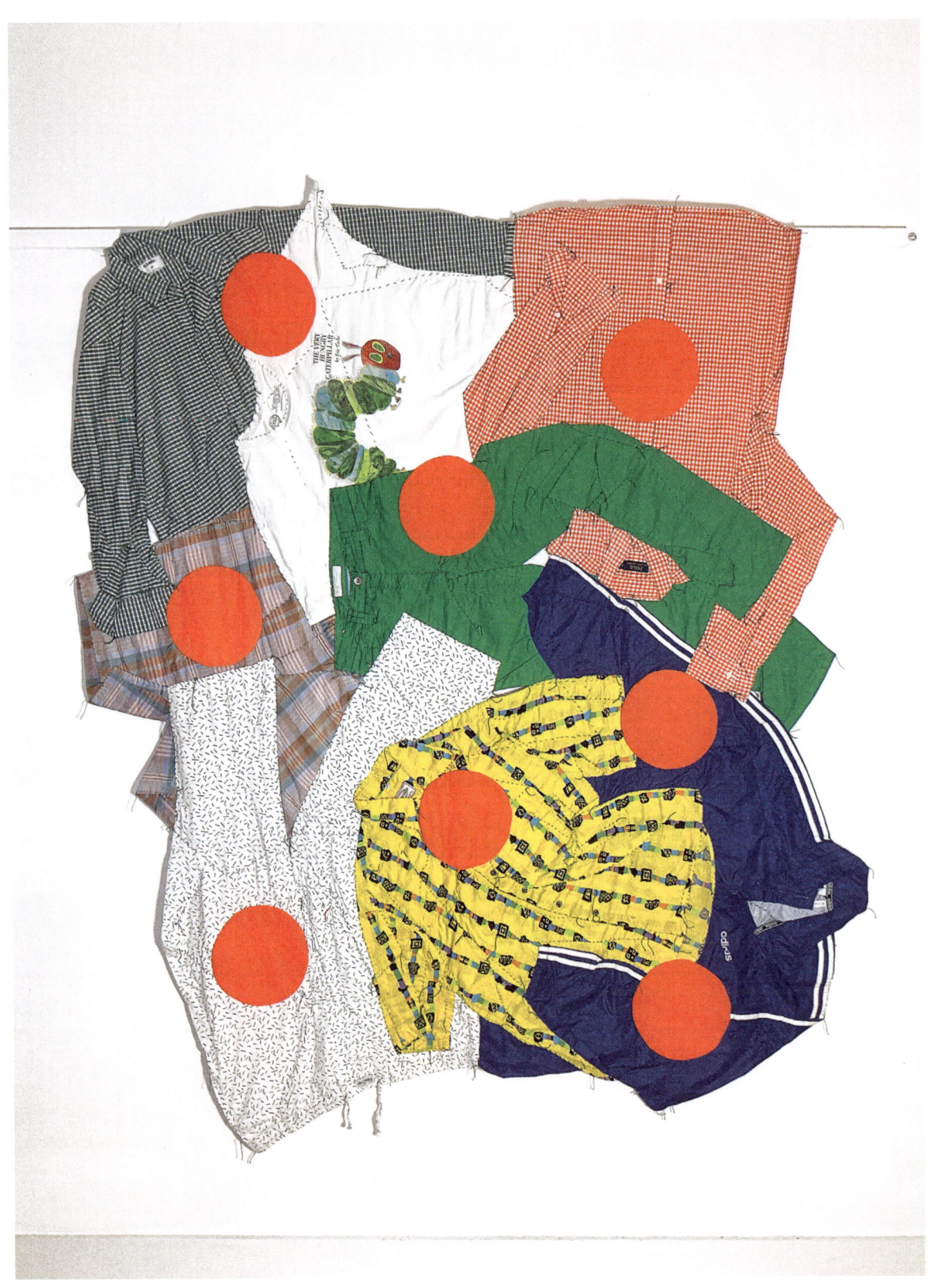

RESISTANCE FOR EXISTENCE

Textile Waste: Landfill and Ocean Pollution

A major problem with fast fashion is its disposability. Fast fashion trends and high-turnover wardrobes lead to a throwaway culture that creates significant environmental pollution.

Each year 92 million tonnes (over 100 million tons) of textile waste ends up in landfill, and much of this is made up of non-biodegradable synthetic fibres, which can take up to 200 years to decompose. In the UK, it is estimated that £140 million worth of clothing ends up in landfill every year.

The solution to the problem includes a move towards ethically sourced raw materials and a circular economy, a reduction in consumption, longer-lasting fashion and more sustainable practices. The '6 Rs' – Reduce, Reuse, Recycle, Refuse, Rethink and Repair – are now common household terms which connote a sustainable approach to managing resources by minimizing waste, extending the life of products and transforming materials for further use, whilst examining our relationship to them.

Within the industry, there is a move to innovate and create fashion which is sustainable and ethical. Several companies and social enterprises are pioneering and promoting ways to do this, including Patagonia (California) who have been producing fleece jackets from recycled bottles since 1993 and repair previous purchases; KoliKoWear (Ghana) who engage unemployed young people to make footwear from collected textile waste; Freitag (Switzerland) who upcycle tarpaulins into bags and backpacks; and Wintervacht (Netherlands) who make new coats and jackets by repurposing blankets and curtains found in charity shops.

As awareness grows that our clothes need to last longer, and our choices need to be greener and more ethical, artists and activists are increasingly upcycling their raw materials, and using them to make a statement about the environment, protest against ocean pollution, or emphasize the themes and importance of sustainability.

Through her wearable art installations made from ocean rubbish, Australian-based activist artist Marina DeBris draws attention to ocean pollution and the 'waste we create that comes back to haunt us'. Recycling is also at the heart of British textile artist Russell Barratt's practice, whose artwork, left, explores pressing issues of fast fashion and the journey of unwanted clothing, which often ends up in the Global South.

Dead White Man
(2023–)

Jeremy Hutchison

Every year, 24 billion garments enter the second-hand clothing market: the majority of these are shipped to Africa. Most are sold in street markets, but 40 per cent have no market value. These are dumped, burned, or heaped on mountains of landfill. In Ghana, these garments are known as *obroni wawu*: 'dead white men's clothes'. In his ongoing project 'Dead White Man', British artist Jeremy Hutchison transforms himself into a zombie of textile waste. Wearing a series of wearable sculptures made from clothes sourced in West Africa, this caucasian monster reverses the supply chain – returning to the Global North to haunt the high streets, shopping malls and corporate headquarters of the major fashion brands.

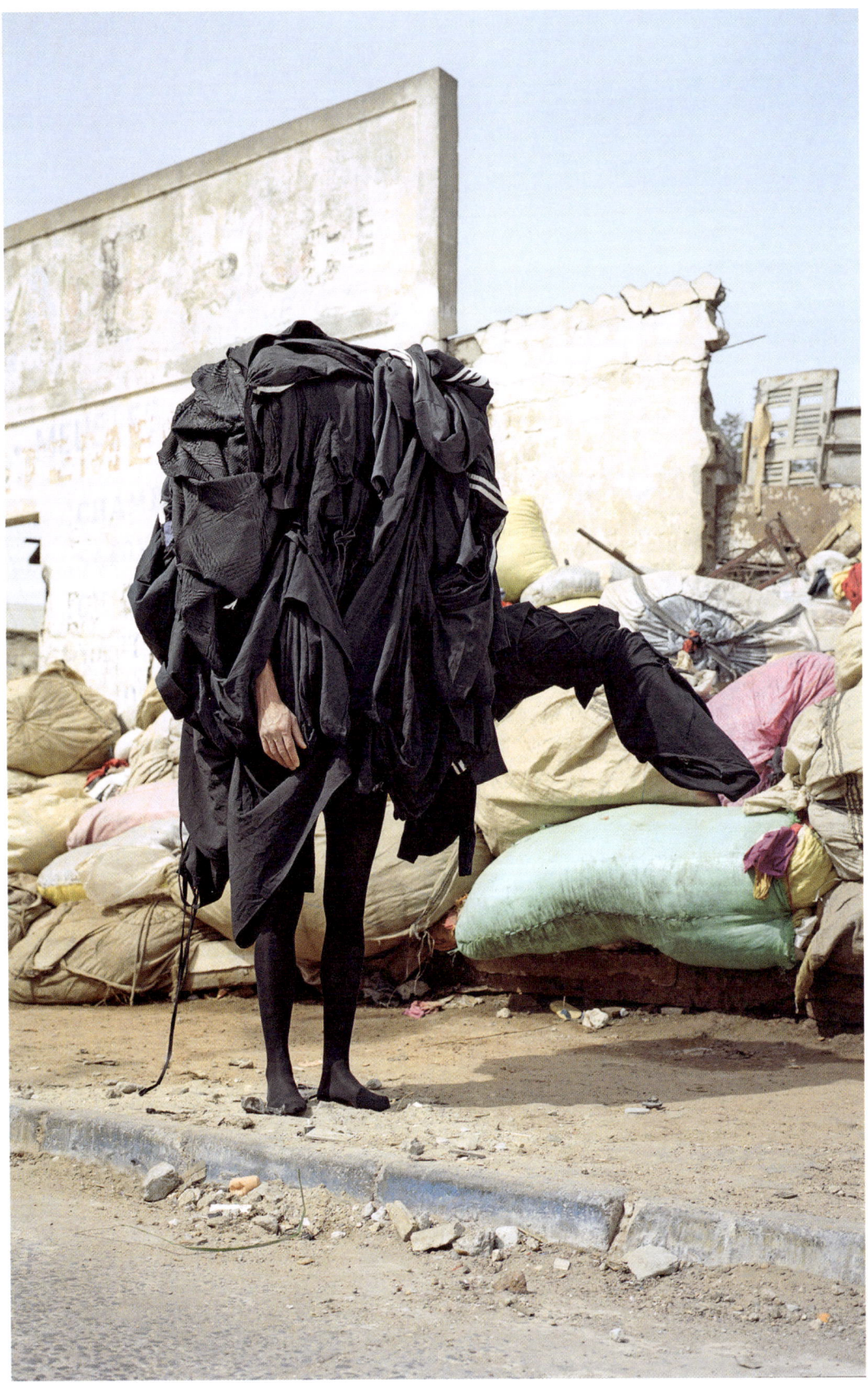

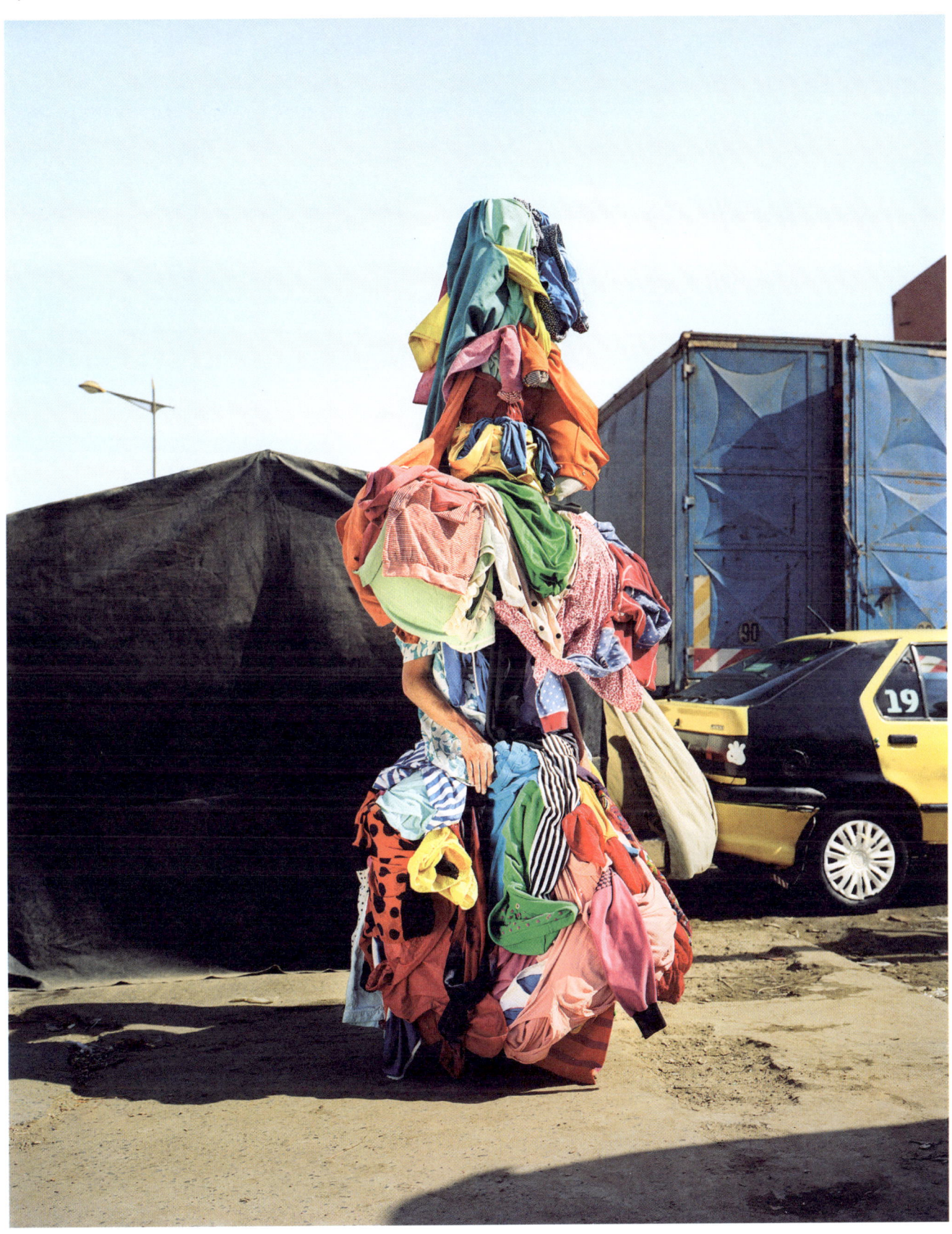

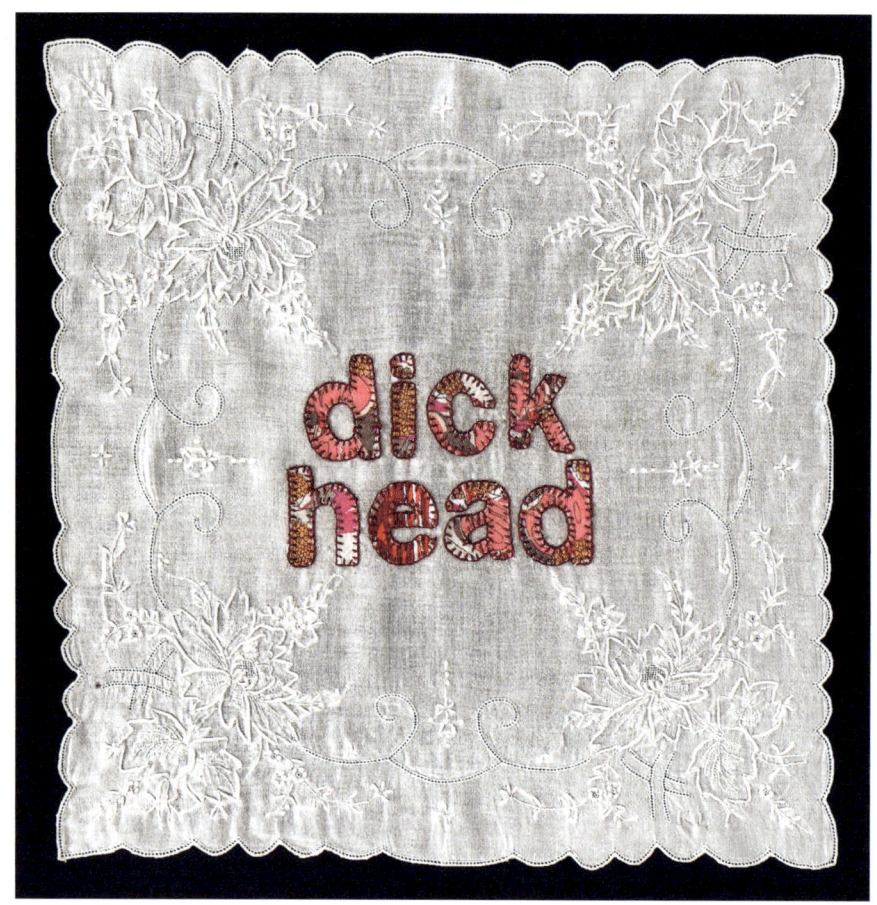

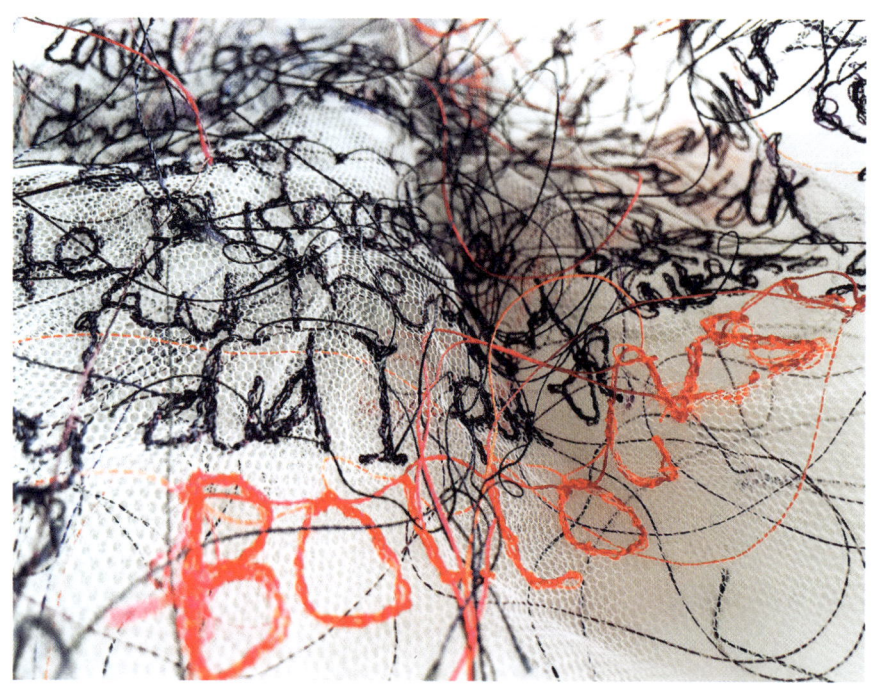

SWEAR IT WELL

SWEAR IT WELL

'The duster is a powerful object that embodies the invisibility of domestic labour through our cultural knowledge of it as a mundane, cleaning cloth. Embroidery transforms it into a voice of protest, defiance and solidarity for women!'

VANESSA MARR

From wearable garments and installations to small and intricate exhibits, protest textiles come in many forms. They can be mass-produced, a limited-edition series or a one-off.

They can be an outlet to express a personal viewpoint or made in response to an event or exhibition title, or simply created for the sheer pleasure of satisfying a rebellious urge. Protest textiles can be intriguing and compelling, mischievous, defiant or even cryptic: only identifiable to those 'in the know'.

Protest textiles can educate, raise awareness and get viewers to question their own situation or beliefs or make them laugh out loud. They can be offbeat, funny, vulgar or kitsch, hand-stitched quickly or professionally made, or may even become a sought-after or collectable cult classic. But what is most important for many makers is that they are subversive. They are made with passion and represent a freedom of expression.

Fashion and Costume

For thousands of years, clothing, in its vast array of forms, has been used to tell stories and express identity, conformity, power, status and belonging.

Traditional dress and corporate uniforms, military wear and religious regalia, all promote a constant, a national identity, a sense of cohesion and commonality, a loyalty to a code of conduct, or cult, where styles, colours and emblems are easily recognized and are symbolic, confirming authority, inviting respect and promoting control.

For centuries this standardized clothing was the norm, because textile making or printing processes were expensive, unmechanized and accessible only to 'the state' and the wealthy. Historically, colour, embroidery and opulent fabrics, such as silks and velvets, were reserved for royalty and higher classes under strict sumptuary laws that reinforced class distinctions and social hierarchies. Whilst the nobility revelled in luxury, members of the lower social classes had no choices: they were restricted to wearing poor-quality drab clothing.

Thanks to technological and scientific advancements, the development of dyeing, printing and construction processes has meant that textiles are widely available and affordable in a vast array of colours and textures. In turn, these developments have revolutionized fashion and the way we express our personalities and protests through clothing.

Clothing is our second skin and the act of dressing is a powerful visual tool. As well as being used to manipulate and oppress, fashion has a strong history of being used as a vehicle to liberate, express defiance and dissent, and communicate solidarity, as cloth in its many wearable forms is an accessible and instant canvas for protest and rebellion.

From overtly compelling T-shirt slogans and symbols, to discreet and deliberate rebellious embroidered motifs on traditional costume, messages of protest are often succinctly and powerfully summed up in one recognizable emblem, phrase, colour or pattern.

OPPOSITE

George Michael and Andrew Ridgeley of the pop group Wham!, arrive at London Heathrow Airport. Michael wears a 'Choose Life' T-shirt.

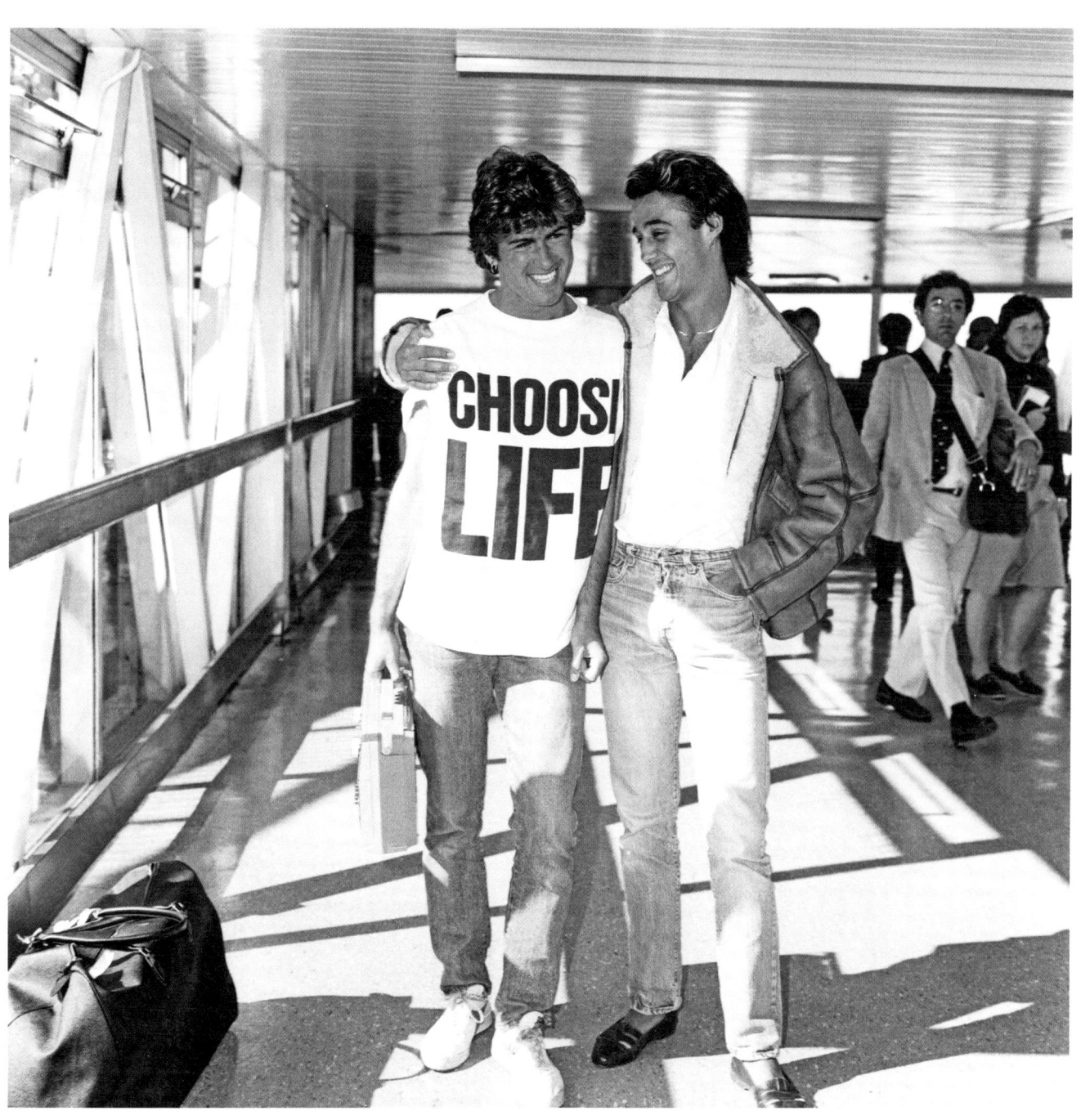

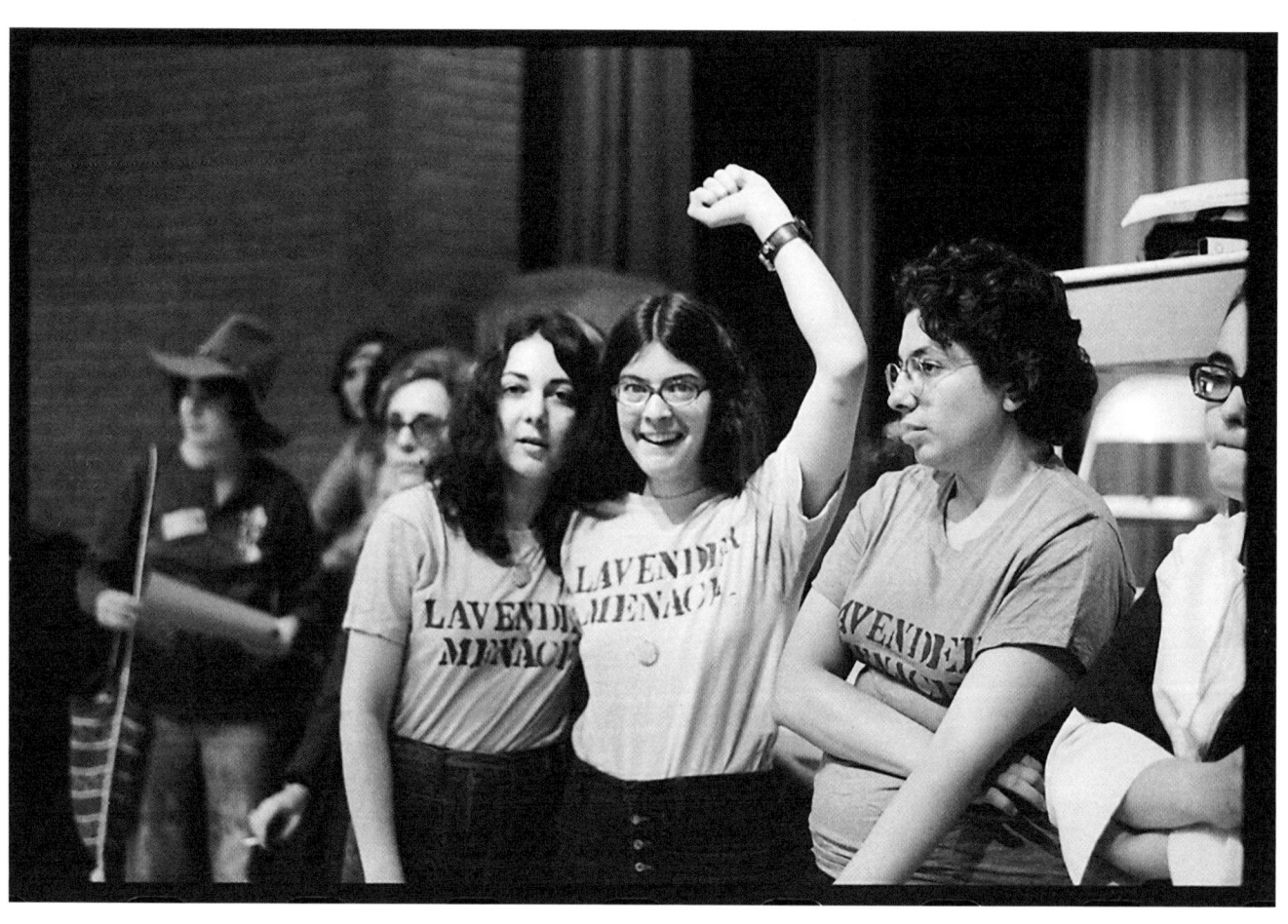

SWEAR IT WELL

OPPOSITE

Lavender Menace
at Second
Congress to Unite
Women, New York
City, May 1970.

OVERLEAF, LEFT

Former Prime
Minister Margaret
Thatcher greets
fashion designer
Katharine
Hamnett who
wears a T-shirt
with a nuclear
missile protest
message at 10
Downing Street,
where Thatcher
hosted a reception
for British Fashion
Week designers.

OVERLEAF, RIGHT

British fashion
designer
Dame Vivienne
Westwood and
her son Joe Corre
stage an anti-
fracking protest
with campaigners
outside Downing
Street, London, 5
June 2018.

Slogan T-Shirts

T-shirts are a relatively affordable item of clothing, easily accessible and worn by millions, and they have been used as a protest textile by many individuals and campaign groups. Slogan T-shirts can represent an identity, perhaps associated with a movement or one that signifies an allegiance, for example to a band, campaign or political party; wearing a slogan makes it more visible, encouraging comment and conversation.

During a protest in 1970, an outspoken lesbian group who were calling for equal rights within the feminist movement as well as wider society, and who had previously been dismissed as 'lavender menaces' by the National Organization for Women (NOW), rose up wearing T-shirts with the slogan 'Lavender Menace' emblazoned across them. They had reclaimed the label positively to confront the mainstream feminists who had pushed them to the fringes of the Women's Liberation Movement. This action brought results; NOW apologized and lesbian rights became an important part of the feminist agenda, and the iconic design and its adaptions (such as Transexual Menace and Bisexual Menace) are still available today.

During the punk era that dawned in the mid-1970s, T-shirts were a popular medium for individual expression – they were torn, ripped, scrawled over with anarchist symbols and swear words, or printed on, and usually held together with safety pins or left gaping to reveal flesh beneath. For punks, they became a signifier, an everyday uniform, and the T-shirt was redefined.

Vivienne Westwood and Malcolm McLaren (manager of the Sex Pistols) were at the forefront of shaping the aesthetic of the punk style. They had a major influence on this anti-establishment subculture with their collaborations and collections, and contributed significantly to the development of fashion with their T-shirt logo designs for punks.

Westwood went on to launch her own label and became a pioneer in pushing boundaries in the fashion landscape by reviving silhouettes in a funky way and challenging stereotypes in clothing. Her visionary approach was championed by marginalized groups as she questioned gender norms in garment design and became an outspoken sustainable-fashion advocate.

Katharine Hamnett, a British fashion designer, is well known for her political T-shirt logos – bold, stark words printed in black

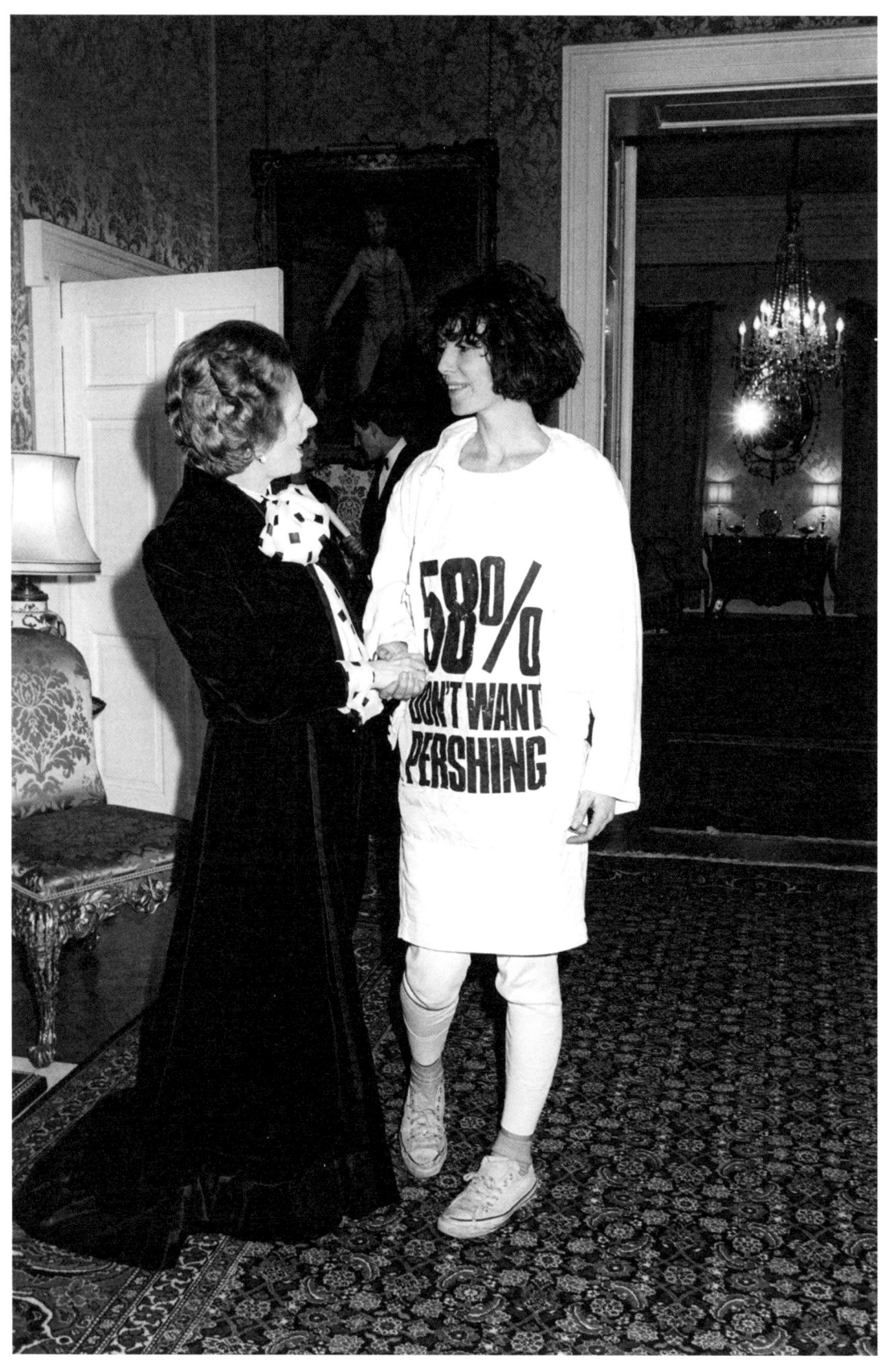

SWEAR IT WELL

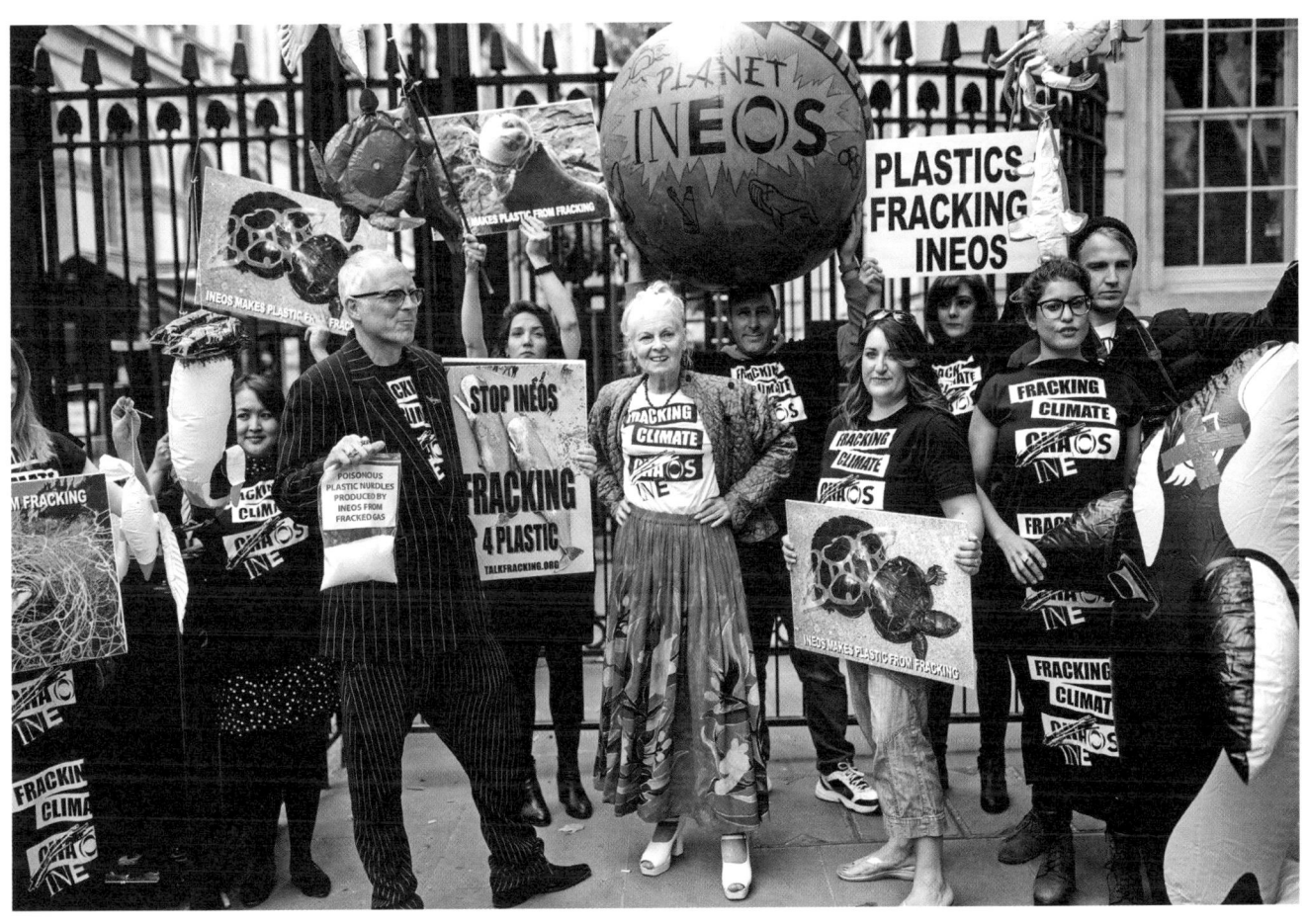

capital letters on a white background which cannot be ignored. Her first slogan, launched in 1983, was 'CHOOSE LIFE'; it became an instant hit, and was adopted by many celebrities. This iconic design, which is still on sale today, is based on Buddhist philosophy, although the anti-abortion lobby have tried to appropriate the slogan against Hamnett's wishes.

Hamnett came to prominence as an activist when she wore her '58% DON'T WANT PERSHING' oversized anti-nuclear-missile T-shirt when she met Margaret Thatcher, the then British prime minister, in 1984 during London's inaugural fashion week. *Vogue* described this action of protest as one of the most iconic moments in fashion.

Hamnett has continued to use fashion as a platform for protest, and promotes ethical and eco-friendly practices. Her slogans have always addressed topical issues, such as expressing disgust with the fur trade, saving the bees and tackling the problem of plastic in our oceans. Hamnett has also highlighted important political issues with her slogans, such as 'CHOOSE LOVE' for Help Refugees, and 'VOTE', which she says is 'the most powerful tool to get the world we want'. In 2024, filmed by her son, she dumped her CBE in a rubbish bin whilst wearing her 'DISGUSTED TO BE BRITISH' T-shirt, in angry protest at Britain not calling for a ceasefire in Gaza. Hamnett posted the footage online to publicly express her outrage.

Many celebrities have drawn attention to campaigns by wearing 'feminist T-shirts'. The slogan 'This Is What A Feminist Looks Like' first appeared on T-shirts designed by the Feminist Majority Foundation in 1992, five years after the US-based organization was established. The slogan was adopted and popularized by the UK-based feminist organization, The Fawcett Society (a charity campaigning for gender equality since 1866) in 2014, and has been worn by thousands since, including Barack Obama, to demonstrate the diversity and inclusivity of feminism. In 2004 Gloria Steinem unapologetically wore an 'I had an abortion' T-shirt, and the 'NO MORE PAGE 3' slogan was notably worn by Caroline Lucas in the UK parliament in 2013.

'The Future is Female' (a slogan dating back to the mid-1970s) is frequently seen on T-shirts at demonstrations, and 'THIS P****Y

OPPOSITE

'This Is What A Feminist Looks Like' T-shirt.

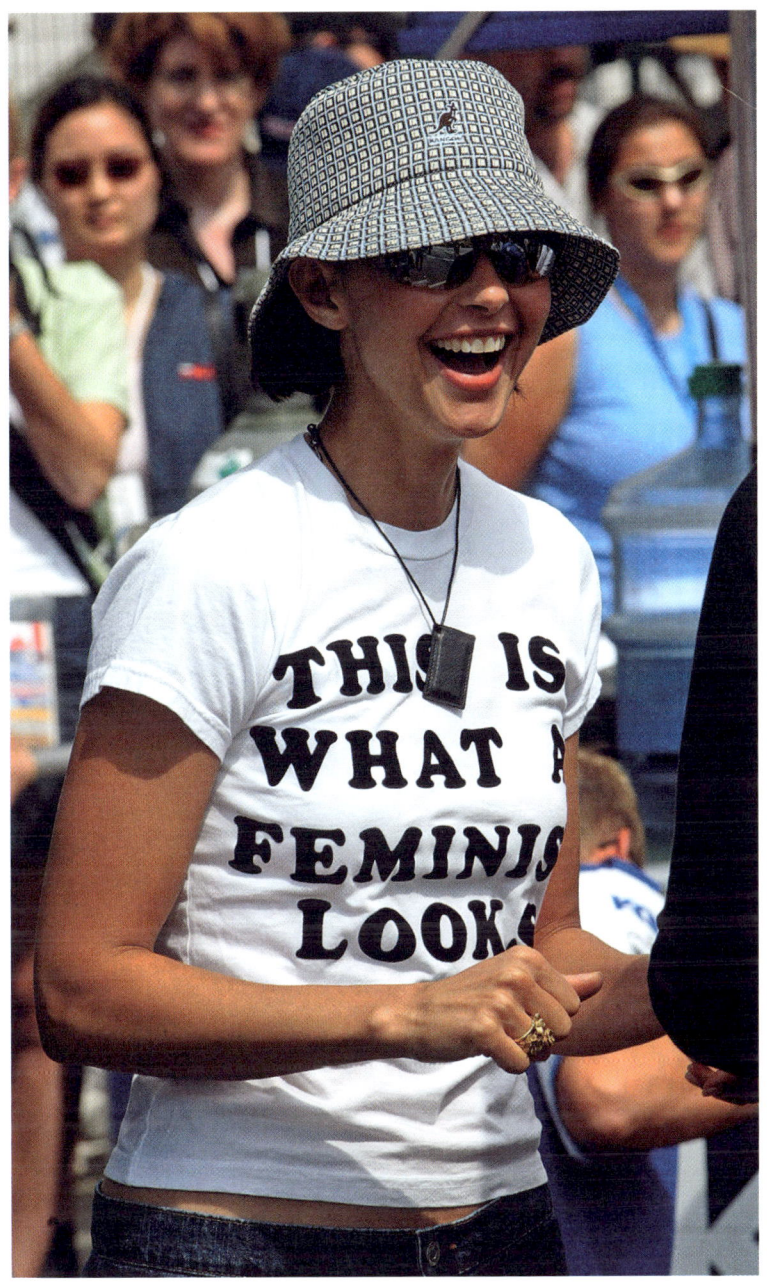

GRABS BACK' has been a humorous feminist response to subvert the misogynistic political culture that is on the rise.

Political slogans on T-shirts have also become popular with sports personalities, particularly in the wake of the Black Lives Matter movement and the #SayHerName campaign. Televised sports have enabled these protest slogans to reach millions of viewers worldwide.

Cultural Dress

National dress and cultural cloths are imbued with meaning. Whether they are worn every day or reserved for special occasions, they represent a cultural heritage reflecting the identity of a community or a nation.

Embroidered or woven patterns and stylized folk motifs reflect regional characteristics that have been passed down for generations, preserving collective memory and pride. Some colours symbolize power or fertility, some motifs are believed to offer protection or ward off evil, and some designs pinpoint belonging to an ethnic group. These can all be subverted to tell a coded tale of protest as the political landscape shifts and people look for a way to express their defiance and resistance to unwanted changes, oppression or displacement.

Throughout history there are many examples of traditional garments that have been overtly worn in cultural assertion against laws that repressed identity. For example, kente cloths in Ghana (against colonialists), vyshyvanka blouses in Ukraine (against Russification), tartan in Scotland (against English laws) and sarapes in Mexico (to signify allegiance in the Mexican Revolution).

Traditional dress has been worn with covert messages too. Rural Palestinian women began to covertly embroider motifs of resistance onto their *thobes* in protest against the Israeli occupation; this was their way of joining the First Intifada in 1987. At the time, the Palestinian flag was banned by the Israeli occupation in Palestine – a calculated attempt to systematically erase Palestinian identity. To avoid suspicion, women individually bought, then shared, embroidery threads in the colours of the Palestinian flag, and secretly stitched at night embroidering symbolic Palestinian landmarks, such as the Dome of the Rock or Al-Aqsa Mosque, onto their 'Intifada dresses'.

Textiles travel with the displaced and the heritage of these embroidered *thobes* has thus been preserved and brought to a wider audience in some notable exhibitions and collections.

In 2021, the Taliban implemented Sharia law across Afghanistan, dispensed with the Ministry of Women's Affairs, and brought back the Ministry for the Propagation of Virtue and the Prevention of Vice under their new regime. Women's dress code

OPPOSITE

A man on horseback wears a serape, a symbol of resistance during the Mexican Revolution.

OVERLEAF

The Intifada Thobe (2023)

Deerah Corporation

Hand embroidered.

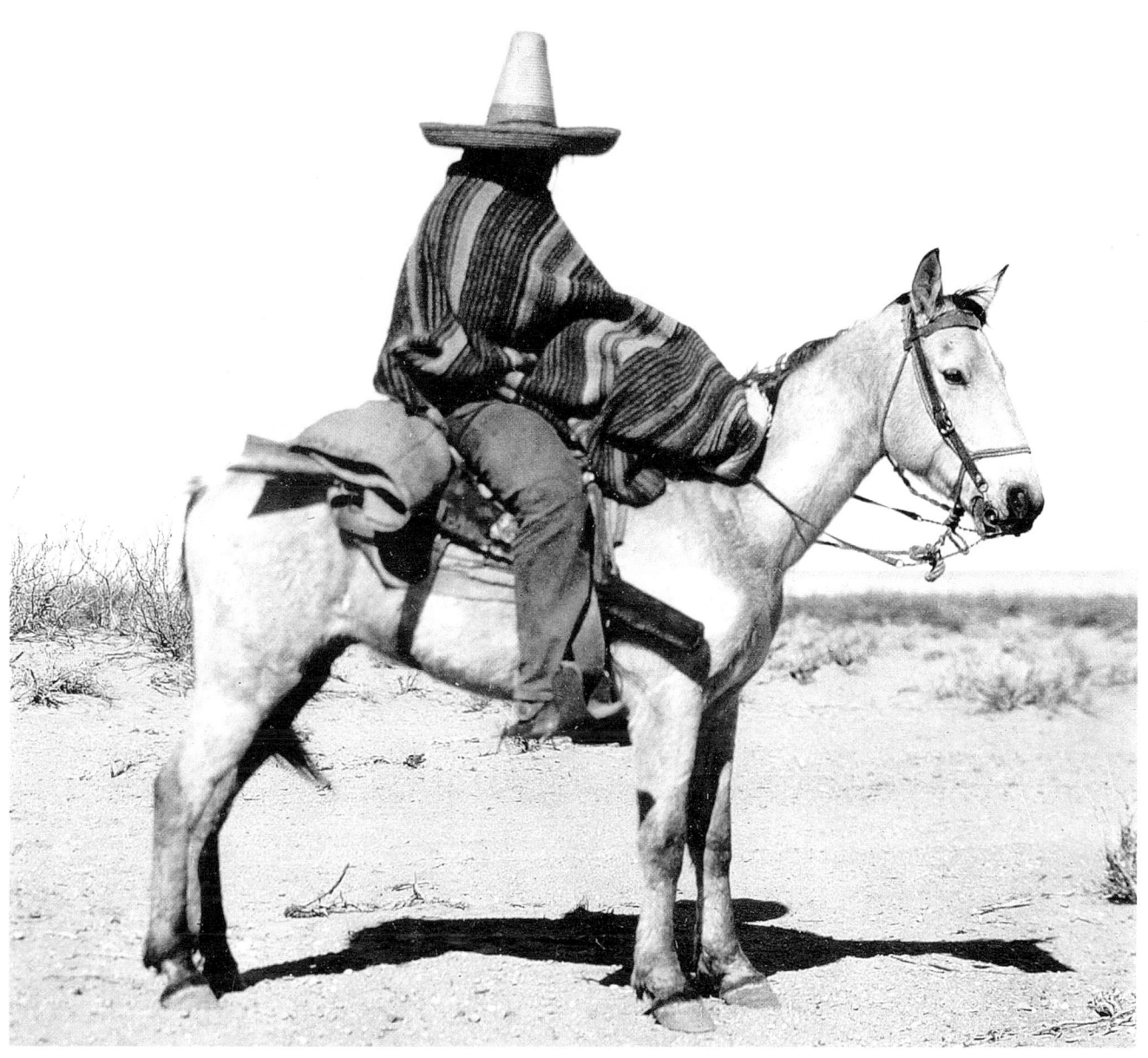

was severely restricted, with the enforced wearing of full black abayas and niqab for female university students – which is not an Afghani tradition and is a misrepresentation of their culture. In the protests that followed, Afghan women defiantly posted pictures of themselves on social media platforms wearing their bright and vibrant national dress, accompanied with the hashtag #DoNotTouchMyClothes, in response to an online campaign launched by Dr Bahar Jalali (an Afghan-American gender studies historian). The campaign went viral, and embroidery, colour and ornament on clothing emerged as another protest.

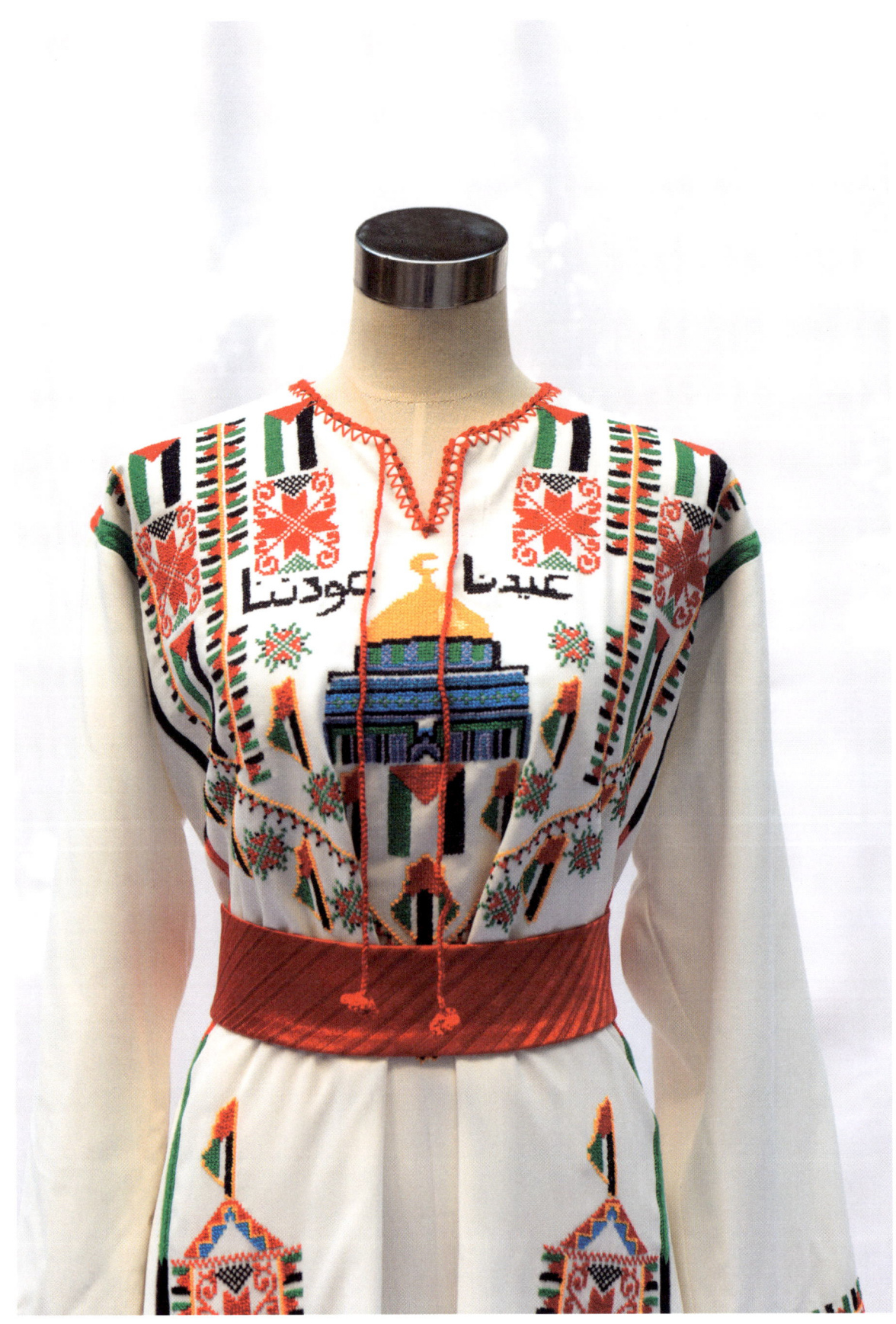

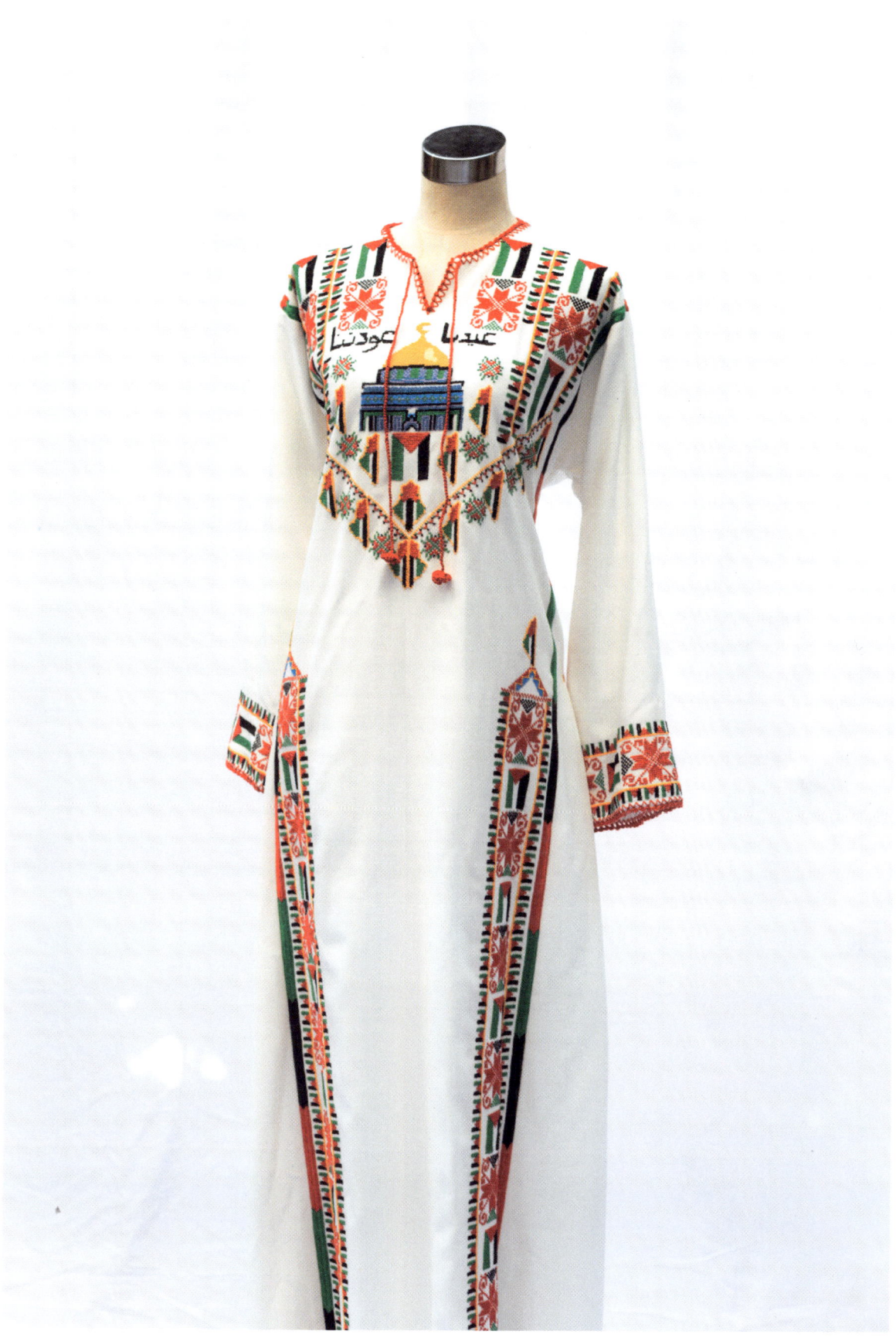

Everyday Textiles

Everyday textiles are the perfect background for printed, appliquéd or embroidered messages of resistance. Defiant slogans and motifs have appeared on utilitarian cloth surfaces from pillowcases and sheets to hats, handkerchiefs, bags and old clothes. Found garments and household linens have also been deconstructed, reconstructed and transformed into installations, wearable art, banners or hangings.

Dusters

The Domestic Dusters project was established in 2014 by artist and academic Vanessa Marr. This ongoing collaborative arts initiative asks women and girls to embroider their experiences and feelings about domesticity and the expectations surrounding responsibilities in the home environment onto a duster.

The duster is an inexpensive cloth used for mopping, wiping and polishing surfaces, and is closely associated with low-paid cleaning jobs and mundane household chores, traditionally assigned to women. But in this project, the duster is reclaimed as a surface for protest and opinion, feminist statements and wit. Participants are asked to embroider with red thread; not only is this a stark contrast to the yellow cloth, but the colour traditionally signifies power and represents feminine sexuality and fertility.

There are multiple aims of the project, which include working with those whose domestic situations are compromised, for example through displacement or unpaid caring responsibilities, but fundamentally its purpose is to empower women to make their own domestic choices, to challenge the gender bias towards domestic chores, and to become a voice for women who are silenced, ignored or unheard. The hundreds of dusters in the collection are a powerful message of defiance and solidarity, which continues to grow as it encompasses more voices and reaches new audiences.

OPPOSITE

Domestic is Not a Female Word! (2022)

Vanessa Marr

Textile cleaning cloths.

Banner created by Domestic Dusters founder Vanessa Marr, often hung alongside the collection when on display to draw attention to the domestic inequality still experienced by many women.

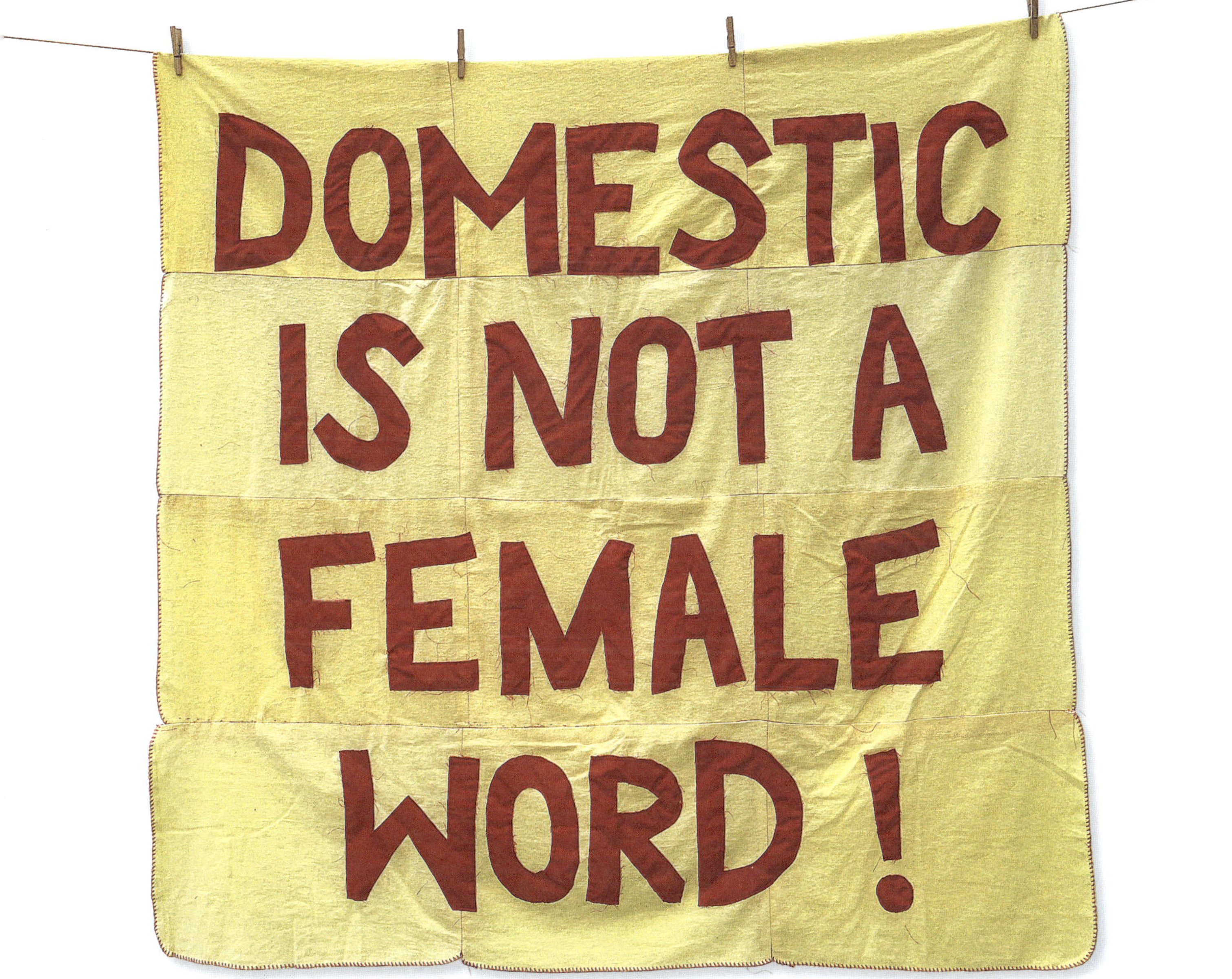
DOMESTIC
IS NOT A
FEMALE
WORD !

A selection of dusters embroidered by women who joined in the Domestic Dusters collaboration with Profanity Embroidery Group, PEG. The combination of gentle embroidery with foul language was a powerful and an enticing mix. Over 150 dusters were submitted, making it the most popular themed call for submissions in the ten-year history of the project.

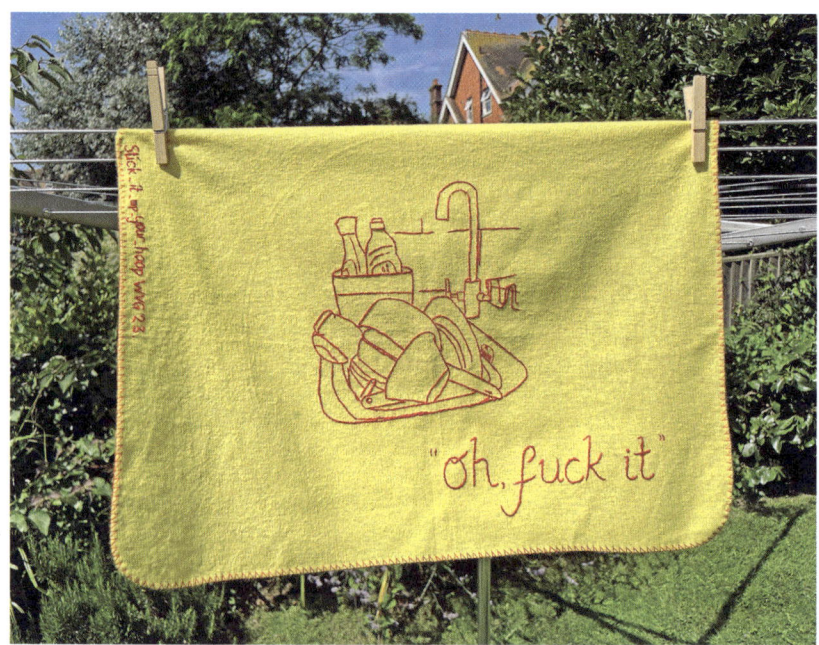

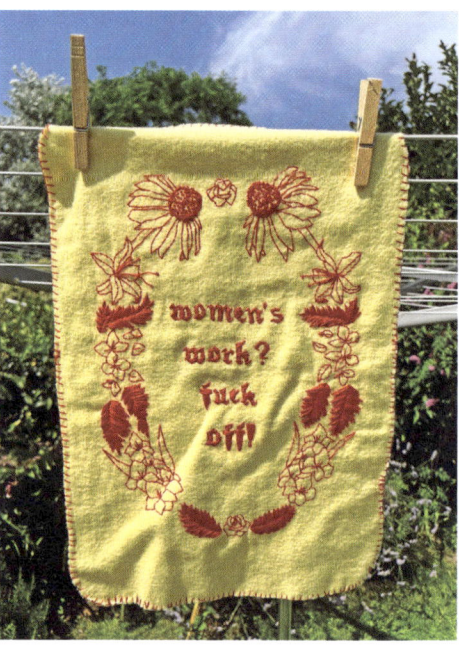

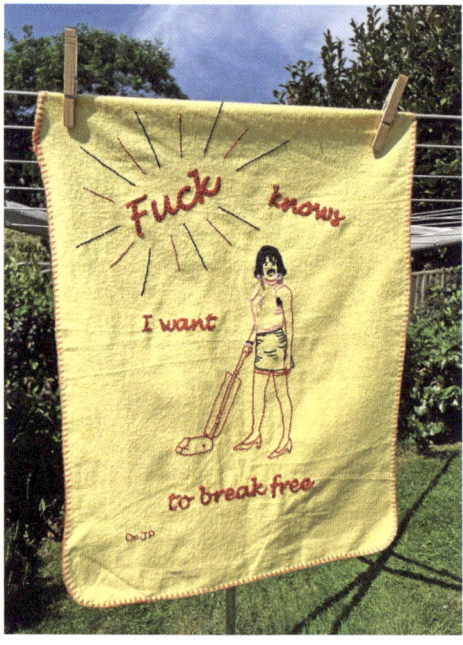

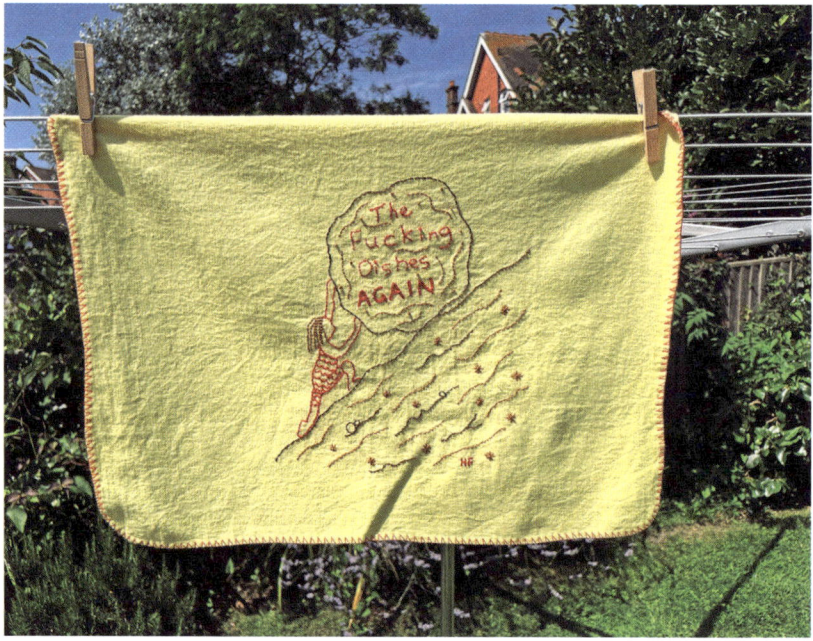

Many of the project participants play with the meaning of words and use humour to get their point across. These dusters poke fun at the monotony of domestic chores whilst making wry observations of the gendered expectations associated with them.

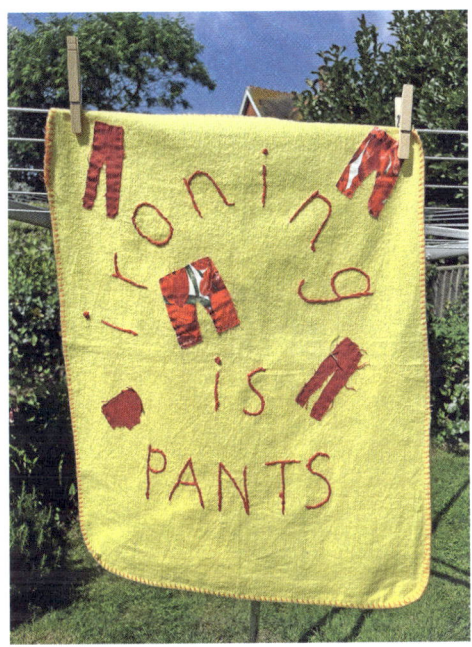

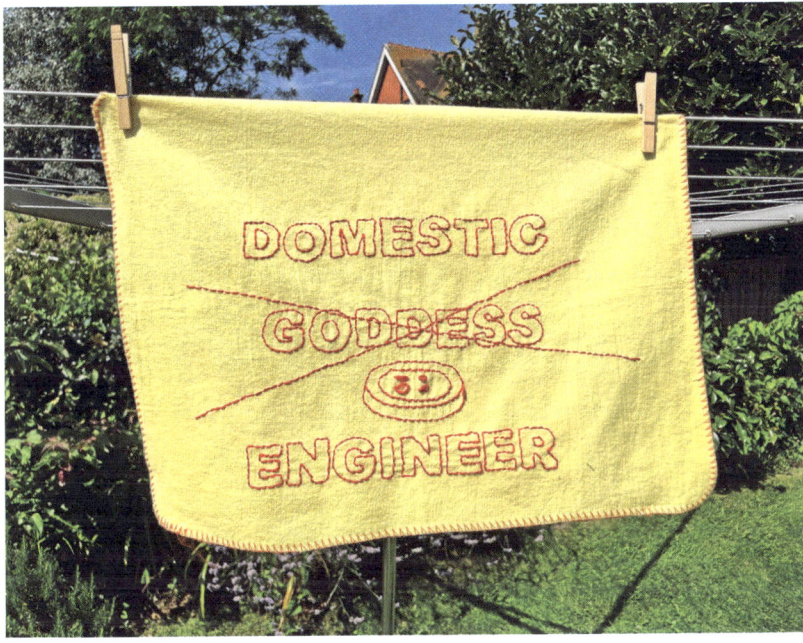

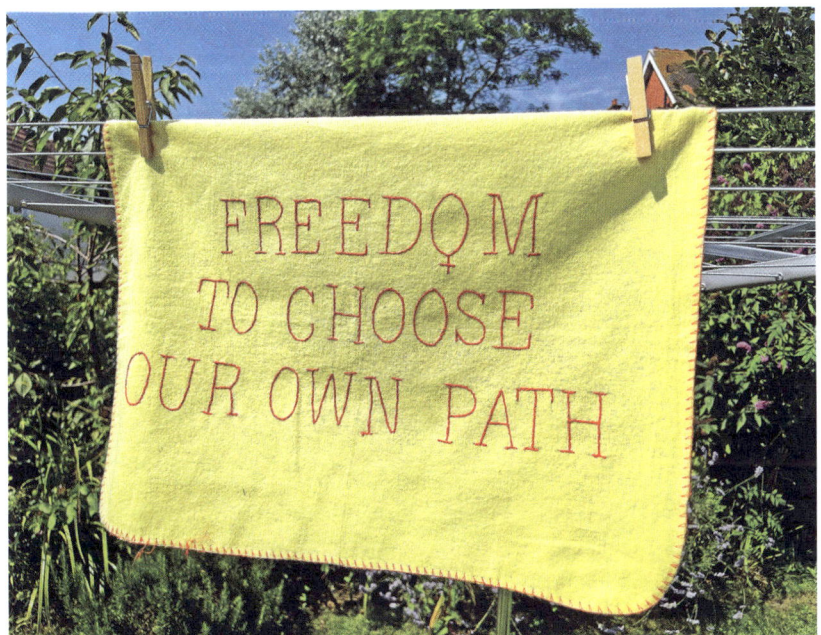

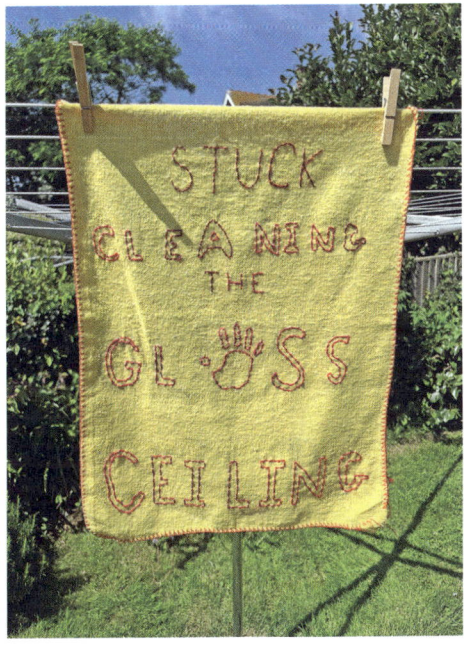

Tea Towels

Tea towels may be viewed as humble and ubiquitous items of household linen but as a canvas for political and artistic expression they have long surpassed their everyday utility. As an object deeply embedded in domestic life, tea towels carry a potent symbolism when repurposed for protest as they transform an ordinary textile into one of dissent. This transformation changes the identity of the tea towel, reclaiming it from a functional cloth in the home to one calling for action in the public domain, therefore bridging domesticity and activism.

The upcycling of tea towels for protest also embodies resourcefulness and sustainability, aligning with the broader message of the rejection of wasteful consumerism and the importance of environmental consciousness.

In my own practice I often use tea towels as a background for appliquéd text to make personal or political statements. I embrace the surfaces as they are; cotton and linen tea towels are often well-washed and show signs of wear and tear. The faded colours, textures and boundaries of the cloths, or the embroidered initials upon them, echo past memories or fashions adding character to my new artworks.

Holly Searle, aka The Subversive Stitcher, uses vintage tea towels extensively in her work as a means of protest against issues such as climate change, greed, corruption and misogyny. Searle appliqués felt letters across the printed surfaces to make bold and subversive statements that succinctly summarize social injustices, frustrations with inept governments, and important issues such as sewage in our waterways.

Searle says: 'The work I make helps me signpost a more realistic narrative than the one I have been fed. It's how I see the world and this is how I share it.' (See also page 47).

BELOW

We Are Not Amused (2022)

Holly Searle

Vintage linen tea-towel with appliquéd felt letters stitched by hand.

OPPOSITE

Fuck The Tories (From the mini banner series 2023–4)

Julia Triston

50×74cm (19.68×29.1in).

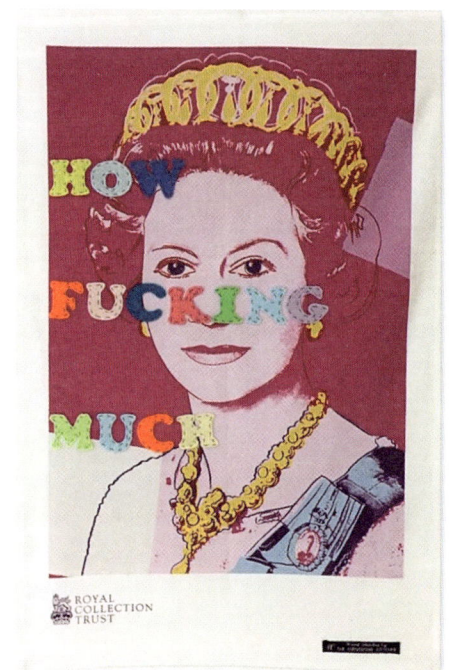

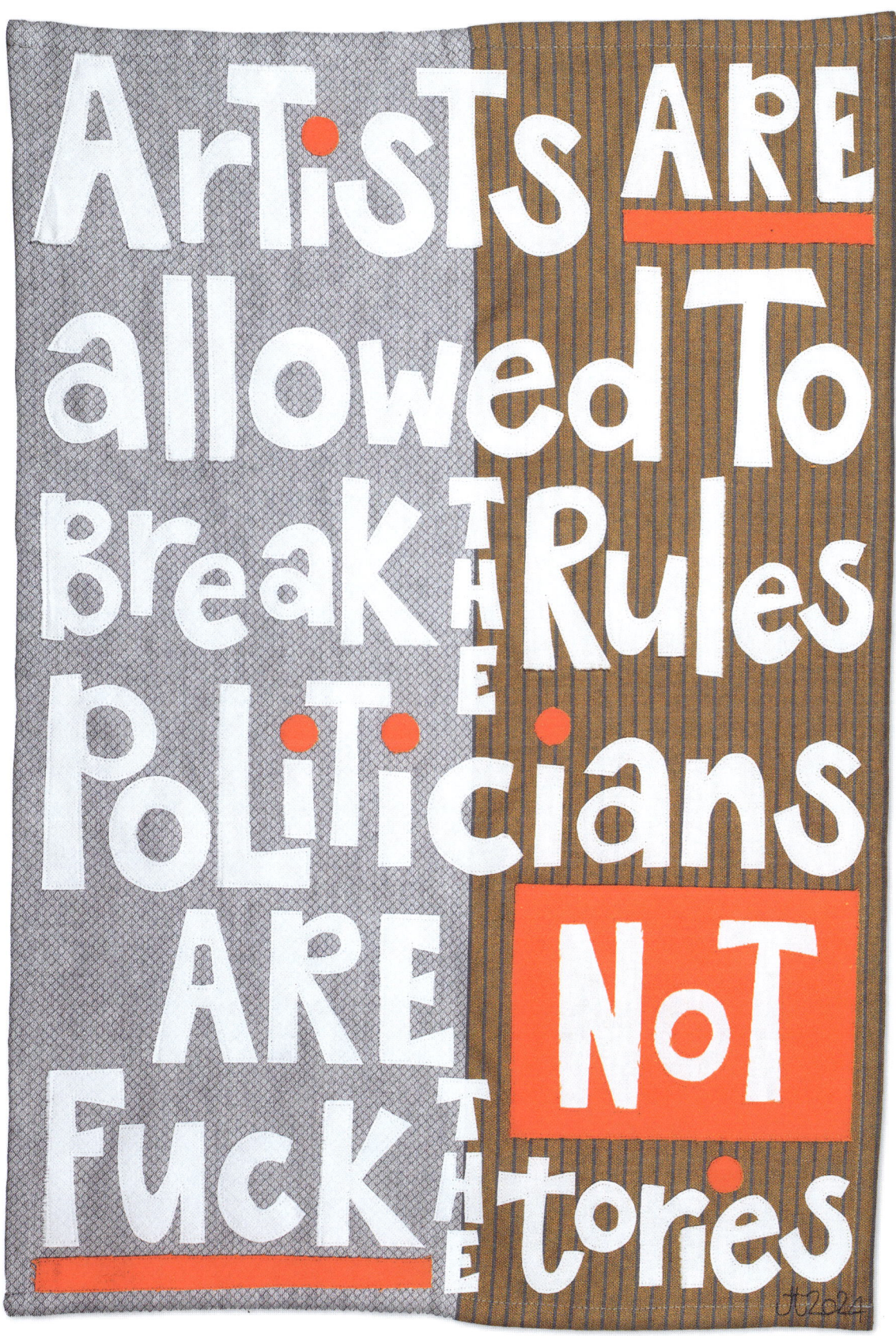

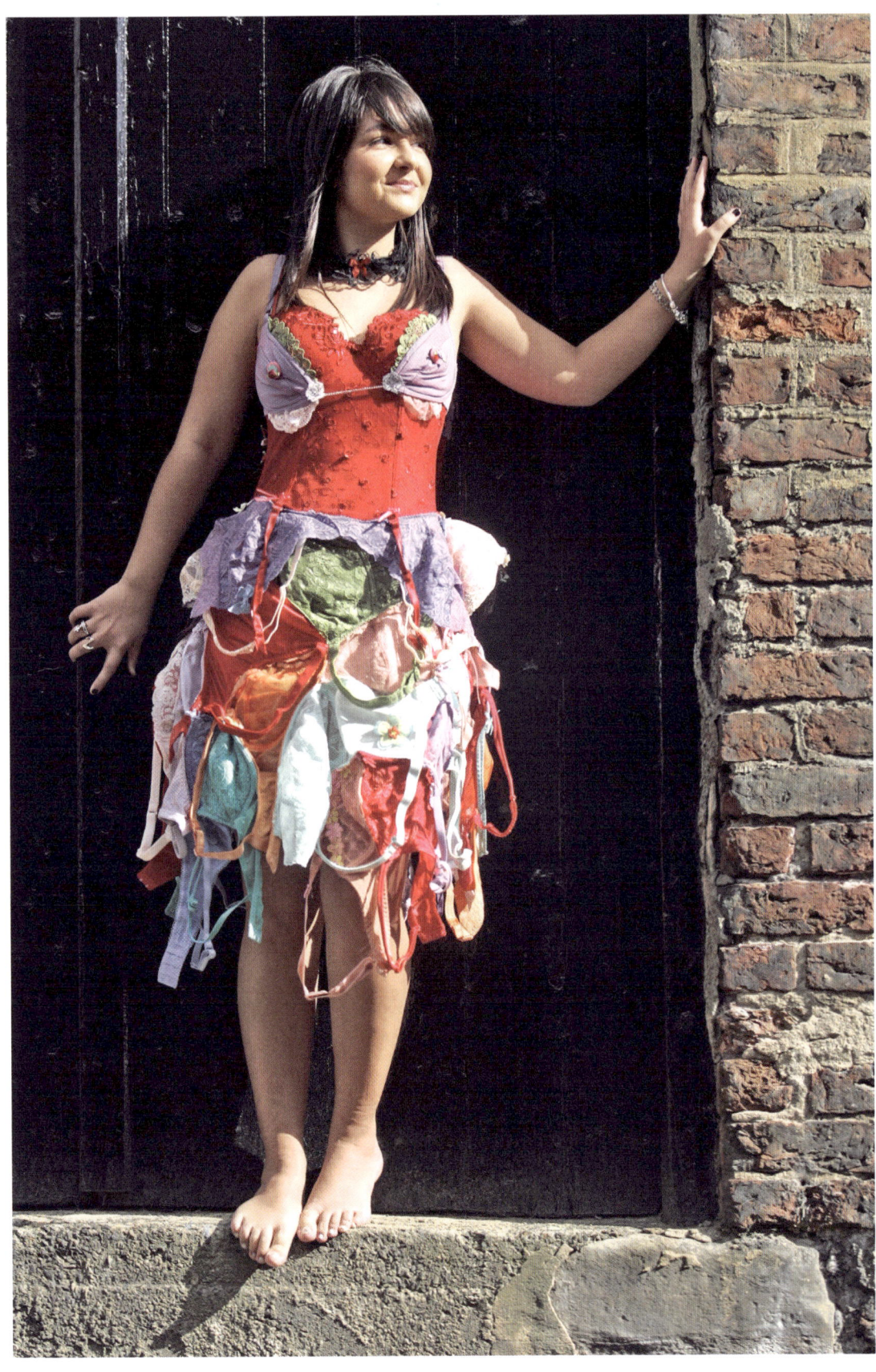

SWEAR IT WELL

*Wild At Heart
Bra-ra-dress
(2008)*

Julia Triston

Made from donated
bras in response to a
call out for previously
worn underwear for
an exhibition and
long-term project
about identity.
Modelled
by Nina.

Underwear

Underwear can be a powerful raw material. Whether to shock or rebel, surprise or subvert, underwear has been used by fashion designers as outerwear, painted on by activists and stitched upon by embroiderers.

As an artist myself, I have used previously worn bras and knickers in my textile artworks since 2008, as part of an inquiry into identity, body image and the exposure of self through the subversive use of intimate clothing. My wearable artworks and installations make a feminist statement about who we are as women and what we really wear, challenging and protesting against the media's perception of what they think we should wear, and how they think we should look.

Each donation of underwear comes with a story that forms part of the narrative behind the artworks. They tell tales that are funny, moving and emotional, and comment on how our bodies change over time, giving women, whose voices may not otherwise be heard, a platform to speak through my art. As I transform and upcycle the bras and knickers into finished pieces, I put on display what is (usually) unseen: evidence of wear and tear, marks, stains and holes, which are preserved as 'landmarks' that hold memories of owners and echoes of former identities.

'My Knicker Bunting' is an ongoing project; I work with women's groups to create installations that stimulate discussions about feminism, activism, self-image and body positivity.

The Umbrella

The umbrella became the iconic everyday textile of resistance during the pro-democracy protests in Hong Kong in 2014 when demonstrators initially used them as protective shields during tear-gas and pepper-spray attacks from the police. The 79-day protest, during which tens of thousands of protestors occupied key areas of Hong Kong, became known as the Umbrella Movement or the Umbrella Revolution, and the yellow umbrella in particular became the adopted political symbol of peaceful resistance, used in demonstrations ever since. The colour yellow symbolizes power in Asia, and was traditionally a colour only used by royalty; the Umbrella Movement claimed it for the people.

One of the central sites of protest during the Umbrella Movement was Admiralty, a key financial district in Hong Kong, originally developed by the British military in the 19th century. Home to the government headquarters and the Legislative Council it became the focal point of the 2014 occupation where resilient demonstrators staged peaceful sit-ins, erected barricades and road blocks and set up a permanent camp on the streets. The camp became a vibrant hub for the duration of the protest and became a symbol of the struggle for democracy, with countless students, well-known activists, and citizens joining the movement.

The occupation of Admiralty represented a bold act of civil disobedience and inspired many to challenge Beijing's increasing control over the region and its decision to impose restrictions on the election of Hong Kong's Chief Executive.

Despite this large scale demand for universal suffrage and greater political autonomy and high profile coverage in the international media, police presence was stepped up. Hundreds were arrested, many detained, and the Admiralty camp was cleared by the authorities in December 2014.

The demands of the protestors were not met, and Beijing imposed a national security law in 2020 which carries a life imprisonment penalty for displays of public dissent, effectively ending mass protests. But the Umbrella Revolution will forever mark a pivotal point in Hong Kong's political history.

OPPOSITE

Umbrellas used during the pro-democracy protests in Hong Kong, 2014.

OVERLEAF

Protestors occupy Admiralty on 24 October 2014 during the Umbrella Revolution.

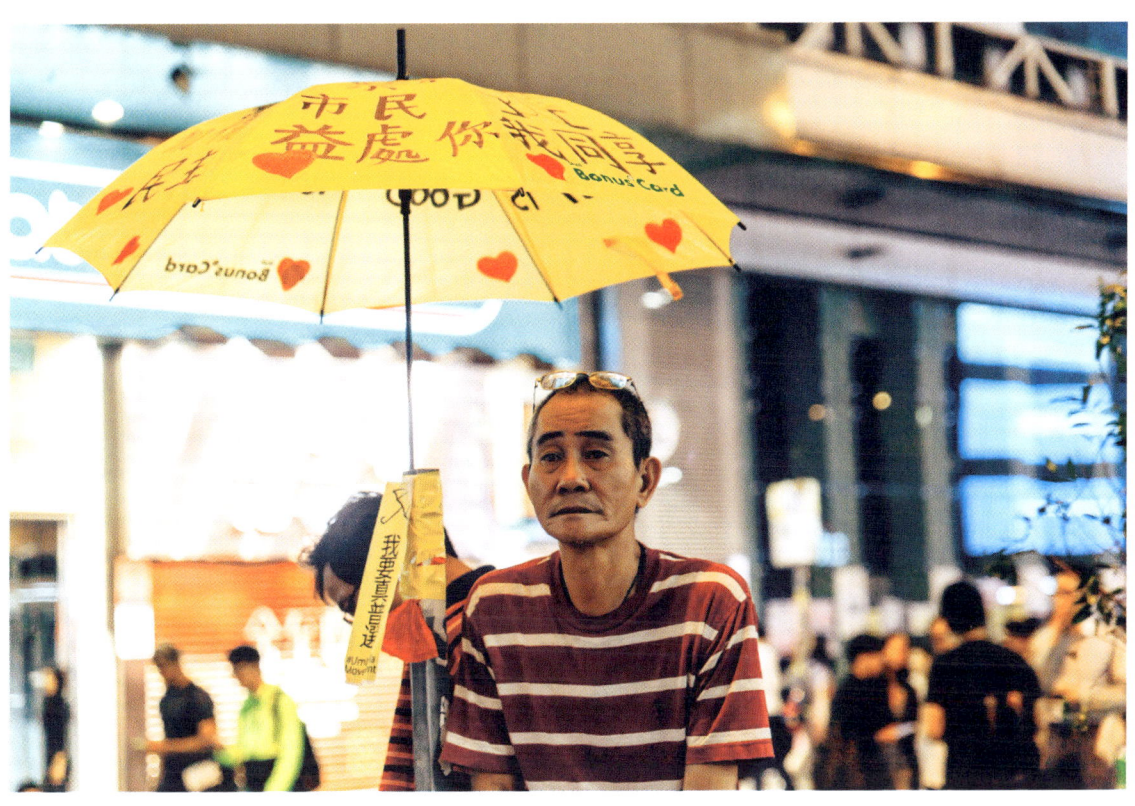

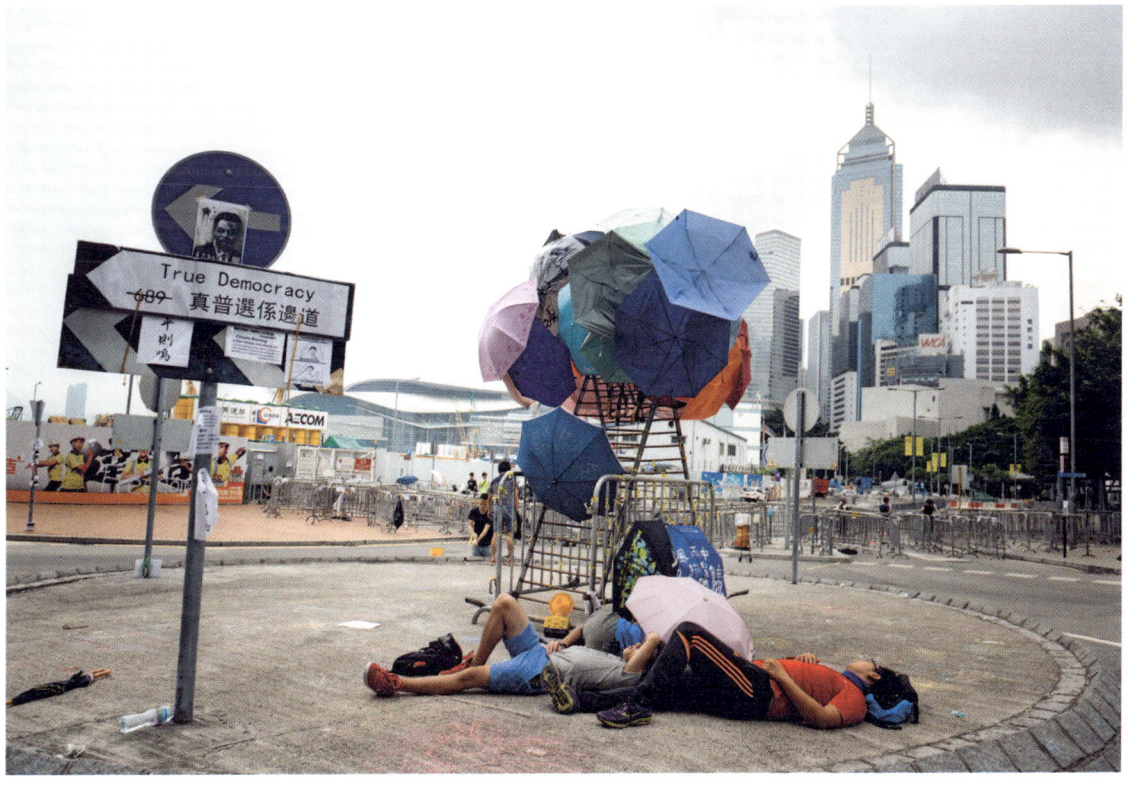

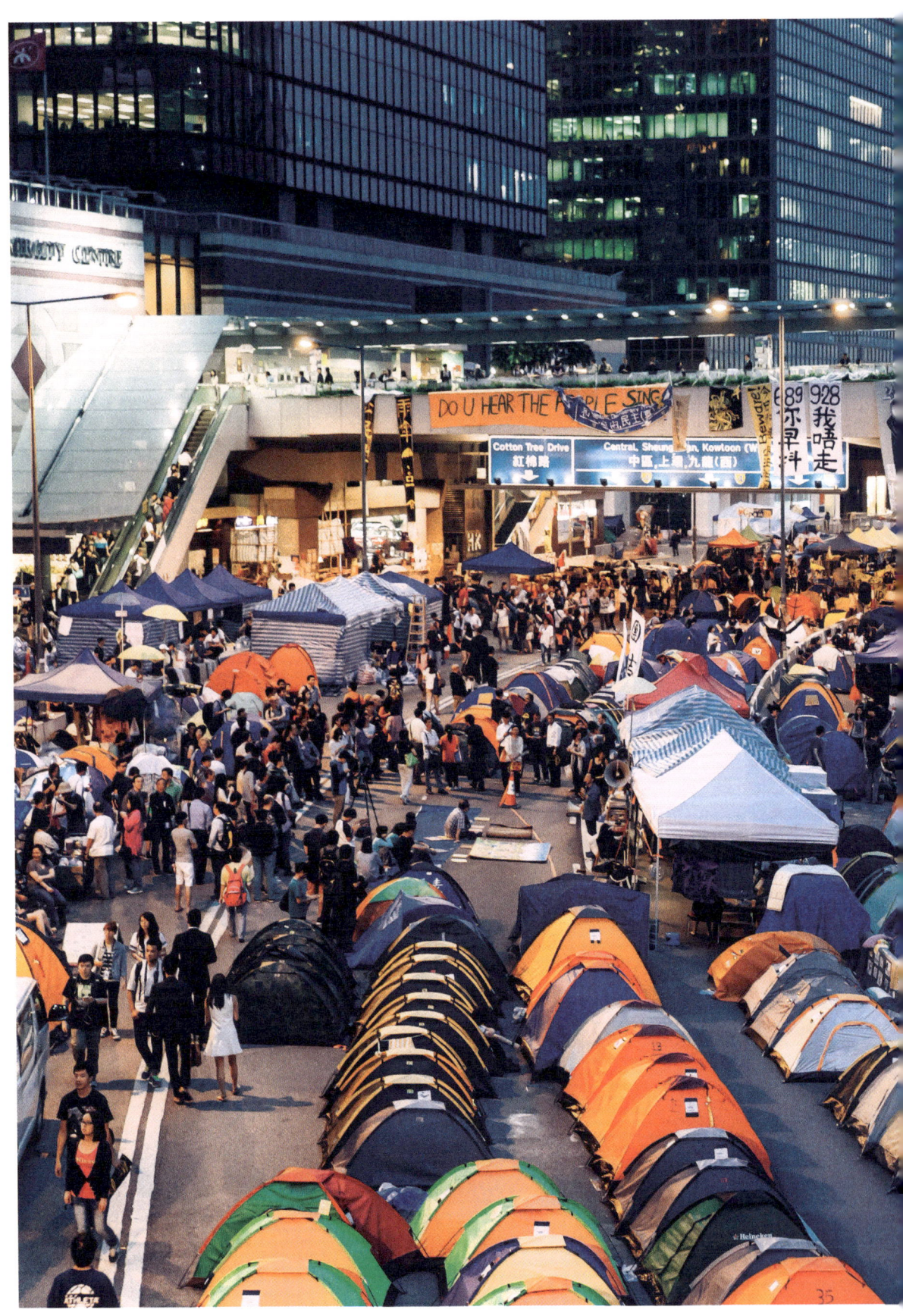

SWEAR IT WELL

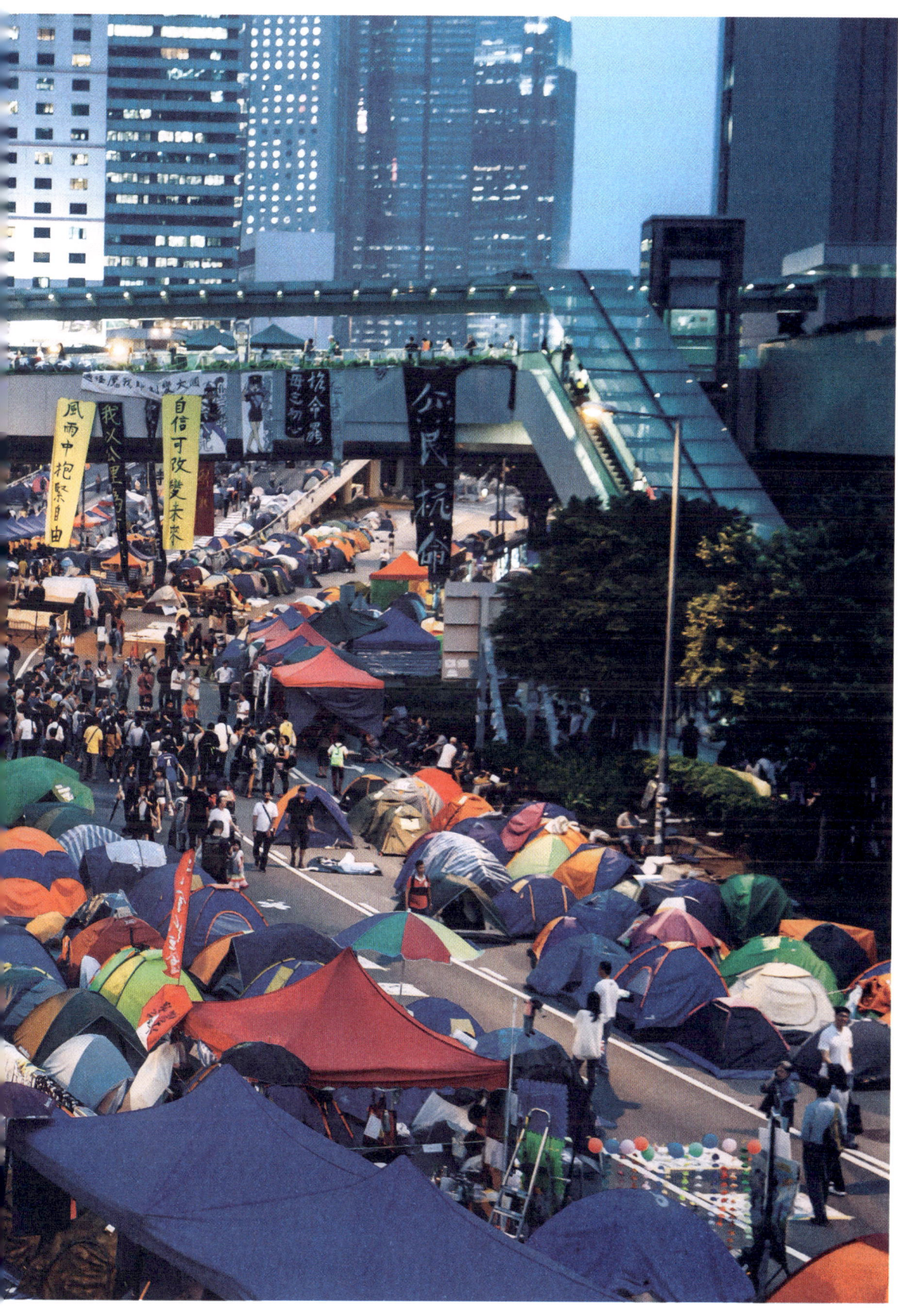

Craftivism

Although there are different approaches to craftivism, most embrace and foster a supportive and community approach towards activism, invoking change one slow stitch at a time. Using the handmade to promote social and political change is the key to craftivism, and is an empowering and engaging practice for those who seek justice and want to make a difference without making a big noise, but still want to be heard clearly.

The Craftivist Collective was founded in 2009 by the award-winning activist Sarah P. Corbett, who has been recognized for her 'Gentle Protest' methodology, which combines neuroscience, positive psychology and campaign strategies with beautifully embroidered objects, some of which are placed as 'street craftivism' in locations relevant to the issue addressed. Betsy Greer coined the word 'craftivism' in 2003 (an intersection of craft and activism) and gave permission for Corbett to use the term for her own approach to craftivism; a style of activism which Corbett describes as 'quiet, compassionate and inclusive.'

As outlined in her 'A Craftivist's Manifesto', Corbett states that gentle craftivism is about using the repetitive and meditative *process* of handicrafts to channel anger and sadness into strategic, not reactive or 'hate-filled' protests.

The emphasis on the aesthetics of small and handmade objects is an empowering practice for those who want to make a difference but worry about fuelling more polarization. The resources of Craftivist Collective have been implemented by professional campaigners, as well as burned-out activists and new protestors, and are used around the world as a tool, not to replace other forms of activism, but to add to the activist's toolkit.

OPPOSITE

Mini Protest Banner (2015)

Sarah P Corbett

17×12cm (6.69×4.72in). Upcycled fabric and Aida, cross stitched. Hung in Brick Lane 2015, East London (see also page 180).

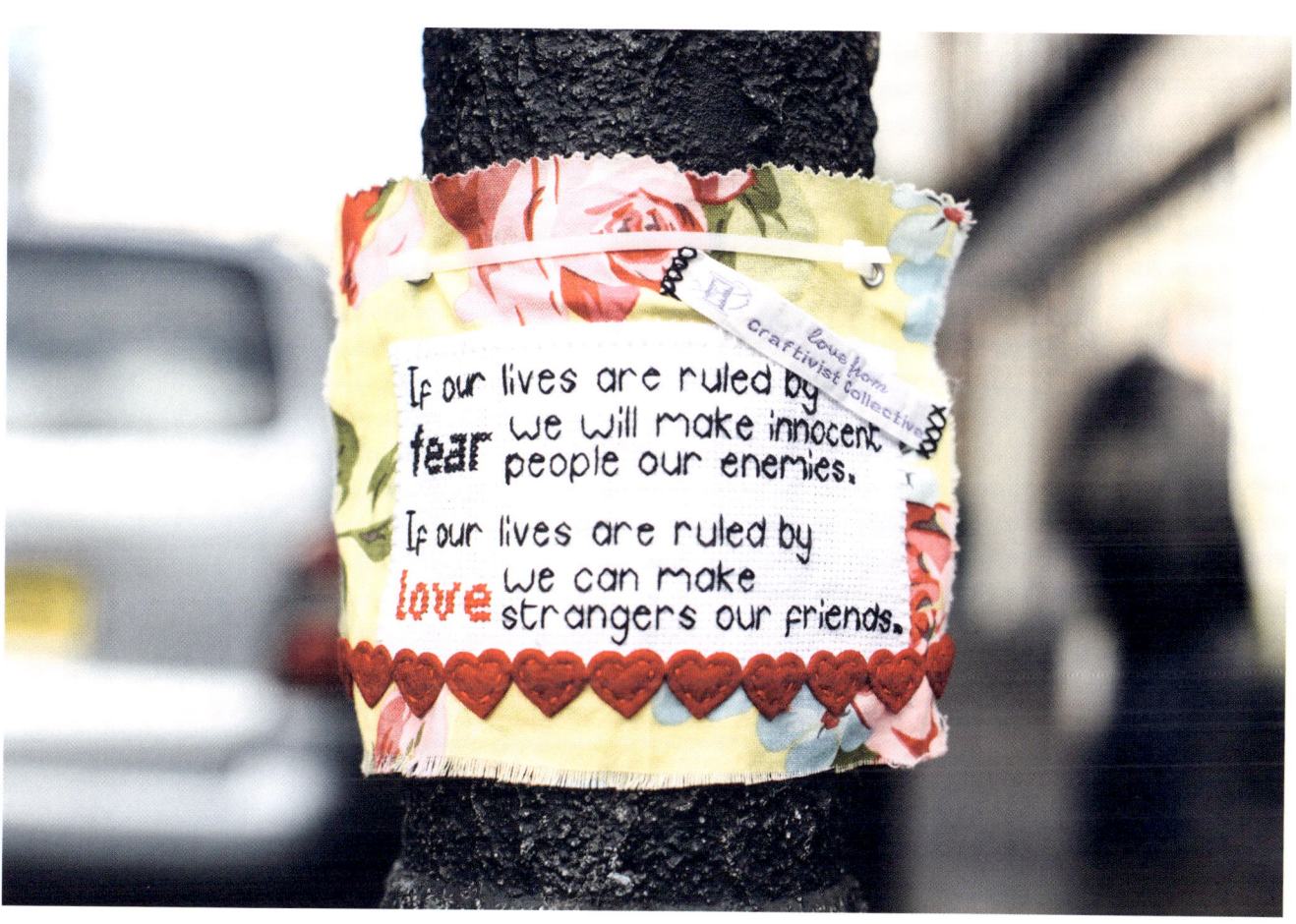

If our lives are ruled by **fear** we will make innocent people our enemies.

If our lives are ruled by **love** we can make strangers our friends.

love from craftivist collective xxx

Embroidery

Embroidery, particularly in the form of cross-stich (traditionally used by women and girls to practise and perfect their embroidery skills in the form of samplers), is experiencing a revival, and has become a medium of strong personal protest for many craftivists and contemporary embroiderers. In traditional samplers, text is stitched centrally in a uniform manner, surrounded by symmetrical borders and motifs. Protesters often keep this format in their stitching, but rebelliously subvert the content of the text; instead of Bible quotations favoured by the Victorians, when embroidery was regarded as a skill for 'esteemed ladies', many now use embroidery to expressively spell and stab out their words of frustration, rage and protest with humour and vigour.

Humour, along with many swear words and expletives, has been the basis for the embroideries stitched by the Profanity Embroidery Group from the UK, which was founded by Annie Taylor and Wendy Robinson in 2014. The pair were inspired by Rina Piccolo's cartoon of an older woman embroidering 'Fuck the Whole World' onto a cushion. The group successfully combine stitching and swearing and have produced many individual and collaborative textile artworks that have been the subject of articles, exhibitions and festivals, all creatively challenging and subverting the traditional 'gentle art of needlework'. Whilst the majority of their embroideries convey personal indignations and observations, quotations, humorous innuendos and plays on words, they also use their high-profile platform to highlight and raise awareness about important community projects such as the Grenfell Memorial Quilt. Their embroideries are to the point, they are amusing and inspiring, and they are empowering more women to take up the needle and boldly and expressively stitch their sweary protests.

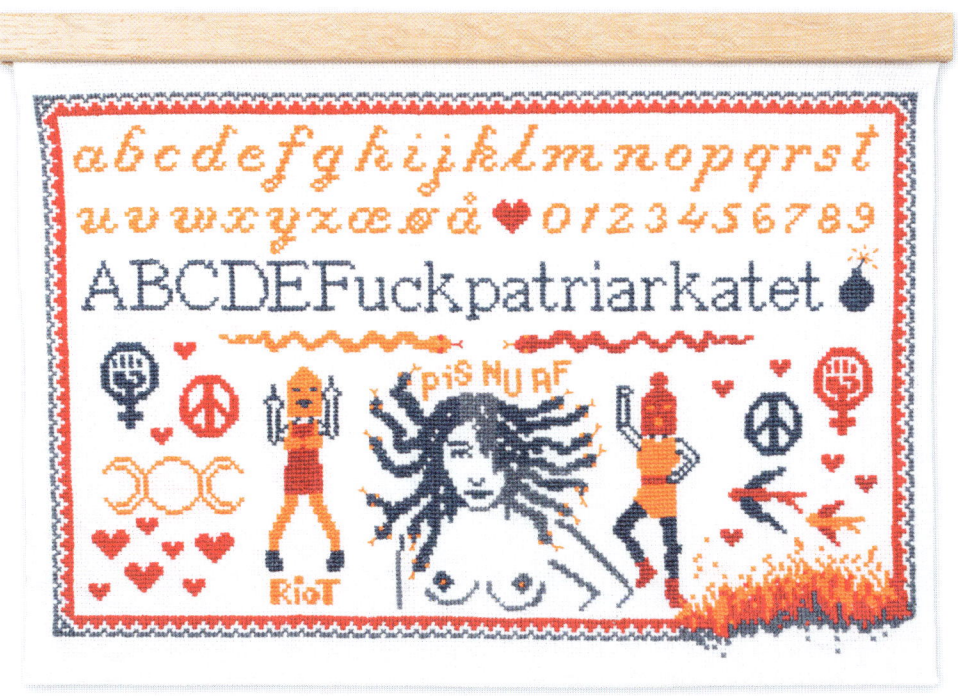

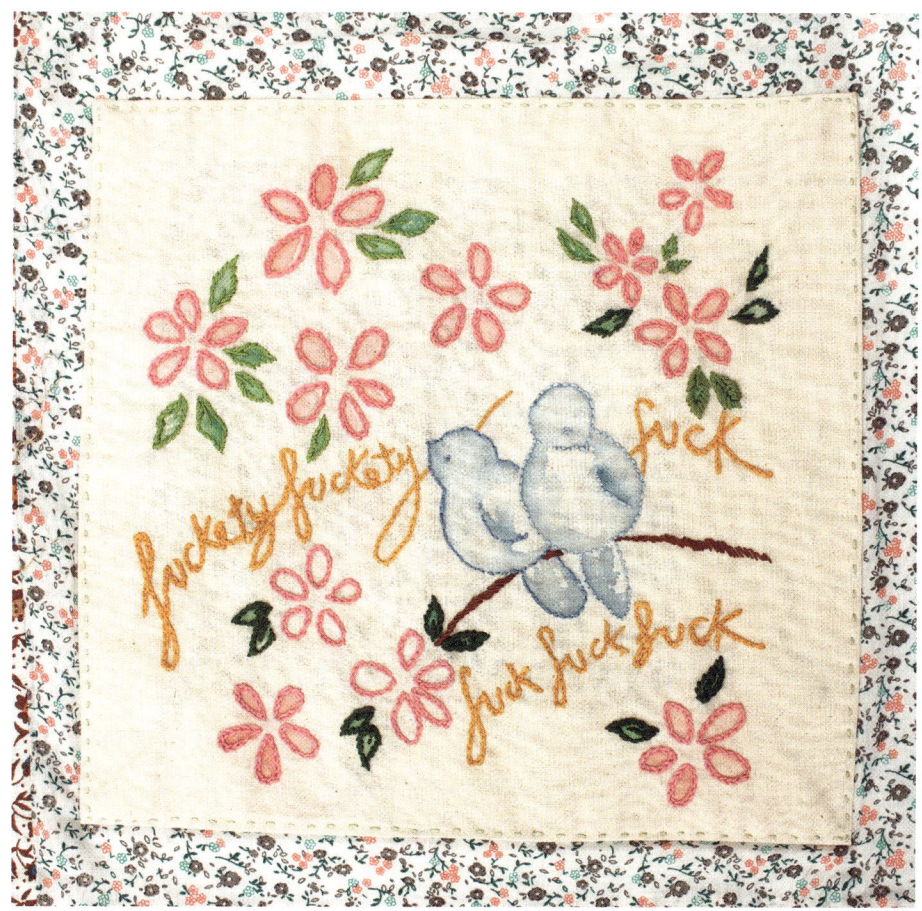

Yarn Bombing

In recent years, knitting and crochet have entered the public domain in a new format by transforming many sterile urban areas with imaginative and colourful site-specific installations in the form of yarn bombing, also known as guerrilla knitting; essentially textile graffiti. This phenomenon, where traditional women's skills have been exhibited in a new context outside the home, has inspired a global movement that celebrates this subversion. Whereas graffiti is permanent and often viewed as a male-dominated form of protest (and sometimes seen as 'vandalism' of communal spaces), yarn bombing is a temporary form of street art and protest, predominantly carried out by women who are disrupting the stereotypical views of women's 'homely' skills by taking them from the home and into the public realm. Thus yarn bombers are challenging the norms of ownership of community spaces with their skilfully constructed sculptures, protective wrappings, hangings and accessories that protest peacefully about anything from the ripping up of mature trees for urban development programmes, to protecting wildlife and campaigning against climate change.

Thanks partly to activists, and the craftivism revolution, there has been a revival of all forms of embroidery, knitting and crochet, and an increase in the cultural value of these crafts; now no longer just labelled as 'women's work', they are all being taken seriously as an art form.

OPPOSITE AND OVERLEAF

Examples of yarn bombing.

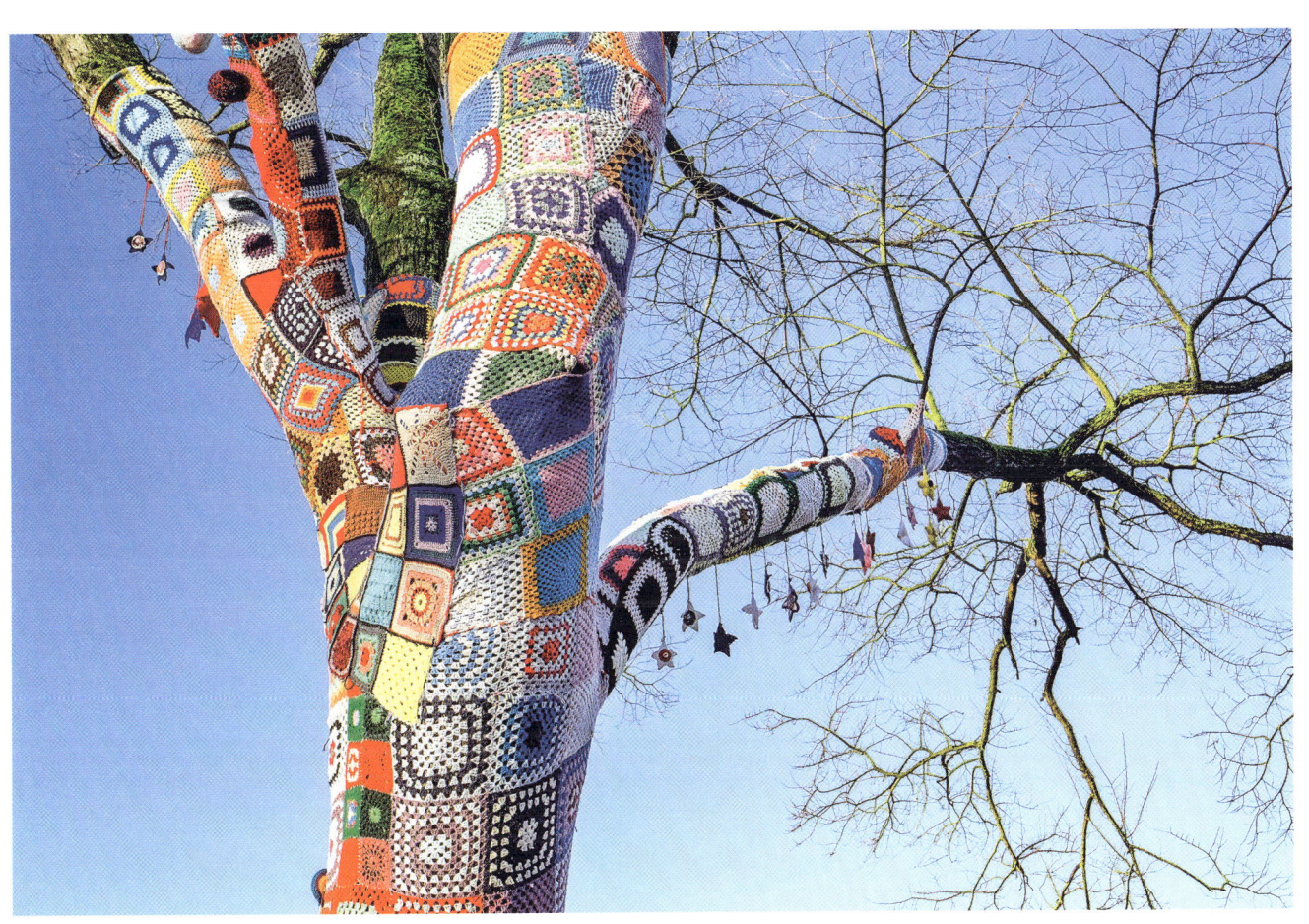

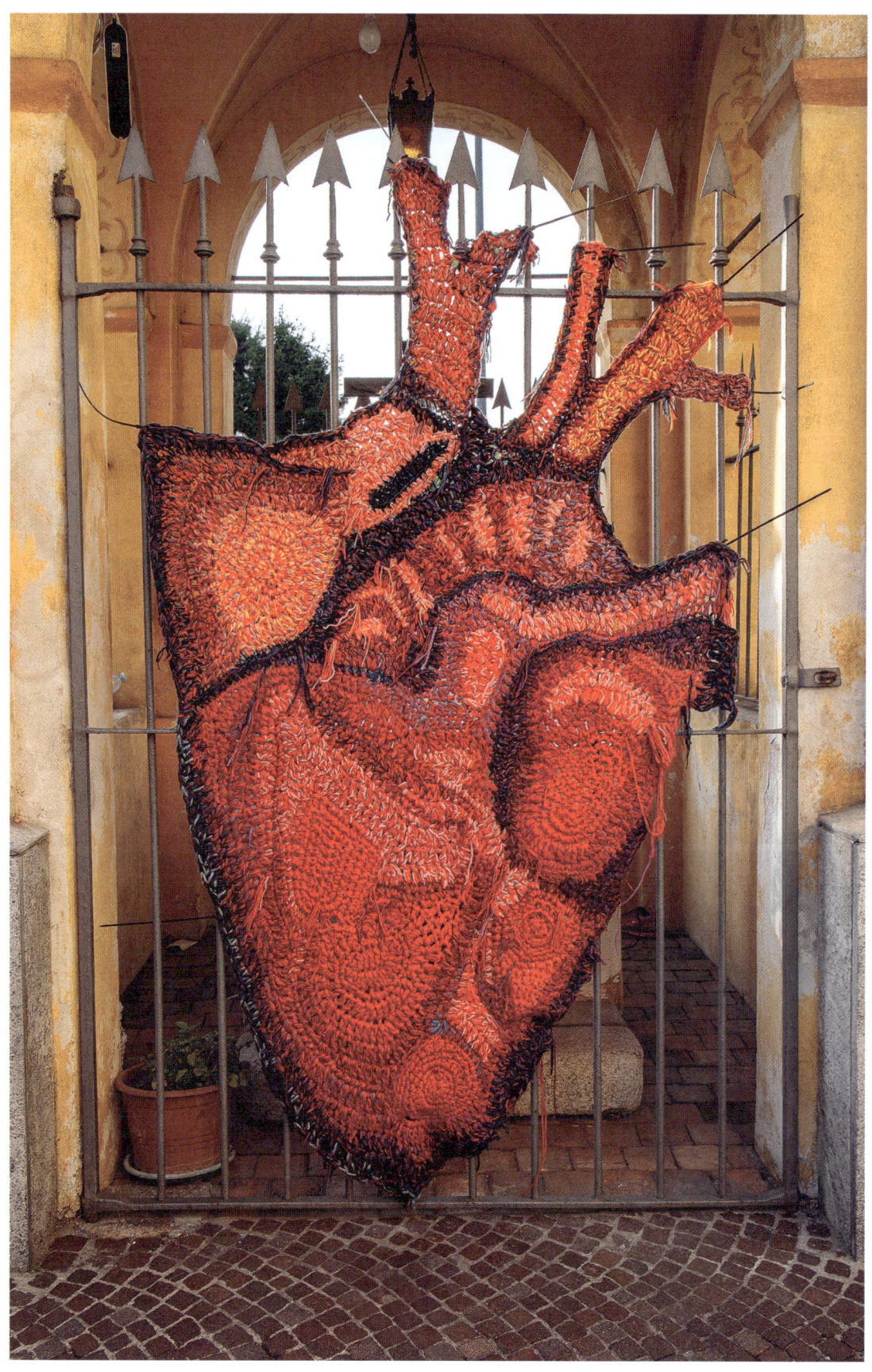

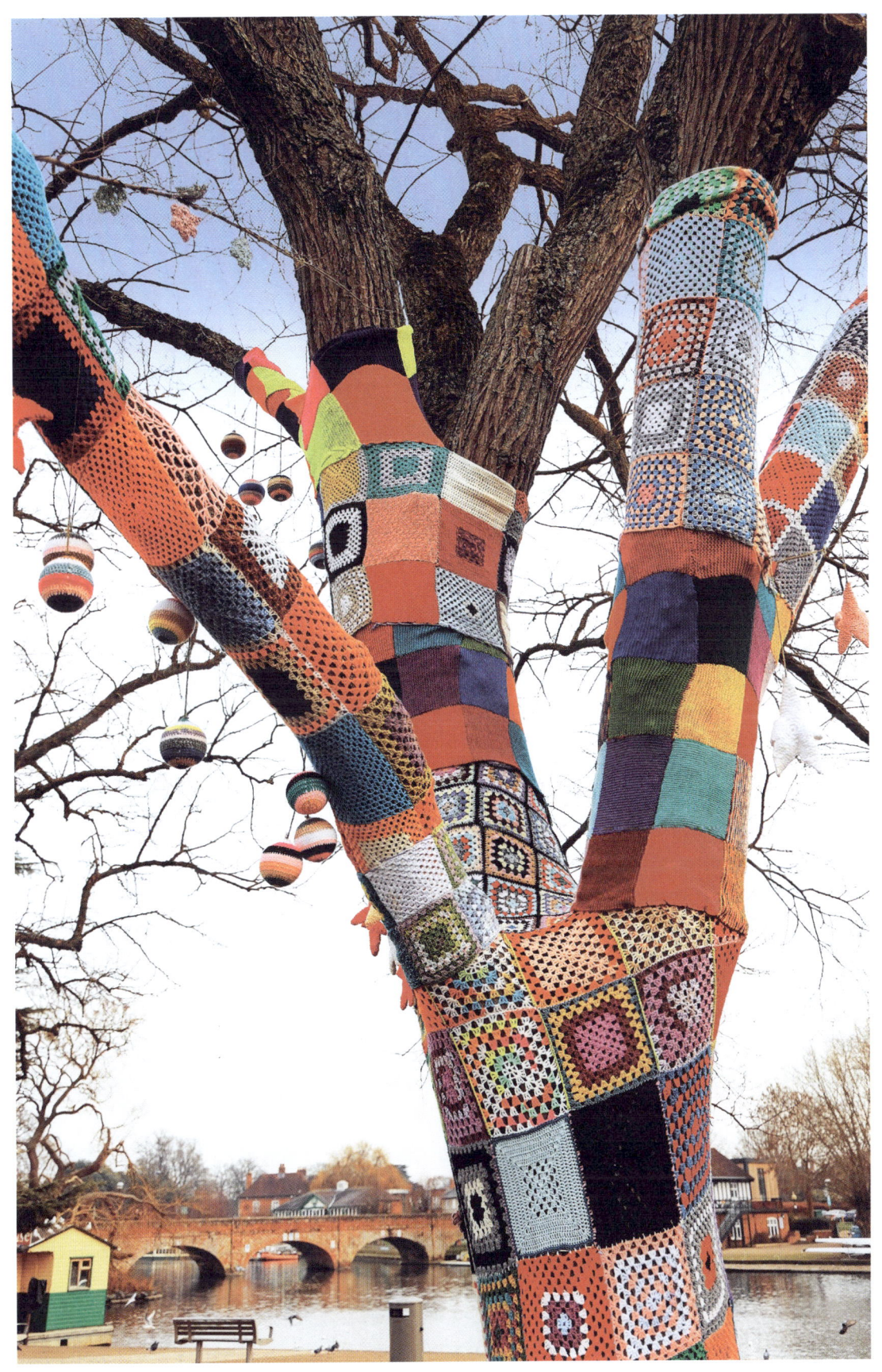

I can't Believe I Still Have To PROTEST This FuAckNing Shit

JL2024

REFLECTIONS

REFLECTIONS

OPPOSITE

Still Protesting...
(From the mini
banner series
2023–4)

Julia Triston

65×62cm (26×24.4in).

Our world is amidst wars, political instability, racial, gender, social and economic inequality, and we are on the brink of a climate disaster. I feel, therefore, this book is timely.

People, including me, are raging. And, whether it's with a quickly made response, or a beautifully crafted permanent artwork, we are expressing our anger, frustrations and outrage through the medium of textiles in increasingly creative ways. Our passionate voices of defiance, resistance and rebelliousness are there for all to see, calling for change, solidarity and justice.

In the process of writing this book I have carried out extensive research by reading seminal texts, significant documents and archive materials. I have visited key exhibitions and analysed a wealth of protest textiles from around the world. I have had conversations with incredible artists and passionate makers, collectors, curators and human rights advocates.

This topic is vast, and could have filled multiple volumes. I am aware that there are many more activists, artists, craftivists, collectives, movements and campaigns that are missing from this book. But I had to be selective and it was difficult to choose what to include, yet be as representative as possible.

The research for my writing has been affirmative, enraging and, at times, distressing. I have learned about and uncovered shocking truths and lies, but I have also been heartened by the hope and passion of people calling attention to their campaigns, and taking positive action to fight injustice, whether personally or collectively, locally or globally through textiles.

In *Textile Protest* I share the work of those who care, and those who dare.

Viva protest textiles!

WORLDWIDE DESIGNATED DAYS

Days that commemorate, celebrate, remember or raise awareness about issues, protests and movements related to the themes in this book are listed below.

JANUARY

Third Monday	Martin Luther King Jr Day (US)
27	International Holocaust Remembrance Day

FEBRUARY

20	World Day of Social Justice

MARCH

8	International Women's Day
21	International Day for the Elimination of Racial Discrimination
22	World Water Day
30	International Day of Zero Waste

APRIL

22	Earth Day

MAY

1	International Workers' Day (also known as May Day or Labour Day)
8–9	Time of Remembrance and Reconciliation for Those Who Lost Their Lives During the Second World War
16	International Day of Living Together in Peace
28	World Menstrual Hygiene Day

JUNE

First Friday	National Gun Violence Awareness Day or #WearOrange Day (US)
Second Saturday	International Yarn Bombing Day
5	World Environment Day
8	World Ocean Day
16	Day of the African Child
17	World Day to Combat Desertification and Drought
19	International Day for the Elimination of Sexual Violence in Conflict
20	World Refugee Day
26	United Nations International Day in Support of Victims of Torture

JULY

18	Nelson Mandela International Day
30	World Embroidery Day

AUGUST

9	International Day of the World's Indigenous Peoples
19	World Humanitarian Day
21	International Day of Remembrance and Tribute to the Victims of Terrorism
23	International Day for the Remembrance of the Slave Trade and Its Abolition
30	International Day of the Victims of Enforced Disappearances
31	International Day for People of African Descent

SEPTEMBER

15	International Day of Democracy
18	International Equal Pay Day
21	International Day of Peace
26	International Day for the Total Elimination of Nuclear Weapons

OCTOBER

2	International Day of Non-Violence
7	World Cotton Day
8	World Circular Textiles Day
10	World Mental Health Day
15	World Craft Day

NOVEMBER

18	World Day for the Prevention of and Healing from Child Sexual Exploitation, Abuse and Violence
25	International Day for the Elimination of Violence against Women
29	International Day of Solidarity with the Palestinian People

DECEMBER

1	World AIDS Day
2	International Day for the Abolition of Slavery
3	International Day of Persons with Disabilities
9	International Day of Commemoration and Dignity of the Victims of the Crime of Genocide and of the Prevention of this Crime
10	Human Rights Day

SELECT BIBLIOGRAPHY
AND FURTHER READING

Adams, Jacqueline, *Art Against Dictatorship: Making and Exporting Arpilleras Under Pinochet* (Louann Atkins Temple Women & Culture Series), University of Texas Press, 2013

Angelou, Maya, *And Still I Rise*, Random House, 1978

Bailey, Dr Jess, *Many Hands Make a Quilt; Short Histories of Radical Quilting*, Common Threads Press, 2022

Barker, Meg-John and Scheele, Jules, *Queer: A Graphic History*, Google Books, 2016

Bender, Camille, *Dressing the Resistance: The Visual Language of Protest Through History*, Princetown Architectural Press, 2022

Bryan-Wilson, Julia, *Fray: Art and Textile Politics*, University of Chicago Press, 2017

Corbett, Sarah, *How to be a Craftivist: The art of gentle protest*, Unbound, 2017

Crawshaw, Gill, *Rights Not Charity: Protest Textiles and Disability Activism*, Common Threads Press, 2023

Dew, Charlotte, *Women For Peace: Banners From Greenham Common*, Four Corners Books, 2021

Emelife, Aindrea, *A Brief History of Protest Art*, Tate Publishing, 2022

Fahs, Breanne (ed.), *Burn It Down! Feminist Manifestos for the Revolution*, Verso, 2020

Gipson, Ferren, *Women's Work: From feminine arts to feminist art*, Frances Lincoln Publishing, 2022

Gorman, John, *Banner Bright*, Scorpion Cavendish Ltd, 1986

Guerrilla Girls, *Guerrilla Girls: The Art of Behaving Badly*, Chronicle Books, 2020

Henderson, P L, *Unravelling Women's Art*, Supernova Books, 2021

Johnson, Lotte, Pinath, Amanda and Fray-Smith, Wells (eds), *Unravel: The Power and Politics of Textiles in Art*, Prestel, 2024

Light, Melanie and Ken, *Picturing Resistance: Moments and Movements of Social Change from the 1950s to Today*, Ten Speed Press, 2020

Lorde, Audre, *Your Silence Will Not Protect You*, Silver Press, 2017

Mansfield, Nick and Wright, Martin, *Made by Labour: A Material and Visual History of British Labour* c. 1780–1924, University of Wales Press, 2023

McQuiston, Liz, *Protest! A History of Social and Political Protest Graphics*, White Lion Publishing, 2019

Mid Pennine Arts, *Banner Culture*, Pendle Radicals Publication, 2022

Mullins, Charlotte, *A Little Feminist History of Art*, Tate Publishing, 2019

Munroe, Silus, S*trikethrough! Typographic Messages of Protest*, Letterform Archive, 2022

Parker, Rozsika, *The Subversive Stitch: Embroidery and the Making of Feminine*, The Women's Press, 1984

Plummer, Dr Sharbreon, *Diasporic Threads: Black Women, Fibre & Textiles*, Common Threads Press, 2022

Profanity Embroidery Group, *Fuck Off, I'm Sewing! Swearing and Sewing That Will Have You in Stitches*, Flint, 2020

Rosner, Isabella, *Stitching Freedom: Embroidery & Incarceration*, Common Threads Press, 2024

Sauermann, Barbara (ed.), *2/15: The Day the World Said NO to War*, AK Press, 2003

Weymar, Diana, *Crafting a Better World*, Harvest, 2024

Young, Linsey (ed.), *Women in Revolt! Art and Activism in the UK 1970–90*, Tate Publishing, 2023

DEDICATION

Dedicated, with huge love and massive thanks, to Zoë Triston, Tim Triston, and Joan Baker – three amazing humans who enrich my life endlessly.

To the memory of my beloved Dad, Peter John Triston, and my much missed friend Kay Livingston.

For the inspiring people I've written about within these pages, and to the artists and activists who rise up to protest against crimes against humanity.

ACKNOWLEDGEMENTS

I'm extremely grateful and deeply indebted to Joan Baker for being a brilliant grammarian and wordsmith, and for her superb editing skills on my first draft; thanks Mum. My heartfelt thanks go to Zoë Triston for her guidance and sensitivity with my use of language; your suggestions were very welcome. Big thanks to Tim Triston for enlightening debates on political and historical events. The three of you continue to teach and inspire me.

I'd like to extend a huge thank you to all contributors: activists, academics, artists, banner makers, craftivists, curators, embroiderers, human rights advocates, installation artists, makers, photographers, quilters, sculptors, textile artists, and all those who sew for justice. This book is much richer for your contributions. Keep on doing what you do so brilliantly.

Thanks to Brenda Saunders (for sewing support) and to Lee Edward (for the photography shoot) in Denmark, Kristian Buus for images from protests on the streets of London, and all other photographers whose images capture moments and record movements and protests that are highlighted in this book. And to Jen Veall, my tenacious picture researcher, for finding permissions and access to important archive images.

Last but not least, many thanks to the Batsford team – Frida Green, Nicola Newman, Rebecca Armstrong and Eoghan O'Brien – for commissioning and believing in my ambitious book project and for your patience with my continuous questions, suggestions and edits.

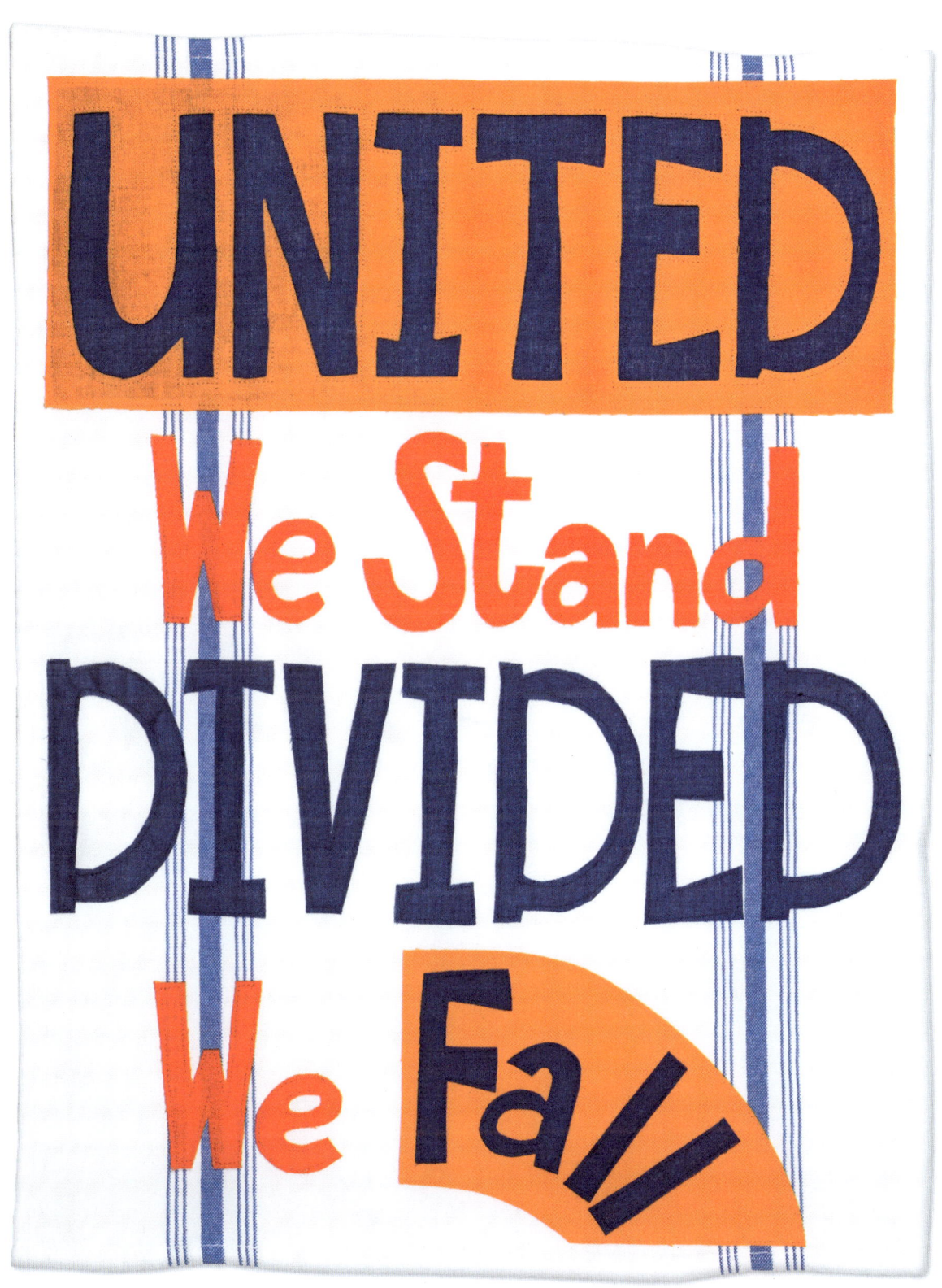

ACKNOWLEDGEMENTS

PICTURE CREDITS

7 © Julia Triston, photograph by Lee Edward; 8 © mark reinstein / Alamy; 11 (above) © Associated Press / Alamy; 11 (below) © Richard Ellis / Alamy; 12 © Directphoto Collection / Alamy; 13 © Richard Ellis / Alamy; 15 © Every Second Media / Alamy; 17 © Jansos / Alamy; 18 (above) © Tuesday Greenidge. All Rights Reserved, DACS 2025. Photograph by Catherine Hill; 18 (below) © Tuesday Greenidge. All Rights Reserved, DACS 2025. Photograph by Catherine Hill; 21© Alison Aye. Photo: Phil Shelly; 22 © Alison Aye. Photo: Phil Shelly; 23 © Alison Aye. Photo: Phil Shelly; 24 © Caren Garfen; 27 (left) © Caren Garfen; 27 (right) © Caren Garfen; 29 © Vince Laws; 30 © 2024 2025 Anyone Can Fly Foundation / DACS. Photograph: Glenstone Museum; 33 (above) © London Museum; 33 (bottom) © PA Images / Alamy; 35 © Photo 12 / Alamy; 36 © Ghada Amer. Courtesy of the artist and Marianne Boesky Gallery, New York and Aspen; 37 © Ghada Amer. Courtesy of the artist and Marianne Boesky Gallery, New York and Aspen; 39 © Susan Fleischmann; 40 © Julia Triston, photograph by Lee Edward; 42 © Nneka Jones @artyouhungry; 43 © Nneka Jones @artyouhungry; 45 © Trinity Mirror / Mirrorpix / Alamy; 46 © Chelsea Guglielmino / Contributor / Getty; 48 © Charlotte Doyle; 49 © Holly Searle; 51© Manasi Sawant; 52 © Manasi Sawant; 53 © Manasi Sawant; 55 (above) © Associated Press / Alamy; 55 (below) © Associated Press / Alamy; 56 © Mark Kerrison / Alamy; 59 © Casey Jenkins Sh; 60 © Bee Hughes, photograph by Milos Simpraga; 61© Bee Hughes, photograph by Milos Simpraga; 62 © Lee Edward; 63 © Viva Ruiz; 64 (above) © Kathy York; 64 (below)©Brian Allen/Voice of America; 66 (left) © Bjanka Kadic / Alamy; 66 (right) © 2023, Mish Aminoff, www.mishaminoff.com; 68 (above) © Guerrilla Girls, courtesy guerrillagirls.com; 68 (below) © © Guerrilla Girls, courtesy guerrillagirls.com; 69 © © Guerrilla Girls, courtesy guerrillagirls.com; 70 © Judy Chicago. ARS, NY and DACS, London 2025. Photograph: Joe Quinn / Alamy; 71 (above) © Judy Chicago. ARS, NY and DACS, London 2025. Photograph: B.O'Kane / Alamy; 71 (below) © Judy Chicago. ARS, NY and DACS, London 2025. Photograph: David Grossman / Alamy; 72 © Zak Foster; 74 © Kristian Buus; 76 © Courtesy Alice Gabb; 79 (above) © Associated Press / Alamy; 79 (below) © Robert Clay / Alamy; 80 (above) © Gavin Hellier / Alamy; 80 (middle) © rfranca / Alamy; 80 (below) © Ink Drop / Alamy; 81 (above) © Robert K. Chin / Alamy; 81 (middle) © Freelance Fotograf / Alamy; 81 (below) © Maxim Ermolenko / Alamy; 83 © Gavin Hellier / Alamy ; 85 © Thatcher's Thugs Banner, Thalia and Ian Campbell, The Campbell Archives, Courtesy of The Peace Museum; 89 (above) © Dawn Williams Boyd. Courtesy of the artist and Fort Gansevoort, New York; 89 (below) © Dawn Williams Boyd. Courtesy of the artist and Fort Gansevoort, New York; 91 (above) © Collection of the Smithsonian National Museum of African American History and Culture; 91 (below) © Everett Collection Inc / Alamy; 93 (above) © DON EMMERT / Contributor / Getty; 93 (below) © Associated Press / Alamy; 95 (above) © John Tweedle / Alamy; 95 (below) © Chicago History Museum / Contributor / Getty; 96 © Precious D Lovell; 97 © Precious D Lovell; 98 © Hew Locke. All rights reserved, DACS/Artimage 2023; 99 © Hew Locke. All rights reserved, DACS/Artimage 2023; 100 © Courtesy the artist and Artists Band Together Campaign; 101 © ARS, NY and DACS, London 2025. Photography: Directphoto Collection / Alamy; 103 (above) © Michael Noble Jr. / Stringer / Getty; 103 (below) © OLIVIER DOULIERY / Contributor / Getty; 104 © Precious D Lovell; 105 © Previous D Lovell; 107 (above) © Associated Press / Alamy; 107 (below) © NurPhoto SRL / Alamy; 109 © Imagespace / Alamy; 111 © Sinai Noor / Alamy; 112 © Ed Hall; 113 © Vince Laws; 114 © Julia Triston, photograph by Lee Edward; 116 © Mary Evans / Marx Memorial Library; 117 © The Estate of Alexander Wheeler Wainman, John Alexander Wainman; 119 (above) © Marx Memorial Library & Workers' School, London, photography Ian Lillicrapp; 119 (below) © Marx Memorial Library & Workers' School, London, photography Ian Lillicrapp; 121 (above) © Europa Press News / Contributor / Getty; 121 (below) © NDavidsonSFC001/Nick Davidson/ Nick@Outside_Left/Clapton Community Football Club; 123 © Bernard Bisson / Contributor / Getty; 124 © Visions of America, LLC / Alamy; 125 © Africa Media Online / Alamy; 126 © Frauen in der Einen Welt/Women in One World. Photo: Gaby Franger; 127 © M.Sobreira / Alamy; 129 © Zak Foster; 130–131 © Zak Foster; 133 (left) © Photo Martin Melaugh, © Conflict Textiles; 133 (right) Photo Martin Melaugh, © Conflict Textiles; 134 © dpa picture alliance archive / Alamy; 136 (above) © Kristian Buus / Alamy; 136 (below) © Sinai Noor / Alamy; 139 © SOPA Images Limited / Alamy; 140 © Associated Press / Alamy; 142 Photograph by Lee Edward; 143 Photograph by Lee Edward; 145 (above) © Associated Press / Alamy; 145 (below) © Guy Corbishley / Alamy; 147 (left) © Findlay / Alamy; 147 (right) © Evening Standard / Stringer / Getty; 148 (above) ©

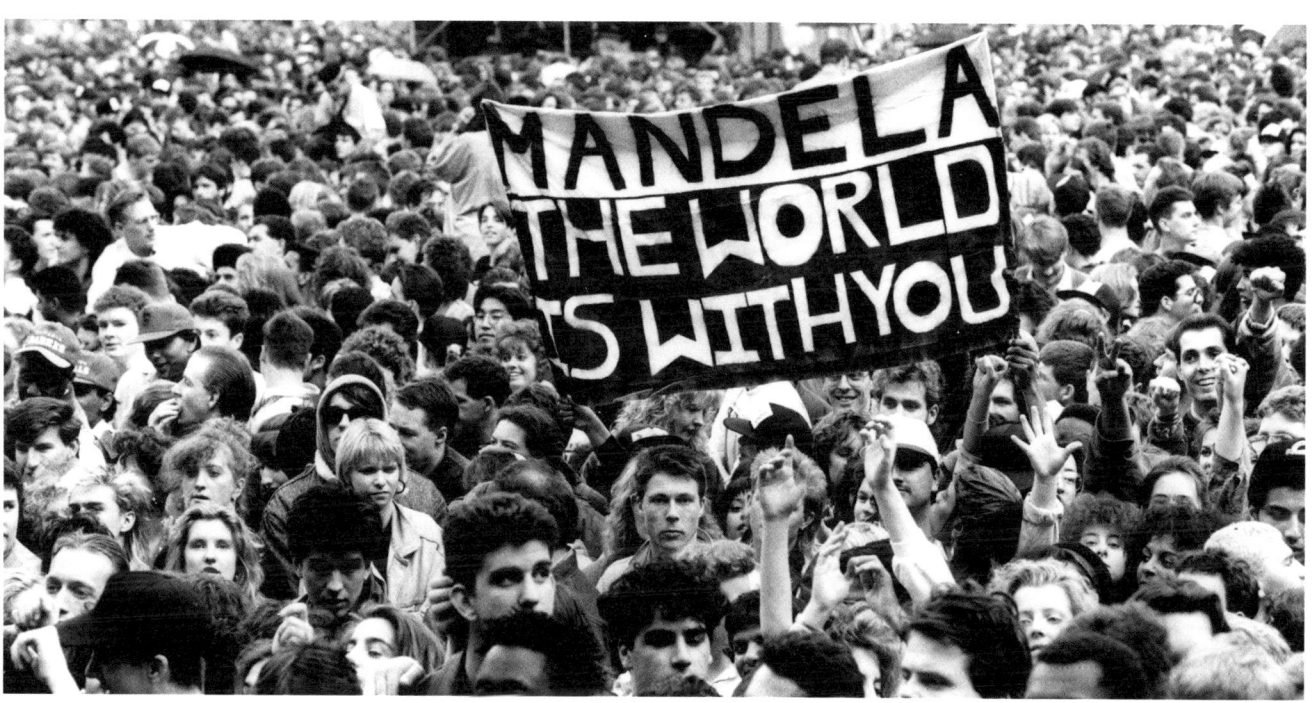

SOURCES

Direct quotations from artists and activists were recorded in interviews and correspondence, or sourced from articles featuring their work:

Amer, Ghada: https://ghadaamer.com/about-ghada-amer/

Aye, Alison: https://www.alisonaye.com and https://covidquilt2020.com

Bacic, Roberta: https://cain.ulster.ac.uk/conflicttextiles/

Barratt, Russell: https://russellbarratt.com/

Campbell, Thalia: https://www.itsnicethat.com/features/women-for-peace-greenham-common-banners-four-corners-thalia-campbell-art-publication-260821

Corbett, Sarah: https://www.craftivist-collective.com

DeBris, Marina: https://cairnscalendar.com.au/event/beach-couture-a-haute-mess-exhibition-by-marina-debris/2023-01-30/

Foster, Zak: https://www.zakfoster.com

Gabb, Alice: http://www.alicegabb.com/

Garfen, Caren: http://www.carengarfen.com

Greenidge, Tuesday: Instagram (@grenfellmemorialquilt)

Hall, Ed: http://www.edhallbanners.co.uk/

Hughes, Dr Bee: https://www.lectitopublishing.nl/Article/Detail/challenging-menstrual-norms-in-online-medical-advice-deconstructing-stigma-through-entangled-art-3883

Hutchison, Jeremy: https://jeremyhutchison.com

Jenkins, Casey: https://casey-jenkins.com

Jones, Nneka: https://www.artyouhungry.com/

Laws, Vince: Facebook – DWP Deaths Make Me Sick

Marr, Vanessa: https://domesticdusters.wordpress.com

Searle, Holly: https://www.thesubversivestitcher.com

Lovell, Precious D: https://www.preciousdlovell.com/

Vickery, Susie: http://www.dharavibiennale.com/provoke-protect

Williams Boyd, Dawn: https://www.dawnwilliamsboyd.com/

The following websites were accessed for historical information, statistics and mission statements:

https://www.who.int

https://www.un.org/en/

https://www.amnesty.org/en/

https://www.greenpeace.org.uk

https://ahf.nuclearmuseum.org/ahf/key-documents/russell-einstein-manifesto/

https://www.sandyhookpromise.org

https://www.everytown.org

https://wearorange.org

https://www.bradyunited.org

https://studentsdemandaction.org

https://naacp.org

https://cnduk.org

https://rebellion.global

https://juststopoil.org

Quotations have been taken from the following websites and articles:

https://www.theguardian.com/uk-news/2016/apr/26/hillsborough-inquests-jury-says-96-victims-were-unlawfully-killed

https://www.cdc.gov/museum/timeline/covid19.html

https://www.un.org/en/coronavirus

https://en.wikipedia.org/wiki/Suffragette_bombing_and_arson_campaign

https://www.legislation.gov.uk/ukpga/1970/41/enacted

https://www.blackpast.org/african-american-history/combahee-river-collective-statement-1977/

https://www.womenshistory.org/education-resources/biographies/tarana-burke

https://www.csmonitor.com/World/2016/1207/Why-Lebanese-women-are-protesting-a-decades-old-rape-law

https://www.huffpost.com/entry/menstrual-blood-art-carina-ubeda_n_3499027#:~:text=Chilean%20artist%20Carina%20Úbeda%20has,soiled%20fabric%20until%20inspiration%20struck

https://brooklynrail.org/2022/05/criticspage/Viva-Ruiz-with-Aliza-Shvarts/

https://www.pussyhatproject.com/our-story

https://www.internationalwomensday.com/Activity/15586/The-history-of-IWD

https://en.wikipedia.org/wiki/International_Women%27s_Day

https://www.millionwomenrise.com

https://www.guerrillagirls.com/about

https://www.history.com/topics/black-history/rosa-parks

https://www.history.com/topics/black-history/martin-luther-king-jr

https://www.theguardian.com/uk-news/2019/feb/22/macpherson-report-what-was-it-and-what-impact-did-it-have

https://www.theguardian.com/uk-news/2023/mar/21/louise-caseys-report-on-the-met-police-the-fall-of-a-british-institution

https://blacklivesmatter.com/about/#vision

https://www.internationaldisabilityalliance.org/content/history

https://en.wikipedia.org/wiki/Pussy_Riot

https://cain.ulster.ac.uk/conflicttextiles/search-quilts2/fulltextiles1/?id=250

https://cain.ulster.ac.uk/conflicttextiles/search-quilts2/fulltextiles1/?id=424

https://www.widewalls.ch/magazine/watermelon-palestine

https://www.theguardian.com/environment/2018/nov/17/thousands-gather-to-block-london-bridges-in-climate-rebellion

https://www.theguardian.com/fashion/article/2024/jun/16/stay-angry-as-hell-with-our-politicians-katharine-hamnett-on-politics-the-planet-and-slogan-t-shirts

INDEX

First published in the United Kingdom
in 2025 by
Batsford
43 Great Ormond Street
London
WC1N 3HZ

An imprint of B. T. Batsford Holdings Limited

ISBN 9781849949071

A CIP catalogue record for this book is available from the British Library.

10 9 8 7 6 5 4 3 2 1

Reproduction by Rival Colour Ltd, UK
Printed by Vivar Printing Sdn. Bhd., Malaysia

Sensitivity read by Helen Gould

This book can be ordered direct from the publisher at www.
batsfordbooks.com, or try your local bookshop

Distributed throughout the UK and Europe by Abrams & Chronicle Books,
1 West Smithfield, London EC1A 9JU and 57 rue Gaston Tessier, 75166
Paris, France

www.abramsandchronicle.co.uk
info@abramsandchronicle.co.uk

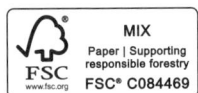

MIX
Paper | Supporting
responsible forestry
FSC
www.fsc.org   FSC® C084469